The Euro, Capital Markets, and Dollarization

The Euro, Capital Markets, and Dollarization

Edward B. Flowers and Francis A. Lees

ROWMAN & LITTLEFIELD PUBLISHERS, INC.
Lanham • Boulder • New York • Oxford

ROWMAN & LITTLEFIELD PUBLISHERS, INC.

Published in the United States of America
by Rowman & Littlefield Publishers, Inc.
4720 Boston Way, Lanham, Maryland 20706
www.rowmanlittlefield.com

12 Hid's Copse Road, Cumnor Hill, Oxford OX2 9JJ, England

British Library Cataloguing-in-Publication Information Available

Library of Congress Cataloging-in-Publication Data

Flowers, Edward B., 1939–
The euro, capital markets, and dollarization / Edward B. Flowers and Francis A. Lees.
p. cm.
Includes bibliographical references and index.
ISBN: 978-0-7425-1305-1
1. Euro. 2. Money—European Union countries. 3. Monetary policy—European Union countries. 4. Capital market—European Union countries. 5. Dollar, American. I. Lees, Francis A. II. Title.

HG925 .F574 2002
332.4'94—dc21

2001041689

Printed in the United States of America

∞™ The paper used in this publication meets the minimum requirements of American National Standard for Information Sciences—Permanence of Paper for Printed Library Materials, ANSI/NISO Z39.48-1992.

To Sara, my wife
E. B. F.

To Kathryn, my wife
F. A. L.

Contents

Tables

Acronyms

ADR	American depository receipt
AIM	alternative investment market
APT	automated pit trading
BIS	Bank for International Settlements
CAP	Common Agricultural Policy
CATS	computer-assisted trading systems
CECI	Establissement de Credit et des Enterprises d'Investissement
CEE	central and eastern Europe
CIS	Commonwealth of Independent States
CMEA	Council for Mutual Economic Assistance
CMF	Conseil des Marches Financiers
COB	Commission des Operations de Bourse
DTB	Deutsche Termin Börse
EC	European Community
ECB	European Central Bank
ECN	electronic communications network
ECS	euro clearing system
ECSC	European Coal and Steel Community
ECU	European currency unit
EEC	European Economic Community
EFTA	European Free Trade Association
EIB	European Investment Bank
EMI	European Monetary Institute
EMU	European Monetary Union
EMS	European monetary system
EONIA	euro overnight index average
EPU	European Payments Union

ERP	Euro Recovery Program
ERM	exchange rate mechanism
ESCB	European system of central banks
ETF	exchange traded fund
EU	European Union
EVCA	European Venture Capital Association
FDI	foreign direct investment
GCC	Gulf Cooperation Council
GDP	gross domestic product
IGC	intergovernmental conference
IMF	International Monetary Fund
IPO	initial public offering
IT	information technology
LBO	leveraged buyout
LIFFE	London International Financial Futures Exchange
LTRO	longer-term refinancing operation
M&A	mergers and acquisitions
MNC	multinational corporation
MPT	modern portfolio theory
MRO	main refinancing option
NCB	national central bank
NYSE	New York Stock Exchange
OECD	Organization for Economic Cooperation and Development
OEEC	Organization for European Economic Cooperation
PYG	pay-as-you-go
RTGS	real-time gross settlement system
SPD	Social Democratic Party (German)
SPDR	Standard & Poor's depository receipt
SWIFT	Society for Worldwide International Financial Telecommunications
TARGET	Trans-European Automated Realtime Gross Settlement Express Transfer System
TMT	technology, media, and telecommunications
TOCA	theory of optimum currency areas
VAT	value-added tax
WEBS	world equity benchmark shares

Preface

Europe is changing more rapidly than most other regions of the world. Part of the stimulus to this dramatic change is the introduction of a single currency. But there are other stimuli, including globalization of business and a growing tendency for regional trade and payments arrangements. Europe is carrying this regionalization further and faster than other parts of the world, creating a political institutional framework of which the European monetary union is the latest and most creative.

When we began to develop this book-writing project, we were uncertain how far Europeans would take their new currency. Early in 1998 we knew only that a great deal of effort and negotiation had been necessary and that in May the EU-15 would meet for another round of discussions.

Thirty-eight months later we can look back at a startling period in European history, in which a new currency is bringing major changes in capital markets, financial and business innovation, and growing shareholder democracy. In 1998 we could not fully comprehend or in any way anticipate the almost revolutionary changes that lay ahead. Since the euro was introduced, Europe's capital markets have demonstrated an amazing ability to reform and reorganize. New stock markets have been created, and older ones are merging or forming alliances.

Corporations in Europe are responding to the new realities of pan-European competition. Companies find themselves in a fishbowl environment, with everything they do more visible and transparent. Unfriendly takeover bids, based on the rising purchasing power held by new sector firms, are becoming accepted as part of the ordinary financial system. Spin-offs have become the newest means of discovering hidden corporate treasure.

Where is Europe headed, and will we discover even more revolutionary changes? Will the new economic sectors, rising shareholder democracy, and expanding financial markets generate even greater change?

Europe appears more prepared to assert itself in business-financial competition, corporate initiatives, defense preparedness, and global political muscle. Will this continue, and will we enter a period of European renaissance accompanied by a shift of economic, financial, and political power and influence that challenges the United States? Will the twenty-first century become the European century, and, if so, in what ways will it lead to a world of better governance?

Chapter 1 summarizes the historic antecedents of the EMU from the Marshall Plan through Maastricht, and concludes with a comparative analysis of Euroland and the United States. Chapter 2 examines the dual issues of resource mobility in the Eurozone and the theoretical requirements of an optimal currency area. Both capital mobility and labor mobility are discussed. Chapter 3 analyzes macroeconomic conditions and issues in a single currency area. These issues include fiscal balance, the Growth and Stability Pact, pensions systems, and euro currency weaknesses in the foreign exchange markets. Chapter 4 considers the impact of the euro on the profitability of the European banking sector, prospects for bank merger and consolidation, and focuses its analysis on banking and financial activities in the Eurozone. Chapter 5 examines the legal and operative framework for the European Central Bank.

Chapter 6 compares capital markets on the eve of the introduction of the single currency, and the impact of the euro on capital market development. Proposed stock market consolidation and competitiveness is analyzed. Three merger cases are discussed in detail. Chapter 7 examines bond market development in the Eurozone, noting the increase in issuance and changes in practices. Chapter 8 examines equity market development, the evolving structure and operation of the stock exchanges, and the expansion of venture capital markets.

Chapter 9 compares the single currency with proposals for dollarization. The theory of optimal currency areas is reviewed, and its applicability to NAFTA and Mercosur. Chapter 10 considers EU enlargement and Eurozone expansion. Considerable attention is given to prospects for the UK entering the single currency system, as well as access to the EU for central and eastern European nations.

Acknowledgments

When we began to research this volume in 1998, we wondered if a single currency and a European-wide financial system could succeed. Although the experts hailed the single currency as the most important, revolutionary monetary event of the century, they were divided on the likely outcome.

We cast our net across the Atlantic searching for materials and information for this study. We sought to obtain viewpoints, insights, and perspectives from those based in Europe, those working in the Eurozone, and those most directly exposed to the political, economic, and financial discussions and debate. We are particularly indebted to the following people who evoked an early interest focused on these subjects. Of these people, we would like to thank particularly Dr. Nicholas Bruck, formerly with the World Bank, Economic Development Institute.

Many individuals in the private sector also provided necessary information and ideas. These include Hugh Baxter at Standard & Poor's (London office); Catherine Claydon at Goldman Sachs (London office); Keith Mullin at IFR-Thomson (London office); Dan Adler at 3i; Robert Darwent at Hicks Muse Tate & Furst (London office); Oliver Haarmann at KKR (London office); Jonathan Meggs and Philip Rattle at Chase Capital Partners (London office); William Northfield at Deutsche Bank Capital Markets (London office); Charles Brealey at William M. Mercer (London); Eric de Bodard at Moody's (London office); Ian Davis and Jonathan Day at McKinsey & Co. (London office); Clifford Dammers at International Primary Market Association (London); Kelly Streatley at Deutsche Morgan Grenfell; Peter Churchill-Coleman at Dresdner Kleinwort Benson (London office); Loretta Murphy at Commerzbank (London); Susan Falks and A. Wilkins at Cable & Wireless; and Elaine Cole at J.P. Morgan (London office).

A number of individuals in the governmental sector and regulatory agencies assisted by providing information. These individuals include John Barrass and Lieselotte Burdorf-Cook at Financial Services Authority (FSA) in London; Elaine Trimble, Eric Meyer, and Nicola Nathan at the European Bank for Reconstruction and Development in London; Ekkehart Boehmer at the Securities Exchange Commission (Washington, D.C.); Ida Reeve and Lynne Fordrad at the Bank of England; and Andrew Jackson at the Department of Trade and Industry of the British government.

The following organizations were helpful in providing information and data: British Venture Capital Association (London); the U.S. embassy in London; Schroders Investment Bank; OECD; the Bank for International Settlements (Basel); and the Federal Reserve Bank of New York.

Naturally, we accept full responsibility for all errors of commission and omission.

Chapter One

The Road to Euro

In 1991 the member states of the European Union (EU) confirmed the goal of achieving a single European market. Further, they agreed to work toward European monetary union. This is the first time that a group of countries moved toward a common currency on such a scale without also forming a political union. Never before had political leaders worked for so long to overcome historical, language, and cultural differences.[1]

The lowering of the iron curtain and breakup of the centrally planned economic system in eastern Europe had removed a fundamental political assumption on which the architects of the European Economic Community had based their economic strategy. Reunification of Germany expanded the European Union (EU) eastward, in defiance of the cold war political assumptions that provided incentive for European economic cooperation.

Indeed, the disappearance of the monolithic Soviet Union fostered a new political philosophy—liberty is necessary because it serves the interests of Western power and capital.[2] This is different from the idea that liberty, as an abstract philosophical principle, is fundamental to the West. This idea also seems peculiarly suited to explain the advent of the EU, which is occurring in the economic arena (because it is necessary to capital) rather than in the political arena, where union may be less important.

This chapter examines the role of the euro as it comes into operation and analyzes the historical and political basis for postwar European economic cooperation.

HISTORICAL BACKGROUND

Postwar Economic Cooperation

In September 1947 Secretary of State George C. Marshall presented to the U.S. government a report urging that the European countries be assisted in undertaking concerted action, marking the advent of "a new stage of European economic cooperation." This was the basis for the European Recovery Program (ERP). European nations were expected to undertake cooperative efforts among themselves and organize a joint recovery program. Economic integration would be a means as well as an end.[3]

The Marshall Plan that evolved from this report was an "economic recovery program" based on the "supremacy of political aims." As stated by Howard S. Ellis:

> Europe is a continent of half a billion people, seat of the world's dominant powers for more than two thousand years. Even today, and even if we assume that we can save only that part of Europe which is not now controlled by Russia, Europe is important.[4]

Political aims become implemented by economic objectives. The ERP transferred close to $14 billion in aid and credits to European recipients over the six-year period from 1947 to 1952. The Organization for European Economic Cooperation (OEEC) was organized to monitor progress on European economic recovery, while the European Payments Union was established to further multilateral trade and payments and ultimately currency convertibility.

By 1953 European production had regained prewar levels, and investment expenditures were providing a base for renewed competitiveness. In 1951 the European Coal and Steel Community (ECSC) was established, a forerunner of the Common Market, but was restricted to the coal and steel sectors. Soon after, western European nations were discussing closer economic cooperation in the form of a free trading zone in industrial product.

The European "Exception"

According to Abba Eban, the European Community (EC) and the EU are the optimistic exceptions in the recent history of global diplomacy.[5] The conventional wisdom was satisfied with the fatalistic expectation that the cold war would continue for a few more decades and that it would end in a bloodbath. There was a fatalistic acceptance of the "balance of terror."

Thus it was a great surprise when global economic growth brought an end to the Soviet Union, unified world capital markets, and set the stage for both the Asian crisis and the EU. Yet international law never celebrated a golden age even after the end of the cold war. According to Eban, "Throughout the Cold War, events had more power than ideas, and pragmatic interests, empirically defined, took precedence over written agreements. The 'scourge of war' did not recur in its full range or scope, but many limited wars proved that military power was still a major element of international relations."[6]

Eban sees the EEC and the EU as the largest happy accident in a passive and fatalistic recent history of international relations. He feels that "the cherished hope of creating international solidarities in what were optimistically called 'nonpolitical' or 'humanitarian' issues was frustrated by East–West and North–South rivalries. Regional institutions multiplied, but, with the important exception of the EU, they have not succeeded in modifying national sovereignties through a meaningful degree of integration. The world is fragmenting and integrating at the same time."[7]

Perhaps, from this point of view, the EU, based as it partly is on the World War II experiences and the political-economic visions of Europe and the United States that grew out of that war, was merely fortuitous. But Eban's point of view may not give enough credit to the staying power of democracy or the changes that steady economic change will bring.

From Treaty of Rome to Maastricht

The European Economic Community (EEC) was organized by the Treaty of Rome (1957) and became operational in 1958. The treaty created a Common Market, initially consisting of six nations—Belgium, Luxembourg, Netherlands, France, Germany, and Italy. The customs union committed members to remove all tariff barriers on internal trade in industrial products over a phased ten-year period and to adopt a common external tariff by the end of the phase-in period. The customs union was seen to generate more trade-creation benefits as opposed to trade-diversion costs for several reasons:

- The industrial similarities of their respective economies
- The high proportion of intraregional trade, prior to customs union, thus minimizing potential for costly trade distortion
- The close proximity (and low transport cost factor) associated with internal trade routes of Common Market countries

Big losers among the former trade partners were ex-colonies in Asia and Africa as well as European nations not included in the six-country group (UK, Scandinavia, Spain, and Portugal).[8]

The customs union led to the creation of a rival bloc, the European Free Trade Association (EFTA) in 1960, consisting of the UK, several Scandinavian nations, Portugal, Austria, and Switzerland. Rivalry between the EFTA and Common Market groups placed Europe in a sixes and sevens quandary that endured until 1973, when EFTA members became full members of the EC.[9]

A second development that altered the nature of the customs union was the import of capital and technology, primarily from the United States, and labor, primarily from Spain and Portugal (to France) and Turkey (to Germany).[10] The inflows of capital and labor made possible high and sustained economic growth rates in western Europe over a decade and a half. This set the stage for easier acceptance of liberalization of capital and labor movements in later years by the EU.

In 1985 the EU Commission issued a policy document known as the Single Europe white paper. Jacques Delors, the president of the Commission, provided support and inspiration for this initiative to remove all existing nontariff trade barriers within the Community. The European Council passed the Single European Act two years later. At this time twelve member countries constituted the EU. Examples of types of nontariff barriers are provided in table 1.1. Some three hundred specific trade barriers were originally identified. Measures were enacted in the form of Council "directives" that required specific national legislation to be enforced.

Table 1.1. Nontariff Barriers Covered by Single European Act

Type of Barrier	*Method of Removal*
Local content and rules of origin	Lower the percentage of local content required by manufacturers.
Fiscal frontiers	Narrow the range of value-added tax (VAT) rates so that individual states will feel no difficulty in allowing goods to pass freely.
Technical standards	Require uniform standards. At one point the twelve member countries had eighteen different electrical plugs. These standards are worked out on a product-line-by-product-line basis.

Source: Larry Neal and Daniel Barbezat, *The Economics of the European Union and the Economies of Europe* (London: Oxford University Press, 1998), 10–12.

Maastricht and European Monetary Union (EMU)

The meetings at Maastricht in December 1991 set the agenda for the European monetary union. The Maastricht treaty (Treaty on European Union) envisaged three stages to achieve a single currency. These are described in table 1.2. The three stages provide for promoting intercurrency competition (stage 1), development of cooperation among independent central banks (stage 2), and eventual centralization of control over the EU money stock (stage 3).

Table 1.2. Summary of the Maastricht Treaty for European Monetary Union

Stage 1–Before Ratification of New Treaty (from July 1, 1990)
Liberalization of capital movements inside Community Multilateral surveillance procedure for economic policy coordination Strengthened monetary cooperation
Stage 1–After Ratification of New Treaty (1993)
Freezing of currency composition of ECU basket Irrevocable commitment to single currency (ECU) Reinforced multilateral surveillance in the context of broad guidelines for economic policies and convergence programs of member states
Stage 2–From January 1, 1994
Liberalization of capital movements to or from third countries Prohibition on direct access to central banks and on privileged access to financial institutions for the financing of public deficits No bailout rule for member states Start of procedure to avoid excessive public deficits (nonbinding) Continued balance of payments support European Monetary Institute (EMI) set up, prepares complete framework for stage 3 Start of process leading to independent central bank Stage 2–After decision on start date of stage 3 (before July 1, 1998) Establishment of European System of Central Banks (ESCB) and European Central Bank (ECB) and adoption of necessary legislation
Stage 3–January 1, 1999, at the latest
Members must meet specific fiscal rules (or show credible progress toward meeting them) to join: • A government debt/GDP ratio of below 60 percent • A government deficit/GDP ratio of below 3 percent • An inflation rate and long-term interest rates within l.5–2.0 percentage points of the average of the three lowest inflation and interest rate countries • Irrevocable fixing of exchange rates to the euro (which will replace the ECU) and to each other, followed by the replacement of the national currencies by the euro (planned for 2002) as the single currency • Single monetary policy conducted by independent ECB • Single exchange rate policy determined between Council of Ministers and ECB • Binding procedure (including sanctions) aimed at avoiding excessive public deficits (the Stability Pact)

Source: Larry Neal and Daniel Barbezat, *The Economics of the European Union and the Economies of Europe* (London: Oxford University Press, 1998), 142.

Why have a common currency? One answer lies in the theory of optimum currency areas discussed in chapter 2. A second answer follows, as we consider the historical evolution of European currencies since 1946.

To amplify the force of the Marshall Plan, in 1950 the European Payments Union (EPU) was established. At that time European currencies were inconvertible, and intra-European trade suffered from a thicket of complicated payments and clearing arrangements that inhibited the growth of regional trade. The EPU provided partial relief with incentives. EPU member countries could clear intra-European trade multilaterally and settle residual claims half in dollars and half in their own currencies. Net importer countries paid an increasing proportion of residual regional trade deficits in dollars. Fixed exchange rates were obligatory within EPU. Gradually the EPU "hardened" settlements, increasing the dollar component. By 1958 the EPU had worked itself out of existence and members could afford to settle all regional trade imbalances in hard currency, as reserve positions improved. At that time European currencies became fully convertible and progressively hardened as the Common Market was phased in and as Europe experienced a strong economic recovery.

By 1970 the Werner report introduced a plan for achieving a common currency in three stages by 1980. Unfortunately, collapse of the dollar-based Bretton Woods system in 1971–1973 forced European currency unionists to return to the drawing board. By March 1979 seven European nations were ready to embark on a European monetary system (EMS) in which fixed exchange rates would operate (Belgium, Denmark, Germany, France, Italy, Ireland, and the Netherlands). A parallel currency was introduced—the European Currency Unit (ECU). The seven EMS member currencies plus the Luxembourg and UK currencies became components of the basket currency. Each currency was assigned a fixed weight in the ECU, and a value of the ECU in terms of the national currency units is determined for each country.

Originally equal to one U.S. dollar, the value of the ECU against the dollar would reflect the variation of component currencies against the dollar on a weighted basis. An exchange rate mechanism (ERM) was established, and every member country participated in the float against the rest of the world. Eventually Great Britain opted out of the ERM. Even if Britain eventually decides not to join the monetary union, it will have to make adjustments within the EU and in fact has already been undertaking these adjustments. In November 1998 the EU economics commissioner, Yves-Thibault de Silguy, praised Britain for publishing procedures for parallel invoicing in both the British pound and in the euro.[11] From 1985 to 1992 the EMS was praised in achieving its goal of stable exchange rates among member states. In this period the deutsche mark replaced the U.S. dollar as the key currency for European central banks. Unfortunately, in 1992–1993 a series of incidents derailed the European monetary union train. The Danish electorate failed to approve the Maastricht treaty, a weaker U.S. dollar placed trade balance pressures on the European region, Germany maintained high interest rates in the wake of reunification, and Finland was forced to float the markka. The period 1992–1993 witnessed a number of currency devaluations (Spain, Italy, Portugal, Ireland, and the UK). To avoid a French withdrawal from the ERM in August 1993, the bands of fluctuation were widened to ±15 percent of central parity.

The August 1993 climax to the EMS crisis was followed by a renewed period of currency convergence. In 1995 a series of discussions led to adopting a compromise name "euro" for the single currency-to-be. By this time the European Monetary Institute had begun operation in Frankfurt, assembling a technical staff to monitor progress of member states toward fulfillment of the Maastricht criteria for convergence.

Decision to Go Ahead

In January 1998, it was still not clear whether attempts at European union would put Europe more on a par with the United States or widen existing European national divisions.[12] But over the May 1–2 weekend in 1998 the political leaders of the EU gathered in Brussels to make a historic decision. The fifteen EU heads of government agreed that eleven EU nations would be initial members of the monetary union. This marked a cultural revolution enshrining conservative economics on a continental scale. The introduction of the euro was expected to bring a new era of prosperity to Europe, built on stable prices, market transparency, and fiscal discipline.[13]

Among the eleven chosen were Germany, France, Italy, Spain, the Netherlands, Belgium, Portugal, Finland, Ireland, Austria, and Luxembourg.[14] Britain, Denmark, and Sweden declined membership for mixed reasons, including the loss of their national identity and the loss of their currencies. Greece was left out because of its poor economic performance. Luxembourg, which might seem an unlikely member, is home of one of Europe's most powerful banking firms, the European Investment Bank (EIB) (see chap. 7 in this volume).[15] Although the EIB is the EU's financing arm,[16] its administration is wholly independent of the European Commission.[17] The EIB draws no fluid funds from the EU budget.

The Legal Framework

As of January 1, 1999, the currency of the EU was agreed to be the "euro."[18] This idea is the core of the monetary law of the member states of the EU as expressed in the third state of the economic and monetary union. The main part of the legal framework for this union is laid down in the Council regulations for the introduction of the euro and the Council regulation (EC) no. 1103/97 of June 17, 1997, which contains provisions prescribing the introduction of the euro.

In January 1999 responsibility for monetary policy, exchange rate policy, and currency law for member states of the EU was transferred to the Community level. The European System of Central Banks (art. 105 of the treaty) will implement the monetary policy.[19] The Council will determine the exchange rate policy, and the ESCB and the Commission will consult according to the provisions of article 109 of the treaty.

A Gamble

In 1998 the creation of the European monetary union was a gamble. It extends beyond the northern fiscally conservative countries to Italy and Spain, countries that have endured inflation-prone conditions for most of the past several decades. While there are unanswered questions concerning degree of success and failure, origins extend back several decades, when Europe was seeking to respond to the breakdown of the Bretton Woods international monetary system.[20]

From an economic and social point of view the survival of the Union will depend on the interaction of three key forces:[21] (1) European integration, (2) the demographics of an aging population, and (3) the strength of European technological development. The single currency is bringing rapid institutional change and accelerating market securitization in the bond and equity markets. These markets now compete with European banks as a major source of credit in the EU.

The idea of one market and one money has an attractive ring. But the euro's success will be decided by the following key factors:

- Sustainability of economic convergence inside the Eurozone
- Strength of political commitment to financial discipline among all member states
- Credibility of the new European Central Bank

Agreement to launch the euro was finalized over the May 1–2 meetings, despite strong disagreement between France and other EU nations concerning the presidency of the European Central Bank.[22] Although Britain was not in the first wave of countries signing on to the euro, Tony Blair and Gordon Brown were at the forefront of efforts to broker a compromise between France and its partners over who should be the first president of the ECB.[23]

Although the EU is not a political union, the side effects of the policies necessary to create convergence through fiscal and monetary policies have created a much higher level of agreement among these countries than before. One evidence of this was the tough new antipollution rules announced in July 1998 by the fifteen-member EU.[24] Under these rules the use of leaded gasoline will be banned for many car engines, and all fuels will be required to be cleaner by 2000. Even tougher standards will go into effect in 2005, anticipating a 70 percent cut in the pollutant emissions from cars that foul Europe's cities. The compromises made on all sides of the long and fiery negotiations to reach these regulations were probably enabled by the successful negotiations that led to the agreement for the EU in May 1998.

The Euro as a Single Currency

On January 1, 1999, eleven European nations introduced a new common currency. In 2002 this currency will replace marks, francs, guilders, lire, and the rest. An optimistic view is that the coming of the euro will bring about growing economic efficiency throughout Europe. This will make the Continent a more competitive industrial region. Further, the peace dividend will take the form of minimizing need for defense expenditures, given the fading cold war. Economic integration is seen as the most effective insurance against backsliding.[25]

Michael Camdessus, the managing director of the International Monetary Fund, made a speech before the European Banking Forum in Prague on March 19, 1996, describing the glowing world that was ready to spring from the EU and the euro.[26] In the single-currency Euroland, markets were expected to become larger, deeper, more complex, and more closely integrated. The adoption of the euro would activate many factors to bring about the following:

- One very strong currency would anchor macroeconomic policy and denominate European trade and investment.
- The euro would aid the development of a unified market for government securities issued by members.
- The euro would produce a large and increasingly dynamic internal market, expanding trade with the rest of the world.
- Larger amounts of European savings would be available for investment in Europe and abroad, would lower interest rates, and would lower risk.
- The creation of a highly liquid capital market would help debt managers reduce funding costs.[27]

Despite the promise of unified capital markets, it was generally believed in 1996 that the extremely narrow spreads and high liquidity of U.S. debt markets—the deepest, most liquid, and most credit-conscious pool of capital in the world—would provide advantages that European and Asian capital markets would not be able to match for some time.[28] But structural change was occurring quickly in the U.S. market, where portfolio managers wanted to diversify their holdings by buying foreign assets.

But with more countries pursuing sound policies, and with markets continuing to channel capital into promising investments around the globe, there would be a continually expanding number of new players in the international economy. The continued expansion of world trade, direct foreign investment, and other international capital flows should make the cost of exchange rate misalignments and the benefits of exchange rate stability all the more apparent.

Practical Preparations for the Euro

Europe's preparations for conversion to the euro made the problem of the millennium bug look simple:[29]

- Making computer systems euro-compliant cost up to $175 billion, according to the IBM Corporation. The Gartner Group estimates $150 billion–$400 billion.
- In the spring before conversion, KPMG found that few European companies understood the real extent of the impact of monetary union on their organizations and their markets.
- Large banks and insurance companies were making preparations for the euro for at least two years, according to Eric Coursin of Sema Group in Paris.
- Small European companies often reduced the euro conversion to a question of software upgrades, "which it definitely isn't," said Coursin.
- The conversion to euro was a bonanza for Germany's SAP[30] and Holland's Baan, which supply business software with comprehensive, firm-wide scope. These programs, which manage payrolls, inventories, orders, and invoices, had to be rewritten. Enormous amounts of historical data had to be converted.
- Automated teller machines, computer recognition programs, and other computer interfaces had to be revamped. Cash registers had to be reprogrammed, employees retrained, and export-import operations reorganized.

The process of conversion has been described as transition and triangulation. Corporations were preparing for the euro while they simultaneously operated on the old, dual-currency system as the system was phased in during the transition period from 1999 to mid-2002. "It's a huge challenge," said Nick Jones, a research director with the Gartner Group Europe in London.[31] The conversion might cost large corporations hundreds of millions of dollars. Paribas, a large French bank, thought that its cost would be nearly $85 million.

How Large Is Euroland?

In May 1998 eleven countries decided to enter the euro system, locking their exchange rates to the new currency. The eleven-country Euroland will become a major economic and monetary bloc in world affairs. The debt markets of united Euroland are expected to be second only in size to those of the United States.[32]

As of 1998 the population in Euroland exceeded that of the United States and was more than twice that of Japan (table 1.3). Euroland contains 19 percent of world gross domestic product (GDP), close to the 20 percent held by the United States. Euroland is the world's largest trading group, accounting for 19 percent of world exports. Finally, the combined stock markets of Euroland are approximately 40 percent as large as the U.S. stock market capitalization, but considerably larger than that of Japan (table 1.3). Should the UK become a participant in the euro system, the stock market capitalization would increase by a wide margin.

Table 1.3. Euroland Compared with the United States and Japan

Economic Component	*Euroland*	*U.S.*	*Japan*
Population (millions)	290	267	127
Share of world GDP (%)	19	20	8
Share of world trade (%)	19	17	8
Stock market value (U.S.$ billion)	$3,560	$9,460	$2,000

Sources: International Monetary Fund (IMF), World Bank, *Wall Street Journal*, and authors' calculations.

The political expansion of the Eurozone should be considered in evaluating overall size. The Eurozone could expand from any of the following developments:

- Decision by eligible countries that are able to become participants in the single currency system (UK, Sweden, or Denmark)
- Greece met eligibility conditions in 2000 and entered the euro system in January 2001
- Eastward expansion (not expected before year 2003)

What Is the Euro?

Most commentators and analysts address the euro as a fairly simple monetary unit, created by combining eleven currencies into a single unit of account. But it is more than that. It is a political, economic, and financial revolution in the European scene.

Former German chancellor Helmut Kohl regards the euro as a way to ensure peace in Europe. It is a first step toward closer ties between national governments.[33] European big business has a different perspective. Business sees the euro as a means of achieving greater efficiency by cutting transaction costs via cross-border mergers and sales competition. Once-bitter rivals are coming together, for example, the proposed merger between the London and Frankfurt stock exchanges or between the LIFFE (London International Financial Futures Exchange) and German DTB (Deutsche Termin Börse).

Consumers see the euro as reorganizing Europe into a buyer's haven. This suggests that retailing will be transformed into an intensely competitive driving force that benefits households. This revives interest in the Galbraithian concept of "countervailing power" in which consumers become unified via larger retail distribution systems.

For people outside Europe the single currency represents a new competitive factor. The Eurozone rivals the U.S. economy and almost dwarfs Japan. American business groups are taking a hard look at Euroland as a potentially stronger trading and investing bloc. European business firms are finding competitive strength by demanding that suppliers invoice in euros, and they will experience a lower cost of capital as the Eurozone capital markets become integrated and further developed.

Can the Euro Work?

The euro is a novel experiment, and there is no prior experience in such a large-scale monetary changeover. When has so large a bloc of nations ever surrendered central banking sovereignty to a regional controller of money supply? The idea of one central bank setting interest rates for economies as diverse as Austria and Spain is daunting.

The euro will work if the governments of member states demonstrate a willingness to align their economies, and if the timetable for phase-in is realistic. EU governments have made considerable progress during the 1990s in bringing their economies and finances into alignment. The Maastricht convergence criteria were targeted successfully by EU members, as well as by G-7 countries (table 1.4). Whereas the G-7 improved their central government financial balance dramatically between 1991 and 1998, the three EU countries represented also achieved striking improvements. These three (Germany, France, Italy) brought their average government financial balance to nearly 2 percent of GDP. As we observe in a following chapter, the original eleven countries in total achieved dramatic success in attaining macroeconomic convergence.

Table 1.4. Central Government Financial Balances, Surplus (+) or Deficit (–) as a Percentage of Nominal GDP

Country	*1991*	*1992*	*1993*	*1994*	*1995*	*1996*	*1997*	*1998*	*1999*
United States	–3.5	–4.7	–3.9	–2.7	–2.3	–1.4	–0.2	0.2	0.1
Excluding social security	–4.4	–5.5	–4.6	–3.5	–3.2	–2.4	–1.3	–1.0	–1.3
Japan	–0.2	–2.1	–2.8	–3.7	–4.1	–4.4	–3.7	–3.4	–2.7
Germany	–1.9	–1.3	–2.1	–1.5	–1.5	–2.2	–1.7	–1.5	–1.4
France	–1.7	–3.0	–4.5	–4.8	–4.3	–3.9	–3.1	–3.4	–3.0
Italy	–9.6	–9.6	–9.8	–9.4	–6.7	–6.7	–2.7	–2.6	–2.5
UK	–1.1	–5.6	–7.3	–5.8	–5.1	–4.0	–1.7	–0.7	–0.3
Canada	–4.6	–4.3	–4.8	–3.6	–3.2	–1.5	0.8	1.5	1.6
Total of above countries	–2.9	–4.1	–4.3	–3.7	–3.3	–2.8	–1.5	–1.1	1.0

Source: OECD Economic Outlook, 1998.

Notes: Organization for Economic Cooperation and Development (OECD) secretariat estimates derived from fiscal year data converted to a calendar year basis.

For the fiscal years beginning April 1 of the year shown.

The 1998 deficit would rise by 5.2 percentage points of GDP if account were taken of the central government's expected assumption of the accumulated deficits of the Japan Railway Settlement Corporation and the National Forest Services.

The timetable for introduction of the euro is outlined in table 1.5. As noted in table 1.2, introduction of the euro signifies the beginning of stage 3 of EMU. During stage 2 the European Monetary Institute (EMI) was set up, and the European System of Central Banks (ESCB) was organized. Also during stage 2 members moved toward conformity with the Maastricht criteria.

As noted in table 1.5, in the final year of stage 2 (1998) participating member states were chosen, bilateral conversion rates were announced (May 1998), and the executive board of the European Central Bank (ECB) was organized.

Table 1.5. Planned Timetable for the Introduction of the Euro in First-Wave Member States

Calendar Period	*Activity*
1998	Stage 2
	Publication of 1997 outturn data
	Informal ECOFIN meeting publication of Commission and EMI Article 109j(1)
	Convergence Reports
	Early May Meeting
	Participating member states chosen
	Bilateral conversion rates announced
	Recommendations for executive board of ECB
	Publication of EMI report
	ECB formally established and EMI enters liquidation
	ECB operational decisions
	Testing of systems
	Conversion weekend at end 1998–begin 1999
1999	Stage 3
	Irrevocable locking of conversion rates
	Euro becomes currency in its own right
	Single Monetary Policy commences
	ECB operations and new issues of government debt denominated in euro
	Redenomination of existing government debt to euro
	Wholesale financial activity to move rapidly to euro
2000	National banknotes and coin remain legal tender
2001	No compulsion, no prohibition in use of euro
2002	Date for introduction of euro notes and coin
	Probable mass changeover of retail activity to euro
	End of legal transition period
	Dual legal tender period (ends at yearend)
2003	Latest date for withdrawal of legal tender status from national currency notes and coin

Sources: European Union.

With the establishment and operation of the ECB, the EMI enters into a liquidation period. Finally, ECB operational decisions take place in preparation for the testing of the new central bank system.

On January 1, 1999, stage 3 commenced. At this point the irrevocable locking of currency conversion rates took place and the euro became a currency in its own right. Most important, a single monetary policy commenced. ECB financial operations include transactions in new issues of government debt denominated in the euro. Also, existing government debt of the eleven member states was redenominated into euro. Wholesale financial activity in euros, as listed below, was phased in:

- central bank system clearings and settlements
- bank-to-bank transactions
- government debt-financing transactions
- government-to-government payments
- EU governmental accounts and fiscal transactions with member states

National bank notes and coin (retail) remain legal tender through the period 1999–2001. But in the year 2002 a conversion will take place, with euro banknotes and coinage coming into circulation. December 2002 is the final month for withdrawal of legal tender status from national currency notes.

As the above description indicates, there is a lengthy transitional period (1998–2002) in which the various aspects of the euro will be phased in. This suggests that the flexibility is sufficient to ensure a reasonably successful transition.

NOTES

1. Edmund L. Andrews, "Eleven Nations Take Key Step toward Unified Currency," *New York Times Interactive*, April 26, 1998.
2. David Gress, "Chapter One. From Plato to NATO: The Idea of the West and Its Opponents," *Free Press Interactive*, 1998.
3. Howard S. Ellis, *The Economics of Freedom* (New York: Council on Foreign Relations, 1950), 369.
4. Ellis, *Economics*, 3.
5. Abba Eban, "Diplomacy for the Next Century," in *The Cold War Remembered* (Cambridge: Yale University Press, 1998), chap. 1.
6. Eban, "Diplomacy," chap. 1.
7. Eban, "Diplomacy," chap. 1.
8. Larry Neal and Daniel Barbezat, *The Economics of the European Union and the Economies of Europe* (London: Oxford University Press, 1998), 7.

9. Emile Benoit, *Europe, at Sixes and Sevens: The Common Market* (London: University Press, 1961), chap. 3, 69–84.

10. Neal and Barbezat, *Economics*, 9–10.

11. "Euro Markets: Firms outside Euro Zone Urged to Adopt Euro as a Parallel Unit," *Dow Jones Newswires*, November 16, 1998.

12. Craig R. Whitney, "Ready or Not, Europe Draws Closer to One Currency," *New York Times Interactive*, January 5, 1998.

13. Lionel Barber, "Let the Great Experiment Begin," *Financial Times*, April 30, 1998; "Special Survey: Birth of the Euro," 1; and Edmund L. Andrews, "Official Stamps of Approval for the Euro Plan," *New York Times*, March 26, 1998, D4.

14. Associated Press, "European Union Selects Eleven to Join Currency Bloc," *New York Times Interactive*, March 25, 1998.

15. Peter Lee, "The World's Best Borrower: EIB," *Euromoney* 338 (June 1997): 73–78.

16. European Investment Bank, "Overview," L-2950 Luxembourg, June 18, 1998, m.bello@eib.org.

17. Alan Osborn, "Luxembourg: European Investment Bank Europe," *Europe* 361 (November 1996): 29–30.

18. Directorate General II, Economic and Financial Affairs, "Legal Framework for the Use of the Euro," Commission of the EEC–Euro Papers, ideas.uqam.ca/ideas/data/JEL/F3.html; and ideas.uqam.ca/ideas/data JEL/F3.htmlJEL.

19. Directorate General II, Economic and Financial Affairs, "The Legal Frame-Work for the Use of the Euro: Questions and Answers on the Euro Regulations," Commission of the EEC–Euro Papers, January 1998, ideas.uqam.ca/ideas/data/JEL/F3.thml, and ideas.uquam.ca/ideas.uqam.ca/ideas/data/JEL/F3.thmlJEL.

20. Graham Bird, "From Bretton Woods to Halifax and Beyond: The Political Economy of International Monetary Reform," *World Economy*, March 1996, 149–173.

21. Graham Bishop, "EMU on Track," *Euromoney*, August 1997, 37–39.

22. Craig R. Whitney, "Eleven Countries Move Ahead with Changeover to the Euro," *New York Times Interactive*, May 3, 1998.

23. Toby Heim and George Jones, "Stage Is Set for Launch of the Euro," *Daily Telegraph* (London), May 2, 1998, 1. The British prime minister and chancellor of Exchequer both indicated a favorable viewpoint concerning the possible future entry of the United Kingdom into a single currency system.

24. "European Union Bans Leaded Gas Starting in 2000," *Houston Chronicle*, July 3, 1998, 29.

25. Richard L. Hudson, "A Safe Haven?" *Wall Street Journal*, September 28, 1998, R4.

26. Michel Camdessus, "Europe in the Global Financial World," *Vital Speeches of the Day*, May 15, 1996, 450.

27. Graham Bishop, "The Key to a Single Market," *Euromoney*, July 1996, 119.

28. Danielle Robinson, "All Aboard the Yankee Debt Train," *Euroweek*, November 1996, 6–22.

29. Bruno Giussani, "Euro Changeover Makes Year 2000 Bug Look Easy," *Interactive New York Times*, April 21, 1998.

30. Matthew Rose, "Prototype: With American Flair, Hasso Plattner Leads Europe's Tech Revival. His Software and His Style Influence a Generation of Young Entrepreneurs, Mooning Ellison's Minions," *Wall Street Journal*, July 2, 1998, A1, A8.

31. Rose, "Prototype," A1, A8.

32. Hannes Schneider, "The Introduction of the Euro—Expectations of a Capital Markets Lawyer," *International Financial Law Review*, April 1988, 7–8.

33. Dagmar Aalund, "What's the Euro?" *Wall Street Journal*, September 28, 1998, R6.

Chapter Two

Resource Mobility in a Suboptimal Currency Area

Many chapters of this book focus on the benefits of a single currency. However, the adoption of a single currency can involve costs as well as benefits. An important "cost" is that the twelve nations of Europe have given up their ability to exercise independent exchange rate policy. A second, and closely related, cost is that exchange rate policy has been abandoned as a means of accommodating economic shocks and balancing the external payments positions of members of the single currency area.

We can understand this as follows. Consider a country that experienced a decline in the demand for its exports. Based on traditional circumstances, it could devalue its currency or allow the currency to depreciate. This could facilitate regaining international competitiveness. The extent of economic openness will determine how costly the currency depreciation must be in terms of lower real incomes.

If this country were a member of a currency union, the decline in the demand for its exports might originate from within the currency union. In this case, a currency depreciation would not be an available remedy. However, other adjustment mechanisms could come into play to offset the consequences of this economic shock, for example, a shift of productive resources from the export sector to other industry sectors, price and wage adjustments, and public sector transfer payments to at least temporarily replace some of the income lost to workers in the export sector.

This chapter considers the costs of a single currency by reviewing the theory of optimal currency areas and its applicability to the European case. In addition, the chapter explores the flexibility and mobility of markets for labor and capital in the European twelve-country group and the potential role of mobility of labor and capital vis-à-vis other economic adjustment mechanisms.

THE THEORY OF OPTIMAL CURRENCY AREAS

Basic Theoretical Approaches

The theory of optimal currency areas (TOCA) emerged midstream during the Bretton Woods era. It was part of the dialogue in which the relative merits of fixed and floating currency systems were debated.[1] Since coming on the scene, TOCA has been refined as a potential justification for a European single currency. In that discussion, the European conditions for introduction of a single currency have been compared with conditions in other currency areas (most especially the United States).

In a classic article, Richard Mundell demonstrated that unless labor and capital can move freely between regions, a shock involving a shift in global demand away from the products of one region will create unemployment.[2] If wages and exchange rates are fixed, devaluation may mitigate the decline in employment (table 2.1). Mundell further argued that western Canada and eastern Canada should be separate currency areas because of the difficulty of moving capital and labor between these regions.[3]

Two years later, Ronald McKinnon demonstrated that the effectiveness of the exchange rate to restore external balance in an economic region adversely affected by an external demand shock is likely to be greater the less open the region is to foreign trade (table 2.1). For example, in an economy with a small

Table 2.1. Development of Conceptual Foundation for European Currency Union

Proponent and year	*Conditions Required*	*Comment*
Mundell (1961)	High mobility of labor and capital	Can factors of production move from a depressed area within currency zone to a more prosperous area?
McKinnon (1963)	Intensity of trade between subregions	Size of the optimum currency area depends on degree of openness.
Kenen (1969)	Industrial diversification	Most highly developed nations enjoy high level of industrial diversification.
de Grauwe (1992–1994)	Political will to form and implement fiscal transfers required	Shocks can be softened by fiscal transfers from one region of the currency zone to another. Fiscal transfers can substitute for labor and capital mobility.

Sources: See notes 2, 3, 4, 5, 6 in this chapter. Richard Mundell, "A Theory of Optimal Currency Areas," *American Economic Review*, September 1961; Richard Mundell, "Capital Mobility and Stabilization Policy," *Canadian Journal of Economics and Political Science*, November 1963; Ronald I. McKinnon, "Optimal Currency Areas," *American Economic Review*, September 1963; Peter Kenen, "The Theory of Optimal Currency Areas: An Eclectic View," in *Monetary Problems of the International Economy* (Chicago: University of Chicago Press, 1969); Paul de Grauwe, *The Economics of Monetary Integration* (Oxford: Oxford University Press, 1992).

foreign trade sector, the exchange rate change required to transfer a given amount of production resources into the foreign trade sector will be relatively small, and the effects on domestic inflation (price levels) minor.[4]

According to McKinnon, the more open an economy, the less likely it is that there will be money illusion or that workers will contract their pay in terms of domestic money only. It is clear that trade unionists fully understand that real wages are affected by devaluation when their workers are fully exposed to international competitive forces. In such cases the exchange rate can become an irrelevant policy measure. Taking this reasoning to its limit, a very small open economy is not a feasible currency area because there would be no reason for it to possess its own exchange rate system.

Several years after McKinnon made his contribution, Peter Kenen demonstrated that the impact of a shock on an economic region will be smaller as the industrial diversification and range of goods and services produced in the region are greater. Economies that specialize in a narrow range of products have a greater need for exchange rate flexibility.[5]

More recently, Paul de Grauwe has argued that the issue of whether two (or more) countries constitute an optimum currency area is ultimately a political one (table 2.1). The political will to form the union and carry out fiscal transfers necessary to maintain it can be as important as the underlying economic structure. The argument by de Grauwe applies specifically to German reunification, which called for unprecedented and enormous fiscal transfers.[6]

The European Union (EU) demonstrates a similar commitment as it expands its structural funds in response to the increased integration resulting from the completion of the unified internal market and the expected European monetary union (EMU).

Does Europe Constitute an Optimal Currency Zone?

The basic principles enunciated above provide an engineer's rough plan for building a highway. The actual construction phase may be hampered by unseen snares and tangles. The operational aspects of an optimal currency zone call for numerous and complex trade-offs. In this regard, Corden put forward a distinction between *optimal* and *feasible* currency areas. Feasibility depends on the effectiveness of the exchange rate as an adjustment measure. Addressing the key question of labor mobility in Europe, Corden noted that

> the mobility of the native-born inhabitants of northwestern Europe is probably now quite low. There would have to be very large wage differentials and substantial unemployment . . . for labor to move on a significant scale among Britain, France and Germany . . . an assumption of low labor mobility among countries seems, in general, more realistic.[7]

More recent analysis appears to support the view concerning labor mobility. A report by Larry Neal and Daniel Barbezat carries a pessimistic view concerning most conditions for currency union.[8] They note that according to three criteria—labor mobility, capital mobility, and fiscal transfers—the countries of Europe fail to fully meet the conditions for currency union. They note that European labor markets are more rigid than those in the United States and that wage elasticities are low in Europe, and they suggest that shocks might be felt for long periods with wages being slow to adjust. These observations are confirmed by the relatively high rates of unemployment persisting in Europe. Only in terms of the criterion of openness and intensity of trade relations do the European countries qualify as an optimum currency area. The smallest countries in Europe are most likely to benefit from a common currency with their larger trading partners. The small countries outside the European Community (EC) can also be expected to find that their trade ties are strongest with the Eurozone. These small countries will find it beneficial to join the common currency. These countries include many nations in eastern and central Europe, as well as the European Union countries that have delayed entry to the single currency system.

LABOR MOBILITY IN EUROPE

Labor Market Shifts

It has been well stated that continental Europe's labor markets are too rigid and need serious deregulation. The Organization for Economic Cooperation and Development (OECD) repeatedly has bemoaned the lack of political will for reform. A turning point could emerge as the euro exerts its influence as the regional currency. One nation that might surprise many by introducing reforms is France, which in the past has been the bastion of state control and regulated labor markets.

When the Jospin government introduced the thirty-five-hour week, it might have been maneuvering to gain flexibility in other areas. The thirty-five-hour week earned Lionel Jospin considerable political goodwill. When visiting the United States in mid-June 1998, he stated that he had come to assess the sources of American economic dynamism. In handling the Air France strike, the government held out against the strikers until they agreed to negotiate. This was a departure from previous experience because in the past the government had frequently capitulated to labor's demands.

Further, the French government has moved ahead with privatization and has actively encouraged entrepreneurship. With France's unemployment rate stuck above 11 percent from 1987 to 1989, Jospin had good reason to advance more flexible, market-oriented reforms. The coming of the EMU and related competitive pressures makes addressing labor market problems of utmost urgency. The EMU will affect other member states in a similar way, and they will see labor market reform as a means of ameliorating high unemployment.[9] Table 2.2 provides comparative May 1997 and May 1998 unemployment rates in selected countries. In most cases the levels are unacceptably high and are not improving in any significant way. Data provided by the European Central Bank (ECB) at year-end 1999 indicated that between the third quarter of 1998 and the third quarter of 1999, the unemployment rate in the Eurozone had moved from 8 percent to 10 percent.[10]

Table 2.2. Movement in Unemployment Rates, Selected European Countries, May 1997–May 1998

Country	*May 1997*	*May 1998*
Austria	4.3	4.5
Portugal	6.6	6.4
Sweden	10.3	8.9
Belgium	9.3	8.9
Ireland	10.2	9.2
Luxembourg	2.6	2.2
Germany	9.9	9.8
France	12.4	11.9
Finland	13.8	12.7
Spain	21.0	18.8

Source: "Continental Shifts," *Financial Times*, June 23, 1998, 19.

Europe's Labor Dilemmas

Since the launch of the euro, it has been possible to observe how well the single-currency area can adapt to world competitive conditions and requirements. Conventional wisdom asserts that the EMU will improve Europe's competitive position. This argument is based on expected larger-scale economies in a single-market area, a more open trading system, and increased capital market efficiencies.

We must remember that the EMU alone can neither (1) reduce the Continent's high labor costs in manufacturing nor (2) improve the efficiencies in Europe's regulated services sector. On the manufacturing side, Germany has been regarded as Europe's economic engine. In 1995, hourly wages in German manufacturing were 88 percent higher than they were in the United States. By 1997 the disparity had narrowed to 54 percent. If we adjust labor costs for productivity, the German cost disadvantage appears less serious. In recent years manufacturing productivity has advanced faster in Germany than in the United States.

There is wide belief that the single currency will enhance labor productivity by making Europe's capital markets more efficient. But the single currency may not be sufficient to bring this about. Pressure exerted by the capital markets is a highly circuitous way of dealing with Europe's structural labor market problems.[11] The political process may ultimately determine the outcome. This is because the root source of high labor costs in Europe is the deeply entrenched social contract. In 1996 benefits and social insurance accounted for 28 percent of hourly compensation in U.S. manufacturing but 45 percent in Germany. The social contract accounts for two-thirds of the disparity between U.S. and German compensation in 1996.

Germany may not represent the full picture in Europe. In 1997, German compensation was 40 percent above the European average ($20.26 per hour). At the opposite end of the spectrum are low-cost labor in the UK ($14.01), Italy ($15.27), and France ($18.53). These wage rates compare with an hourly compensation in Germany of $27.81.

In 1995, on average, hourly compensation in euro manufacturing was 32 percent higher than in U.S. manufacturing but only 12 percent higher in 1997. There is no mistaking the narrowing in overall cost disadvantage. Can this continue?

In recent years European privatization and corporate restructuring have played a growing role in promoting labor market flexibility. Here the service sector plays the role of shock absorber to accommodate the job shedding in tradable goods industries. Europe needs a dynamic and competitive service sector to assist in this restructuring by absorbing workers who may be shed as manufacturing adopts a leaner operation.

Information technology represents a second problem area. European investment in IT is lagging as a percentage of gross domestic product (GDP) when compared with investment in the United States and Japan. Europe has only 52 business personal computers per 100 white-collar workers (1996), half the UK level of 103 per 100 workers. However, these statistics are indicators that Europe is shifting its focus toward developing IT sectors more aggressively.

Over the short run, the shift in competitiveness may hinge on currency fluctuations. This poses a tactical challenge for Europe. It would require (mid-1998) a substantial dollar exchange rate adjustment to make U.S. and German compensation balance (rate of 2.7 DM/$). At midyear 1998 the rate was 1.77. At midyear 2000 the rate was 3.4. But it would take a much smaller depreciation of the euro to achieve similar conditions of wage-cost parity for other countries in Europe. The 1999–2000 depreciation of the euro vis-à-vis the dollar has accomplished much in restoring wage-cost parity.

Attached to Home

How mobile are Europe's workers? Or, how attached are they to home? If jobless Europeans, and there are many of them (table 2.3), do not change their

Table 2.3. Labor Costs and Productivity in the Eurozone, 1997

	Index of Productivity	*Index of Labor Cost*	*Jobless Rate*
Austria	90.9	89.5	4.4
Belgium	97.6	107.6	9.2
Finland	81.4	93.8	14.0
France	95.3	95.6	12.4
Germany	92.9	95.3	9.7
West	100.0	100.0	8.3
East	60.4	74.4	15.7
Ireland	69.5	71.8	10.2
Italy	85.0	79.9	12.1
Netherlands	85.4	94.4	5.2
Portugal	34.5	37.4	6.8
Spain	62.0	66.9	20.8
UK	71.7	68.0	7.1

Source: Peter Norman, "Productivity Study Shows Dangers of Euro Wage Clauses," *Financial Times*, July 7, 1998, 3.

stay-at-home habits, the EMU could run into a serious difficulty. Lack of labor mobility clearly contributes to European unemployment. The euro has taken away much of the ability of individual countries to stimulate economic activity as a means of fighting unemployment.

The International Monetary Fund (IMF) cautioned, in a report issued in May 1998, that failure to reform Europe's labor markets could become the Achilles' heel of the euro. Economic and monetary union limits the use of monetary and fiscal policy, since a new ECB is setting interest rates for all Euroland.

Labor mobility would be less of a problem if unemployed workers would move to find jobs as they do in the United States. For example, the U.S. Census Bureau estimates that 9 percent of all American households move to a different state every five years. With no comparable figures for Europe, economists estimate that European mobility is far lower.[12]

What factors make European labor less mobile than its American counterpart? One factor is culture, pride of home, family, and social protection. A second is language. Nevertheless, many are persuaded that Europe is changing and that the direction is toward higher worker mobility.

Loosening Labor Laws

New terminologies are making their way into Europe's labor market, terminologies such as "shared workers" and "rented employees." Saab and Ericsson, two large Swedish companies, are enthusiastic about sharing workers on a day-to-day basis. Moreover, they can let them go when they don't need them, avoiding severance bonuses or formal action by the union.

The European market has added a new dimension. Manpower Europe, a temporary job unit of Manpower U.S., is actively serving European employers needing workers for short-term or temporary employment. It is easier and less expensive to rent employees than to hire them. Europe is adopting an obvious solution to its high unemployment problem—labor flexibility.[13]

Many governments are allowing companies to hire workers on short-term contracts. Aided by relaxed labor laws, some European countries are enjoying a net increase in jobs for the first time in over a decade. In the past, many companies avoided adding any workers, due to the difficulty and expense of dismissing them when not needed. Countries that have eased labor laws the most have experienced the biggest gains in new jobs. Between 1994 and 1997 employment rose 6.2 percent in Spain, 6.9 percent in the Netherlands, and 4 percent in Britain. By contrast, in Germany, where employment fell 3.3 percent (1994–1997), labor laws have remained more restrictive.

European companies are pushing Europe toward deregulation. This is reflected in large gains in temporary work and short-term contracts. The temporary market is growing more than 10 percent a year. It is reported that the Netherlands has the highest proportion of temporary workers at 3.2 percent, compared with 2.2 percent in the United States and 1.9 percent in Britain. Spain is experiencing a driving growth of temporary agencies in Europe.

While Europe has the strictest worker protection laws, the situation is changing. In Spain the standard severance pay was reduced from forty-five days to thirty-three days, in return for lengthening the duration of labor contracts. In France, Labor Minister Martine Aubry notes that "30 percent of new hires are on short term contracts," usually six months. Also, employers can fire without prior authorization. France is now relatively flexible.

Sweden is experiencing an unofficial loosening of labor market rules. In one case manufacturers favored a local labor pool, which they can use to add and give back workers on a flexible basis. Nevertheless, many workers consider flexibility a bad trend.

European companies are joining the temp job bandwagon. Moulinex S.A., a French household appliance maker, illustrates the use of temporary workers. In 1996 the company chairman decided to close two plants and cut 2,700 jobs. In 1998, after five years of losses, Moulinex is in the black and is expected to remain profitable after 1998. Also, the company has cut the workweek of its remaining employees to thirty-three hours from thirty-nine, with almost no loss in pay. This is in return for greater flexibility in working hours.

Productivity, Wages, and Competitiveness

Labor market equilibrium at full employment is a goal no politician can scoff at. Is it achievable in the new Eurozone? What is the best way to achieve it—

worker mobility, wage adjustment, or some other mix of economic micropolicies? These are key questions bedeviling economists, researchers, and politicians.

A Divergent Productivity Picture in Europe

Individual countries in the Eurozone have assembled labor productivity data for analytical use. Unfortunately, the statistical bases and methods are different, making intercountry data not comparable. Horst Siebert, head of the Kiel Institute of World Economics and one of five economics professors on the German government Council of Economic Advisers, has undertaken pioneering work on labor productivity in the E-11. In a newly published Kiel working paper Siebert has produced the first comparable figures on labor productivity among the euro-11 member states.[14]

Siebert's study reveals several important facts. First, wage-setting and social security systems cannot be Europeanized. They will have to remain anchored on their present national structures for the foreseeable future. This can be a troublesome finding, since trade unions in Europe are preparing to develop cross-border activities to replace the former nationally based wage and fringe benefits negotiations. The euro and its transparency of prices and wages reinforce this cross-border wage setting trend.

A second part of the Siebert study indicates divergent productivity levels in the Eurozone. A Europeanization of wages would likely increase unemployment, most especially in countries or areas suffering lower productivity levels. Table 2.3 uses former West Germany as a base (equal to 100) case. From this we can observe the degree to which countries differ in productivity and in wage costs.

Regarding this productivity, four countries fall within 10 percent of the West German level (Austria, Belgium, France, and Germany). Three countries fall between 81 and 86 percent (Finland, Italy, and the Netherlands). Another three fall between 60 and 70 percent (East Germany, Ireland, and Spain). Portugal falls at a low 34.5 percent of the West German productivity level. Siebert estimates UK labor productivity at 71.7 percent of the West German level.

The middle column of table 2.3 shows how labor costs vary with lower labor productivity and higher costs in countries with higher productivity. Exceptions are the Netherlands, East Germany, Finland and Belgium with somewhat higher levels of labor costs on a relative basis.

Decentralized Wage Setting

The data in Siebert's study must be used with care. They apply to only one year (1997), whereas trends are changing the relationships over time. Also, unemployment levels vary (col. 3, table 2.3), a factor that is part of the labor market picture. The informal economy plays a somewhat different role in each country. In the Netherlands, substantial part-time workers could influence measured productivity.

Nevertheless, Siebert and others argue that the different productivity levels indicate the need for decentralized wage formation. This could operate on a company-wide or national level. Differential wages allow for hiring a greater number of workers where labor productivity is lower, providing for a fuller employment level, and avoiding the need to incur high social insurance expenses.

In this connection, the Siebert study has important implications for social policy. Social security and social insurance schemes in Europe are financed by levies on employment. Ultimately, these revenues depend on productivity (the value of wages). Divergence in labor productivity means that the costs of social security systems in countries will be different. This strongly suggests that social security benefits cannot be harmonized very easily in Europe.

Population Migration in the European Union

One of the goals of the EC is to reduce regional differences in well-being as defined by per capita income and employment. In this connection the European Union has made EU-wide projections of regional population, and analyses of population migration. Eurostat (Statistical Office of the European Communities) has been closely involved in much of this work.

In considering population migration in the European Union, three types of flow can be distinguished: (1) flows between EU member states and the rest of the world, (2) flows between EU member states, and (3) flows between regions within EU member states.[15]

External Migration

The period 1990–1995 witnessed significant immigration to the EU countries. However, due to the unusual happenings in Europe during that period (Aussiedler returns to Germany, asylum seekers, and refugees), national projections anticipate substantial new and continuing inflows after 1995. Direct additions to the E-12 population between 1990 and 2020 are likely to be substantial, as indicated in table 2.4. These high estimates may be politically unacceptable, and already measures are being taken to control population movements.

Table 2.4. Projections of In-Migration to the EU-12, 1990–2020

High estimate	23.7 million
Moderate estimate	15.3 million
Low estimate	8.3 million

Source: Philip Rees, "Projecting the National and Regional Populations of the European Union Using Migration Information," in P. Rees, J. Stillwell, A. Convey, and M. Hupiszewski, eds., *Population Migration in the European Union* (New York: Wiley, 1996), 346–348.

Intermember State Migration

One of the aims of the treaty of Maastricht is to ensure freedom of movement for EU citizens among member states.[16] Intermember migration has declined from the peak years of the 1950s, 1960s, and 1970s. Reasons for this decline include an aging population, lower economic growth in former magnet states, reduced demographic pressure in traditional emigration countries, and improved economic conditions in Ireland.

Three categories of the population are viewed as likely to be most affected by closer integration: young persons, highly skilled workers, and some migrant workers outside the European Union. Student exchanges among member states have been increasing. The ERASMUS program, funded by the European Commission, aims at attaining a 10 percent level of student participation. This will bring about an upward shift in international worker migration throughout Europe. There is already evidence of increasing short-term migration among managerial and technical workers.

While intra-EU worker exchanges are moderately small and unlikely to achieve a Rostowian "takeoff," they are increasing and possess a somewhat different content. We can expect that migration between member states will represent more highly skilled, managerial, and technical workers. It will be responsive to improvements in per capita income and focused mostly on higher income countries.

Interregional Migration

Interregional population and labor flows, within country, are subject to reversible factors. For example, between 1989 and 1992 there was a heavy outflow from the eastern *Länder* of Germany. Improved economic conditions have reduced these flows. Similarly, in the UK interregional migration has followed the upswings and downswings of local regional economics in a complex way.

In northern Europe, high-density urbanized regions are becoming less attractive, while low-density, less urbanized regions are becoming more attractive. Alternatively, in southern Europe urbanization is still in its final stages of development.

Regional Population

The geography of future population and labor flows suggests that countries and regions will experience gains and losses in their respective share of the EU total. Gaining countries are, in order of percentage gains, Luxembourg, France, the Netherlands, the UK, and Portugal. The largest loser is Germany. Italy, Denmark, and Belgium follow as share losers, in that order.

A significant number of regions in the European Union face prospects of substantial population loss over the next thirty years, some expected to record declines of over 5 percent. These regions include eastern and northern Germany, north-central Italy, and central and northeastern Spain.

Gaining regions include Luxembourg, the Brussels region, southwestern Scotland, and the northern UK. France is expected to experience population shifts to the Mediterranean region and to other EU states.

As a whole, the European Union faces a future of zero population growth over the medium term. This overall projection conceals a number of varied regional trends.

Migration Policy

In terms of migration policy, the treaty of Maastricht was a milestone. Fully ratified, the treaty came into effect on November 1, 1993. The treaty states that "every person holding the nationality of a member state shall be a citizen of the Union." Included among these rights is freedom to move and reside freely within the territory of the member states. To date, policy toward internal EU migration is becoming increasingly liberal. At the same time, policy toward non-EU citizens crossing the external boundaries of the Union becomes increasingly controlled.

From the point of view of international migration policy, each member state controls a number of "gates" that regulate inflow and settlement of foreigners. These gates include the following:

- entry visa requirements
- border external controls
- long-term work and residence permits
- internal controls
- permanent residence permits
- naturalization

States can open or close these gates. Within the European Union three categories of aliens are recognized:

- citizens of other EU countries
- citizens of the remaining European Free Trade Association (EFTA) countries
- citizens of third countries

The first two categories compose the European economic area. Each category has a different (unequal) legal position.

Entry Visa Requirements

Citizens of EU member states need no visas to enter another EU country. Citizens of EFTA and most OECD countries enjoy the same privileges. Within the EU, admission policies differ from one country to another. EU countries require visas from citizens of all states of the Commonwealth of Independent States (CIS). Citizens of Visegrad countries are much less restricted. There is no recognition within the European Union of a need to develop a common visa policy.

In effect, from a policy perspective, a resident of one EU state has the ability to travel to, reside, and undertake an employed position in any other EU state.

External Border Control

The Benelux countries abolished border controls at their national boundaries in 1960. The Schengen Accords, which came into being on March 26, 1995, for seven of the fifteen EU member states (Belgium, France, Germany, Luxembourg, the Netherlands, Portugal, and Spain), relaxed the border check. This accord also set the goal of abolishing this control. Abolition of border checks reduces states' control over their territory—and gives criminals more favorable working conditions.[17]

In July 1991 the former EC prepared the Convention on the Crossing of EC External Borders. This sought to regulate a number of technical matters and stipulated creation of EC visas. Signing was suspended due to British refusal to do away with intra-EC immigration controls. Additionally, they argued that in the absence of an identity card system internal policing is more difficult.

More recent practice in EU countries has tended toward tightening border checks. This is related to greater numbers of illegal immigrants with the mirage of lucrative employment, African economic distress, atrocities in former Yugoslavia, and instability in East Europe.

Long-Term Residence Permits

It is important to understand that a citizen of the European Union does not need a work permit to get a job in another member state. There is freedom to move and take paid employment anywhere within the member states. There are some limits. This right was given initially only to those taking employment. EC legislation extended this right of relocation and residence to employee families and to those at retirement age. They can remain in the country in which they were formerly employed.[18] Following this, students and retired persons have been given the right to move freely within the EC. Citizens of third countries are closed from such privileges. They must apply for entry visas, and they face greater difficulties in getting employment or regularizing their stay.

Association agreements between the EC and other countries usually vary with regard to freedom of movement. Temporary work and residence permits normally are issued for a specific time period. The main condition for obtaining a residence permit is stable employment. The protection of national labor markets is the focus of policies in these areas.

Internal Controls

Internal controls protect the internal labor market against illegal employment of a foreign labor force. Little or no international cooperation may be expected. In Germany a stringent system requires all workers to possess a social security identification card, to be used for identification as well as for social security office procedures. Employers hiring foreign labor must report this to social security officials. In the Netherlands employers must cover the cost of illegal labor expulsions, and in France they must return all taxes and fees. Small companies are particularly affected (in services and construction), as it is important to keep costs under control.

Permanent Residence Permits

Permanent residence permits are obtained in various ways, often related to prolonged residence and employment. The UK requires four years of uninterrupted legal residence and employment. One of the most important streams of permanent migrants consists of those who reunite with members of their families already lawfully residing in the host country. In all EU countries, spouses and juvenile children are admitted.

EU countries are reported to be housing large numbers of illegal migrants. Many countries attempt to "regularize" clandestine migrants (in the south of Europe). Some countries (Germany, Netherlands) stand firmly on the side of regularizing only those residing in their country legally.

Naturalization

There are several avenues for acquiring citizenship in a country, including (1) place of birth, (2) parents' citizenship, and (3) a mixture of the first two. The EU countries adhering to one or another of these approaches are outlined in table 2.5. From the perspective of migration policy, naturalization becomes an important factor. The final stage of the migration process can be acquiring citizenship via naturalization.

Table 2.5. Methods and Determination for Achieving Citizenship

Type of Citizenship	*Theory*	*Countries in Practice*
Jus solis	Place of birth determines citizenship.	Spain, the Netherlands, Luxembourg, and Greece
Jus sanguinis	The parents' citizenship determines the child's citizenship.	Germany, Denmark, Ireland, and Portugal
Mixture of jus solis and jus sanguinis	Both place of birth and citizenship of parents can control citizenship of the child.	UK, France, Italy, and Belgium
Naturalization	Administrative procedure	All provide this method

Countries prefer to have new citizens integrated as fully as possible into the local community. This explains the long period of residence generally required. In EU countries this varies from as few as five years (France, Ireland, Italy, Netherlands, and the UK), to as many as ten (Belgium, Germany, Luxembourg, and Spain).

Social Security and Health Care

Once migrants cross an EU frontier, they come into contact with other (secondary) elements of national or Union policy. Social security provisions are a long-standing feature of employment legislation in all EU member states. With regard to the movements of workers, the social chapter of the Maastricht treaty highlights several features relating to freedom of movement:

- To ensure at least minimum levels of social security protection are afforded to migrating workers
- A discussion of supplementary retirement schemes to ensure wider trans-frontier worker mobility
- A proposed amendment to existing EEC legislation to ease the coordination of existing schemes, national and European
- A communication on the living and working conditions of citizens in frontier regions

All member states have social security regulations that make a full range of benefits available to all inner migrants who have residence and work permits.

Health care forms part of the social chapter of the Maastricht treaty. Normal medical services have been made available to all EU nationals for some years. This policy does not cater to persons staying in another country for more than a year. Therefore, this system is not especially helpful to migrants, who are normally dependent on medical care available through the national social security systems.

CAPITAL MOBILITY

One aspect of the identification of an optimum currency area is capital mobility. In this section we consider several perspectives on capital mobility, especially in connection with the Eurozone, including the mechanisms through which capital mobility takes place and an assessment of future prospects for European capital mobility.

Perspectives on Capital Mobility

Extensive preparations were made for both the single currency and the parallel single market for capital across most of Europe. A single currency implies a unified capital market. However, two important dimensions of how well the unified capital market will operate should be considered. These are (1) the changes in the volume of capital available and (2) the structural-competitive factors.

Volume of Capital

The unified European capital market will develop in an efficient way if there is a steady expansion in the available flow of capital funds. Perceived or anticipated shortages will cause "rationing and hoarding behavior," not unlike the petroleum markets in the mid-1970s. What are the prospects for a steady expansion in the available flow of capital? Writing in 2000, we consider the prospects favorable for several reasons.

- Expansionary macroeconomic policies are expected in the Eurozone, as required. In 2000 most Eurozone countries had socialist democratic governments, and this suggests a lack of tolerance for high unemployment and a willingness to follow somewhat expansionary policies to alleviate this problem.
- Positive wealth effects (discussed in another chapter) will provide an incremental supply of capital and expand the pool of available capital on a permanent basis.

- Governments in Europe have been striving to improve their budget and debt positions and to reduce deficits. This should continue as the euro is phased in, releasing funds that central governments otherwise would need to borrow.
- The E-11 region will become a more attractive focus for foreign investors and for European investors who otherwise might undertake investment outside the Eurozone. This attraction is already reflected in foreign direct investment (FDI) flows. In the 1980s E-11 outflows represented 29 percent of global total, but in the 1990s they were only 27 percent. Similarly, portfolio inflows will accelerate as the European stock exchanges compete more aggressively for investors.
- Personal saving and investment to finance retirement will be encouraged by government policy. Already, steps have been taken through European Commission directives to promote unit trust investment plans throughout the Continent. Also, the rising burden of social security is forcing governments to rethink public policy approaches to incentives for funding self-financed retirement plans.

Structural-Competitive Factors

Several factors have been operating to encourage the development of a unified European capital market, including the code of liberalization of capital, development of a more level playing field for European banks, and privatization.

European banks are finding the playing field across the Continent more level in a competitive sense. A basic reason for this is that worldwide cooperation by banking supervisors has increased international harmonization. This harmonization takes place through the activities of the Basel Committee on Banking Supervision. This committee has sought to strengthen various banking functions that affect the provision of capital:[19]

- Prudential oversight
- The development of the core principles for effective banking supervision with specific rules for supervisory collaboration
- Agreements on extending capital adequacy that include "market risk" and "credit risk"
- The development of enhanced transparency of derivative activities
- Proposals for a codified directive relating to unifying the existing legal instruments in banking legislation
- The development of drafts of recommendations concerning disclosure of financial instruments in bank annual reports

There should be a capital supply related stimulus from greater efficiency from reduced transaction costs and more transparent markets. Following the first year (1999) of the single currency, it is possible to assert that the corporate bond market in the Eurozone has benefited in a substantial way from these factors.

EU directives regarding bank loan exposures, simplification of banking supervision, and prudential supervision are being incorporated into the national banking laws for all institutions, irrespective of nationality.[20]

Mechanisms for European Capital Mobility

The introduction of the euro is increasing the mobility of capital throughout the twelve-country Eurozone. Key reasons for this include the removal of currency risk from moving capital funds from one country to another, lower transaction costs, and the wealth and income effects that expand the amount of capital.

At the same time, the quality of capital flows has been improved in at least two respects. First, the transaction costs related to cross-border capital flows in Europe have declined. This is reflected in the lower trading spreads on typical bond transactions, as well as on foreign exchange market transactions. Second, the quality has improved in connection with the greater variety and range of types of cross-border capital flows. As we shall observe in the following discussion, at present there exist at least a half dozen key mechanisms for promoting and facilitating trans-European capital mobility.

Six Mechanisms Promoting Capital Mobility

We identify six key mechanisms that promote capital mobility in Europe (table 2.6). Each of the six plays an important role. Some of these activities are arranged by investment banks (mergers and acquisitions). Some are supported by the activities of large commercial (or universal) banks of the type that operate in euro currency markets and make syndicated loans.

Table 2.6. Six Mechanisms Promoting European Capital Mobility

Mechanism	*Type Cross-Border Capital Flow*	*Description of Enabling Activities*
Cross-border mergers and acquisitions	Merger between two companies, domiciled in two different countries	Competitive forces following euro will expand mergers and acquisitions (M&A) activities. This includes spinoffs and LBOs.
Foreign direct investment	Control investment by one company into a second country	The Eurozone will become a more attractive locus for inward FDI. It will provide European-based multinational corporations (MNC) with a larger and stronger currency base.

Table 2.6. *Continued*

Mechanism	*Type Cross-Border Capital Flow*	*Description of Enabling Activities*
Eurobond issurance	New issues of Eurobonds involving European issuer and/or European investor	Greater competition will further narrow spreads on euro issues. New type bond issues, including high yield, pfandbrief, others.
Eurocurrency market and syndicated loans	Eurocurrency deposit and medium-term loan syndication activities of large international banks	A more efficient euro-denominated syndicated loan market will expand rapidly as the euro is phased in.
MNC finance operations in Europe	System-wide, cross-border financial management, including European-based parent firms and subsidiaries	Working capital management will be facilitated by development of a euro-denominated money market. European corporations shift to euro for internal accounting and sourcing inputs.
European portfolio Investment	Institutional and individual securities transactions for the purpose of managing investment funds	Equity culture is growing. Role of institutional investment is changing. Pension plans are diversifying by type.

Three of these mechanisms relate to the cross-border financial activities of multinational corporations (MNCs) across Europe. European portfolio investment is a rapidly expanding business activity, and we discuss it in detail in a later section.

Cross-Border M&A

Cross-border M&A (mergers and acquisitions) in Europe may not have attained the level and scale of activity witnessed in the United States, but a dramatically increased pace of such activity is taking place across Europe although Europe is still preoccupied with the institution of the single currency in 1999.[21] In Europe M&A is changing more fundamentally than in the United States, with a high likelihood of deals being contested and/or another party emerging in the bidding. Politics is very important, witness the Parisian governmental insistence on "reciprocity" in the wake of Germany's Allianz takeover of French AGF. Europeans are also concerned with the impact of M&A on jobs. The DaimlerChrysler deal was made easier by the complementary nature of the two companies and probable limited effect on jobs.

Britain leads Europe in M&A activity, as can be observed in table 2.7; three of the twenty companies involved are based in the UK. The value of M&A in

Table 2.7. Top Ten Cross-Border M&A Deals

Target	*Acquirer*	*Status*	*Value $ Millions*	*Target Advisers*	*Acquirer Advisers*
Chrysler (U.S.)	Daimler-Benz (Ger)	Pending	39,513.4	Credit Suisse First Boston	Goldman Sachs Deutsche Bank
Generale de Banque (Fr)	ABN Amro (Nl)	Withdrawn	12,249.9	Goldman Sachs	ABN Amro Merrill Lynch
Energy Group (UK)	Texas Utilities (U.S.)	Unconditional	10,947.0	Morgan Stanley Lazard Freres	Lehman Brothers Merrill Lynch
Polygram (Nl)	Universal Studios (U.S.)	Pending	7,970.2	Goldman Sachs	Morgan Stanley Bear Stearns
Société Generale de Belgique (B)	Suez Lyonnais des Eaux (Fr)	Pending	5,938.9	J.P. Morgan	
Store Kopperbergs (Swe)	Enso (Fr)	Pending	4,913.2	Morgan Stanley	Goldman Sachs
DSC Communications (U.S.)	Alcatel Alsthom (Fr)	Pending	4,685.3	Goldman Sachs	Lehman Brothers
Simon & Schuster (U.S.)	Pearson (UK)	Pending	4,600.0	Morgan Stanley	Goldman Sachs
STR Global Packaging (UK)	Owens-Illinois (U.S.)	Completed	3,600.0	Goldman Sachs	Salomon Smith Barney Morgan Stanley
Norcan Energy Resources (CA)	Union Pacific (U.S.)	Completed	3,448.5	Goldman Sachs	Salomon Smith Barney Nesbitt Burns

the UK in first half 1998 was £42 billion, 60 percent ahead of a year earlier. Six other European nations are represented in this list of top ten cross-border deals in the first half of 1998.

Based on 1997 data, western Europe accounted for 35 percent of M&A sales, and 31 percent of M&A purchases (table 2.8). In that year there were 2,350 cross-border M&A sales of western European enterprises, and 2,620 purchases of western European enterprises. Interestingly, North America ranked second to western Europe in number and value of cross-border M&A activity (table 2.8). On the buying side, Eurozone countries globally ranked as follows: France (5), the Netherlands (6), Germany (7), and Spain (8). Based on value of transactions on the selling side, Eurozone countries ranked as follows: Germany (3), France (4), Italy (9), the Netherlands (10), Belgium (13), and Spain (14).

Table 2.8. Cross-Border Mergers and Acquisitions by Region ($ Millions)

	Sales			*Purchases*		
	Cases	*Value*	*Share %*	*Cases*	*Value*	*Share %*
Total	5726	341	100	5726	341	100
Western Europe	2310	118	31	2620	168	49
North America[a]	1301	86	29	2111	100	31
Asia	830	34	11	821	46	13
Japan, Australia, NZL	77	2	1	390	18	1
ASEAN	264	13	4	174	10	3
Other Asia[b]	489	19	6		18	1
South America	330	32	9	38	4	1
Central, eastern Europe	154	5	1	6	3	0

Source: KPMG Corporate Finance 1997.
[a]United States, Canada, Mexico.
[b]Chinese Taipei, Hong Kong (China), Korea, and China.

In 1999 Europe accounted for over 12,000 M&A deals, with mega-mergers and hostile bids creating new breakthroughs. The year saw Vodafone make a £131 billion hostile bid for Mannesmann (completed in 2000). Elf Aquitaine merged into total Fina (worth $58.8 billion), and Hoechst and Rhone-Poulenc completed a $28.5 billion merger. The year saw the creation of a Trillionaire's Club, with investment banks Goldman Sachs, Morgan Stanley Dean Witter, and Merrill Lynch each advising on deals in 1999 with a cumulative value of more than $1 trillion.

Foreign Direct Investment

In a compilation of annual foreign direct investment, the OECD reported that in 1997 European companies located in the Eurozone accounted for $102 billion or 29 percent of the estimated global total of FDI outflows (table 2.9). In

Table 2.9. Foreign Direct Investment by European Companies and Entering European Countries, 1997 (U.S.$ millions)

Eurozone	*Inflow (entering)*	*Outflows (by European companies)*
Denmark	—	—
France	14,842	24,945
Germany	–188	33,243
Ireland	126	26
Italy	3,779	12,164
Netherlands	8,678	20,157
Portugal	1,728	1,856
Spain	5,540	10,142
Subtotal	34,505	102,533
As % OECD total	13.7	29.0
Non-Eurozone		
Czech Republic	1,252	25
Finland	1,542	4,405
Greece	—	—
Hungary	2,085	431
Iceland	—	—
Norway	3,692	4,114
Poland	3,077	36
Sweden	9,665	11,382
Switzerland	—	—
Turkey	873	319
UK	36,972	58,313
Subtotal	59,158	79,025
As % OECD Total	23.3	22.3
OECD global total	254,702	354,909

Source: OECD, "Recent Trends in Foreign Direct Investment," *Financial Market Trends,* June 1998.

the same period the eleven-country group in Europe was host for $34 billion or close to 14 percent of the estimated global total.

Between 1990 and 1996 nine Eurozone countries accounted for $610 billion (34 percent) of the estimated global FDI outflow (table 2.10).

Over the same period eight Eurozone countries accounted $386 billion (27 percent) of the estimated global FDI inflows. As the euro is introduced, European companies should find themselves in a stronger competitive position and therefore should be expected to play an even more important role as direct investors on a global basis. Also, we might expect the euro to increase the attractiveness of the region for direct investors located outside the Eurozone.

The ECBs now publish comprehensive data concerning the net international investment position of the Eurozone. In its December 1999 *Monthly Bulletin,* the ECB noted that the net direct investment stake of the eleven-country group had risen from European Currency Unit (ECU) 114.4 billion at year-end 1997 to

Table 2.10. Total FDI Outflows and Inflows, Selected European Countries, 1990–1996 (U.S.$ millions)

Outflows	*Amount*	*Rank*
France	189,049	3
Germany	166,071	5
Netherlands	111,100	6
Belg.-Luxembourg	49,061	9
Italy	45,423	12
Spain	23,067	13
Denmark	16,867	10
Austria	9,938	22
Subtotal	610,576	
As % OECD total	33.9%	
Inflows	*Amount*	*Rank*
France	126,390	4
Belg.-Luxembourg	71,483	5
Spain	62,528	6
Netherlands	62,065	
Italy	26,615	14
Germany	21,663	17
Denmark	15,810	19
Subtotal	386,554	
As % OECD total	27.3%	

Source: OECD, "Recent Trends in Foreign Direct Investment," *Financial Market Trends,* June 1998.

ECU 164.6 billion at year-end 1998. Figures for the first nine months of 1999 reflect higher direct investment abroad by euro area residents and lower foreign direct investment into the euro area.[22] Several Eurozone countries are experiencing a shift in the location of corporate assets to areas within the zone where operating costs are low, as well as a shift of assets to regions beyond the Eurozone.

This relocation of corporate investment has been particularly noticeable for countries with relatively high social labor costs, such as Germany. Since the beginning of the 1990s, German enterprises have spent almost DM0.5 trillion on loans and the acquisition of equity interests abroad. This amounts to more than one-tenth of their total allocation of funds in this period.[23]

Eurobond Issuance

The coming of the euro has increased bond issuance denominated in euros. First, prior to 1999, European corporations were more willing to issue bonds denominated in other European currencies, given the "lock-in" of exchange rates in preparation for the euro in 1999. For example, in July 1998 Saint-Gobain, the French glassmaker, issued a DM590 million offering, fungible with a

French franc 2 billion bond launched a month earlier.[24] This was the company's first offering in a European currency other than the French franc. The offering was an exercise in building a European investor base prior to monetary union.

Second, European bond issuers anticipate that investors across Europe will become receptive to security types formerly considered of interest only to national bond investors.

Third, European corporations need to fund their increasing number of mergers and acquisitions. The liquid euro-denominated corporate bond market provides a convenient and relatively low-cost means of financing these activities. For example, in July 1998, Landesbank Rheinland-Pfalz made the first offering by a German state bank of a global pfandbriefe issue. This was the bank's largest debt offering. Both European and American investors purchased significant amounts of this issue.[25]

Finally, the European junk bond market exploded in the first half of 1998. In that period $4.2 billion of euro currency high yield bond issues came to market, compared with only $314 million of such issues in the same period 1997. Junk bonds are emerging as one of the main growth areas in the European financial (and Eurobond) markets following launch of the euro.[26] By early 2000, large-ticket high yield issues had become a reality. For example, in January 2000, United Pan-Europe Communications, a Dutch cable operator, launched a $1.6 billion bond issue, denominated in both euros and dollars. The company has a single B rating.[27] Junk bond issuance in Europe grew from $12.6 billion in 1997 to $17.6 billion in 1998 to $17.6 billion in 1999. Telecom and media companies account for 70 percent of the 1999 volume.[28]

Demand has come from European fund managers trying to boost portfolio returns following the narrowing of government bond yields. High yield bonds are becoming a standard means for financing acquisitions in Europe, as in the case of William Hill and the HMV and Waterstone's retail chains. Europe is slowly building up a new breed of investor who can assess credit risk and is prepared to back these deals.

European Portfolio Investment

European institutional investors are growing in importance, adopting Anglo-Saxon perspectives, and becoming more willing to take risks to achieve improved portfolio results. As part of this change, the equity culture is growing. In part, this stems from government efforts to bring about more focused interest in equity investing, as in Germany. But it also follows from the growing privatization activities of governments in Italy, France, and Spain.

Institutional investors are becoming more important as are fund managers, and the managers of unit trusts, insurance companies, and pension funds. Governments are happy to see a private pension trend. This is especially so as it is becoming understood that social security systems are overburdened while tax levies are bloated by the need to support social insurance, which is at saturation levels.

Managers and business leaders throughout Europe are aware of the need to supplement or reinforce publicly administered social insurance programs with personal savings and retirement programs. Realization of this need is reinforced by the advent of a single currency.

Any government reforms will dramatically expand financial markets. It is estimated that such reforms could increase European-managed pension assets ninefold to $9 trillion by the year 2020. According to Paul M. Achleitner, head of Goldman Sachs's German division, pension reform is the single most important legislative change expected to cause the growth of competitive capital markets in Germany and the rest of Europe. Expectations of this growth opportunity were behind Merrill Lynch's $5.2 billion bid for Mercury Asset Management Group PLC in November 1997.[29]

These changes are already taking hold across Europe. In 1988 Britain started giving tax deductions for personal pensions. In 1996 such products accounted for 27 percent of the $88 billion in long-term premiums generated by its insurance industry. In the Netherlands the civil servants' pension fund was privatized in 1996 and now holds $110 billion in assets. This fund is second only to the California Public Employees Retirement System (CALPERS) fund.

Since 1991 European mutual fund assets nearly tripled to $1.8 trillion (midyear 1997). Fidelity's European pension assets doubled between 1995 and 1997 to $9.3 billion. Between 1996 and 2000 European private sector pension assets grew from 32 percent of GDP to 40 percent.

Within Eurozone countries there has been a major shift from domestic to Eurozone investment. Both the equity and bond markets are looked upon as a European totality, meaning that portfolio allocations eventually will bring about increasing mobility of investment funds across the Continent.

NOTES

1. Christopher Taylor, *EMU 2000? Prospects for European Monetary Union* (London: The Royal Institute of International Affairs, 1995), 23.
2. Richard Mundell, "A Theory of Optimal Currency Areas," *American Economic Review*, September 1961.
3. Richard Mundell, "Capital Mobility and Stabilization Policy under Fixed and Flexible Exchange Rates," *Canadian Journal of Economics and Political Science*, November 1963.
4. Ronald I. McKinnon, "Optimal Currency Areas," *American Economic Review*, September 1963.
5. Peter Kenen, "The Theory of Optimal Currency Areas: An Eclectic View," *Monetary Problems of the International Economy* (Chicago: University of Chicago Press, 1969).

6. Paul de Grauwe, *The Economics of Monetary Integration* (Oxford: Oxford University Press, 1992), 22.

7. W. M. Corden, *Monetary Integration: Essays in International Finance*, International Finance Section 93 (Princeton: Princeton University Press, 1972), 12–13.

8. Larry Neal and Daniel Barbezat, *The Economics of the European Union and the Economics of Europe* (New York: Oxford University Press, 1998), 144.

9. "Continental Shifts," *Financial Times*, June 23, 1998, 19. While France has moved toward flexible labor markets in June 1998, it advanced its minimum wage by more than the current inflation rate. Robert Graham, "French Minimum Wage Rise Will Be Higher Than Inflation," *Financial Times*, June 25, 1998, 2.

10. European Central Bank, *Monthly Bulletin*, December 1999, 31*.

11. Stephen Roach, "Europe's Dilemmas Revisited," *Financial Times*, May 27, 1998, 14.

12. Helene Cooper, "European Attachment to Home Could Pose Problem for Euro," *Wall Street Journal*, June 24, 1998, 14.

13. H. Cooper and T. Kamm, "Loosening Up: Much of Europe Eases Its Rigid Labor Laws, and Temps Proliferate," *Wall Street Journal*, June 26, 1998, Al, A6.

14. Peter Norman, "Productivity Study Shows Dangers of Euro Wage Clauses," *Financial Times*, July 7, 1998, 3.

15. Philip Rees, "Projecting the National and Regional Populations of the European Union Using Migration Information," in P. Rees, J. Stillwell, A. Convey, and M. Hupiszewski, eds., *Population Migration in the European Union* (New York: Wiley, 1996), 245–246.

16. This also is an objective of the Treaty. At present there are virtually no legal impediments to this movement. Obstacles are being reduced via policies such as the ERASMUS scheme for promoting student exchanges. Rees, "Projecting," 348–350.

17. A. Convey and M. Kupiszewski, "Migration and Policy in the European Union," in *Population Migration*, 311–324.

18. Ibid., 320.

19. Deutsche Bundesbank, *Annual Report 1997*, sec. 5, "The Bank's Participation in Banking Supervision and Changes in Banking Supervision Legislation," 141–146.

20. Ibid., 146–149.

21. William Lewis and Clay Harris, "The Year to End All Years," *Financial Times*, Merger and Acquisition Special Section, June 26, 1998, I.

22. European Central Bank, *Monthly Bulletin*, December 1999, 54–55.

23. Deutsche Bundesbank, *Monthly Report*, June 1999, 22.

24. Edward Luce, "Saint-Gobain Raises DM 590m," *Financial Times*, July 7, 1998, 32.

25. Jeremy Grant, "Global First by Bundesbank," July 8, 1998, 24.

26. Simon Davies, "High Yield Issuance in Europe Jumps," *Financial Times*, July 7, 1998, 32.

27. Rebecca Bream, "UPC Launches $1.6 bn Bond Deal," *Financial Times*, January 17, 2000, 20.

28. Rebecca Bream, "Bulls Drag Junk bonds Off the Scrap Heap," *Financial Times*, February 24, 2000, 23.

29. "A Pension Bonanza Beckons on the Continent," *Business Week*, December 15, 1997, 58.

Chapter Three

Macroeconomic Environment

In chapter 1 we noted that at the December 1991 meeting of the European Council, the Treaty on European Union (Maastricht treaty) was agreed. Ratification by national parliaments ran into difficulties, and it took close to two years to complete the ratification process.

The Maastricht treaty is essentially a series of amendments to the Rome treaty, according to which detailed convergence criteria must be met during stage 2 of European monetary union (EMU). We discuss these criteria in the first section of this chapter. Stage 3 of EMU calls for introduction of the new central banking system. At the same time, convergence must continue and must be reinforced. The second section of this chapter discusses the Stability and Growth Pact providing this reinforcement. In the third section of this chapter we consider how entry into stage 3 impacts fiscal coordination and budget reform. Finally, we consider the performance of the euro in the foreign exchange market.

FISCAL AND MONETARY CONVERGENCE

When the Maastricht treaty was drafted, it set the following agenda for member states: "the adoption of an economic policy which is based on the close coordination of member state economic policies."[1] Economic policy activities of member states include the irrevocable fixing of exchange rates leading to the introduction of a single currency. They also include the conduct of a single monetary policy and an exchange rate policy.

Further, the treaty states:

> Member States shall regard their economic policies as a matter of common concern and shall coordinate them within the Council.[2] . . . The Council shall, on the basis of

> reports submitted by the Commission, monitor economic developments in each of the member states and in the community . . . where it is established . . . that the economic policies of a member state are not consistent with the broad guidelines . . . or that they risk jeopardizing the proper functioning of economic and monetary union, the Council may acting by a qualified majority make the necessary recommendations.[3]

As previous passages from the Maastricht treaty indicate, member states bind themselves to rigorous and demanding economic criteria, which cover four principal areas: price stability, fiscal position, exchange rate stability, and interest rate convergence (table 3.1). We now examine the rationale for these criteria.

Table 3.1. The Convergence Criteria

1. Price stability: a rate of consumer price inflation over the previous year no more than 1.5 percentage points above that of the three best-performing states.
2. Government financial position: a government deficit that is not judged by the Council to be excessive, according to two tests:
   - A ratio of general government net borrowing to gross domestic product (GDP) no greater than 3 percent, unless it has declined substantially and continually and comes close to 3 percent, or the excess is only exceptional and temporary, and the deficit remains close to 3 percent
   - A ratio of general government gross debt to GDP no greater than 60 percent, unless it is sufficiently diminishing and approaching 60 percent at a satisfactory pace
3. Exchange rate stability: participation of a state's currency in the exchange rate mechanism of the European monetary system (EMS) while respecting the "normal margins of fluctuation" for at least two years previously, without devaluing "on its own initiative."
4. Interest-rate convergence: an average nominal interest rate on long-term government bonds over the past year no more than 2 percentage points above that of, at most, the three best-performing states in terms of price stability.

Why Convergence Is Important

Convergence is important for three reasons. First, member countries are surrendering one of their key economic policy adjustment mechanisms—changes in the exchange rate of their currency. Second, member countries are giving up another key economic policy adjustment mechanism, central banking activities. Finally, they are entering into a joint economic policy accord, according to which their economies move as one vis-à-vis the rest of the world. For this historic experiment to succeed, strict convergence criteria must operate to give greater assurance of success.

Within EMU, individual nations surrender their ability to depreciate their national currencies. In the past this has been an important means of strengthening or regaining international competitiveness and external payments equilibrium. The eleven nations undertake a joint effort to maintain external financial stability. A joint effort may be feasible in the following cases:

- All members of the group practice financial policies that assure financial balance.
- The group enjoys a fairly homogeneous international trading system vis-à-vis the rest of the world.
- An improved degree of labor-capital mobility has been achieved within the multicountry group.
- All members of the group are committed to the single market concept.

The first condition listed above, all members practice financial policies that assure financial balance, is represented by the four convergence criteria listed in table 3.1. These point toward fiscal as well as monetary balance in Europe. Monetary stability operates directly through price stability and interest rate convergence, and indirectly via exchange rate stability. Fisher conditions prevailing, price stability in all countries virtually guarantees convergence of interest rates. Under Fisher parity, interest rates contain a margin for the rate of inflation.

Monetary equilibrium is not possible without fiscal discipline. Government budget deficits must be small or there must be a balanced budget. Government debt must be small enough that interest payments represent a relatively unimportant component of government expenditure.

We can observe in table 3.2 the performance of the EU-15 with respect to the ratio of government debt to GDP. By 1997 nine countries were at or close to the target 60 percent ratio, and two others were within reasonable range of the target ratio.

In chapter 1 we noted that three large European countries, Germany, France, and Italy, had improved their central government budget balances between 1991 and 1997, and they appeared ready to enter the single currency arrangement (table 1.4).

Only one country of the EU-15 failed to meet the convergence criteria in 1998—Greece. But two months before the coming of the euro, Greece indicated that it was getting serious about joining the EMU.[4] Greek Prime Minister Costa Simitis stated that he was determined to make Greece part of the single-currency group, convinced that membership would strengthen the economy and promote greater internal social and political harmony. Simitis pushed ahead with plans to privatize Greek banks, airlines, and commercial enterprises. Additionally, he got tough with tax evaders as part of the attempt to bring the budget deficit under control.

Table 3.2. Maastricht Definition of General Government Gross Public Debt as a Percentage of Nominal GDP

Country	*1991*	*1992*	*1993*	*1994*	*1995*	*1996*	*1997*	*1998*	*1999*
Austria	58.1	58.0	62.7	65.4	69.3	69.5	65.2	64.8	64.4
Belgium	127.5	129.0	135.2	133.5	131.3	126.9	122.4	118.4	115.4
Denmark	62.3	66.4	77.4	73.8	69.0	61.8	61.8	57.3	53.2
Finland	23.0	41.5	58.0	59.6	58.1	57.6	55.8	53.4	54.6
France	35.8	39.7	45.2	48.3	52.5	55.4	57.7	58.9	59.5
Germany	41.5	44.1	48.0	50.2	58.0	60.4	61.3	60.7	60.5
Greece	92.3	98.8	111.6	109.2	110.0	111.5	108.4	108.2	105.6
Ireland[a]	95.3	92.3	96.3	89.1	82.3	72.7	65.3	57.0	50.3
Italy	101.5	108.7	119.1	124.9	124.2	124.0	121.6	118.5	116.0
Luxembourg	4.2	5.1	6.1	5.7	5.9	6.5	6.7	—	—
Netherlands	78.8	79.6	80.8	77.1	78.5	76.6	71.4	69.5	68.9
Portugal	69.0	61.5	64.3	66.3	69.1	68.7	65.3	63.4	61.9
Spain	45.8	48.3	60.5	63.0	65.9	70.6	69.3	68.5	67.5
Sweden	53.0	67.1	76.0	79.3	78.0	77.2	76.9	74.5	71.1
UK	35.5	41.6	48.3	50.3	53.7	54.5	53.3	52.1	50.5

Source: OECD Economic Outlook, 1998.
Note: The Commission of the European Communities provided the debt figures, in national currencies, from 1991 to 1997, whereas the GDP figures are national definitions (except for Ireland). The 1998 and 1999 debt ratios are projected forward in line with the OECD secretariat's projections for general government gross financial liabilities and GDP.
[a]The debt ratio is calculated using the same definition of GDP in the Maastricht debt ratio. For Ireland, this GDP is higher than GDP under the national definition.

On March 14, 1998, the Greek government devalued the drachma by 14 percent and committed itself to participating in the single currency. Greece joined the single currency group in January 2001.

European Exchange Rate Mechanism

We should note that euro interest rate convergence operated extremely well throughout 1998, the final year before the coming of the single currency (table 3.3). In October 1998, the range between the highest and lowest money market interest rates was 2.55 percent (5.75–3.20). At that point Ireland had the highest short-term rate, and Austria the lowest. Germany was at 3.30 percent, the expected convergence interest rate for early 1999. The convergence achieved represented considerable lowering of interest rates in many of the eleven countries.

Lower interest rates, converging toward 3.30 percent, had the following implications for Euroland:

- Lower cost of borrowed funds for European companies should spur business spending for capital goods and improvements, spurring economic activity.
- Lower cost of capital should give Eurozone companies a greater competitive edge in world business.

Table 3.3. Euro Interest Rate Convergence, October 19, 1998

Country	*Interest Rate %*	*Type Local Rate*
Ireland	5.75	Short-term
Italy	5.00	Discount
Portugal	4.00	Repo
Spain	3.75	Repo
Finland	3.40	Tender
Germany	3.30	Repo
France	3.30	Intervention
Belgium/Luxembourg	3.30	Central
Netherlands	3.30	Special advance
Austria	3.20	Repo

Expected convergence rate: 3.30%

This chart shows the official interest rate of the eleven countries that will participate in Europe's forthcoming single currency. Analysts surveyed by Standard & Poor's MMS International expect the short-term interest rates of the eleven countries to converge at a 3.30 percent initial rate for the European Central Bank at the beginning of 1999.

Source: Financial Times.

- Lower cost of borrowed funds should cause European investors to reevaluate their options between equity and debt securities.

Maintaining Convergence

Whereas monetary and fiscal policy represents more traditional means of maintaining progress on macroeconomic convergence, other methods are to be used as well. For example, the German chancellor, Gerhard Schröder, has a plan to cure high unemployment. If successful, this plan would allow disciplined monetary-fiscal policy to maintain convergence.

Under his "Alliance for Jobs" proposal, Schröder would seat management and union representatives together and encourage management to promise more jobs in return for union labor flexibility, including wage costs. Industry has been hostile to former initiatives in this direction. Hans Peter Stihl, president of the German Chamber of Industry and Commerce, expressed serious doubts. Klaus Zwickel, head of IG Metall, Germany's largest union, stated that the battle against unemployment would move ahead only gradually. Labor has its own proposals for increasing jobs, which include restricting overtime work and lowering the retirement age to sixty.[5]

Germany is the only country in Europe that has decreasing unit labor costs, states Wolfgang Scheremet, a labor economist at the German Institute for Economic Research. Some economists are stating that the only possible source for additional jobs will be the service sector.

A second approach to maintaining convergence is adjusting the length of time necessary for the transition into a single currency. In Europe, France has been at the forefront in implementing measures for the single currency. France was the first to announce its plans to shorten its period of transition into the new currency. Retail groups and business lobbyists in France and elsewhere have been complaining that a long transitional period would make their operations too costly and cumbersome. The French Socialist government statement suggests that the lengthy transition is unrealistic. It is expected that the French will push other European Union (EU) nations to adopt a similar approach toward implementation.[6]

STABILITY AND GROWTH PACT

How can the world be assured that member states will practice and conform to strict fiscal and monetary discipline? In stage 2, leading up to the introduction of the euro, the five separate convergence criteria (table 3.1) were pursued. In stage 3 the question of discipline continues to be relevant and important. In this context, a crucial role will be played by the so-called Stability

Pact, which aims at ensuring that fiscal discipline is maintained in the period after the euro is introduced.

Nature of the Pact

The Stability and Growth Pact is derived from the Dublin Summit, held in December 1996. The Maastricht treaty obliges member states to avoid excessive budget deficits in stage 3. The Council of Finance Ministers adopted regulations on surveillance to preserve budget discipline and to correct budget deficits. These regulations, together with the European Council Resolution, make up what we refer to as the Stability and Growth Pact.

Each member state adopting the euro is obliged to submit a stability program, and it is subject to sanctions for failure to act properly to limit budget deficits. The stability programs contain the following information:

- Budgetary objectives
- An adjustment path for governmental surplus/deficit and the expected path for the government debt ratio
- The main assumptions regarding economic conditions
- A sensitivity analysis of the deficit and debt position

This information enables the European Commission to give early warning of any significant deterioration in the fiscal position in a member state.

Member states will be able to deal with normal cyclical fluctuations but must keep the government deficit within the 3 percent reference range. However, an "excessive deficit procedure" will trigger the issuance of recommendations that must be followed. A Council regulation will provide clear definitions and deadlines for steps to be taken. If member states have failed to comply with such a decision, the Council will impose sanctions.

The "excessive deficit procedure" calls for (1) deciding when an excessive deficit exists, (2) corrective recommendations, (3) a Council judgment regarding whether effective action has been taken, and (4) consideration of appropriate sanctions. A government will be exempt from sanctions if its economy is held to be in undisputed recession.

Structure and Scale of Sanctions

The burden of proof falls on the government charged with running an excessive deficit. The government must show that its recessionary economy is the cause for such deficits. Should sanctions be applied, they will consist first of a non–interest bearing deposit. This deposit is converted into a fine after two years if the deficit continues to exist. If the member state is found to be in noncompliance, the amount of the fine will be the combination of a fixed and a variable component. The fixed component is equal to 0.2 percent of GDP, while the variable component is equal to one-tenth of the excess of the deficit over the reference value of 3 percent of GDP.

The rationale of the stability pact is the concern that one or more member countries could take advantage of their protected position within the single-currency zone to borrow heavily. Large and continuing budget deficits in one or more member states would damage the credibility of the euro and impair the creditworthiness of all member states. Enhanced creditworthiness is one of the expected benefits from the euro. It would be an unfortunate development if the fiscal profligacy of a few member states proved damaging to all.

Political Challenges to Stability

As the third stage progresses, many questions arise concerning the desire and willingness of the twelve member states to maintain the level of fiscal control needed for success. A "hard" euro can attract inward business investment, and with it technology and rising competitiveness. A "hard" euro depends on continued fiscal austerity measures. Possible changes in government policy are a key question mark.

At midyear 1998, Yves Thibault de Silguy, chairman of the EU Monetary Commission, warned that the eleven founding members of the Eurozone were falling behind in their efforts to curb public deficits before the launch of the single currency. At the same time, a new monthly forum of finance ministers known as the Euro-11 was organized. Without progress on fiscal deficits, de Silguy voiced concern that the European Central Bank (ECB) would be required to adopt a more stringent monetary stance.[7]

In the three-year run-up to introduction of the euro, national elections shifted the focus of government in a number of member states to the left. This also happened in other countries such as the UK, where Tony Blair became prime minister in 1997. Another case in point was the election in October 1998 of German Socialist Party leader Schröder, who attracted more votes than former Chancellor Helmut Kohl did. At that point in time, parties of the left controlled or were key participants in government coalitions in thirteen of the fifteen EU countries.

Italy's political crisis in October 1998 underscores the challenge for Europe and the many left-of-center governments as they seek to achieve a balance between appeasing their radical coalition partners and staying on track for Europe's single currency.[8]

Early in October 1998 the communist group in the Italian government voted to not support the 1999 budget bill, placing the viability of their coalition government in doubt.[9] At this point the hard-line communists pulled their support over a budget dispute. Only four months earlier Italy and ten other European nations had launched the single currency. President Oscar Luigi Scalfalo tapped Massimo D'Alema, a former communist, as the country's next prime minister. D'Alema is the leader of the Democratic Left, Italy's largest party, which accounted for 21 percent of the national vote in the previous election.

The new government was expected to bring Marxists into the cabinet for the first time ever in Italy. A hard-line communist party, Italian Communists, planned to lend its votes to the D'Alema government. An economist at Paine Webber International in London stated that the new government would be too weak to make any change. He said that the government had to keep on the budgetary path already laid down to avoid risking monetary union or hampering the operation of the new ECB.[10]

Governments in France and Germany include parties that reject further budget cutting and/or tough structural reform. Both environmentalists and left-leaning hard-liners are becoming emboldened by the defeat of Helmut Kohl in Germany. Kohl's defeat raises the possibility of making job creation a higher priority than monetary orthodoxy. A shift in tone seems to have taken place in France, where Prime Minister Lionel Jospin said, "European construction must follow a new course, possibly more political, in any case more social." The French coalition government relies on greens and communists for a majority. The communists have raised their voice, and a break with the socialists would raise the question of the government's commitment to fiscal stability.

Europe may find a way to steer a course toward fiscal orthodoxy and at the same time move toward higher economic growth in order to absorb the unemployed. This could take the form of an easier monetary policy. In October 1998 the Bank of Spain initiated a larger-than-expected interest rate cut. This came on the heels of an apparent global financial crisis. At that time a credit crunch was pressing company and other borrowers in Asia and Latin America. According to ECB executive board member Tommaso Padoa-Schioppa, strong domestic demand is supporting European economic growth while historically low long-term interest rates provide a favorable investment environment. Padoa-Schioppa noted that the ECB is closely monitoring the situation.[11]

Spain's unexpectedly large half percent interest rate cut to 3.75 percent in October 1998 reflected more than technical concerns. About half of the cut was for convergence; the other half was a political step that reinforced greater flexibility. The Spanish rate cut brought that country close to Germany's repo rate of 3.30 percent. This interest rate level is considered to be the practical floor for Eurozone rate easing.

The strong, independent stand of European central bankers is well-known. At year-end 1998 they were holding to a conservative policy designed to establish the euro's credibility. But political leaders, particularly in France and Germany, bluntly attacked these policies and pushed for easier money as a way to spur economic growth and job expansion.[12]

Oscar Lafontaine, chairman of the Social Democratic Party who was named finance minister in the new German government, stated, "I find it wrong that the Bundesbank conducts its monetary policy as if these problematic developments in global finance weren't there." But Hans Tietmeyer, president of Germany's central bank, made it clear late in 1998 that he would not cut interest rates in the near future. Nevertheless, pressure was growing for more rate cuts in Europe in the October–November period prior to introduction of the euro. This pressure came from volatile stock markets, a hedge fund crisis in the United States, and stronger European currencies that would eventually hurt exports.

Although the center-left governments in Europe were calling for interest rate cuts, their intention seemingly was to exert more political control over the ECB. Lafontaine has been very critical of "hawkish" monetary policies. French political leaders share these views and want a monetary policy geared to job creation.

In short, the worst pitfall for the euro would be a social revolt, forcing one or more nations to withdraw from the twelve-nation Eurozone. Such a choice would develop into the most radical political play by a democracy since the end of World War II. Not only would that country have to reestablish its national currency, but it would also be pulled from other EU institutional arrangements, shaking the entire Brussels-centered system on the way.[13]

No clear procedures exist for exiting the euro, but governments can always break treaties by invoking the national interest. Legal complications would be a relatively minor factor because of the enormous economic and financial costs of such an action. A nation that went its own way could lose thousands of jobs as doubts escalated about its economic prospects. Departure of a major country would "poison the economic climate" badly.

Government leaders throughout Europe see an important advantage in the euro. It is like a harness for European power that masks their basic aim of taking unpopular measures to help Europe meet intensifying international economic pressures. It is no accident, that the single currency came into existence at precisely the time when globalization was about to hit Europe with full force. The implications of globalization are corporate restructuring, job transitions, and intense pressure on social program budgets.

Job Solutions

Clearly, the need for jobs has posed a potential threat to success of the euro. Preparations for the euro were accompanied by no visible gain in creating jobs in Europe. Europe's 18 million unemployed (midyear 1998) were in stark contrast to Europe's growing financial stability, economic convergence, and currency unification. In the larger countries—Germany, France, and Italy—the degree of abstinence needed to create low inflation and smaller indebtedness has not matched up well with the labor market liberalization necessary to break the cycle of European joblessness.

The more liberal European labor market has not brought lower unemployment rates. A downward convergence of interest rates has spurred economic prosperity, but joblessness remains a sticky factor. According to *Le Figaro*, Jack Lang, the socialist chairman of the French National Assembly's foreign affairs committee, has described Europe's economic circumstances as "gray, toneless, and boring."[14] While Europe expects consumers will win out with the euro, the expectation also is that workers may lose.[15] The dismal prospect for workers is based on the belief that greater transparency in wages will not make it easy for unions to negotiate increases.[16]

Those who fear adverse effects have given the euro the title "esperanto money." With monetary policy "outsourced" and fiscal policy constrained by the Stability Pact, three avenues remain for dealing with unemployment. First, wage flexibility could attract new investment and create jobs. Unfortunately, wages in Europe are not sufficiently flexible and tend to be kept uniform through union agreements. Second, workers can move to where jobs are more plentiful. But again, past experience does not offer much hope for this remedy. European workers tend to be much less mobile than American workers.

Third, transfer payments on a European-wide scale could be introduced. Such automatic stabilizers have worked well in the United States but require, much more than monetary union, political union, and that is an arguable goal for Europe at present. The EU taxing power is limited to 1.7 percent of GDP. This is nowhere near the amount required to support American-style transfer payments.[17]

FISCAL DISHARMONY: WITHHOLDING TAX

At midyear 1998, shortly after the momentous May meeting at which eleven EU nations declared that they would enter the Eurozone, the European Community criticized EU member states for failing to make sufficient progress in consolidating their public finances. The warning came at a meeting of finance ministers and was the first policy confrontation since the May decision to start economic and monetary union.[18]

To compound the issue, the UK warned that it expected difficulties in reaching an agreement on the harmonization of withholding taxes on savings accounts. Meanwhile, Austria's finance minister, Rudolf Edlinger, stated that the harmonization of withholding on savings accounts and a simplification of value-added tax rules were priority areas for reform.

Helen Liddell, the UK economic secretary to the Treasury, noted that the UK was, in principle, prepared to act on tax evasion issues but could not approve measures that might damage UK financial markets. Previously, the UK opposed attempts to introduce a common or minimum withholding tax, fearing that this might damage the City of London's financial standing. By spring 2000, the UK had brought the debate to a point where many European governments would accept "tax transparency in reporting" in lieu of a system-wide withholding tax.

The Commission's warning on public finances reflected concern that governments, after qualifying for the euro, might cave in to political pressure to relax spending targets. According to the Commission, the eleven Eurozone countries reduced their structural budget deficits from 6.5 percent of GDP in 1991 to approximately 2 percent in 1997. The ECB also expressed concern about fiscal policy in its member states.

Harmonization–Coordination

Tax policy is one of the last bastions of national sovereignty. Will the single currency promote or hinder harmonization of fiscal policy? In Europe the politics of fiscal harmonization or fiscal coordination are delicate.

All decisions must pass the unanimity rule in the EU, so that progress in areas such as the value-added tax, the withholding tax (discussed in a later section titled "Fiscal Reform"), and a revision of the tax burden limits is halting at best.

In 1997–1998, tax policy rose to the top of the EU economic agenda. Anticipating the impact of the euro in connection with tax poaching or, alternately, tax competition, in December 1997 the EU finance ministers agreed to a voluntary code of conduct on business taxation.[19]

They also made a commitment to consider a minimum withholding tax on nonresidents' income on savings. Further, they agreed to consider a directive that would make it easier for companies to transfer royalties and interest across borders without the risk of double taxation.

Luxembourg declared that it would not go along with an EU-wide withholding tax unless it was counterbalanced with legislation to enforce a minimum corporate tax. The UK and Ireland reacted unfavorably to this proposal.

The EU is edging very slowly toward tax coordination. Mario Monti, the Italian commissioner responsible for the single market, unveiled proposals for a directive eliminating withholding taxes on interest and royalties paid between associated companies.

The withholding tax, on the other hand, could allow for anonymity but, at the same time, generate taxes for the EU Treasury. This creates a further question, How are the revenues from this tax to be shared?

More fundamental is the question of tax rate differentials throughout Europe. These tax differentials act competitively to either attract or repel commercial and investment activity in regions and member states. A case in point is the tax haven status that gives Dublin Docks a comparative advantage in attracting financial services and commercial operations. Logic points to some kind of agreement or understanding that sets minimum standards on tax and social security.

EU directives also are expected to limit predatory competition. Without a common tax regime, money will flow from member states into tax havens such as Geneva or Zurich. The British government announcement that it was reviewing the status of the Channel Islands could be an indication of changes to come. Investment bankers have warned that a directive on taxes on savings could damage European capital markets, notably the Eurobond market.[20]

Fiscal Reform

As noted above, EU governments are moving closer to bringing tax systems more closely into line, with a proposed 15 or 20 percent tax on savings and investment income. This is part of a comprehensive plan to combat tax evasion and unfair tax competition. It is feared the proposal could lead investors to move their money outside the EU. The measure would remove a significant distortion in the single market. EU countries compete for capital by levying little or no taxes on individuals based in other nations. This practice has led to tensions among some EU member states. For example, some German politicians have accused Luxembourg of helping German citizens evade taxes.[21]

The EU initiatives are not unrelated to actions considered elsewhere. The world's wealthiest nations are planning a crackdown on international tax evasion. The plan announced in 1998 by the Group of Seven finance ministers argues that tax-related crimes be attacked with the laws that are used against the laundering of drug proceeds. It follows a campaign announced by the OECD against "harmful tax competition" that calls for severe counter-measures against tax havens that flagrantly cater to tax cheats.[22]

Industrial countries are looking for ways to pierce the veil of bank secrecy in tax havens by requiring offshore banks to divulge information on depositors under investigation for tax evasion. The initiatives, if successful, could hurt the economies of Ireland and other financial centers built on the twin pillars of zero taxation and bank secrecy.

The EU scheme could cause a political row in Britain, with Tory officials claiming that this is the first step on the path to tax harmonization across Europe. If it is, Britain's low tax status is likely to be among the first victims. Tax harmonization would test whether Blair's New Labor is really ready to march opposite to the rest of Europe on this issue. Graham Mather, a former banker who is a Tory Member of Parliament, has warned that the single currency will spearhead an inexorable drive toward a single European tax system.

Germany supports the withholding tax proposal and estimates that it loses $16 billion a year in taxes because cash is squabbled away in foreign bank accounts—often those in Luxembourg. French and Belgian businesses reregister as British to take advantage of the low UK taxes. As a result of these "continental differences," the withholding scheme, at times, assumes an anti-British flavor.[23] Harmful tax competition is Brussels-speak for the widely resented low tax regimes of countries such as Britain.

The British are not united in this debate. A draft version of the Edwards report on financial supervision in the "offshore UK" islands harshly criticizes their role in overseas criminal investigations. It refers to several cases of involvement in financial scandals, including BCCI in the Isle of Man, the Barings collapse in Guernsey, and the Cantrade private banking scandal in Jersey. The Cantrade case involved a subsidiary of UBS, the Swiss bank, where a rogue trader concealed losses.

Andrew Edwards, a UK Treasury official, suggests providing statutory protection for whistle-blowers and strengthening the number of financial regulators in the islands. There are also UK recommendations, including the introduction of regulation for trust companies in the UK, to bring the mainland in line with new rules on the islands.[24]

EU Budget Reform

EU budgetary reform is more difficult to achieve than fiscal reforms in the eleven nation member states of the single currency. This is due to the persistent lack of transparency in EU budgets, the large Common Agricultural Policy (CAP) component on the spending side, and the unanimity rule required for changes in revenue structure.

In October 1998 the European Commission published a comprehensive report on the EU budget. The report reflected how complicated but nontransparent the EU budget is. It revealed the full scale of Germany's role as the primary paymaster with a net contribution of around ECU11 billion. France also is a net contributor to the EU of ECU1 billion, less than 10 percent of Germany's net contribution. The report also demonstrates how the so-called British budget rebate, negotiated by Baroness Thatcher (the former prime minister) in the early 1980s, is no longer as justified as it was because farm spending has dropped from 70 percent to 50 percent of total EU budget expenditure. The UK is now the fifth largest net contributor to the EU budget.[25]

While this report is mainly factual and makes no formal recommendations, it outlines alternatives for making EU finances more transparent and efficient. This has aroused strong reaction. For example, the Spanish government has declared that the document itself is not acceptable. Luxembourg questions whether EU administrative spending should be included in its data. This data transforms Luxembourg from the status of the second largest net contributor to the second largest net recipient as a percentage of GNP. It is interesting that the European Commission's own Eurobarometer shows that the popularity of the EU in different member states matches closely the state of net contributions (table 3.4).

Table 3.4. Comovement between Budget Net Recipient Position and Public Support for EU

Country	*Budget Net Recipient Position in European Union (as % of GDP)*	*Public Support for EU (%)*
Ireland	5.1	76
Luxembourg	4.9	65
Greece	4.1	50
Portugal	3.1	54
Spain	1.2	47
Belgium	0.8	33
Denmark	0.1	34
Italy	–0.01	64
France	–0.1	37
Finland	–0.1	11
UK	–0.3	22
Netherlands	–0.3	72
Austria	–0.4	17
Germany	–0.6	28
Sweden	–0.6	–6

Source: Quentin Peel, "Europe's Hard Sums," *Financial Times,* October 20, 1998, 16.

When German Chancellor Gerhard Schröder attended the European Parliament before his election, he appeared to criticize Helmut Kohl for wanting to cut contributions. Since then he has suggested that inequities should be resolved through spending, not through changing the revenue side of the budget. Political reality suggests that only limited changes should be made in the EU budget. This is because any change in EU revenues requires a unanimous decision and ratification by national parliaments, a highly unlikely event.

German Federalism: A Slow Process

In the race to convert their accounts to the euro, German companies ran up against a bureaucratic slowdown. In 1999, although they were able to prepare their accounts, set prices, and work with suppliers in euros, large parts of their tax bills had to be declared in deutsche marks. This was a result of Germany's federal system. The administration of the tax system is a responsibility of the sixteen German states (or *Länder*). Germany's local tax collectors decided that allowing all taxes to be declared in euros beginning January 1999 would be too costly.[26]

State finance ministers complained that separate software is needed to run euro taxation alongside the deutsche mark in the transition period (1999–2000). Also, there was fear that running two systems would raise taxpayer suspicions that they were being dealt with unfairly. Given the strong complaints from business, state finance ministers decreed that only in two areas would tax declarations be possible in euros from January 1, 1999: monthly and annual value-added tax (VAT) declarations and taxes on incomes deducted by employers on behalf of employees.

Nevertheless, this leaves Germany trailing other countries, notably the Netherlands and France, in converting their tax administration into the euro. According to surveys, more than half of German companies plan to be using euro accounting systems before 2002, but this message does not appear to have fully penetrated the German civil service.

While Germany may be slow in implementing euro-denominated taxation at the *Länder* level, the new coalition of the Socialist Democratic Party (SPD) and the greens quickly initiated discussions for overall tax reform (October 1998). This initiative included the proposal to cut income tax rates by six percentage points by 2002. Lafontaine of the SPD said an average family would be $1,677 a year better off with these changes. Company tax rates would be capped at 36 percent by 2002, compared with rates of up to 47 percent at the election of September 1998. Offsetting lower rates would be a tightening of "loopholes" and the inclusion of favorable treatment of corporate financial reserves. The SPD stated that the aim of these reforms was to bring Germany into line with international standards.[27]

German Fiscal Reform

In October 1999 the German business community and international press were ready to write off Chancellor Schröder as an ineffective populist with a proclivity for government meddling.[28] After the embarrassing departure of Finance Minister Oscar LaFontaine in March 1999 and a string of local election defeats for his SPD, his government was perceived as in danger of collapse. In November 1999 Schröder pressured Deutsche Bank CEO Breuer to support the rescue of the illiquid builder Philipp Holzmann. Since the rescue of Holzmann, Schröder has quietly organized a "kitchen cabinet" of German CEOs that includes Schremp (DaimlerChrysler), Sommer (Deutsche Telekom), Frenzel (Preussag), Breuer (Deutsche Bank), Schulte-Noelle (Allianz), and von Pierer (Siemens).

Although Schröder has been dubbed "the accidental reformer," Germany's initiatives toward fiscal reform and economic restructuring were no accidents. These were carefully orchestrated efforts to move the largest Eurozone national economy (and third largest in the world) from stable and static traditionalism toward a more dynamic and competitive capitalist system.

The range of structural reforms required is daunting, but the Schröder government has taken a strong initiative in two of the key areas outlined in table 3.5: tax cuts and deficit reduction. But there are several places into which Schröder is less willing to move, especially labor reforms. He has kept very quiet about regulations that make it difficult to lay off workers. Also, the government has moved carefully in the area of pension reform, despite the urgent need. For example, in year 2020 over half of Germany's adult population will

Table 3.5. Schröder's Structural Reform Agenda: Need and Reality

Area of Reform	*Need*	*Reality*
Tax System	Reduce corporate and personal income tax rates. Eliminate capital gains tax in sale of corporate holdings.	Included by Schröder in proposed budget for 2001.
Budget deficit	Fiscal austerity program to reduce deficit from 1.5% of GDP to 0.5% in year 2001.	Budget proposal for 2001 provides for deficit reduction.
Bureaucracy	Remove red tape that hinders business ventures and new start-ups.	May initiate such changes.
Labor market	Change labor laws to provide more flexibility in hours, wages, and staffing.	No plans yet to revise laws.
Pension reform	Relate retirement benefits to inflation, not wage scale. Provide tax breaks for private pension plans.	May initiate some reforms to promote private pensions.

Sources: Ralph Atkins, "Germany's Coalition Argues on Cut in Bank Tax," *Financial Times,* October 12, 1998, 18; "The Accidental Reformer," *Business Week,* May 1, 2000, 60–61.

be over the age of sixty. This will impose a heavy strain on government resources. We discuss this in a later section.

The Holzmann rescue could be considered a turning point. When Schröder approached Deutsche Bank, the bank was ready to let Holzmann go under. Breuer, Deutsche Bank's CEO, pointed out to Schröder that the Holzmann case was a symptom of a broader problem in Germany and Europe–punitive taxes on corporate income and capital gains. The capital gains tax prevented Deutsche Bank from selling its 15 percent stake in Holzmann and other companies. The day after Schröder announced the Holzmann rescue, the DAX stock market index plunged.

Schröder wasted no time in developing and unveiling a tax reform plan in December 1999. This plan called for cutting the top corporate tax rate to 38 percent and the personal income tax rate from 53 percent to 45 percent by the year 2005. Buried in the complex fiscal proposal was elimination of the capital gains tax on profits from sale of shares held in publicly listed companies. Elimination of this part of the tax system is significant in Germany, where a complex of share cross-holdings ties banks and insurance firms to older economy industrial giants like Siemens, Hoechst, and BMW.

Shortly after this tax reform was unveiled, the Deutsche Bank–Dresdner Bank merger was proposed. While the deal fell apart (discussed in chapter on banking), other mergers and related share disposals will no doubt follow, given the introduction of capital gains tax reform.

Budget deficits also are on track for reduction in the Eurozone. Eurozone countries were experiencing higher economic growth in 2000, and this growth is projected to continue for several years. As a result, the average budget deficit in the Eurozone may fall from 1.2 percent of GDP in 1999 to 0.7 percent in 2001. Should European countries continue to enjoy strong economic growth and rising tax revenues, they face the dilemma of shrinking government bond issuance and a growing illiquidity in their respective government securities markets. The Dutch solution to this problem is to concentrate debt issuance in a few segments of the yield curve. In particular, Europe faces a sharply reduced availability of long (over ten years) maturity government bonds.[29]

However, not all Eurozone nations will meet the strict Growth and Stability Pact requirement that the budget position be balanced or in surplus in the medium term. For example, Germany is somewhat behind the European Commission recommendation that it aim for a budget deficit that is less than 1 percent of GDP in 2000.[30]

The French Way

France and Germany do not always agree on economic policy matters, and in the first eighteen months of the single currency, several divergences in policy approach manifested themselves. For example, at a meeting of finance ministers in May 2000, an unprecedented public statement was made aimed at boosting the ailing single currency. But this display of unity was spoiled when Hans Eichel, German finance minister, and Laurent Fabius, his French colleague, differed in public over whether support measures should include an EU-wide agreement on the use of revenues from the sale of mobile phone licenses for government debt reduction.[31] Joaquim Pina Moura, Portuguese finance minister, stated at the same meeting that the eleven ministers were determined to speed up fiscal consolidation and structural reforms. He also hinted at central bank intervention to support the euro.

The differing statements by Eichel and Fabius concerning the use of mobile telecoms licensing revenues caused confusion in the financial markets. It was estimated that European governments could raise well over $100 billion by selling third-generation mobile licenses in competitive auctions. The UK raised close to $39 billion in its auction, and France, Germany, and Italy conducted several large auctions in 2001. Whereas Eichel has pledged to use virtually all of the auction proceeds to reduce debt, Fabius is expected to use a part of these proceeds for job creation schemes, especially with a presidential vote approaching in France.[32]

A more fundamental divergence on economic policy matters is the French interest in the EU's adopting a more radical social agenda. Prime Minister Lionel Jospin does not wish to abandon the social model built by Europe over the past half century and does not accept the arguments of those economists who argue that the plunge of the euro in 1999–2000 is tied to Europe's regulatory maze. Jospin would rather strengthen the euro by giving the E-12 finance ministers a hand in determining Euroland's monetary policy, now the sole responsibility of the ECB.[33]

Jobs Mismatch

In the first half of 2000, over 15 million Europeans were unemployed in the labor markets of the E-11 countries. Meanwhile, millions of jobs went begging for lack of qualified applicants.[34] There is no technological fix for closing this jobs gap, and many wonder if macroeconomic policy can do much about it. Many agree that Europe's jobs problem is due to an inflexible educational system, high labor taxes, and barriers to worker mobility.

EU countries spend billions on unemployment benefits but cannot afford to spend more on information education to prepare workers for the revolution in information technology (IT). The shortage of IT professionals in the year 2003 is projected to be 1.7 million. But there are other regional disconformities as well. Several regions in France need thousands of construction workers, whereas such skilled workers are unemployed elsewhere in Europe. Europe now faces shortages of machine tool workers and accountants.

Europe now has a two-speed labor market in which millions of poorly trained workers fall further behind those in high demand. As a result, employers must pay new people with needed skills more than they are worth. Europe needs to retool its concept of education, as the United States has recently had to learn as well.

One proposed solution, issuing temporary work permits for foreign IT workers, has brought vehement protests. The idea of importing labor has met with sharp criticism from labor unions and xenophobic radicals. Cultural barriers and outdated restrictions on working conditions also prevent a solution to the jobs-skills mismatch in Europe. Ireland is a case in point. Where Ireland was once a source of surplus workers, it is now reimporting those who left.

The new economy sectors in Europe are not waiting for governments to act on the labor shortages. Big corporations are seeing talent lured away by headhunters and job agencies. Online job search companies are spreading throughout Europe to assist firms that have critical worker shortages. Younger Europeans are more willing to relocate than their parents were.[35] Nevertheless, democratic governments will need to address this fundamental problem. Worker mobility is developing in Europe, but this change is in a very early stage. Governments will be required to tackle the dual requirements of providing more timely educational training and fostering an environment in which job mobility is increased.

Pension Reform

Pension reform is an issue facing all countries in the Eurozone. The issue is pressing due to the need to meet global competition with a more flexible and fluid labor market. Across Europe an aging population is imposing greater stress on the pay-as-you-go (PYG) pension plans currently in use. These PYG pension plans are the main source of worker retirement benefits, so governments face an urgent need to initiate reforms before the tax burden from pension transfers makes European labor noncompetitive in world markets. In part, we focus our attention on Germany in this discussion, since it is the largest economy in the Eurozone and seems determined to come to grips with these problems.

The German social market economy has been geared toward achieving an optimal balance between competitive market capitalism and a system with a workable social safety net. In the past, the typical German worker could rely on employment stability and adequate health insurance and could expect a carefree retirement.

Several developments in the 1990s have caused many to wonder how long it will be before Germany and other European nations must modify the costly and restrictive social safety net financed by burdensome taxation. The growth of shareholder capitalism is putting more companies "in play" on the stock exchanges; witness the Vodafone takeover of Mannesmann early in 2000. More important, the aging of Germany's (and Europe's) population indicates that PYG pension plans cannot continue as the core of the retirement system in the future. In 2015, 33 percent of Germany's population (over age twenty) will be over age sixty, and in 2035 this will rise to 41 percent (table 3.6).

Germany and other European nations enjoyed a cyclical growth upswing in 1999–2000, which reduced government budget deficits and need to borrow on the capital markets. But in a decade or so a surging elderly population will put serious pressure on government budgets across all of Europe.[36]

According to one analyst, the big demographic changes developing in Europe "could generate very large capital exports." The preretirement savings being accumulated at present "will head for more dynamic economies." Growth-minded European companies will behave the same way, taking their capital to regions where labor is not burdened by high social tax systems and where labor markets are more flexible.[37]

These trends seem to be manifesting themselves already. The Eurozone is now exporting capital in the form of direct cross-border investment by companies. In the first twenty months since the euro was launched, investment outflows from the Eurozone have exceeded inflows by more than $200 billion. One illustration of this is the $18 billion offer by Unilever to acquire Bestfoods, a U.S.-based company.

Table 3.6. Population Aging in Eurozone Countries, U.S., and UK: Percentage of Population over 20 Who Will Be 60 and over in 2015 and 2035

Country	*2015*	*2035*
Italy	36	45
Spain	31	44
Germany	32	41
Sweden	35	40
Netherlands	30	40
France	32	38
UK	30	35
U.S.	27	34

Source: Gene Koretz, "Europe Faces a Retiree Crisis," *Business Week*, May 15, 2000, 38.

Rising life expectancy, declining births, and overly generous benefits are pushing public pension systems in major Continental countries to the verge of crisis. In Italy, pension reform is falling victim to political crisis. In France, Prime Minister Lionel Jospin has ruled out relying heavily on private pensions, which he considers too much a part of the volatile Anglo-Saxon capital market system. In Germany the labor unions would like to increase their economic influence by managing occupational pension funds.[38]

The European public pension systems rely on government transfers financed by special taxes on labor income. These pay-as-you-go systems rely on intergenerational redistribution of income. The demographic trends have led politicians to "solve" the financing problem through higher taxes. This discourages economic initiative and causes workers to cut back their willingness to work (or have children).

Privately funded pensions enjoy several advantages over PYG systems. First, tax policy makes workers want to expand their pension contributions by working more and setting aside larger amounts of their wages for retirement. Second, the system adjusts better to demographic change. Third, private pensions do not discourage savings, whereas PYG systems give workers the "false security" of a government-guaranteed pension.

European governments need to solve the pension problem quickly. The solution requires political as well as economic and financial balancing. The issues extend beyond social stability and retirement incomes. The issues extend to fiscal stability and the preservation of investor confidence in the European region by investors.

Companies and workers are busy seeking solutions to the pension problems they individually face in Europe. In 1999 the European Roundtable of Industrialists, which includes the chairmen of forty-three EU companies, called for a pan-European approach to prevent pension system "self-destruction."

The European Commission is considering legislation that would allow workers to transfer pensions across borders. The lack of the ability to transfer pension assets is seen as a hindrance to the free movement of workers throughout the EU. The Commission also is debating whether it should coordinate the tax and regulatory treatment of pensions in the EU. The Commission also suspects it should broaden the scope of investments allowed for pension funds, including the ability to invest in EU markets outside the home country.

Luxembourg Funds Markets

The government of Luxembourg hopes to match its success in developing a successful investment funds industry by creating the appropriate environment for the sale of private pension funds. In June 1999, the Luxembourg government passed a law allowing the creation of a private fund industry. This sets the stage for the growth of a fund management industry in Luxembourg that could control pension assets for multinational companies on behalf of their employees. Unilever has decided to base its pension fund in Luxembourg.

The Luxembourg legislation permits two types of fund vehicles. The Sepcav is an open-ended pension savings company that operates on a defined contribution basis. It pays benefits upon retirement based on the performance of the fund and the previous level of contributions. The Assep is a pension savings association that operates according to a defined benefits system, in which the level of benefits is set in advance and contributions conform to the projected benefit level.[39]

Luxembourg is in a good position to play an important role as a center for European pension fund management. First, it is centrally located. Second, Luxembourg has extensive treaties in place against the double taxation of investment income. Finally, most other countries in Europe do not possess the financial and communications infrastructure in place, as does Luxembourg. Luxembourg's investment funds sector is the largest in Europe, with assets managed in April 2000 of €848 billion.[40]

MACROECONOMY AND EURO EXCHANGE RATE

The euro currency demonstrated persistent weakness in its initial sixteen months. By May 2000, the new currency had depreciated 24 percent against the U.S. dollar. Several theories compete for attention in explaining the determination of foreign exchange rates and changes in such rates, notably those that revolve around macroeconomic conditions and monetary trends. The following sections follow the ECB analysis of the path of the euro in 1999–2000, consider political and other noneconomic analyses, discuss economic explanations, and then evaluate the performance of the euro in its first thirty months.

ECB Reviews the Euro in 1999

In its first *Annual Report* the ECB discussed the euro's behavior in the foreign exchange market and provided a review of the factors related to the single currency's weakness. The report noted that the euro declined against the currencies of most trading partners during 1999 and into the first few months of 2000.

Considering the 12 percent depreciation of the euro vis-à-vis the dollar in first half of 1999, the ECB described the strength of the dollar as tied to the respective cyclical conditions for the United States and euro area. Continuous strong growth of the U.S. economy subdued inflationary pressures and translated them into dollar appreciation.

For part of 1999 the Japanese yen demonstrated even stronger tendencies to appreciate against the euro than the dollar. According to the ECB, "this strengthening occurred mainly against the background of significant current account surpluses and in parallel with a turnaround of the economy, which started to record slightly more positive growth."[41]

Focusing more directly on the euro area, the ECB noted that (1) there was a reduced current account surplus and (2) euro area residents increased their foreign direct investment while portfolio investment outflows declined.

The ECB commentary on the euro in the foreign exchange markets was very brief and mostly factual. This brevity was in part due to the concern over giving incorrect signals to the financial markets, as well as the dismay apparently felt by ECB officials at the currency's dismal performance.[42] It was not until May 2000 that ECB officials began to "talk intervention" in order to inject a stabilizing tone into foreign exchange market psychology.

Political Explanations

Of the political and other noneconomic explanations for the weakness of the euro, the strongest was the political explanation. This argument said that a weak euro was caused by the creation of the single currency as an act of political compromise, without any rational economic basis. In 1990, when the Berlin Wall fell, the West German government was anxious to reunify the nation. The French were not favorably disposed to this reunification and only accepted it if Germany would pledge to give up the deutsche mark for the single currency.[43]

When France and Germany agree, the European agenda moves ahead. Unfortunately, some sharp differences in thinking underlie the surface ease between these two largest members of the Eurozone. These differences relate to (1) the need for structural reforms, (2) the need to maintain progress in reducing government budget deficits, and (3) the need to more closely align and integrate national economies within the EU and Eurozone.

Related to the political argument is the realization that the Eurozone encompasses nations that are in different phases of their economic cycles, so that a single monetary policy cannot be appropriate for all parts of the union. For example, Ireland entered the monetary union with a record domestic growth rate and higher inflation than most other Eurozone countries. The ECB monetary policy of low interest rates and monetary stimulus was not well suited to Ireland's needs in 1999–2000. Ireland no longer has control over its interest rates or exchange rate movements, and increasingly in the first eighteen months of the single currency found inflation creeping up, to over 5 percent in June 2000.[44]

Some analysts blame the weak performance of the euro on market perceptions that the ECB lacks any power over the exchange rate. The ECB pursues a policy of internal, not external, stabilization. The problem lies in the fact that nobody is in charge of exchange rate policy.[45]

A final set of explanations for the weak euro focuses on financial market behavior and inherent market instability. One commentator argued that the euro slump was nothing more than a currency overshooting. Lack of confidence in the euro based on psychology could send the currency lower and lower.[46] Finally, several financial writers ascribed the euro's weakness to the herdlike behavior in financial markets. Ernst Welteke, president of the German Bundesbank, expressed this view.[47] Welteke maintained that the "current valuation of the euro may not be entirely justified by economic fundamentals." He noted that the European economic growth rate differential with the United States has been narrowed, but this has not been reflected by a recovery in value of the euro. He attributes the lag in recovery of the euro to currency overshooting and the herdlike behavior of traders in the financial markets.

Economic Analysis

Economic commentary on the depreciation of the euro strongly emphasizes two factors. These factors are the investment flows from Euroland to the UK and United States, and the higher economic growth rate in the United States as compared with the E-12 group.

According to Martin Essex, money is pouring into the United States and UK, forcing up the exchange rates of the dollar and the pound, leaving the euro behind.[48] International investors recognize that the Americans and British are ahead in the development of the new economy, putting their funds into Internet start-ups and other new ventures. In addition, both the U.S. and UK economies are benefiting from currency strength. Similarly, equity investment in Japan buoyed the yen vis-à-vis the euro. Edward Dove, chief investment officer of Julius Baer Asset Management in London, put funds into Japanese stocks in 1999 and stayed fairly light on European equities. Equity investment inflows to Japan aggregated €83 billion, with the countries in the euro experiencing a net outflow of €56 billion. Similarly, in 1997–1998 and

Table 3.7. Real GNP Growth Rate, 1998–2001

Year	Eurozone	U.S.
1998	2.7	4.3
1999	2.1	4.0
2000	3.0	4.0
2001	3.0	3.0

Source: "The Sick Money of Europe," *Business Week*, May 15, 2000, 60–61.

1999 foreigners bought a net $70 billion, $50 billion, and $108 billion, respectively, of U.S. shares. In each of these three years, Eurozone investors accounted for more than half of these purchases.[49]

The second most common explanation for the weak euro is the differential in economic growth rates between the U.S. and Eurozone economies (table 3.7). The financial press has described this as a torrent of money rushing out of Europe as businesspersons and investors flee the continent's anemic economies.[50] In economic theory, the appropriate explanation lies with the monetary explanation of exchange rate determination. That is, in high-growth economies, the transaction demand for money may be outpacing the central bank's willingness to pump liquidity into the system. Demand for money exceeds supply. By contrast, in a slow-growing economy, the demand for money based on transactions may be lagging behind liquidity creation and the supply of money exceeds demand. When these two regions are put together, money should flow from the region where supply exceeds demand (the Eurozone) to the region where demand exceeds supply (United States). This money flow is likely to bring about an appreciation of currency of the money-receiving region, and a depreciation of the currency of the money-sending region.

While investment flows and differential economic growth rates have tended to predominate in explanations concerning the weak euro, several other theories also warrant discussion. These include (1) low euro interest rates and the carry trade distortions and (2) worries about ECB credibility. ECB credibility was questioned increasingly in January–May 2000, as the central bank resorted to timid twenty-five-basis-point rate increases and avoided currency market intervention.[51] The *International Herald Tribune* referred to the ECB as "powerless" when it raised interest rates for a fourth time (April 27, 2000) and the currency plunged to a new low against the U.S. dollar.[52] At that point the euro was worth $0.9095 and had depreciated by over 22 percent against the U.S. dollar since early January 1999. The euro would decline in value by another $0.02 before reaching its seventeen-month low point.

Low interest rates in the Eurozone encourage so-called euro-carry trades, the borrowing of euro to be switched into higher yielding dollar assets. Carry trade distortions can generate persistent exchange rate trends but can also cause sudden sharp reversals when the risks of currency mismatching become obvious and positions are unwound. Much of the euro's slide can be linked to the rapid development in 1999 of euro-denominated financing encouraged by low interest rates. Also important was the perception by borrowers that the euro would prove to be a persistently weak currency.[53]

Evaluation of Euro Trading on the Foreign Exchanges

The early weakness of the new currency persisted until October 2000. Many reasons, both political and economic, were given for this weak performance. The fact that the monetary unification was one of the most revolutionary changes of its type ever attempted in itself provides a good reason for a lack of confidence in the currency in its early months. Reticence on the part of officials of the new ECB added fuel to the uncertainties in the minds of investors and businesspersons.

Over the period from January 1999 to October 2000, the euro depreciated almost 30 percent against the U.S. dollar. Over the next several months the euro strengthened, appreciating approximately 16 percent against the dollar by January 2001. The new ECB agonized over euro depreciation, and only in September 2000 did it relent and organize a massive central bank intervention in the foreign exchange markets to support the currency (table 3.8). From January 2001 to July 2001 the euro showed its weakness by declining 10.5 percent against the U.S. dollar.

The increased strength of the euro late in year 2000 can be partially explained by the coordinated foreign exchange market intervention. Another scenario, suggested by a *Business Week* analysis was that European investors might repatriate some of their massive stock market investments in the United States, while European governments could attract inward bond investment if they issued an additional $120 billion in extra debt paper in 2001.[54] While the United States accounts for 30 percent of world output, it has absorbed two-thirds of all funds leaving capital-exporting countries.[55] For this reason the European capital flow into the United States in 2000 is thought to be unsustainable. So perhaps this flow might reverse itself, flowing into the Eurozone to support the euro. Finally, the opposite cyclical positions of the United States and the Eurozone economies when the single currency was introduced appear to have been an important factor in euro currency weakness. The reversal of these economic cycle positions in 2000 probably helped strengthen the euro from October 2000 to January 2001.

Table 3.8. Chronology of the Euro in Foreign Exchange Markets

Date	*Event Description*
January 1999	Euro starts trading at approximately $1.17.
May 1999	EU eases Italy's deficit requirements and euro falls to a record low of $1.05.
November 1999	ECB tightens monetary policy. ECB initiates first of seven increases in money market interest rates in the Eurozone, through October 2000.
July 2000	Reports indicate European investment flows to the United States in first half 2000 exceed $180 billion.
September 2000	German Chancellor Gerhard Schröder announces that the German government is not concerned about euro weakness on foreign exchange markets. Goldman Sachs economist notes there is doubt central bankers would intervene when Europe's most important politician does not think the euro's valuation is a problem.
September 2000	European Central Bank and the United States launch coordinated intervention on foreign exchange markets with G-7 central banks. Stabilizes euro temporarily.
September 2000	Denmark voters reject the euro in popular referendum.
October 2000	Euro has declined in value from $1.17 to $0.82 since January 1999, a 30 percent fall.
November 2000	United Nations agrees to Iraqi demands that it be paid for its oil exports in euros rather than in dollars. Should increase monthly demand for euros by $1.7 billion.
November 2000	Companies report sharp drop in third-quarter dollar-valued earnings from their European units.
November 2000	Evidence developing that European capital flows to U.S. slackening, possible source of new strength in euro.
December 2000	Third-quarter economic growth in U.S. falls to 2.2% as the Eurozone growth accelerates to 3.4%. This is followed by strength of euro on exchange markets.
December 2000	Investors react to gloomy economic news in U.S. and Japan by selling these currencies against the euro, giving further strength to the currency.
January 2001	Greece joins the Eurozone, the first additional member since the euro was introduced. Euro reaches value of $0.952, a 16 percent appreciation, since October 2000.
July 2001	Euro declines to $0.8515, a depreciation of 10.5 percent since January 2001.

NOTES

1. Maastricht treaty, title II, art. G 3 a.
2. Maastricht treaty, title VI, chap. 1, art. 103.
3. Maastricht treaty, title VI, chap. 1, art. 103.

4. Helene Cooper, "Greece Gets Serious about Joining EMU," *Wall Street Journal*, October 7, 1998, A17.
5. Brian Coleman, "German Alliance for Jobs Needs Allies, *Wall Street Journal*, October 9, 1998, A10.
6. *Wall Street Journal*, "France to Adopt Shorter Transition for Euro Currency," July 6, 1998, A11.
7. Lionel Barber and Liam Halligan, "Euro-11 Warned on Public Deficit Slippage," *Financial Times*, June 6, 1998, 2.
8. Thomas Kamm, "Governmental Crisis in Italy Reflects Challenge for Europe's Leftists on EMU," *Wall Street Journal*, October 6, 1998, A19.
9. A change in the schedule of payments by the Italian government made it more difficult to evaluate the budgetary balance in 1998. James Blitz, "Italian Deficit Drift after Tax Shortfall," *Financial Times*, July 3, 1998, 2.
10. Maureen Kline, "A Leftist Is Tapped to Lead Italy in Europe's Latest Political Shift," *Wall Street Journal*, October 19, 1998, A21.
11. Dagmar Allund, "Spanish Rate Cut Suggests a Shift in Europe," *Wall Street Journal*, October 7, 1998, A8.
12. Edmund L. Andrews, "Politicians Seek Wider Role in European Central Bank," *New York Times*, C2.
13. Joseph Fitchett, "Worst Pitfall for the Euro: Social Revolt Could Force a Nation to Withdraw," *International Herald Tribune*, May 2–3, 1998, 20.
14. John Vinocur, "Single Currency Marks Triumph of Political Will: But Public's Enthusiasm Is Muted by Jobs Crisis," *International Herald Tribune*, May 2–3, 1998, 18.
15. Tom Buerkle, "Will Consumers Win and Workers Lose?" *International Herald Tribune*, May 2–3, 1998, 18.
16. This view is expressed by Bernadette Tesch, who heads the Brussels office of IET, the federation of European unions in banking, insurance, and other services.
17. Josef Joffe, "The Euro: A Huge, Dangerous Gamble for Europe," *International Herald Tribune*, May 2–3, 1998, 6.
18. Wolfgang Münchau, "Santer Warns on EU Public Finances," *Financial Times*, July 7, 1998, 2.
19. Lionel Barber, "Harmony a Sensitive Issue," *Financial Times*, March 29, 1998, VI.
20. Lionel Barber, "EU Moves Nearer Deal on Savings Tax," *Financial Times*, May 21, 1998, 2.
21. Julie Wolf, "EU Tax Proposal Will Test Ability to Unify Systems," *Wall Street Journal Europe*, May 22–23, 1998, 13.
22. Michael Allen, "A Gathering Storm Threatens to Swamp Offshore Banking," *Wall Street Journal Europe*, May 22–23, 1998, 13.
23. Martin Walker, "EU Will Put Squeeze on Tax Havens," *Guardian* (London), May 21, 1998, 25.
24. Robert Wright, "Tax Havens' Role in Financial Scandals Attacked," *Financial Times*, October 12, 1998, 8.
25. Quentin Peel, "Europe's Hard Sums," *Financial Times*, October 20, 1998, 16.
26. Ralph Atkins, "Euro Gives Germans a Taxing Problem," *Financial Times*, June 23, 1998, 3.
27. Ralph Atkins, "Germany's Coalition Agrees on Cut in Basic Tax," *Financial Times*, October 12, 1998, 18.

28. "The Accidental Reformer," *Business Week*, May 1, 2000, 60–61.

29. Astrid Wendlandt, "Safe Havens Become Endangered Species," *Financial Times*, March 30, 2000, 25.

30. Tony Barber, "Ambitious Reforms in Store," *Financial Times*, Special Germany Supplement, May 22, 2000, X.

31. P. Norman and C. Swann, "Display of Euro-Zone Unity Spoiled," *Financial Times*, May 9, 2000, 1.

32. Stanley Reed, "Europe Shouldn't Squander This Telecom Windfall," *Business Week*, May 22, 2000, p. 68.

33. "Jospin's Laundry List," *Wall Street Journal*, May 11, 2000, 10.

34. James Graff, "Europe's Jobs Challenge," *Time*, May 8, 2000, 29–31.

35. John Tagliabue, "Europe Lags in High Tech Hunt," *International Herald Tribune*, May 6, 2000, 1, 16.

36. Gene Koretz, "Europe Faces a Retiree Crisis," *Business Week*, May 15, 2000, 38.

37. Barry Riley, "The Euro Dilemma," *Financial Times*, May 6, 2000, XXVI.

38. Thomas Mayer, "The Time to Fix the Pension System Is Now," *Wall Street Journal Europe*, May 5, 2000, 10.

39. Deborah Hargreaves, "Finding a Solution to a Pressing Problem," *Financial Times*, Luxembourg Supplement, June 15, 2000, III.

40. Neil Buckley, "Prosperous, Robust State Marches On," *Financial Times*, Luxembourg Supplement, June 15, 2000, I.

41. ECB, *Annual Report 1999*, "The Global Macroeconomic Environment," 42.

42. David Shirreff, "Still Off-Centre," *Euromoney*, April 2000, 104. The author notes that paranoia may be too strong a word, but the ECB appears frustratingly cautious in giving messages to the market.

43. R. Graham and H. Simonian, "Europe's Rocky Relationship," *Financial Times*, May 18, 2000, 14.

44. John M. Brown, "Ireland Struggles to Settle in the Euro-Zone," *Financial Times*, May 26, 2000, 26.

45. Wolfgang Münchau, "Euro Suffers the Perils of Benign Neglect," *Financial Times*, April 24, 2000, 17.

46. Eduardo Cue, "The Woes of the Euro," *U.S. News and World Report*, May 8, 2000, 33.

47. Ernst Welteke, "A Currency Hobbled by the Herd Instinct," *Financial Times*, May 31, 2000, 13.

48. Martin Essex, "Britain Buoyed by the New Economy," *Sunday Business* (London), April 30, 2000, 29.

49. Bill Spindle, "Brighter Prospects Send Capital Flowing to Japan," *Wall Street Journal Europe*, May 10, 2000, 1, 13.

50. "The Sick Money of Europe," *Business Week*, May 15, 2000, 60–61.

51. M. R. Sesit, "Euro Keeps Sliding as Currency Fails to Find Bottom," *Wall Street Journal Europe*, May 4, 2000, 1, 14.

52. Edmund L. Andrews, "European Interest Rate Rise Fails to Halt New Euro Slide," *International Herald Tribune*, April 28, 2000, 1.

53. Barry Riley, "The Euro Fights Back," *Financial Times*, June 10, 2000, XXVI.

54. David Fairlamb, "Back from the Depths," *Business Week*, January 8, 2001, 52–53.

55. Tony Barber, "A Tentative Recovery," *Financial Times*, November 3, 2000, 14.

Chapter Four

European Banking and the Euro

As continental Europe experiences the phase-in of the euro, its banking sector is one part of the economy most impacted by these changes. In the 1980s, European banking followed a strategy of stability and slow change. But by the mid-1990s the coming of European monetary union (EMU), global competition changes in information technology, and rapid evolution of capital market sectors began to put pressure on banks throughout Europe.

The introduction of the euro has accelerated forces of change in European banking. In this chapter we analyze prospects for bank profits and revenues on the eve of the single currency, consider bank and financial sector restructuring and mergers, and analyze the growing emphasis on investment banking and changes in regulation and management of bank capital. A final section considers the need for large European banks to focus on maximizing shareholder wealth using Commerzbank as a case study.

PERSPECTIVE ON EUROPEAN BANKING ON THE EVE OF SINGLE CURRENCY

On the eve of the creation of the single currency in Europe, most banks were ill prepared. While many large European banking institutions had tackled information technology (IT) and operational challenges, they had not addressed more difficult strategic issues involving the single currency. The euro has wiped out big chunks of traditionally important sources of profit in foreign exchange, corporate finance, and government bond trading. The following discussion provides a perspective on European bank profits in 1998, shortly prior to adoption of the single currency.

Areas of Profit Change

In 1998, European banks faced a dilemma. The coming of the single currency offered opportunities for them to be part of a single banking market that could challenge the United States. The United States might now be challenged in overall economic size (GDP and population), in its government bond market, in its equity market, and in its management of personal financial assets (table 4.1). On the other hand, the coming of euro meant the loss of a considerable part of the profits these same banks had derived in the areas of foreign exchange, government bond trading, and corporate lending. In 1997 these business activities accounted for a major part of the profit base of most large- and medium-sized European banks. As a result of competitive and other changes, revenues from government bond trading, foreign exchange, and corporate lending is expected to shrink from $64 billion in 1998 to $49.5 billion in 2006. Government bond trading will be more competitive. Government bond trading will be concentrated mostly in a single currency, and it will take place in a more liquid market place. Since twelve currencies will be collapsed into one, trade and financial transactions between Euroland nations will become "domesticated" and cleared/settled in euros; much of the foreign exchange revenues earned by European banks will disappear. Corporate lending will be intensely more competitive as banks from all around the Eurozone can lend to a corporation in a uniform currency. Equally important, corporate bond financing will grow and will displace a sizeable chunk of the former bank lending.

Alternately, the single currency is seen as creating opportunities for banks. However, only a small number of the most effective and strategically driven banks will be in a position to benefit from these opportunities. Revenue growth will be concentrated in investment banking, in areas such as equities, corporate bonds, and mergers and acquisitions. In the following sections we analyze these opportunity areas.[1]

Table 4.1. Comparison of Europe (E-15) and United States, 1997

	United States (U.S.$ billions)	*Europe (U.S.$ billions)*
Real GDP	6,485.0	7,304
Population (millions)	265.8	372.8
Central government bond market	2,682.0	3,655
Corporate bond market	1,910.0	370
Equity market capitalization	8,059.0	4,327
Total personal financial assets	24,406.0	17,921

Source: Jonathan Davidson, Alison Ledger, and Giovanni Viani, "Wholesale Banking: The Ugly Implications of EMU," *McKinsey Quarterly* 1 (1998).

Table 4.2. Projected Impact of Single Currency on European Wholesale Banking Revenues (U.S.$ billions)

Revenue-Generation Activity	*1998*	*2006*
M&A	2.5	3.0
Equity	8.5	17.0
Bond[a]	3.0	8.0
Foreign exchange	6.0	5.0
Payments	14.0	20.0
Deposit	21.0	9.0
Lending	55.0	42.0
Total	110.0	104.0

[a]In 1998 all were from government bond trading; in 2006 from municipal bonds (3.3), corporate bonds (2.2), and government bonds (2.5).

Corporate Banking

Prior to the single currency, corporate banking generated about $90 billion of bank revenues. Approximately $76 billion of this was accounted for by lending and deposit activities. Another $14 billion was generated from payments services. With the single currency, these revenues could shrink to $71 billion. We should note that within this broad category, although profits will decrease, revenues from payments services should increase because of the large number of banking institutions, the complex correspondent relationships, and the introduction of new cross-border payments systems Trans-European Automated Realtime Gross Settlement Express Transfer System (TARGET).

Lending overcapacity has prompted European banks to offer companies low-cost loans. With the single currency, greater focus on bank shareholder returns, and government efforts to eliminate state subsidies to banks, fewer banks will want to continue to operate corporate lending services that generate zero or substandard profits. The new European Central Bank has set minimum reserves on banks, which cost must be passed on to customers.

The creation of a more liquid corporate bond market in the Eurozone will allow corporations to fund themselves more cheaply by shifting from bank loans to bond issuance. Competition for any remaining corporate lending business will be fierce. Only the largest, most efficient, and best-capitalized banks will survive in the new corporate loan business.

Deposit and Money Market

The deposit and money market business was worth about $21 billion in revenues on the eve of the single currency. With the euro, the volume of this business will be reduced. Corporate customers will no longer need to hold deposits in many European currencies they now trade in. Moreover, there will be no use of the money market to take advantage of interest rate differentials between EMU currencies. Deposit revenues will decline. In addition, margins will shrink as the twelve currencies collapse into one, and as all banks compete for corporate deposit funds. Money market banks will have to compete with many players in the now enlarged euro money market. Winners will be the large banks that are able to operate cost-efficient centralized trading systems and those that enjoy access to the most up-to-date market information.

Payments

On the eve of the euro, the payments business was worth $14 billion in revenues. Much of this comes from correspondent banking, where smaller banks hold accounts with other banks to make and receive payments in foreign currencies. The single currency is eliminating these intra-European currency payments business relations. The introduction of TARGET, a bank clearing system that operates in real time, will further reduce the need for correspondent bank services. But cross-border payments will rise as trade expands, so that revenues could reach $20 billion by 2006.

Declining costs also represent a plus for European bank earnings. A study by Boston Consulting Group forecasts that the average price of a domestic payment in Europe will fall from $1.08 to $0.55 by 2005. The decline will be steeper in the wholesale market. In cross-border payments the average rate worldwide is likely to drop from $57 to $31. Three large banks are expected to emerge as dominant global providers of payment services.[2]

Corporate Bonds

In the past, corporate bonds have played an insignificant role as a source of capital within Europe. A more liquid euro-denominated bond market will reduce the borrowing cost and encourage a shift away from bank loans as a method of financing companies. A shift by European corporations toward the use of bonds would generate additional revenues of $2.2 billion a year in origination fees and bond-trading income for banks.[3] American investment banks likely would participate in this activity, based on their strong experience in such financing.

Collateral with the development of corporate bond financing, higher yield bond financing, should also develop. Traditionally, European investors have demonstrated an interest in holding European government bonds when they offer relatively high yields. Therefore, such investors may demonstrate a similar strong interest in high yielding corporate bond issues. This bond market sector is discussed in chapter 7, which focuses on bond market development.

Equities

On the eve of the introduction of a single currency, many European equity markets were less well developed than counterparts in the UK, Switzerland, and Luxembourg (table 4.3). These countries exhibited stock market capitalizations below 50 percent of GDP (Germany, France, Italy, Spain, Belgium, Denmark, Finland, Norway, and Austria).

Several factors explain this retarded development. First, supply is limited by high corporate tax rates, which encourage companies to remain privately owned and to more easily shelter income in offshore accounts. Also, bank loans are relatively cheaper than equity finance. Second, many corporations are state-owned. This has been changing recently; witness the numerous telecoms privatizations, spurring the growth of European stock markets since 1997. Third, investor demand for equities has been constrained by lack of large institutional pensions and by the (until 1998) availability of high yielding government bonds.

The single currency is increasing both the demand and supply of equities. Banks that will benefit from more rapid development of equities markets are those with top tier status as investment banks, as well as those that can

Table 4.3. European Stock Markets, Market Capitalization, Relative to GDP (percentage)

Country	*U.S.$ Billions*	*% GDP*
UK	1,643	143
Germany	664	28
France	587	38
Switzerland	400	137
Netherlands	375	75
Italy	257	24
Sweden	240	96
Spain	192	33
Belgium	119	45
Denmark	71	38
Finland	61	49
Norway	57	36
Austria	34	15
Luxembourg	32	191

Source: Jonathan Davidson, Alison Ledger, and Giovanni Viani, "Wholesale Banking: The Ugly Implications of EMU," *McKinsey Quarterly* 1 (1998).

originate and distribute equity issues on a global basis. Later we describe the efforts of several large European banks to become leaders in these sectors.

One immediate effect of the single currency is to shift the asset allocation of investors from a domestic to a European sector focus. Assume that a Dutch investor has 85 percent of its equity portfolio in Dutch stocks. To give proper weight to all of the share issues in the Eurozone, the Dutch investor would have to reduce the Dutch stock market component to approximately 17 percent of the portfolio. Such portfolio rebalancings will generate large commission business for stockbrokers. Those banks with the better-regarded equity research departments will be able to compete for such trading business.

At the same time, competition will be narrowing the commission fees that banks earn on this growing business. Estimates of the impact of such pressures on the equity-related revenues of European banks are summarized in table 4.4. Here we note that origination fees are projected to rise from $3 billion (pre-euro) to $8 billion after the single currency is introduced. Trading revenues will increase but only by a small percentage because competition will reduce the size of trading commissions. Institutions that do not already have strong equity capabilities and a well-regarded research group may be discouraged from participating in the equities business because of the costs of building the necessary skills. As we note later in this chapter, existing equities trading and research institutions are being acquired eagerly by banks intent on surviving in this business.

The cost structure of equities trading is complex, consisting of at least a half dozen elements. Their relative importance is outlined in table 4.5. The functional areas of sales, trading, and settlement clearing all play an important role

Table 4.4. Changes in Equity Business Revenues, 1998–2006

	Pre-Euro	*Post-Euro*
1. Origination	3.0	8.0
2. Trading	5.5	9.5
Total	8.5	17.5
Analysis of Changes in:		
1. Origination		
Growth		9.0
Fall in Fee Levels		−4.0
Net Change		5.0
2. Trading		
Growth		8.0
Fall in Trading Commissions		−4.0
Net Change		4.0

Source: Jonathan Davidson, Alison Ledger, and Giovanni Viani, "Wholesale Banking: The Ugly Implications of EMU," McKinsey Quarterly 1 (1998).
Note: Amounts in U.S.$ billions.

Table 4.5. Equities Trading Cost Elements as Percentage of Total Cost, Mid-1990s

Trading Cost Element	*Cost Element (%)*
Sales	20–25
Trading	10–15
Research	25–30
Settlement-clearing	10–15
Office and telecoms	20
Risk Capital	5
Total	100

Source: Jonathan Davidson, Alison Ledger, and Giovanni Viani, "Wholesale Banking: The Ugly Implications of EMU," *McKinsey Quarterly* 1 (1998).

as cost factors. Risk capital appears as a relatively small item, but it is a definite cost element. The largest single cost element is research. While research expenditure may seem to be exorbitant, research powerfully influences the quality of investment advisory services and plays a unique role in sustaining the bank's reputation. Table 4.6 indicates the number of equity researchers of the top equity investment banks in the mid-1990s.

Table 4.6. Number of Equity Researchers, 1995

Company	*Number*
SBC Warburg	263
Merrill Lynch	262
James Capel	221
CSFB	199
NatWest	153
DMG	131
Goldman	128
Salomon	115
Morgan Stanley	108

Source: Jonathan Davidson, Alison Ledger, and Giovanni Viani, "Wholesale Banking: The Ugly Implications of EMU," *McKinsey Quarterly* 1 (1998).

M&A Advisory

On the eve of the euro's introduction it was well understood that a large increase in demand for mergers and acquisition (M&A) advisory services would be created. Cross-border consolidation in 1999–2000 proved this to be true. Many of Europe's industries are restructuring to improve their cost structures and achieve higher productivity levels. Individual companies are seeking higher growth opportunities and new core businesses.

Banks will be best positioned to profit from a growing merger advisory business when they possess the required skills and connections. These connections include institutions with expertise in specific industrial sectors, with a proven track record in M&A work, with strong contacts with CEOs, and with office networks in the countries in which such activities take place.

Banks outside Eurozone Get Ready

As the euro changed the dynamics of competition in European banking, banking institutions across the Continent were getting ready. Equally important, banks outside the Eurozone were preparing for the competitive onslaught. Chase, a leading American bank, began preparing for a unified Europe in 1988 when it started to strip data processing out of its European branches and focus it in an operating center located in Bournemouth, England. Since that initiative, Chase has spent hundreds of millions of dollars on the facility.[4] Shortly after these changes, Chase started thinking of the euro as equivalent in importance to real-time payments in the United States, where payments flow through the same system and are geographically transparent. Chase uses the Society for Worldwide International Financial Transactions (SWIFT) banking network between the UK and continental centers. Chase ranks as the number three payment system player in Germany, behind Deutsche Bank and Dresdner Bank.

Citibank started preparations for the retail side of the euro in October 1996. Citibank views the EMU as a business project but with strong compliance content needs for year 2000. A central team of twenty-five people has worked on coordinating technical projects into the business of foreign exchange, transactions, cash management, trading, and securities. The currency integration in Europe is designed to create efficiencies that can be adopted at other financial centers outside Europe.

In 1997 Bank America completed year 2000 conversions and has remained well focused on the euro. Its global banking system is in place (since 1980s) in all thirty-nine countries where the bank is directly represented. Bank America may be the only bank that runs its global system off a single network. The bank has had a team of forty people focused on the euro at facilities in London.

While the UK remains outside the Eurozone, its banks offered euro accounts as soon as the euro implementation began. It may be several years before the UK joins the single currency system officially, but large British banks are bulk mailing information, conducting seminars for clients, and persuading UK corporate officers to join their programs for servicing euro financial needs. Barclays PLC has offered 30,000 clients euro accounts. Barclays spent $250 million in preparations for the euro.[5]

FINANCIAL SECTOR RESTRUCTURING AND MERGERS

At midyear 2000, conditions were ripe for pan-European bank consolidation. Banking remains one of the Continent's more fragmented sectors. In 2000 there were some 3,400 German banks, including various types of savings, mortgage, and cooperative banks. In Italy there are close to 1,000 banks.

The biggest banks are reaching growth limits in domestic markets, but few have developed a clearly convincing strategy for expanding across Europe. Cross-border mergers have been carried out mainly in smaller countries. Only in the case of HSBC acquiring Credit Commercial de France (CCF) has a large bank successfully acquired another sizable institution in another country (table 4.7).

Table 4.7. Selected Banking Mergers in Europe, 1992–2000

Year	Country	Deal Size	Bidder	Target
2000	UK/France[a]	10,517	HSBC	CCF
	UK	32,352	RBS	NatWest
	Spain	11,300	BBVA	Argentaria
	Spain/Port[a]	1,527	BSCH	Banco Totta & Acc
1999	Spain	16,639	Banco Santander	
	France	12,525	Banque Nat. de Paris	Paribas
	Italy	8,400	Banca Intesa SpA	BCI
	Sweden/Ger[a]	1,656	SEB	BFG Bank
	France/Lux[a]	1,045	Dexia Group	Banque Int. Luxembourg
1998	Switzerland	23,244	UBS	SBC
	Italy	10,916	Credito Italiano	Unicredito
	Italy	8,504	Instituto Bancario	IMI
	Sweden/Fin[a]	4,675	Nordbanken	Merita Oyj
	Neth/Belg[a]	1,514	Fortis	ASLK-CGER
1997	France	2,644	Paribas	Compagnie Banc
	France	2,109	Paribas	Cetelese
1996	Sweden	3,374	Svenska Handelsbank	Statshypotek
	France/Belg[a]	1,600	Credit Local de France	Credit Communale
	Belg/Neth[a]	1,457	Fortis	MeesPierson
1995	UK	9,236	Lloyds Bank	TSB Group
	Switz/UK[a]	3,189	SBC	SG Warburg
	Germany/UK[a]	1,568	Dresdner Bank	Kleinwort Benson
1994	UK	2,652	Lloyds Bank	Cheltenham & Gloucester
	Italy	2,442	Credito Italiano	Credito Romagnolo
1993	Switzerland	1,092	CS Holding	Schweizerische Volksbank
1992	UK	6,518	HSBC	Midland Bank

Source: John Wallman, "Fear of Becoming Token Candidates," *Financial Times*, Banking in Europe Supplement, May 26, 2000, II.
[a]Denotes cross-border merger.

Everyone in Europe expects pan-European consolidation of the banking industry. But there are numerous obstacles:[6]

- The presence in several large countries of mutual and cooperative savings banks that hold large portions of retail business. These institutions have low returns on funds, but are insulated from capital market pressures.
- National governments collude with entrenched managements to protect national institutions.
- A lack of harmonization in tax and legal systems in the banking sector makes it difficult to produce pan-European financial services.

Cross-border mergers have occurred in small countries (Benelux and Nordic), where the big banks must cross borders to expand. Several bank alliances have been attempted, but little has been accomplished outside of blocking attempted takeovers of alliance partners. Some observers believe alliances could lead to better specialization in particular products (credit cards), with each partner specializing in a different product or range of services.

Consolidation

Within each national banking market in Europe there is room for further consolidation. Within-country merger is the simplest way for banks to grow larger and at the same time enhance their bottom-line profitability. Within-country merger also avoids the complicated cultural problems of combining banks with different languages and customers with different expectations.

Domestic consolidation appeals more to shareholders. But when market share attains a certain threshold (30–45 percent), which varies by country, cross-border expansion is the only remaining option. In smaller countries, this threshold is reached quickly (Belgium, Sweden). Consequently, in these cases Europe has seen cross-border mergers in the first year of the euro. In larger countries (Germany) the big four commercial banks have fewer than 20 percent of the market. But their opportunities are limited due to the nature of bank structure. In Germany there are over 2,000 urban cooperative banks *(Volksbanken)*, as well as banks in country areas *(Raffeisen)*. Germany also has hundreds of public sector savings banks *(Sparkassen)* as well as regional *Landesbanken.*[7]

The public sector and cooperative banks dominate German banking. German savings banks dominate with 35 percent of the market. These banks use common advertising and shared IT systems. Cooperatives hold 25 percent of the market and are well entrenched.

In France, the 1999 merger of Banque Nationale de Paris (BNP) and Paribas created the second largest European bank in terms of assets, and the eleventh in terms of stock market value (table 4.8). This merger is discussed in detail in a later chapter. In 2000, HSBC acquired Credit Commercial de France (CCF) (table 4.7), leaving Société Generale in a field of seven groups that dominate the French banking market. In May 2000 HSBC Holdings had a market capitalization over €103 billion, ranking it first among European banks. The French system, like the German one, includes mutual savings banks.

Opportunity for consolidation exists in the UK, with many demutualized mortgage banks ready to be acquired. Synergistic benefits from moves such as

Table 4.8. Top European Banks by Stock Market Capitalization, May 2000

Rank/Company	*Country*	*Market Cap (€bn)*
1. HSBC Holdings	UK	103.2
2. Lloyds TSB	UK	59.0
3. ING Group	Neth	58.1
4. UBS	Switz	58.1
5. Credit Suisse	Switz	54.4
6. BSCH	Spain	47.0
7. Deutsche Bank	Ger	45.4
8. BBV Argentaria	Spain	44.0
9. Royal Bank of Scotland	UK	43.3
10. Barclays	UK	41.8
11. BNP Paribas	France	40.0
12. Fortis	Belg/Neth	34.4
13. ABN Amro Holding	Neth	32.9
14. Hypo Vereinsbank	Ger	26.8
15. Dresdner Bank	Ger	23.7
16. Société Generale	France	23.7
17. Halifax Group	UK	23.0
18. Unicredito Italiano	Italy	22.3
19. San Paolo IMI	Italy	21.6
20. Commerzbank	Ger	20.9
21. Nordic Baltic Holding	Sweden	20.3
22. Banca Intesa	Italy	18.8
23. Abbey International	UK	17.8
24. Turkiye Is Bank	Turkey	16.3
25. Bipop Caire	Italy	16.2
26. Standard Chartered	UK	15.6
27. Credit Lyonnais	France	14.0
28. Bank of Scotland	UK	12.2
29. KBC Bankverzekerung	Belg	12.0
30. CCF	France	11.6

Source: Financial Times, Banking in Europe Supplement, May 26, 2000.

closing branches may be limited by the outcry against Barclays branch closings. The acquisition of NatWest by RBS early in 2000 was a surprise because NatWest ranked fifteenth in Europe in assets at year-end 1999, dwarfing the two Scottish banks that fought to acquire the larger clearing bank. In 2000, two small acquisitions should be noted. Chase acquired Flemings, an asset management specialist with operations in Asia, and Citigroup acquired Schroders, an investment bank with a strong M&A advisory business.

Cross-Border Mergers

At midyear 2000, banking consolidation and cross-border mergers still lagged behind other industrial sectors (telecoms, manufacturing). According to a Commerzbank report, there have been forty-nine European bank merger deals worth more than $1 million over the past decade. Only ten of these have been across borders. These mergers are identified in table 4.7. Only two of the top twenty-five deals were cross-border. These cross-border mergers were the 1998 mergers of Sweden's Nordbanken with Merita of Finland and HSBC's acquisition of CCF in 2000.

One hindrance to cross-border mergers is doubt that these mergers will create value for shareholders. But as the euro and technological change take hold, opportunities will appear more favorable.

Differences in the law and tax regulations between European countries cause complications for cross-border bank mergers. Financial services are not as easily mass-produced as automobiles and TV sets. Financial products are intangibles, subject to regulatory and cultural behavior molds. Within-country bank mergers are not impeded by these differences.

In the case of cross-border mergers, investors may prefer cash rather than shares as payment. With European banks trading at multiples of 2.5 times book equity, the acquirer must write off a large portion of the purchase price as goodwill. This may require issuing new equity to satisfy the capital adequacy regulations of bank supervisors. This makes it difficult for banks to attract shareholders.[8]

Those who acquired UK banks found their margins and returns on equity to be very high. Therefore, buying a bank in a continental country will almost certainly dilute profits and spoil financial performance. In the case of HSBC's acquisition of CCF, the UK bank was prepared to pay a premium to facilitate its first takeover of a large continental retail and commercial bank. The premium underlines the importance to HSBC of implementing its strategic expansion into Europe. Other banks may also face difficulties in doing this. Part of HSBC's interest in CCF was the private banking area, where the French institution is regarded as a strong member of the top end of this market.

Banks fear that failure to act will mean they will be left at the starting gate. If so, they will become targets themselves.

Bank Mergers at Work

In this section we consider bank mergers in several European countries, both in and out of the Eurozone. In all cases, the mergers proposed or completed are within-country mergers.

The Swiss Case

Union Bank of Switzerland (UBS), the biggest in the country, has chosen to list its securities on the New York Stock Exchange (NYSE) as global registered shares rather than American depository receipts (ADRs). ADRs are the traditional vehicle for non–U.S. companies seeking an American share listing. UBS is the first global bank to issue a global share that can be traded round the clock in the world's stock markets. About four hundred non–U.S. companies are listed on the NYSE, but very few multinationals have ventured along this path. The only European companies that have launched global shares on the NYSE are DaimlerChrysler and Celanese.[9]

ADRs involve converting domestic shares into a U.S.–listed security that is registered with the U.S. Securities and Exchange Commission. ADRs do not differ from global shares in terms of disclosure and regulation. They can be used to raise capital and pay for acquisitions. Also, ADRs do not suffer from the "flowback" problem. For example, in two years DaimlerChrysler's global shares have "migrated away." Their U.S. shareholder base has shrunk from 46 percent to 26 percent of shares outstanding, with most of their shares flowing back to Europe.

Global shares enjoy the advantage of allowing seamless cross-border trading. This cross-border trading increases the liquidity and pricing efficiency of the shares of non–U.S. companies. At the same time, global shares give U.S. investors access to the home market shares on the same terms as local investors. Global shares are a fungible security that can be traded anywhere.[10]

The listing of UBS shares on the NYSE came two years after the 1998 merger of UBS with Swiss Bank Corporation. The listing indicates that UBS is starting to enjoy the benefits of the merger and is ready to seek acquisitions with a flexible currency—NYSE listed shares. UBS has enjoyed handsome profits from its investment banking unit, UBS Warburg.[11]

UBS met with a setback when it had to write off a disastrous investment in Long Term Capital Management, a hedge fund that almost went bust in September 1998. But their fortunes rebounded because of a rise in trading profits from investment banking.

Internationally UBS has two big asset management firms, Phillips & Drew and Brinson Partners. Both are value investors that try to buy cheap shares that are expected to outperform the market over time. With a string of acquisitions, including SG Warburg, O'Connor (a derivatives trading firm), and Dillon Reed, the bank has developed a formidable investment banking business. The one partial gap is in mergers and acquisitions.[12]

Now UBS is a hunter, on the prowl for acquisitions in the United States that will strengthen their investment banking operations. Acquisitions would help UBS Warburg, its investment unit. Possible targets include retail-focused groups in insurance, brokerage, or trust companies. UBS is reported to have held a meeting with Paine Webber, the American brokerage firm. Other merger candidates include the broker TD Waterhouse, Prudential of the United States, and E*Trade, an online broker. There also were countless regional brokers in the United States that could be put together to widen UBS's existing investment bank platform.[13]

Deutsche-Dresdner Failed Union

In early March 2000, it was announced that Germany's Deutsche and Dresdner Banks would merge. The €31 billion takeover by Deutsche, Germany's largest bank, and of Dresdner, their third biggest, reflects how quickly German industry and finance were changing at the time. With the involvement of Allianz, Germany's biggest insurer and a holder of large equity stakes in German industry and finance, the future development of the nation's banking sector seemed to have become a clearer picture.

The proposed deal signaled that the old ways of doing business in Germany were coming apart, one reason being the hostile takeover of Mannesmann. Another sign of change was the proposed tax reform that was announced by the German finance minister, Hans Eichel. This reform would cut taxes on income and corporate profits, and it would remove the capital gains tax on sales of large equity stakes held by Allianz and the big German banks. The proposed reform also suggested the end of the Deutschland AG model and a new beginning.[14]

The merger would allow Allianz to shed its large stakes in the two German banks and expand its retail fund management. Allianz's sale of most of its Dresdner holdings would allow it to then purchase from Deutsche its funds manager, DWS, a large piece of the retail bank Bank 24, as well as life insurer Deutsche Herold. Deutsche and Dresdner would then merge via an exchange of shares and combine their corporate, investment, and private banking operations. Their hidden reserves would provide the means to acquire an American investment bank.

Unfortunately, investment bankers in both institutions had not been closely involved in the merger discussions. An early report by the financial press stated that parts of Dresdner Kleinwort Benson (DKB), an investment bank, might be sold or shut down. Dresdner's investment bankers had built a strong capability since its 1995 acquisition by Dresdner. They were ahead of Deutsche in German and UK corporate finance and advisory services. So the investment bankers rebelled at the thought of sale of DKB or, alternatively, of the forced integration of the two investment banking units. Several top executives resigned in protest and dismay over the future prospects of their investment banking operations.[15]

Institutional investors holding shares in the two banks threatened to vote against the merger, arguing that both Deutsche and Dresdner shareholders were losing and that Allianz was getting the best of the transaction. By early April 2000, the proposed merger had come unglued. There were several reasons for the merger losing the support it needed. First, Deutsche Bank was to give up many prized assets, especially its DWS mutual fund business. The Dresdner investment bank unit faced disposal, or even worse, painful integration into the Deutsche Bank investment arm.

Allianz was the big loser when the deal failed. It could have exchanged one-fifth of a bank that had lost direction and focus and gain in domestic mutual fund management and retail distribution. It would have been able to combine DWS with its U.S. funds manager Pimco, purchased in 1999. Also, it could have used Bank 24 offices to distribute its insurance and savings products.

Poor treatment of Deutsche and Dresdner shareholders was a negative aspect of the proposed merger, and the integration of the two banks' investment banking units never made sense. DKB, in the first nine months of 1999, earned pretax profit of €774 million, with a return on equity of 29.5 percent. Integration or sale would have jeopardized this highly profitable operation.[16]

The failure of this merger highlights an overcrowded banking sector in Germany. It also puts pressure on Deutsche and Allianz to find a way to salvage some form of cooperation from the wreckage. Deutsche and Dresdner need to find cross-border merger opportunities, but now, although their choices are more difficult, there still remains the irresistible challenge to create Continent-wide banks.[17]

The Allianz-Dresdner Merger

In March 2001 Allianz, the German insurer, indicated that it was in advanced discussions for a takeover of Dresdner, Germany's third largest bank group. Allianz wanted to build a German version of Citigroup, a group that could offer a full range of financial services and products. The transaction would involve a four-way exchange of assets. Allianz and Munich Re would swap their holdings in Dresdner and Hypo Vereinsbank, Germany's second largest bank.

The merger would create a second bancassurance giant embracing Munich Re and Hypo Vereinsbank.

The transaction was a big step toward unwinding class share holdings in the financial sector. Allianz held a 21.4 percent stake in Dresdner and a 17.4 percent stake in Hypo Vereinsbank. It also held 20 percent of Munich Re. Munich Re owned 5.9 percent of Dresdner and 5 percent of Hypo Vereinsbank, as well as 20 percent of Allianz.[18]

Buying Dresdner would give Allianz an increased retail distribution capacity and access to close to half of all German households. Allianz expected to retain Dresdner Kleinwort Wasserstein as a separate investment-banking unit, and planned to eventually spin part of it off in the stock market. The merger was expected to transform Allianz-Dresdner into a financial services powerhouse.

French Restructuring

The euro also is expected to speed French financial sector restructuring. At the annual conference of Paris in June 1998, Europlace, a lobby group, called for reform of the French financial sector. At that time Marc Vienot, chairman of Société Generale, predicted that in two years only three of the five large French banks would remain as independent units. Rapid progress in transition to the euro will impact banks in all eleven countries in the Eurozone. France's euro committee believes that it would be better to push for rapid implementation, despite logistical problems.[19]

One large French bank, Credit Lyonnais (CL), has experienced financial and organizational problems over the past decade. These problems have required enormous injections of government capital. Its problems can be traced to overexpansion—from 1988 to 1993 its industrial holdings increased 500 percent. Their lending doubled in the five years ending in 1992. But in 1993 Parisian commercial property values declined, causing losses on property loans. The government came to CL's aid with a FF23 billion bailout in 1994, and an additional FF45 billion in 1995. While the government has been criticized for these large bailouts, CL's balance sheet is equal to one-fourth of French GDP. This makes the possibility of a Lyonnais failure a formidable and fearful event. The European Competition Commission mandated that CL dispose of 35 percent of its nondomestic assets by year-end 1998. Success in this endeavor is slow and doubtful.[20]

Italy Needs Consolidation

Italy's large banking sector (close to 1,000 institutions) is under severe pressure to consolidate. The April 1998 merger of Bancario San Paolo di Torino (retail) and Istituto Mobiliare Italiano (IMI), a financial conglomerate, was Italy's third big bank merger in less than a year. The pressure to merge is coming from Europe's single currency. Italy's biggest banks are midgets when compared with the largest in Germany, France, and Britain.[21]

In 1998, two of Italy's largest banks, Banca di Roma and Banca Commerciale Italiana (BCI), were reported meeting with investment bankers to evaluate a merger that would create Italy's largest bank. Banca di Roma was in talks with Goldman Sachs, while BCI was negotiating with Merrill Lynch. BCI has a healthier loan portfolio but Banca di Roma has a sizable profit base.[22]

Greek Banks Must Prepare for Euro

Even in European countries remaining outside the Eurozone, merger activity has picked up. The stakes were raised in 1998 when the government sold Cretabank, a Greek state institution, to EFG Eurobank, a bank controlled by the London based Latsis Group. The government also announced the privatization of two other Greek state-controlled banks, Ionian Bank and Bank of Central Greece. EFG Eurobank paid $305 million for Cretabank, more than double its market value. Cretabank has a large branch banking network, but it has been unable to win back its reputation after an embarrassing loss in the 1980s.[23]

Greece's banking system is dominated by a small number of state-owned groups. These groups have been losing market share to private banks that offer better service to corporate customers. The socialist government's decision to sell five banks in 1998 in a fast-paced privatization program provides an opportunity for private banks to expand. The government has made modernization of the banking sector a priority in order to quality for membership in the Eurozone.

The state-controlled National Bank of Greece, the largest bank, moved consolidation activity ahead by merging with its mortgage subsidiary. Greece's two most profitable private banks, Alpha Credit and Eugobank are the front-runners to acquire Ionian. This wave of mergers is only the first stage in what will be a much broader restructuring of Greece's banking system. In the past, Greek banks have been cushioned by high spreads and generous commissions paid by the Finance Ministry for buying large tranches of government bonds.

INVESTMENT BANKING AND CAPITAL MARKETS

Traditionally, large European banks have mixed elements of commercial banking and investment banking under one roof. This has been given the label "universal banking." Investment banking was not given a distinct emphasis as in the United States. In the past decade, however, American investment banks have rediscovered Europe, and European banks have become more aware of the benefits of focused investment banking. This awareness has been reinforced by the adoption of a single currency.

The following discussion considers how "plain vanilla" (or American-style) investment banking has taken root in Europe, spurred on by the euro. We also examine how ownership changes create opportunities, analyze the surge in M&A, consider the outlook for new bond sectors, and analyze the expansion of the venture capital and private equity business.

Plain Vanilla

Early in 1998, Rolf Breuer, a Deutsche Bank director, unveiled a plan for reorganizing the bank into five operating divisions. One of these divisions, investment banking, focuses on developing a European business base and seems destined to be an important source of profit for the bank. Deutsche Bank is not alone. A number of other large European banks are following Deutsche Bank's lead by emphasizing their investment banking operations. In many cases this emphasis is being accomplished through strategic acquisitions of U.S. or UK merchant and investment banks (table 4.9).

In 1998 ING, a Dutch bank, refocused its business development on Europe. Shortly after the eleven countries had declared their intention to create the euro, ING stated that expansion in Europe was its top priority. The bank denied that it had reduced its ambitions to develop business in the United States, the UK, or emerging markets, but Arjun Mathrani, chief of ING Barings's London-based affiliate, quit after a disagreement over the European strategy. He objected to a new structure that brought together the continental corporate and investment banking operations of ING Barings, ING Bank, and Belgium's Banque Bruxelles Lambert. The new structure will operate under the ING Bar-

Table 4.9. European Acquisitions of Merchant and Investment Banks

Acquirer	*Date*	*Acquired Unit*
Deutsche Bank, Germany	1989	Morgan Grenfell, UK
Hong Kong Shanghai Bank, UK	1990	James Capel, UK
ING, Netherlands	1995	Barings, UK
Swiss Bank Corp	1995	S.G. Warburg, UK
Dresdner Bank, Germany	1995	Kleinwort Benson, UK
Citigroup, U.S.	2000	Schroders, UK
Chase Manhattan, U.S.	2000	Flemings, UK

Source: Various periodicals. These mergers and acquisitions are covered contemporaneously in sources such as *Financial Times* and *Wall Street Journal Europe,* which the authors consulted.

ings name. This reorganization indicated that ING, like other continental financial groups, is placing a new emphasis on activities within the Eurozone.[24]

On the eve of the coming of the euro, European banks could be criticized for being slow in shedding their domestic focus. They recognize the new challenge presented by the euro, which will bring the following key changes in the European banking environment:

- Greater transparency in banking and finance across Europe. All banks will use the same home currency, the euro.
- Removal of currency transaction costs, allowing the unification of Europe into a single banking and financial services market
- A lower interest rate environment, conducive to the use of corporate bond finance in lieu of bank loans
- More unified stock exchange systems and greater efficiency in the equity markets
- Greater competition across national borders, and between banks and other financial institutions

A key part of traditional investment banking, fund management, has witnessed startling growth for American-based firms and certain European banking houses in the UK and Switzerland. However, as the euro phases in, this growth will become more centered in non-UK European investors, particularly in Germany, France, Italy, and the Netherlands. U.S.–based Merrill Lynch expanded its equity analysis, trading, and fund management business in the UK with the 1995 acquisition of Smith New Court (London). The Europeans have learned from this specific case. For example, ABN Amro organized a joint venture with NM Rothschild corporate finance advisory. This has yielded a series of equity deals and advisory relationships.

On the fund management side, low interest rates and a growing corporate debt market are whetting the appetite of continental investors, who no longer have double-digit interest rate government bonds available to them. New debt markets will energize investors who can obtain from forty to sixty additional basis points of yield for the assumption of credit risk on longer-term corporate bond issues and Pfandbriefe.

Where companies formerly could rely on governments to bail them out, they no longer are able to count on this. They must sink or swim on their own. This is demonstrated by European mergers and acquisitions data. Between 1993 and 1997 the value of mergers and acquisitions deals grew from $50 billion to $250 billion. With the euro coming into place, this amount has grown to where, in 1999, European M&A activity exceeded this activity in the United States. This trend is supported by low borrowing costs.[25]

Mergers and acquisitions activity runs high in Europe. In Germany, non-German banks have led the field. However, this may be changing. As can be seen in table 4.10, German banks ranked sixth and tenth among top mergers and acquisitions advisers in 1999–2000.

Table 4.10. Top Advisers on Deals Involving European Companies' M&A Deals Announced and Not Withdrawn, January 1, 1999 to February 15, 2000

Adviser	*Value ($bn)*	*Rank*	*Market Share*	*Number of Deals*
Goldman Sachs	871.5	1	49.2	174
Morgan Stanley Dean Witter	787.3	2	44.4	208
Merrill Lynch	590.8	3	33.3	173
J.P. Morgan	451.6	4	25.5	123
Warburg Dillon Read	356.4	5	20.1	187
Deutsche Bank	275.8	6	15.6	120
Credit Suisse First Boston	257.6	7	14.5	173
Lazard	246.4	8	13.9	137
Rothschild	155.5	9	8.8	193
Dresdner Kleinwort Benson	142.2	10	8.0	83
Salomon Smith Barney	127.8	11	7.2	76
Lehman Brothers	126.7	12	7.2	92
BNP Paribas	119.5	13	6.7	94
Donaldson Lufkin & Jenrette	81.0	14	4.6	84
Credit Agricole-Indosuez	62.4	15	3.5	13
ABN Amro	59.6	16	3.4	125
Mediobanca	56.1	17	3.2	9
Schroders	55.0	18	3.1	111
Chase Manhattan	53.4	19	3.0	53
Wasserstein Parella	47.8	20	2.7	20

Source: "The Dealmakers Reshaping Europe," *Euromoney,* March 2000, 39.

Large European companies are restructuring and divesting unprofitable units. For example, late in 1998 Hoechst, the German chemicals conglomerate, announced the sale of its $3 billion worldwide polyester business to a consortium of Mexican and U.S. investors. J.P. Morgan advised the North American buyers. This gives a boost to Hoechst's disposal program, which will transform the German chemical and pharmaceutical group into a more focused life sciences company. But their recent disposals have run into problems. Stock market turmoil has interrupted Hoechst's sale of several units. More details are provided about M&A activity in Europe in a later chapter.[26]

Ownership Changes

Ownership changes are accelerating on the continent. Germany's *Mittelstand,* the small and medium-sized businesses that are the backbone of Europe's biggest economy, is moving into a period of sweeping change. In this change, an estimated 700,000 companies that constitute the Mittelstand will experience dramatic ownership changes.

Based on a study by the Institute of the German Economy, a leading research body in Germany, in 1998–1999 alone an estimated 120,000 companies employing 1.6 million people will be searching for new owners as former owners retire or die. The IW classifies 2.9 million companies as making up the *Mittelstand.* The issue of succession is one of the most significant developments confronting Germany and other European countries. The issue is becoming more important as the generation of business entrepreneurs that helped restore prosperity after World War II reaches retirement age.[27]

The *Mittelstand* employs over two-thirds of the country's workforce, handles most of the vocational training, and is viewed as one of the pillars of the German "social market" economic model.

The expected ownership structure change, where control passes from founding families, is seen as a two-edged sword. It can be an incentive for a more vibrant stock market in Germany as well as an opportunity for foreign investors. Alternately, it poses problems of transition, at a time when Germany has entered into the single currency system.

In 1997 the family owners of Wankler and Dunnebier, a company that has a strong hold on world envelope-producing equipment, sold 92 percent of the company to Doughty Hanson, a UK venture capital group. There is an estimated DM10 billion (U.S.$5.5 billion) held in German buyout funds, contributed by European and North American financial groups, seeking opportunities to acquire interests in such companies.

IW warns that a smooth turnover of control of Mittelstand companies may be difficult due to lack of expertise among those who inherit ownership. Another reason to expect difficulties is the heirs' reluctance to assume the helm. High taxes may also complicate this transition. The German chambers of industry and commerce said (July 1998) that revised inheritance tax law would be a hurdle for heirs.

Family Firms in Italy

The family firm has also been the backbone of the Italian economy. Names like Agnelli, Pirelli, and De Benedetti have traditionally controlled large parts of Italian industry. But as firms struggle to adapt to changing technology and the single currency environment, Italy's business sector is moving away from business modeled on family ownership and control.

According to Confindustria, the nation's industrial federation, 70 percent of Italian workers are employed in firms with fewer than a hundred employees. In France, the comparable number is 30 percent, and in Germany 20 percent.

Most of these firms are family owned.[28] Italian entrepreneurs have been unwilling to surrender even a small part of equity ownership to other investors. Rather, financing comes from bank loans and internal cash flows. The alliance of Fiat and General Motors in 2000, in which 20 percent of the Agnelli-owned Fiat was exchanged for 5 percent of GM shares, was a significant event.

Family control in Italy is coming under attack, and some owner groups have been tempted to cash in on Italy's buyout stock market. In 1999 some thirty-two firms came to the Milan bourse, compared with eighteen in 1998 and eleven in 1997. Investment bankers assert that early in 2000 at least three hundred firms were waiting to float their shares and the queue was growing. In the early 1990s Italy's stock market capitalization was 15 percent of gross domestic product (GDP), but in year 2000 it reached 65 percent. New listings, market value appreciation, and privatizations (Telecom Italia) all contributed to this upward shift.

As Italian companies seek debt funds in Europe's developing corporate bond markets, firms will issue more information on financial status. This will reinforce the trend of more family firms considering going public.

Mergers and Acquisitions

In 1999 the European M&A market turned into a $1 trillion plus land of opportunity for investment bank advisers. M&A advisers in North America and Europe fought for turf and market share in the evolving, dynamic Eurozone. The mergers taking place in Europe since creation of the single currency are creating a new generation of top global corporations in telecoms, Internet access, and other industrial sectors.

To gain a competitive edge in the mergers business, American and European M&A houses are bidding for top talent, as well as purchasing whole investment banks. In January 2000, for example, Citigroup announced its purchase of the investment banking business of Schroders, the last independent UK investment bank. Citigroup paid $2.2 billion and pledged $250 million to fund retention bonuses intended to retain two hundred high-level individuals on the banks' staff.[29] Schroders is best known for its mergers and acquisitions work in the UK, while Citigroup will use its reputation to boost market share in the profitable European merger advisory business.

In 1999, M&A deals worth $1,200 billion were announced in Europe. Citigroups' Salomon Smith Barney (SSB) advised on thirty-one deals worth approximately $28 billion (table 4.10). SSB ranked eleventh in 1999–2000 with merger deals valued at a total of $127.8 billion. If we add Schroders $55 billion, the total of $182.8 billion in deals would have ranked SSB ninth, just below Lazard (table 4.10).

Deutsche Bank ranks sixth in the league (table 4.10), and including Deutsche, five European dealmakers make up the rankings six through ten in the table. Similarly, five European dealmakers are included in the second tier of the top ten advisers in M&A. Deutsche is on the rise, and a J.P. Morgan report notes that "we consider that there is now no doubt that Deutsche has created a bulge bracket investment bank."[30] Deutsche has outpaced the revenue growth of its U.S. peers and UBS Warburg. In the early part of 2000, Deutsche generated more revenues from investment banking than Goldman Sachs and Merrill Lynch did. In 1999 Deutsche was the most profitable investment bank in Europe, with operating profits of $2.54 billion.

Deutsche also has gained momentum in equities, coming third in the Thomson Financial league table of international equity bookrunners, behind Goldman and Merrill (table 4.11). Deutsche would like to rank higher in its U.S. equity underwriting. But it takes time to develop close relationships with corporate clients. Deutsche is ranked third in the number of IPOs underwritten in the United States. In first quarter of 2000, Deutsche also enjoys favorable status in IPO performance. In the period January 1999 to April 2000, Deutsche Bank Alex Brown ranked first in average IPO performance on offerings measured from the first day of closing price.

A sign of Deutsche's determination to attain and hold the status of a top investment bank was its appointment in May 2000 of two Americans, Edson Mitchell and Michael Philipp, to its *Vorstand* (management board). Deutsche's determination to muscle into the top levels of investment banking marks a shift in the balance of power, recognizing that investment bank profits account for over 60 percent of their group profit.[31]

Table 4.11. International Equity Bookrunners, January–June 2000

Manager	*Total ($m)*	*Share (%)*
Goldman Sachs	17,267.06	21.6
Merrill Lynch	8,550.58	10.7
Deutsche Bank	7,624.01	9.5
Salomon SB	7,561.61	9.4
Morgan Stanley Dean Witter	6.947.79	8.7
CSFB	5,172.89	6.4
ABN Amro Rothschild	3.506.58	4.4
BNP Paribas	2,991.83	3.7
Lehman Brothers	2,713.12	3.4
UBS Warburg	2,231.14	2.8

Source: Charles Pretzlik, "Deutsche Scents Victory in Battle of the Bulge," *Financial Times*, June 14, 2000, 17.

Loans and High Yield Bonds

The coming of the euro places greater competitive pressure on European-based bank lenders, but it also generates new opportunities for bond-issuing houses. The dynamic interaction of the American and European corporate loan and bond markets is becoming a new feature of global corporate finance. The following paragraphs analyze developments in these sectors from the eve of the single currency to midpoint 2000.

The syndicated loan market is one of the largest channels for international capital, with over $1.3 trillion in annual volume. Between 1985 and 1987 heightened competition squeezed bank profit margins (spreads), a condition that partially reversed because of the increased global financial volatility of mid-1998. In the past, three main bank groups, including American, Japanese, and European banks, participated as lender intermediaries. In 1997 the Japanese banks cut back their international lending dramatically. Consequently, from 1997 to 1999 the principal locus of these loan syndications has been American and European banks.

Since 1997, loan spreads improved for bank lenders, as have the loan terms and conditions. Chase Manhattan, the market leader, was the first bank to change the rules with its insertion of "market flex" into its loan underwriting agreements.[32]

Peter Gleisteen, group head of global syndicated finance at Chase, stated that the bank has not lost market share but has derived benefits from its ability to reprice loans and restructure them. He notes that the changing terms written into loan agreements brought their syndicated loan practice more into line with the bond market. While bond volumes were down in 1998, syndicated loan volumes were down by a smaller margin.

At midyear 2000 the trends in the United States and European high yield bond markets began to diverge. In 2000 the U.S. market was suffering as investors grew more distressed over rising defaults. In first half of 2000, many corporate names were trading lower, with discounts of 40–50 percent. These distressed prices produced yields of 10 percentage points over Treasuries. According to one Merrill Lynch analyst, disappointing earnings created a perception of default risk, and this caused sharp drops in bond prices.[33] The 1999 default rate for U.S. high yield bonds (4.15 percent) was well below the 1991 peak of 10.3 percent.

In Europe, however, 1999–2000 saw the European high yield bond market decoupled from the weak U.S. junk bond market, as new issues trended upward. In 1999, two-thirds of European high yield bonds were being purchased by U.S. accounts. But in late 1999 and 2000 greater numbers of European buyers emerged. In 2000 the European high yield sector asserted its stand-alone credentials. Over one hundred different European institutional investors regularly began buying high yields, with France and Germany providing the core of these buyers. In 2000 several euro-denominated deals were sold wholly to European investors.[34]

The telecom and media sectors dominate European high yield issuance. Equity market declines in early 2000 affected the secondary market in these high yield bonds adversely. This made it more difficult for these companies to access the high yield market. Nevertheless, money continues to flow to issuers, and in 2000 the European market was receptive to old economy borrowers. If, however, a significant number of U.S. companies decided to access the European market, the balance of supply and demand in the European market could deteriorate.[35]

Jumbo Pfandbrief

Since its launch in 1995, the jumbo Pfandbrief has enjoyed uninterrupted growth. By April 2000, the sector had grown to €330 billion outstanding, or 30 percent of the entire German Pfandbrief market. Jumbos represent the fourth largest bond market sector in Europe, only exceeded by Italian, German, and French government bonds. Jumbo deals are defined as those of €500 million or more. Most mortgage bank issuers have established benchmark issues, and bond sizes of €5 billion attract institutional buyers due to their liquidity, security, and excess yield over governments.[36]

Mortgage banks issue Pfandbrief bonds, which are bonds that are collateralized by underlying mortgage loans carried as assets. Most mortgage bank issuers enjoy a AAA rating. This and two other factors explain the success of Pfandebrief market development. First, liquidity considerations are important in the planning and execution of these issues. Second, issuers ensure that their bonds qualify for trading on the new Euro Credit MTS platform launched in May 2000. This system encourages higher liquidity by providing investors with lower bid-offer spreads, as well as requiring that each jumbo bond traded on the system be supported by at least five market makers.[37]

The Pfandbrief market provides a unique core sector to the euro-denominated bond market. A number of developments could expand the scope of this market.

These developments are discussed in detail in chapter 7, which focuses on bond market development. The market has been a major success in Germany and has taken hold in many other European countries as well (table 4.12).

Table 4.12. Country Composition of the Pfandbrief Market, 2000

Country	*€Billions*	*Percentage*
Germany	930	71
Denmark	155	12
Sweden	115	9
France	25	2
Italy	25	2
Other	50	4

Source: "Tinkering with the Specialist Principle," *Euromoney,* April 2000, 60–62.

REGULATION AND BANK CAPITAL MANAGEMENT

This section discusses how the single currency has focused attention on capital adequacy and risk management in the banking sector. It also reviews the operation of the 1988 Basel capital rules, as well as other proposals for modernizing the regulation of bank capital.

Single Currency and Capital Adequacy

The coming of the single currency focuses attention on bank capital adequacy. There are many reasons for this.

First, when "currency zones" are removed throughout the euro area, banks will be viewed in a more transparent way. Although the creditworthiness of European banks is closely monitored, their credit ratings will become even more important as the European-wide corporate bond market evolves.

Second, as banks aggressively move into capital market operations, they become subject to a mix of credit and market volatility risks. The banking industry's brightest rocket scientists have been assigned the task of measuring these risks. Credit Suisse Financial Products has developed and launched Credit Risk, a program that provides an actuarial model of loan default risk. J.P. Morgan has developed a similar product called Credit Metrics.

With the help of Taylor-series expansions, Gamma integrals, and negative binomial distributions, these models calculate probabilities of default. Value-at-risk models examine bank trading portfolios to estimate potential one-day losses from financial market price volatility.[38]

Third, the European Union will not countenance large bank bailouts any longer. France's bailout of Credit Lyonnais, once Europe's largest commercial bank, is a horror story well known throughout Europe. Reckless chairmen, operating with unchecked authority, made risky loans to corrupt businessmen. When its enormous losses became known, the French government predictably decided that the bank was too important to fail. Karel Van Miert, the EU competition commissioner, threatened to force CL's bankruptcy. The French banking sector still is in desperate need of consolidation and restructuring.[39]

Fourth, there is no centralized deposit protection system in the European Union. In fact, the Maastricht treaty forbids the European Central Bank to act as a lender of last resort or participate in insurance schemes.[40] Most deposit protection schemes in the European Union have limited guarantees. The participating credit institutions that fund these guarantee schemes argue that full guarantees would erode market discipline.[41]

Regulation and Management of Bank Capital

The Basel risk-weighted capital requirements, instituted a decade ago, are a crude protection. These requirements set minimum Tier I ratios of capital to risk assets at 4 percent, and a Tier I plus Tier II requirement of 8 percent. Risk adjustments weight loans at 100 percent of face value, mortgage credits at 50 percent, and central government security at zero. Since the institution of integrated capital requirements, banks have made far-reaching changes in managing their credit exposure. But bank regulators in Organization for Economic Cooperation and Development (OECD) countries are now looking seriously at how to modernize the rules. The current capital rules make no distinction between loans to banks in North America and loans to banks in South Korea, nor between loans to blue chip companies and to firms on the edge of bankruptcy.

Three developments have brought these inadequacies into focus. First, since the early 1990s banks have become more sophisticated in managing loan portfolios, developing complex computer models to do the job. Second, an expansion in the use of credit derivatives allows banks to trade their credit risk exposures cheaply and to reduce or shift the risk of loan portfolios. Third, new rules early in 1998 differentiate between the assets in a bank's trading portfolio and in its loan portfolio. Banks are more widely using sophisticated risk models to calculate how much capital they need.[42]

Bank mergers in Europe will create larger and, we hope, more sophisticated institutions. As the largest banks diversify into investment banking activities, they will be challenged to more carefully analyze their capital positions relative to the risks they are exposed to.

The review of the international Basel agreement on how much capital banks need is likely to bring a revolutionary change. This review was begun in 1999 and in mid-2000 seemed likely to continue for some time. Much is at stake as banks and regulators fight for their interests. A report in June 2000 gives some insight concerning the likely shape of the finished product.

The most significant change may be that bank regulators will be given explicit powers to order banks perceived to be more risky to hold more capital. This could place UK banks on a more level playing field. This change is due to the fact that UK banks have been required to hold greater amounts of capital than banks on the continent. The UK has taken a conservative approach to administering capital ratios, and consequently institutions operating in London have held more capital relative to risk assets than most other European banks.

Since capital is a costly means of protection, differential capital requirements affect returns to bank shareholders. The proposed EU directive and new regime will provide legislative support for regulators who feel that they should require riskier banks to hold additional capital. Two other changes aim at injecting exactness to the process. First, credit ratings are to be used. These ratings will measure loan risk and will be obtained from the banks' own analysis and from rating agencies (Standard & Poor's and Moody's). Second, an additional capital requirement is to be applied to operational risks such as technology changes and management problems. The United States has supported the use of external ratings of professional agencies, but this is a relatively new phenomenon in Europe.[43]

Regional and smaller banks fear that revised capital guidelines could raise the overall cost of capital and force them out of the lending business.

FOCUS ON SHAREHOLDER WEALTH

European banks are "in play" as potential acquisition targets. These same banks are attempting to play a successful game of acquiring other institutions that enhance share price. Successful acquisitions can elevate share price, making it difficult for unwanted suitors to gain control. We conclude this chapter by examining the status of Commerzbank, fourth largest bank in Germany and a prime takeover candidate.

Commerzbank as Target

At midyear 2000, Commerzbank was facing off against corporate raider Hansgeorg Hofmann, who heads a German holding company called Cobra. Cobra was Commerzbank's largest shareholder, with a 17 percent stake. Hofmann was pushing the German bank to find a suitable cross-border merger partner. Chief executive Martin Kohlhaussen has indicated a commitment to keep Commerzbank independent.

The fight for Commerzbank also put Henri de Castries, chief executive of the French insurer AXA, in contention with Gianfranco Gutty, head of Italian insurer Assicurazioni Generali. Generali owns 5.25 percent of the bank, sells insurance through Commerz's branch banking network, and has expressed their determination to protect this interest (table 4.13).[44]

Table 4.13. Main Stakes in Commerzbank, Mid-2000

Stakeholder	*Percentage*
Rebon, Dutch holding group that holds shares via Cobra	17.00
Assicurazioni Generali, insurance group	5.25
Banco Santander Central Hispano, Spanish bank	4.80

Sources: David Fairlamb, "A Fight to the Finish," *Business Week*, June 19, 2000, 44–45; Tony Major, "Cobra Bares Its Fangs at Commerzbank Meeting," *Financial Times*, May 27, 2000, 9.

On June 6, 2000, Commerzbank's stock market capitalization was $18.6 billion, and its assets were approximately $360 billion. Commerzbank is too small to compete as a major Eurozone bank, but too big to prosper within the confining and low profit German markets. Hofmann's strategy, at midyear 2000, was to find a suitable partner for the bank.

Attending the annual shareholders meeting (May 2000), the Cobra leader stated that he wanted to help the bank forge a European partnership. Kohlhaussen responded by affirming Commerzbank's intent to choose its own alliances, and scolded Cobra for not holding to its stated policy of operating as a passive investor.

Hofmann stated that he had received several interesting partnership offers based on the large stake that he held. Above all, he was keen to improve shareholder value at the bank.[45] Many shareholders asked for a clear statement of policy direction for the bank, in light of the many takeover stories being floated in the financial press.

Commerzbank as Global Player

Commerzbank has been building its investment banking and fund management businesses aggressively. Large equity groups operate in Frankfurt, London, New York, and other locations. The bank is aiming to boost asset management's contribution to profits by extending its global network of distribution channels. Table 4.14 describes the range of initiatives taken by the bank in recent years.

Friedrich Schmitz, who took control of Commerz's asset management department in March 2000, noted that the absence of acquisition opportunities and the high cost of asset management were forcing Commerzbank to start businesses from scratch. In 2000 Schmitz oversaw 2,000 people in twenty-three separate businesses, spread across sixteen countries.[46] The bank had spent heavily to buy companies in France, UK, and the United States (table 4.14).

Table 4.14. Initiatives by Commerzbank to Build Global Asset Management

Location	*Investment Type*
Germany	Purchased Adig, oldest German mutual fund, from Hypo Vereinsbank
Italy	Set up Commerzbank Asset Management Italia, with goal of having 170 financial agents in place by year-end 2000 and 1,000 within four years
Spain	Organized Afina, 51 percent owned by Commerzbank, with focus on institutional business
France	Purchased Caisse Centrale de Reescompte
UK	Bought Jupiter International Group in 1995
U.S.	Bought Montgomery Asset Management, San Francisco
South Korea	Formed a fund management joint venture with affiliate Korea Exchange Bank. Offers CB products.

Source: Tony Major and Stefanie Burgmaier, "Commerzbank Extends Scope of Asset Management," *Financial Times,* May 26, 2000, 18.

Total assets under management control at mid-2000 were DM280 billion. This compares with Deutsche Bank's assets under management of over DM1 trillion. CB's strategy is flexible, emphasizing decentralized control and local expertise. This leads to tailor-made firms that better reflect local market conditions.

CB has established an innovative equity participation scheme to stimulate entrepreneurial drive among its staff. As in the case of Jupiter (UK), CB acted to lock in senior executives and fund managers with generous incentive payments.[47] Staff workers were offered substantial equity participations.

NOTES

1. Jonathan Davidson, Alison Ledger, and Giovanni Viani, "Wholesale Banking, the Ugly Implications of EMU," *McKinsey Quarterly* 1 (1998).
2. George Graham, "Cost of Bank Payments to Plunge," *Financial Times*, July 15, 1998, 3.
3. This estimate is based on annual issuance of $200 billion, with an origination fee of 0.8 percent and trading volume of $100 billion, with a trading margin of 0.6 percent.
4. Carol Power, "Euro May Bring Shakeout among Global Banks," *American Banker*, March 13, 1998, 1–14.
5. Melissa Chancellor, "British Banks Move to Offer Euro Accounts," *Wall Street Journal*, July 1, 1998, B14.
6. John Willman, "Freeze or Jump? That Is the Question," *Financial Times*, Banking in Europe Supplement, May 26, 2000, I.

7. John Willman, "Scope for Further Mergers and Acquisitions," *Financial Times*, Banking in Europe Supplement, May 26, 2000, II.

8. John Willman, "Fear of Becoming Takeover Candidates," *Financial Times*, Banking in Europe Supplement, May 26, 2000, II.

9. William Hall, "UBS Gambles on Value of Going Global," *Financial Times*, May 16, 2000, 22.

10. William Hall, "UBS Listing is Snub for ADRs," *Financial Times*, May 11, 2000, 22.

11. William Hall, "UBS Starts to Reap Profits from Merger," *Financial Times*, May 26, 2000, 21.

12. "The Travails of UBS," *Economist*, March 11, 2000, 76.

13. W. Lewis, A. Hill, and C. Pretzlik, "It's Time for Hunted UBS to Go on the Prowl for US Prey," *Financial Times*, May 24, 2000, 21.

14. "Deutsche's Big Gamble," *Economist*, March 11, 2000, 74.

15. David Shirreff, "No: To the Blender," *Euromoney*, April 2000, 16.

16. "Deutsche's Ruling Tribe," *Euromoney*, April 2000, 5.

17. "Europe's Banking Blues," *Economist*, March 11, 2000, 22–23.

18. C. Pretzlik and T. Major, "Allianz Poised to Become a Financial Services Powerhouse," *Financial Times*, March 29, 2001, 18; and "Allianz in Talks with Dresdner," *Financial Times*, March 29, 2001, 1.

19. Robert Graham and Andrew Jack, "Euro to Speed French Financial Reshape," *Financial Times*, July 4, 1998, 2.

20. A. Santomero and P. Hoffman, "Problem Bank Resolution: Evaluating the Option" (paper presented to the Financial Management Association Seminar, Chicago, October 1998), 27–28.

21. "Cautious Communion," *Economist*, May 2, 1998, 67.

22. Fred Kapner, "Italian Banks Get Ready to Discuss Huge Merger," *Wall Street Journal Europe*, May 14, 1998, 14.

23. Kerin Hope, "Scramble for Greek Banks Speeds Up with Prospect of Euro Zone Application," *Financial Times*, July 16, 1998, 3.

24. Clay Harris, "ING Places Emphasis on Eurozone," *Financial Times*, June 3, 1998, 17.

25. Peter Lee, "The Gold Diggers of Europe 1999," *Euromoney*, September 1998, 49–50.

26. Graham Bowley and Henry Tricks, "Hoechst Completes $3 bn. Polyester Disposal," *Financial Times*, October 16, 1998, 25.

27. Frederick Studemann, "Germany's Small Businesses Enter a Decade of Transition," *Financial Times*, July 22, 1998, 14.

28. "Family Firms in Italy, the Generation Game," *Economist*, March 4, 2000, 65–66.

29. C. Pretzlik, W. Lewis, and G. Silverman, "Citigroup Buys UK Business to Boost M&A Deals in Europe," *Financial Times*, January 19, 2000, 1.

30. Charles Pretzlik, "Deutsche Scents Victory in Battle of the Bulge," *Financial Times*, June 14, 2000, 17.

31. "German Investment Banks: Down but Not Out," *Economist*, May 27, 2000, 81.

32. George Graham, "Lenders Take Initiative in Global Bank Loan Market," *Financial Times*, October 21, 1998, 28.

33. Dena Aubin, "Junk Bonds Plunge as Investors Grow Distressed by Defaults," *Wall Street Journal Europe*, May 5, 2000, 16.

34. "Europe DeCouples from Weak US Junk Bond Market," *Euromoney*, April 2000, 124.

35. J. Chaffin and R. Bream, "Europe's High-Yield Market Matures," *Financial Times*, April 26, 2000, 24.

36. "The Pfandbrief: Progress Report," *Economist*, May 27, 2000, 66A, 66B.

37. "The German Pfandbrief," *Wall Street Journal*, May 22, 2000, B21.

38. "Model Behavior," *Economist*, February 28, 1998, 80.

39. Rachel V. Laffer, "A Bank Bailout and Its Consequences," *Wall Street Journal*, July 10, 1998, A14.

40. Treaty on European Union and Final Act, December 31, 1991, title II, art 4(a), 31 1.1024, 258.

41. Laura Shea, "Deposit Protection in the European Economic Community," *Boston College International Comparative Law Review* 17, no. 1 (1994): 35.

42. "When Borrowers Go Bad," *Economist*, February 28, 1998, 79–80.

43. James Mackintosh, "Balance of Power May Be Changed," *Financial Times*, Banking in Europe Supplement, May 26, 2000, IV.

44. David Fairlamb, "A Fight to the Finish," *Business Week*, June 19, 2000, 44–45.

45. Tony Major, "Cobra Bares Its Fangs at Commerzbank Meeting," *Financial Times*, May 27, 2000, 9.

46. Tony Major and Stefanie Burgmaier, "Commerzbank Extends Scope of Asset Management," *Financial Times*, May 26, 2000, 18.

47. C. Pretzlik and S. Targett, "Commerzbank Aims to Lock in Jupiter," *Financial Times*, June 3, 2000, 8.

Chapter Five

The European Central Bank and Role of the Euro

The Maastricht treaty created the European Monetary Institute (EMI) as a transitional unit to coordinate preparations on monetary policy for the third stage of European economic and monetary union (EMU). An important aspect of the EMI mandate was development of an operational framework for monetary policy for the European System of Central Banks (ESCB). EMI has fulfilled its advisory role and made recommendations to the governing council of the European Central Bank (ECB), as well as identifying issues and options from which the ECB has been organized.

In spring 1989 the Delors Committee, composed of all EC central bank governors plus three outside experts, issued a report on a three-stage approach for the creation of the EMU. The report recommended a first stage (which began July 1, 1990) of increased coordination of monetary and economic policies among the member states. A second stage began on January 1, 1994, for transition to a common currency and creation of a predecessor central banking institution (European Monetary Institute). Located in Frankfurt, the EMI assisted member states in the transition to the third stage. The third stage, which began on January 1, 1999, included the transfer of monetary policy to the ECB. The ECB is responsible for all monetary issues, including exchange market intervention in third currencies, and management of the official reserves of the member states.[1]

EU Summit Installs ECB

The weekend of May 2–3, 1998, witnessed a historic European Union (EU) summit meeting, at which eleven countries agreed to enter the third phase of the EMU. The eventful weekend saw the exchange rates of the eleven currencies set against the euro.[2] The weekend event was marred by a fight over the presidency of the new central bank, the French seeking to appoint Jean-Claude Trichet, and the Germans Wim Duisenberg. Fortunately, a compromise was found as Duisenberg volunteered to serve half of the initial presidential term, to be followed by Trichet for the second half. Both individuals possessed excellent credentials, Duisenberg at the Dutch central bank and Trichet at the French finance ministry and as head of the treasury at the Club of Paris.[3]

However, early in 2000 it was revealed that Trichet was to be investigated by a judicial inquiry for his role in the downfall of Credit Lyonnais in the early 1990s. The purpose of the investigation was to determine Trichet's responsibility in the alleged publication of false information to the market and presentation of inaccurate accounts. Between 1987 and 1993, Trichet was director of the Ministry of Finance's department responsible for overseeing state-owned banks, including Credit Lyonnais. At that time CL teetered on the edge of bankruptcy after huge losses from an expansion spree. It was bailed out with state subsidies. The slow-moving French judicial system raised serious questions about the length of time it would take to decide whether there is a good case against Trichet with respect to his role as director of the treasury in the Credit Lyonnais. A lengthy period of uncertainty could prevent Trichet from assuming the presidency of the ECB.[4] As of June 2001 there were no indications that Duisenberg would be vacating his position.

Institutional Framework

The ECB has a legal existence under public international law. Each of the national central banks (NCBs) has legal personality according to its own national law. NCBs carry out the tasks conferred upon them with rules established by the ECB.

Decision-making bodies of the ECB include the Governing Council and the executive board. The General Council is a third decision body. The General Council is to exist as long as there are member states that have not adopted the euro as their currency. In early 2000 these countries included the UK, Sweden, Denmark, and Greece.

The Governing Council is the supreme decision-making body of the ECB, and it includes all members of the executive board and the governors of the NCBs of member states that have adopted the euro. The main responsibilities of the Governing Council are (1) to adopt the guidelines and decisions needed to ensure performance of ESCB tasks and (2) to formulate the monetary policy of the euro area related to key interest rates and reserve availability. In 1999 the Governing Council met every other week at the ECB headquarters in Frankfurt.

The executive board includes the president, vice president, and four other members appointed by the common accord of the governments of participating member states. The main responsibilities of the executive board are:

- To prepare the meetings of the Governing Council
- To implement monetary policy in accord with the guidelines set by the Governing Council
- To be responsible for the current business of the ECB
- To assume certain powers delegated to it by the Governing Council including those of a regulatory nature.[5] The executive board meets at least weekly to decide on the allotment volume for the main refinancing operations of the Eurosystem.

The General Council includes the ECB president and vice president, plus the governors of all fifteen NCBs. The council is responsible for reporting on progress leading toward convergence by nonparticipating member states and for giving advice on the irrevocable fixing of exchange rates of nonparticipating member states.

Historical Perspective

As the euro replaces the twleve European currencies, some analysts have taken a historical perspective on several of these currencies. The deutsche mark especially had a remarkable history in the fifty years between 1948 and 1998. In 1948, when one new deutsche mark replaced ten Reichsmarks, Ludwig Erhard, economics minister, introduced an economic liberalization plan. This plan, together with the generous U.S. Marshall Plan and the vigorous efforts of the West Germans, allowed the deutsche mark to become part of Germany's *Wirtshaftswunder*. The success of the deutsche mark helped Germans recover their self-esteem. The currency became a symbol of prosperity. This success was further ensured by the Bundesbank's commitment to price stability.[6]

Within one month of its inception, the ECB squared up to the continental finance ministers, warning them that their fiscal policies were inappropriate. The ECB indicated that governments in the Eurozone aim to run balanced budgets. Countries with high levels of debt should be aiming for budget surpluses. These remarks saw Duisenberg engaged in an unprecedented intervention in an area that national governments had traditionally regarded as their sovereign domain.[7]

The ECB has no legal mechanism with which to enforce such fiscal change. But Duisenberg's warning indicated that fiscal profligacy would have consequences for monetary policy. For example, the ECB might be required to set interest rates at higher levels than would otherwise be required. The European Commission issued a similar warning when it published a forecast showing that Eurozone budgetary deficits could remain stuck at 2 percent of gross domestic product for several years.[8]

MONETARY POLICY INSTRUMENTS

The EU has indicated a desire to achieve an appropriate balance between a centralized as opposed to a decentralized role for the ECB. Part of this policy is that national central banks are expected to retain a significant role in executing monetary policy. The EMI and Europe's national central banks prepared a "menu" of market-based monetary instruments with which the ECB operates. These include open market operations, standby facilities, and reserve requirements (table 5.1).

Table 5.1. Operating Procedures of the European System of Central Banks

Procedure	*Description*
Main refinancing	Open market operations: weekly frequency, maturity two weeks, executed through standard repurchase tenders (variable/fixed rate), provides key interest rate signal
Longer-term refinancing	Monthly frequency, maturity three months, executed through standard repurchases tenders (variable/fixed rate), provides longer-term refinancing
Fine-tuning	Variable frequency and maturity, executed through quick tenders or bilateral procedures, used to smooth interest rates
Structural operations	Variable frequency and maturity, executed through standard tenders or bilateral procedures, used to manage structural position of the banking sector
	Standing facilities
Lombard facility	Maturity overnight, interest rate generally above the tender rate, provides a ceiling for market interest rates
Deposit facility	Maturity overnight, interest rate generally below the tender rate, provides a floor for market interest rates
	Reserve requirements[a]
Main features	Maintenance period one month, lagged, averaging permitted, no carryover, eligible assets, correspondent account balances held with the national central bank, end-of-month balance sheet data on liabilities used to determine the reserve base, covers credit institutions

Source: European Monetary Institute, "The Single Monetary Policy in Stage Three: General Documentation on ESCB Monetary Policy Instruments and Procedures," September 1997. Mimeo.
[a]Awaits a decision by the European Central Bank.

Open Market Operations

The main instrument of monetary policy is weekly open market operations. These operations aid in steering interest rates and managing financial system liquidity, and they signal the direction and strength of monetary policy action. Liquidity operations provide refinancing to the banks and financial sector and also function as an instrument of liquidity management.

Longer-term refinancing is carried out monthly and provides only a small part of the ESCB's liquidity. These longer-term operations are not intended to provide a signal concerning monetary policy direction. This signal comes from shorter-term liquidity operations. Therefore, the ESCB will operate as a price taker in the monthly refinancing tenders. The above does not mean that the monthly issued instruments do not reflect (indirectly signal) monetary policy stances.[9]

The ESCB may conduct operations to adjust the structural position of the banks vis-à-vis the European System of Central Banks (ESCB). A long lasting upward shift in demand for currency, for example, may require fine-tuning operations to manage fluctuations in the market. These operations can be affected via currency swaps or through an alternative instrument.

Standby Facilities

Two standing facilities were originally envisaged. These include a Lombard facility through which banks can obtain liquidity overnight (against pledged eligible assets) and a deposit facility through which banks can deposit their surplus funds overnight. The interest rates on these two facilities provide a corridor within which market volatile interest rates may move. These facilities were of very great importance in the early period, when the demand for euros was more difficult to estimate and was also likely to be somewhat unstable.

If the Lombard and deposit facility rates provide a wide ceiling-to-floor range for money market interest rates, banks and financial institutions can find frequent and profitable arbitrage opportunities. If these rates provide a narrow ceiling-to-floor range for money market interest rates, arbitrage opportunities may be limited and constrained. Needless to say, European authorities would like to see an optimal interest rate ceiling-to-floor range, which would provide strong incentives for arbitrage, creating a more liquid money market environment. They would also like to see a not-too-volatile interest rate pattern.

The ECB will be required to exercise good judgment in influencing the width of the interest rate corridor. Techniques that can be used would include the weekly repo (repurchase agreement) interest rate. The repo rate provides a policy signal regarding monetary policy tightening and easing. Alternately, the Lombard and deposit rates serve as the policy signal. Central banks around the world have used various techniques to both signal and impact the money market.

Collateral

Credit operations between the ESCB and financial institutions require collateral. As can be seen in table 5.2, the two tiers of collateral include public and

Table 5.2. Eligible Collateral

Criteria	*Tier 1*	*Tier 2*
Type of asset	• European system of central banks (ESCB) debt certificates • Other marketable financial obligations	• Marketable financial obligations • Nonmarketable financial obligations • Equities traded on a regulated market
Type of issuer	• ESCB • Public sector • Private sector • International institutions	• Public sector • Private sector
Financial soundness	The issuer must be deemed financially sound by the European Central Bank (ECB)	The issuer/debtor must be deemed financially sound by the national central bank that included the asset in its tier two list
Location of issuer	European economic area (EEA) except for international institutions	Euro area Location in other EEA countries can be accepted subject to ECB approval
Location of asset	Euro area	Euro area Location in other EEA countries can be accepted subject to ECB approval
Currency of denomination	Euro (or its national denominations)	Euro (or its national denominations) Other EEA or widely traded currencies can be accepted subject to ECB approval

Source: European Monetary Institute, "The Single Monetary Policy in Stage Three: General Documentation on ESCB Monetary Policy Instruments and Procedures," September 1997. Mimeo.

private paper. Tier 1 would include assets with euro-wide acceptability. Tier 2 includes assets with national or regional acceptability. Risk control measures have to be introduced to protect the ESCB against financial loss if underlying assets need to be liquidated due to the default of a counterparty. For this reason, counterparties (for open market operations) must be selected properly and must all be financially sound. The ESCB counterparties may use eligible assets on a cross-border basis.

Reserve Requirements and Liquidity Management

The minimum reserve system requires credit institutions to hold cash balances with the NCBs in an amount equal to 2 percent of their reserve base (short-term liabilities). This requirement is fulfilled over a one-month "maintenance period," in which institutions average the base and reserve amounts. This has a significant smoothing effect on demand for reserves by institutions and also the interest rates on money market instruments used to achieve reserve adjustment. According to the ECB, this enables the system to "conduct monetary policy efficiently resorting only to a limited number of the instruments available during the first year of implementation."[10]

The ECB focuses on the interbank market for reserves, that is, current account deposits of credit institutions held with NCBs. The supply of such reserves is determined by the effect of monetary policy operations on liquidity, adjusted by autonomous factors such as banknote circulation changes, net foreign assets, and government deposits. The market price of reserves, the short-term interbank interest rate, is a point of reference at the overnight maturity. The widely used reference rate for overnight euro deposits, EONIA (euro overnight index average), is computed as a weighted average of the unsecured overnight lending transactions of a panel of fifty-seven contributing banks in the market.[11]

Credit institutions seek to minimize the cost of holding required reserves. This cost is the difference between the interbank overnight rate and the interest rate paid on the required reserves (the main refinancing operations—MRO) that day. Credit institutions tend to build up reserve surpluses when this difference is low, compared with future expected differences. Past, current, and expected future liquidity conditions will determine interbank rates. Also, the interbank overnight rate is influenced by market expectations of future changes in the MRO rate by the ECB. Reserve holdings of banks fluctuated between €63.0 billion and €126.4 billion in the first year of operations, without producing significant stress in prevailing market interest rates.

Main Refinancing Operations

The MROs are the most important open market operations conducted by the Eurosystem. They are regular liquidity-providing reverse transactions, conducted as standard tenders. They provide the bulk of liquidity to the financial sector, and they are conducted as standard tenders, with a weekly frequency and maturity of two weeks. In 1999 the Eurosystem carried out fifty-two MROs, with allotment volumes ranging between €3.9 billion and €102 billion.

Fixed rate or variable rate tenders can be conducted, but in its initial operating year the ECB used only fixed rate tenders. These tenders are conducted to signal clearly the monetary policy stance, and to allot the amount of liquidity considered necessary. With fixed rate tenders, the interest rate is preannounced. Counterparties submit bids at these rates, and ECB matches the bids with its own estimate of the banking sector's liquidity requirements. Allotment ratios are adjusted (usually) well below 100 percent. In 1999 the average "allotment ratio" was 10.8 percent.[12]

The central bank can control the average overnight rate by determining the quantity of bank reserves. In 1999 the ECB tended to set allotments that insured an interbank overnight rate close to the tender rate. This policy implied that on average, in 1999, the EONIA rate was 2.5 basis points higher than the rate on the MROs.

The Eurosystem also conducts longer-term refinancing operations (LTROs), as well as regular reverse transactions to provide liquidity. These transactions are conducted as standard tenders with a monthly rather than a weekly frequency, and a maturity of three months. LTROs usually are conducted as variable rate tenders with preannounced allotment volumes. On average, a volume of liquidity of €49 billion was provided through this type transaction, with 316 counterparties submitting bids.

Standing facilities aim at providing and absorbing overnight liquidity on the initiative of credit institutions. An upper and lower limit for overnight interest rates is provided by (1) the marginal lending facility interest rate, which provides a ceiling when institutions obtain overnight liquidity from the system, and (2) the deposit facility, which allows institutions to deposit overnight surplus funds with the Eurosystem. The interest rate provides a floor for the overnight interest rate. The two facilities together determine a corridor for the overnight market rate. In 1999 the width of this corridor varied between 50 basis points and 250 basis points (table 5.3). Daily recourse to the marginal lending and deposit facilities averaged €l.0 billion and €0.8 billion, respectively, indicating relatively low system liquidity imbalances.

Table 5.3. Width of Overnight Corridor (Basis Points) in 1999

Period	*January 4–January 21*	*January 22–April 8*	*April 9–December 31*
Width	50	250	200

Source: ECB, *Annual Report 1999,* 51.

Minimum Reserve System and Collateral

In its first year of operation the ECB successfully implemented the minimum reserve system. Both functions of this system, the stabilization of interest rates and the enlargement of the structural liquidity deficit of the banking sector, were carried out as intended. The preceding discussion outlined the manner in which interest rates were managed during 1999. With respect to the enlargement function, during 1999, required reserves generally accounted for more than 50 percent of the refinancing needs of the bank sector.

Eurosystem credit operations must be based on collateral provided by the respective counterparties. To allow for the differences in member state financial structure, a large number of different instruments can be used as assets eligible for credit operations. However, the ECB makes a strict distinction between tier 1 and tier 2 categories of collateral. These distinctions are for purposes of internal euro system operations.

Tier 1 consists of marketable debt fulfilling uniform euro area eligibility criteria. Tier 2 consists of assets of particular importance to the national financial markets and banking systems where eligibility criteria are established by the NCBs. At mid-December 1999 the amount of marketable eligible assets available for Eurosystem operations was €5.7 trillion. Most (96 percent) of this consisted of tier 1 assets. Over 62 percent of these assets were government securities, 33 percent securities issued by institutions, and 4 percent corporate paper. Approximately 93 percent of the assets were longer-term bonds and medium-term notes.[13]

At year-end 1999, approximately 7,900 euro area credit institutions were subject to reserve requirements. Of these, 4,100 had direct or indirect access to the real-time gross settlement system account, an operational condition for participating in monetary policy operations. Of these, 3,800 had access to the deposit facility and 3,200 could access the marginal lending facility. The number of counterparties participating in the MROs ranged from 1,068 (January 1999) to 302 (April 1999).

Money Market Developments

With the introduction of the euro and the monetary policy framework, the money market in the Eurozone experienced a process of deep integration throughout the eleven-country region. This integration *was* not homogeneous across the various market segments. The unsecured deposit market, where banks exchange short-term liquidity without collateral protection, and the derivatives markets experienced faster integration. The repo market, in which participants exchange short-term liquidity against collateral, and the short-term securities markets (Treasury bills, commercial paper, certificates of deposit) still have scope for further integration.

From the beginning of stage 3 of the EMU, cross-border transactions in the euro money market increased substantially. Currently, these transactions represent over 50 percent of overall activity in all segments of the money market. This development was fostered by the smooth functioning of the Trans-European Automated Realtime Gross Settlement Express Transfer System (TARGET) for the transfer of large value funds throughout the euro area. TARGET has proven to be a key factor in the efficient redistribution of liquidity across the Eurozone.

The most far-reaching changes took place in the unsecured and swap segments of the money market. This includes the substantial increase in cross-border transactions. The homogeneity and high level of liquidity are reflected by the limited differences between overnight rates observed in the individual Eurozone countries.

Other structural changes in the money market since introduction of the euro include a surge in the liquidity of secondary markets, increased concentration of euro cash management compared with the situation prevailing in the formerly fragmented money markets, and a larger number of counterparties available to individual banks.

FOREIGN EXCHANGE RESERVES OF THE EUROSYSTEM

The treaty establishing the European Community (EC) and the Statute of the ECSB and of the ECB (Statute of the ESCB) stipulate that the Eurosystem is responsible for holding and managing the foreign reserves of the member states. Both the ECB and NCBs hold foreign reserves. At January 2000 these amounted to around €350 billion, with the ECB accounting for €45 billion. The fact that national central banks continue to hold the major component of foreign reserves speaks to the likely continuing role of NCBs within the Eurozone.[14]

These reserves are held for several purposes, one of the most important potentially being foreign exchange intervention. These reserves are invested in a manner that provides security and liquidity and maximizes their value. The following describes the institutional framework for reserve management within the Eurozone, size and composition, and issues that have arisen concerning foreign exchange management.

Institutional Framework

Foreign exchange operations of the ECB, if and when carried out, would be a component of the single monetary policy. In this regard, they would be bound by the same primary objective, maintenance of price stability. Therefore, any foreign exchange intervention or other operations would necessarily be viewed as part of the Eurosystem's monetary policy strategy.[15]

The Eurosystem may, when needed, conduct foreign exchange intervention on its own or may be coordinated with other central banks. The currency holdings involved include those pooled at ECB and would be carried out directly by ECB and/or by NCBs acting on behalf of the ECB. Also, the ECB can fund intervention through other means, such as foreign exchange swaps, including swaps with other central banks.

The ECB remains independent of the direct intercession of national governments and finance ministers, but it is aware of the need to remain on favored terms with these politically influential agents. A regular monthly meeting of the twelve finance ministers and top officials of the ECB allows for interchange of ideas and perspectives concerning monetary and economic policy. In early May 2000, after such a meeting, the finance ministers were to issue a statement supporting the (declining) euro and, by implication, the policy stance of the ECB. At that time Wim Duisenberg, ECB president, issued a statement to reassure Europeans concerned with the 24 percent depreciation of the euro against the dollar since January 1999.

A statement by the finance ministers emphasized several points:

- The euro's weakness is not justified by the strong European economy.
- Inflation in the Eurozone is under control.
- The currency has the potential to reverse direction and appreciate.[16]

Duisenberg noted on May 8, 2000, that the ECB had raised interest rates four times in the past six months to counter inflation threats and would continue to do everything possible to maintain price stability. Financial markets took these words as a sign the ECB might sell dollars and buy euros on the open market to support the single currency. At this time talk of currency intervention was increasing, but ECB officials maintained that they would consider intervention only if it was done in concert with the United States and Japan. However, U.S. Treasury officials were at that time unwilling to intervene in an attempt to bolster sagging currencies.[17]

By May 15, 2000, the financial press was asked repeatedly, Will the ECB step in to support the euro?[18] Fearing erosion in its export position from a weak euro, Japan appeared ready to support intervention. However, the United States remained unwilling.

At this time a new "theory of euro depreciation" was put forth in the press. It noted that a unified Eurozone requires a smaller money supply than an eleven-country region with separate currencies. The euro has a larger transaction domain and is thus more liquid than the smaller volumes of currencies that preceded it. In the case of the euro, the consolidation of eleven currencies into one produced an excess of central bank reserves, and it also increased the liquidity of outstanding government debt. To preserve the value of the new single currency, the central bank was expected to adopt a tighter monetary policy.[19]

Size and Composition of Reserves

In January 1999, over €39 billion of foreign reserves was transferred from the eleven NCBs to the ECB. Of this amount, 15 percent constituted gold, and the remaining 85 percent was in the two major currencies, the U.S. dollar and Japanese yen. Liquidity and security are the basic requirements for investment of these reserves. The ECB foreign reserves are managed in a decentralized manner. But the strategic and tactical framework is determined centrally by the decision bodies of the ECB. This framework considers the following:

- Trade-off between interest rate risk and return
- Credit risk
- Liquidity requirements

NCBs are advised regarding these investment decisions, in the form of investment limits and investment benchmarks. The Governing Council of the ECB defines the currency distribution of foreign reserves on the basis of prospective operational need, which can change from time to time.

Four key parameters describe the investment of foreign reserves:

- A two-level investment benchmark for each currency (strategic and tactical)
- Permitted deviations from benchmarks
- Eligible instruments and operations
- Limits for credit risk exposure

Information regarding all four parameters is communicated to the NCBs, which implement the investment framework. There is constant consultation between the ECB and all NCBs with regard to operations involving foreign reserve assets.

NCB-held foreign reserves are managed with a view to achieving a desired portfolio position and servicing customer transaction needs. These goals include the management of public debt denominated in foreign currencies. As of November 1999, foreign reserves held by NCBs amounted to €307.5 billion (table 5.4). Table 5.4 illustrates the development of ECB and NCB reserve holdings from January 1999 onward. Reserve holdings increased mainly as a result of revaluations and accruals of income. As of January 2000, the Eurosystem had carried out no foreign exchange intervention.[20]

Table 5.4. Foreign Reserve Assets of the Eurosystem (including gold)

1999	*ECB*	*All NCBs*	*Eurosystem*
January	39.2	289.1	328.3
February	39.4	285.4	324.8
March	42.3	302.1	344.4
April	42.4	300.4	342.8
May	42.5	297.1	339.6
June	43.6	299.2	342.8
July	43.5	298.7	342.2
August	43.7	299.8	343.5
September	44.1	307.4	351.5
October	44.1	307.3	351.4
November	44.3	307.5	351.8

Source: European Central Bank, *Monthly Bulletin,* January 2000, 56.

A "Spoken" Intervention for Euro Rate Management

In the first sixteen months of operation of the single currency, the euro depreciated sharply against all other major currencies (table 5.5). By April 28, 2000, the euro had fallen to $0.9078 and ¥96.52, despite a series of ECB interest rate increases from November 1999 onward. The euro had lost 22 percent of its value against the dollar since early January 1999. The euro's decline against the pound sterling gave the pound its highest level against the deutsche mark and French franc in fourteen years.[21] One analyst noted that nothing the ECB says or does seemed capable of reversing the downward trend of the euro.[22] "With the ECB giving no hint it is contemplating foreign exchange market intervention to support the euro, the currency is a one-way bet."

During the first week of May 2000, pressure was growing for intervention, or signs of willingness to intervene by the ECB, to halt the euro's downslide.[23] This came after the euro had fallen to a rate of $0.8845. On Friday, May 5, the ECB tried to reassure Eurozone residents that their euro-denominated savings

Table 5.5. Euro Valuation on Forex Markets, April 28, 2000

Currency	*Exchange Rate*
Dollars per euro	$0.9078
Yen per euro	Y96.5200
DMark per pound	DM3.4000
French franc per pound	FF11.4000

Source: The Times (London), April 28, 2000, 27.

and pensions remained sound. Wim Duisenberg, ECB president, conceded that the plunging euro had shaken trust in Europe's common currency, and stated that such fears were groundless. Foreign exchange traders bought the euro in the expectation that ECB statements could presage the first intervention in the open market to support the single currency. "Traders increasingly expect the central bank to abandon its hands-off policy, because continued euro weakness threatens to allow an intolerable rate of inflation to leech into Continental economies. Speculation that intervention was no longer ruled out, gave the euro a lift against the dollar. The market saw several European central banks buying euros, although this was attributed to routine foreign exchange operations."[24]

The first two weeks of May 2000 could be considered a small watershed in the early history of the euro. First, ECB officials spoke out in the first week of May to reassure Europeans that the euro was in good shape and remained a reliable store of value for future pensioners. Second, the ECB raised its own informal economic growth forecast and began to publish a regular monthly report analyzing economic trends. According to the *Wall Street Journal Europe*, "Unhappy with the euro's weakness, the ECB and politicians have been on a deliberate campaign to stress the strengths of the eleven-nation region." Tommaso Padoa-Schioppa, ECB executive board member, noted in mid-May that "there will be a moment when the market will recognize it must change its weighting of negative factors in relation to positive factors, and in that moment the market will change direction."[25]

By the third week of May, rumors of impending ECB exchange intervention in support of the euro were in abundance. These helped prop up the currency, despite the apparent unwillingness of the U.S. Treasury to participate in any jointly coordinated intervention.[26] By May 26, speculation was more widespread that ECB intervention would lift the euro to its highest level against the dollar in over a month. Against the pound, the euro hit its highest level in four months. Ernst Welteke, Bundesbank president, underlined concern that the weakness of the euro could trigger Eurozone inflation. The ECB Governing Council echoed this concern.[27]

At month's end (May 2000) supportive rhetoric by European policy makers aimed at maintaining momentum in a rally of the euro. Ernst Welteke noted that "intervention belongs to the toolkit of central bankers." Laurent Fabius, French finance minister, stated that Europe would use the available instruments to favor a solid and stable euro.

By early June, economic data reflected rising consumer confidence and declining unemployment in the Eurozone. Coupled with expectations of an ECB interest rate increase, the improved data helped lift the euro to a seven-week high against the dollar. The euro rose to $0.9550, and analysts saw a diminishing need for a direct ECB intervention in support of the single currency.[28]

On June 8, 2000, the ECB surprised financial markets when it raised interest rates by a larger than expected 0.5 percent. Citing the risk that inflation could breach the ECB target of two percent in 2000, and also in 2001, the ECB raised its main lending rate to 4.25 percent from 3.75 percent. This was the fifth increase since November 1999, when the rate was 2.5 percent. The ECB president, Wim Duisenberg, noted that additional increases were possible in 2000, depending on whether monetary conditions had been restored to a neutral level. The euro fell back to close to $0.95 after this announcement. The euro had staged a recovery in the two weeks preceding the rate increase.[29]

The ECB also announced a change in its refinancing operations. Effective June 28, the bank will switch from fixed rate tenders to variable rate tenders in order to solve the problem of overbidding by banks at the weekly refinancing operations. This was not a change of monetary policy stance but rather a change in technical operations. Overbidding had distorted the distribution of funds across the Eurozone by preventing smaller banks from obtaining money. Under a variable rate system, the central bank invites bids without announcing the rate in advance. It then accepts all bids in descending order of interest rates offered, until it reaches its liquidity target.[30]

Within the nearly eighteen-month period from early January 1999 to early June 2000, the euro declined in terms of the dollar by approximately 24.7 percent and then recovered over 20 percent of this loss in the final two-week period ending June 7. During this period the ECB avoided currency intervention, although it undertook an informal program of "talking up" the value of the currency in early May.

Neutrality in the Gold Market

As a result of the initial transfer of foreign reserves, the ECB holds approximately 750 tons of gold. Transfer of gold from the NCBs to the ECB carries no specific implications for consolidated gold holdings of the Eurosystem. The ECB is a signatory, along with fourteen other European central banks, to the

1999 Central Bank Gold Agreement. The agreement established basic principles concerning the activities and responsibilities of the signatories, regarding their participation in the market for gold, and the intended role of gold as a monetary reserve:

- Gold will remain an important element of global monetary reserves.
- The signatory central banks will not enter the market as sellers except for already decided sales.
- Gold sales already decided will be managed to avoid undue market pressure.
- The signatory central banks will not expand their gold leasings and use of gold futures and options over the next five-year period.
- The agreement is to be reviewed after five years.

Clearly, this agreement aims at achieving a "neutral" effect on the market for gold. This is disappointing news for gold-producing companies and government agencies in countries that customarily export large amounts of gold.

Gold producers were disappointed that the ECB would hold only 10 percent to 15 percent of its reserves in gold. Luis Linde, director general of the Bank of Spain's foreign department, suggested that the bank would follow the example of many central banks and become a "new participant" in the gold financial market. More active gold management is a compromise between net holding gold and holding unproductive gold.

John Wilson, president of Placer Dome, Canada's second-largest gold producer, has denounced central bank gold operations. He insisted that central bank mobilization of gold over the past decade has been a leading factor in gold's falling purchasing power. He stated central banks earned less than $1 billion (since 1996) in lending gold to the market but caused a $100 billion drop in the value of their reserves.[31] Wilson called for better coordination of central bank activity, as well as clarity about their objectives toward gold.

Rudolf Trink, head of Treasury at the Australian Central Bank, stated in 1998 that there was no commercial argument for central banks to hold gold. "Public confidence in central banks is largely based on the idea that [they] . . . are not primarily income-driven institutions." Trink stated that there should be no surprise if ECB held little gold in its reserves.

The ECB's reserves provide it with the ability to intervene in currency markets. Since gold would first have to be converted into U.S. dollars before it could be used in intervention, there is a certain limitation on the share of gold in ECB reserves.

Trink noted that coordination of policy must develop among European central banks. Through this, the ECB would want to demonstrate its leadership role, and the need for it to approve shifts in gold holdings by member central banks.

PAYMENT SYSTEM

A key part of the new euro-based monetary system is to provide for cross-border payments. Commercial banks in the Eurozone need continuous intra-day money transfers and payments, linking together all parts of the money market system throughout the Eurozone.

The Trans-European Automated Realtime Gross Settlement Express Transfer System (TARGET) was ready for testing at midyear 1998. TARGET consists of (1) a national real-time gross settlement system (RTGS) in all member countries and (2) a system that interlinks national systems. All countries had an RTGS system in place in 1998. The TARGET system successfully commenced operation at the end of December 1998.

With entry into the third stage of the EMU, national payment systems are permitted to use both the national currency and the euro. All transfers in TARGET will be in euros. Use of TARGET is mandatory for monetary operations in the EMU. However, TARGET is not intended to be the only cross-border wholesale payment system in Europe from 1999 on. Use of correspondent banks will continue, along with international netting and clearinghouse schemes.

National central banks are responsible for intraday liquidity. They facilitate this through intraday drafts and intraday repos, both fully collateralized. There is no charge for such intraday credit, but central banks will bear little or no risk due to the full collateralization. TARGET will operate from 7 A.M. to 6 P.M., central European time. This will be an important expansion of operational hours for most EU countries, reflecting a global trend toward longer operating hours.

TARGET can be accessed by 34,000 institutions throughout the EU. In 1999 the daily average number of payments processed in the system (cross-border and domestic) was 163,157, with a value of €925 billion. Cross-border payments in TARGET were 18 percent of total volume and 39 percent of total value.[32]

Technically, TARGET was successful in the following respects:

- It was capable of processing many large value payments within short transmission times.
- Its collateralization of intraday credit presented no substantial problems.
- Their price difference vis-à-vis alternative systems did not deter banks from using TARGET extensively.
- Small and medium-sized banks that lacked access to other systems found TARGET an efficient alternative to correspondent banking.

In 1999 the ECB conducted a survey on cross-border payment service provided through TARGET. The main findings of this survey were presented in the report "Cross-border Payments in TARGET: A User's Survey," published in the November 1999 *Monthly Bulletin*.[33] While the survey found many credit institutions satisfied with ongoing TARGET services, large participants prefer a higher degree of harmonization of the service provided by the different RTGS (real-time gross settlements) systems participating in TARGET. It was agreed that TARGET would be a decentralized system, with credit institutions keeping their settlements accounts with their home central bank. Therefore, payments continue to be processed through national RTGS systems.[34]

PRACTICAL ASPECTS OF ECB OPERATION: QUESTIONS AND UNCERTAINTIES

On June 1, 1998, the ECB came into being. The six executive board directors were in place, central bankers from European institutions who had long experience in their respective countries. Credibility and internal harmony seemed to be present within the ECB and member countries at midyear 1998. But more was needed to make a successful central bank. One essential ingredient was transparency. Markets must have some ability to predict or anticipate central bank action, and this requires that key data and information be provided by the central bank and government agencies.

Three Central Problems

Three problems arise with respect to anticipating ECB policy directions. First, the regional issue is important. There are widely differing economic conditions from one country to another, such as unemployment rate, labor productivity, wage levels, labor market flexibility, and government fiscal position. Uncertainties are widespread concerning how monetary policy can bridge the gap from these differences. Will the ECB focus on the problems of the weakest countries, and will political pressures mandate such an approach? Second, monetary and economic statistics are acknowledged to be weak or only developing for euro-wide use. It was feared that monetary data could be misleading in the early period of the euro.[35]

Top ECB officials decided to adopt two complementary policy targets—a monetary growth target and an inflation-cum-interest rate approach. This places the ECB in a halfway house between the German and UK central bank approaches. This complicates monetary policy and the job of tracking monetary policy by financial market analysts.

During the past eighteen years monetary targeting has fallen out of fashion among financial analysts and academics. Thomas Mayer, European economist at Goldman Sachs, defends the use of monetary targeting at the ECB, arguing that it should be a key guidepost. He also argues that consideration of asset price inflation is important for the ECB, especially as the capital market sector begins to expand strongly under the euro system.

Some analysts calculate the ECB will opt for a tight range of monetary growth. Joachim Fels, ECB watcher at Morgan Stanley, estimated that growth of 4 percent would be consistent with price stability in the Eurozone, and a real economic growth of 2.5 percent (allowing for 1.5 percent inflation).[36]

Other ECB policies, such as minimum reserve requirements, are a divisive issue. Some central bankers favor these reserve requirements, since they tie banks closely to the central bank. However, they are costly and could drive financial business away from the Eurozone. London has no such requirement, and has enjoyed a competitive strength from this position.

The ECB attracted controversy when it opted for a system of minimum reserves as a key policy tool. Under a minimum reserve system, commercial banks are obliged to park funds at the central bank as a percentage of deposits (between 1.5 and 2.5 percent according to ECB announcements). These are to be remunerated at the prevailing repo rate or alternative money market rate.[37]

A third question is the relation between the ECB and the national central banks. Power will be at least partly dispersed and the question remains, What level will prevail in the case of serious policy disagreement? This is discussed at a later point in this chapter.

European Central Bank Relations

A key question related to the working of the ECB is its relation to the twelve national central banks. The twelve central banks continue, but not as before. The ECB based in Frankfurt makes the big monetary policy decisions, but the national central banks implement them.[38] Money market operations and foreign exchange market interventions are carried out at the national level. As of 1998 the eleven national central banks had 60,000 employees, contrasted to the ECB staff of 475.

The ECB and national central banks constitute a complex system, labeled ESCB. The central banks are shareholders in the ECB. The ECB has three boards. The first is the executive board, consisting of Wim Duisenberg (president) and five other directors. These six are responsible for day-to-day operation of the ECB.

The second tier board is the most important. It serves as the Governing Council, consisting of six executive board members and the twelve governors of the participating national central banks. This council meets once a month and sets all the important monetary policy decisions, such as changes in interest rates or exchange rate policy. Finally, there is the Governing Council. This extended body consists of central bank governors of all EU countries, including those that do not participate as yet in the single currency (UK, Sweden, and Denmark). This board has no specific policy function.

OPERATING MECHANISMS

It is clear that the ECB is responsible for setting policy, and the twelve national central banks conduct the bulk of money market operations and foreign exchange interventions. The ECB policy council will decide on interest rates. National central banks also will retain much larger staffs than the ECB. Both the Bundesbank and the Bank of France have over 10,000 people on staff. The ECB staff was only 475. However, the nature of duties will be quite different. Many national central bank employees are involved in processing paperwork. ECB employees will be involved more heavily in decision making.

Uncertainties

Daniel Gros, director of the Center for European Policy Studies, Brussels, has expressed concern that the national bank "outsiders" could squeeze ECB personnel by forming coalitions and impeding efforts to gear policy toward the total Eurozone rather than individual nations. Countering this view is the understanding that European central bankers have a long history of close cooperation.

A real test could come when the worlds of politics and central banking collide. How well the ECB can withstand pressures from EU finance ministers still remains an untested variable. It is possible that the EU finance ministers could become a countervailing force vis-à-vis the ECB.

At his confirmation hearings Duisenberg ruled out publication of the minutes of the council meetings. This practice is common in the United States and the UK. By contrast the ECB operates a cabinet-style system. Every member is expected to support and represent the ECB position to the outside world.

Monetary Targeting

The ECB has implemented a policy tool that minimizes reserve requirements on funds that receive interest. Their interest rate structure is similar to Germany's, with several highlighted interest rates. The lowest rate is a deposit rate at which banks can deposit surplus funds at the end of the day with the central bank. The highest rate is the marginal lending rate, for overnight (emergency) borrowing by banks at the central bank. The most important rate is the securities repurchase rate, set between the other two rates.

The ECB is expected to develop a German-style monetary targeting to set how much money should be available in the economy. An inflation target will probably be used, an approach that is somewhat like that of the Bank of England. However, the ECB does not publish forecasts related to these targets.

A fundamental reason for avoiding target forecasts is the quality (and lack) of statistics covering the Eurozone. Many leading academicians have contrasting and even contradictory views concerning monetary theory and the appropriate policy approach. Top officials at the ECB accept the view that today's growth in the money supply causes tomorrow's inflation. Following this model requires high-quality monetary and economic statistics. ECB officials understand that money data provide a useful communications service. If the money supply overshoots a given target, the financial markets will expect interest rates to advance in response to this overshoot.

Unreliable data will interfere with this process of interaction (between central bank and financial markets) and policy adjustment. The ECB may find itself explaining "data blips" as due to this unreliable data. Repeated explanations of this kind could quickly erode confidence in the ECB.

Wim Duisenberg rejected requests to publish the minutes of the monthly meetings of the governing council, since this would subject national central banks to intolerable pressure from their own governments. Also, it would prevent the ECB from accomplishing the psychological change from focusing on the Eurozone rather than the twelve national economies.[39] Duisenberg plans to report in person to the European Parliament regularly in regard to Eurozone monetary policy developments.

THE INTERNATIONAL ROLE OF THE EURO: THE EURO, DOLLAR, AND YEN

According to the ECB, the development of the euro as an international currency will mainly be a market-driven process.[40] French policy makers hope the euro will become a serious rival to the dollar as an international currency. Robert Mundell of Columbia University, father of the theory of optimal currency areas, thinks American complacency is mistaken. To him, introduction of the euro is the most significant world monetary development since the dollar replaced the pound sterling as the dominant international currency during World War I.[41]

Given its economic weight in the world, the euro area is expected to play an important role in the process of international cooperation. Although the gross domestic product of the initial eleven-member Eurozone is only 80 percent of U.S. GDP, the addition of the four EU nonmembers makes the area as big as the United States (table 5.6). Also, the EU-15 account for 31 percent of world trade, over 33 percent of world debt securities, and 35 percent of foreign exchange transactions (table 5.6).

Internationalization of the euro is not an ECB policy objective. It will be neither fostered nor hindered by the Eurosystem. The big doubt concerning the euro is political. Outsiders may well need further evidence of continuing integration before they put their faith in the euro. We should note, however, that at midyear 1998, Italian bond yields were already lower than U.S. yields, suggesting that outsiders may not need much additional evidence.[42]

The advantage of the dollar over the euro, perceived in 1998–1999, is the greater liquidity of dollar-based financial markets. According to Richard Portes of the Center for Economic Policy Research, this could change if transaction volumes were large enough in euro-denominated markets. In mid-1998 bid-ask spreads in the German and French bond markets were 4 basis points, while in the United States they were only 1.6 basis points. Mere fusion of the markets in Europe might be enough to reduce transaction costs to U.S. levels. Further changes are needed in the Eurozone, such as development of larger institutional buying and the inclusion of the UK within the Eurozone.

What impact would the euro have if it became a key international currency? According to Mundell, over the past fifteen years, the cumulative U.S. current account deficit totaled $1.7 trillion. This has been financed by $1 trillion in net capital inflows and a foreign accumulation of dollar reserves of $700 billion.

Table 5.6. The Eurozone as a Potential Monetary Giant

	Percentage of Total		
	U.S.	*Japan*	*EU-15*
Relative economic size			
Shares of world GDP, 1996	20.7	8.0	20.4
Shares of world exports (ex-intra-EU) 1996	15.2	6.1	14.7
Relative use of currencies[a]			
World trade, 1992	48.0	5.0	31.0
World debt securities, September 1996	37.2	17.0	34.5
Developing country debt, end 1996	50.2	18.1	15.8
Global foreign exchange reserves, end 1995	56.4	7.1	25.8
Foreign exchange transactions, April 1995[b]	41.5	12.0	35.0

Source: International Monetary Fund, *Financial Times*.
[a]Shares denominated in currency (or currencies) of country (or EU).
[b]Shares adjusted for double-counting that arises from the fact that each transaction involves two currencies.

If the euro were to rival the dollar, global foreign exchange reserves would increase, much of this denominated in the euro, not the dollar. If this did happen, there could be a devastating impact. The Asian crisis called for an increasing U.S. current account deficit to absorb the rising Asian exports needed to allow these countries to regain prosperity. But a declining role of the dollar as an international reserve currency implies a shift toward current account surplus and a corresponding shift of Euroland toward current account deficit.[43]

If the rest of the world wanted to shift from the dollar to the euro as a reserve holding, there would be an appreciation of the euro vis-à-vis the dollar. This is because the United States already experiences current account deficits, whereas the EU experiences surpluses.[44]

The reality is that the EU region would have to shift from a large current account surplus to a deficit to accommodate the world's desire to hold euro-denominated assets. This would create difficulties for the management of monetary policy in Europe. At the same time, the United States would face an uncertain choice between a weak dollar and/or higher interest rates.

The role of a third currency, the Japanese yen, complicates these issues further. During the first half of 2000, concern was expressed as the Japanese raised interest rates and elicited a massive flow of funds from dollar to yen-denominated holdings. This could put great pressure on the dollar's valuation, forcing the United States to allow interest rates to climb to high levels. A weak euro early in 2000 deflected this kind of pressure.

INTERNATIONAL ROLE OF THE DOLLAR

Over the past fifty years, the U.S. dollar has served as the preeminent international currency. In the 1940s and 1950s the pound sterling provided competition to the dollar in this respect. In the 1980s both the Japanese yen and the German mark rose in importance, fueling speculation that a bipolar or tripolar global currency system could develop. With the coming of the euro, speculation has renewed that a bipolar or tripolar international monetary system could yet come into existence.

International Currency Defined

Basic monetary economics tells us that money carries out three essential functions: a medium of exchange, a unit of account, and a store of value. In the international context these same functions are required. In the context of the Eurozone, an international currency serves as a medium of exchange in direct exchanges of currencies and as a vehicle currency in completing indirect exchanges between two other currencies in foreign trade and investment. An international currency also is used by official agents as a vehicle for foreign exchange market intervention and for financing the swings in external accounts. As a unit of account, it is used to invoice merchandise trade and to denominate financial transactions; official agencies (governments) use it to define exchange rate parities. As a store of value, savers, investors, and companies use it with financial assets. In a similar way, official agents (governments and central banks) may hold assets denominated in an international currency as reserve assets.

There is a fundamental difference in the use of money in a domestic as contrasted with an international use. In the domestic case the government declares by fiat the currency to be used as legal tender. In the international case the choice or selection of currencies used depends on market forces. Since the selection of currency for international money is a market-driven process, the function of money as medium of exchange and unit of account predominate over its use as a store of value. This leads to the use of only one or several international currencies. This can be explained as follows. Modern portfolio theory (MPT) states that to diversify risks, investors typically hold a wide range of international currencies as assets. The amount of each depends on its risk and return characteristics. Therefore, if the choice of international currencies used depends on asset motives, many currencies will be held and the dollar will have no reason to dominate investor portfolios. Over the past quarter century, deutsche mark– and yen-denominated assets have provided higher returns, as measured by nominal yields plus capital appreciation, than dollar-denominated assets. Nevertheless, the dollar is the dominant international currency.

Supporting the dollar's dominant role is its successful dual role as a medium of international exchange and a unit of international account. Equally important, the dollar conveys information about relative prices. This monetary role of the dollar works as follows. When individuals use money, this reduces the amount of information they must acquire and analyze. Money is a transmitter of information. The international role of the dollar is similar to that of an international language. As more people use a language, it conveys more information. Analogously, as more people use the dollar, it conveys more useful information. For example, a Saudi Arabian exporter who does not speak French sells crude oil to a French importer who does not speak Arabic. The transaction may be conducted in English and settled in U.S. dollars. The use of the dollar in the transaction leads to economies of communication in transmitting information. So also does the use of English. The more popular a currency, the more useful it is to those who hold it. Further, if individuals have an incentive to switch to another currency, they would have to convince many others to make the same switch before it would be worthwhile to do so. This so-called switching cost helps us understand why the pound sterling continued in wide use internationally years after the UK lost its position as the world's main economic power.

Requirements for International Currency Status

A number of factors are required for a currency to be widely used internationally:

- Widespread confidence in the currency's value. In part this is related to an absence of home country inflation. Variable inflation generates exchange rate depreciation and uncertainty. The United States has had a good experience in this regard, compared with other nations in the Group of Seven (G-7). Since floating rates began in 1973, only two G-7 nations (Germany and Japan) have enjoyed lower inflation than the United States (table 5.7). In terms of industrial prices, the same two countries enjoyed an edge over the United States, and France experienced almost the same price increase.
- There must be confidence in the political stability of the issuing government.
- The issuing country should possess financial markets that are free of controls, containing a wide variety of financial instruments. Such markets contribute to the international demand for a country's currency. The U.S. capital markets are the largest in the world.
- The issuing country's economic characteristics are important. Especially important are the country's share of world trade and size of its economy. The larger a country's share of world trade the more comfortable and knowledgeable are traders of that currency. With over 15 percent of world exports, the United States is the leading exporter. Accounting for approximately 20 percent of world gross domestic product (GDP), the United States has the largest productive system and largest consuming market.

Table 5.7. Comparative Inflation Rates, 1973–1997

Country	*Measured by CPI*	*Measured by Producer Prices*
United States	263.2	181.6
United Kingdom	575.0	545.6
Germany	113.1	86.3
France	345.0	181.1
Italy	920.1	746.1
Canada	283.1	262.6
Japan	154.4	51.4

Source: International Monetary Fund (IMF), *International Financial Statistics.*

Benefits from International Currency Status

The United States derives benefits as a major issuing country for international money. First, it gains seigniorage, as non-interest-bearing or low-interest-bearing claims are denominated in U.S. dollars. The board of governors of the Federal Reserve estimates that seigniorage for the United States is between $11 billion and $15 billion per year.[45] Second, as international use of a currency expands, loans, investments, and purchases will be executed increasingly through the financial institutions of the issuing currency. Financial sector earnings likewise will expand. Third, with world trade generally denominated in U.S. dollars, the U.S. economy becomes less vulnerable to changes in the value of its currency than other economies. For example, with petroleum prices quoted in U.S. dollars, an appreciation or depreciation of the dollar against other currencies has less impact on the United States and oil-using sectors, but more impact on other national economies that import and export oil.

There may be costs associated with having a currency that is used internationally, such as the following:

- In the case of a pegged exchange rate, a shift in preferences by international holders of that currency can lead to large capital flows, undermining the monetary authority's ability to control the monetary base and domestic economic conditions.
- In the case of a floating exchange rate, there also could be limits on the ability of the authorities to stabilize the domestic economy. This would operate as changes in portfolio preferences perceived by the government lead it to restrict the international use of the currency. This problem manifested itself when the German and Japanese governments took restrictive measures on the international use of their respective currencies in the 1970s and 1980s.

International Use of the Dollar

The relative importance of a currency as a unit of account and medium of exchange is reflected in the trading volume of that currency in foreign exchange markets. Table 5.8 provides trading volume data reported by the Bank for International Settlements, collected by central banks from 1989 to 1995. While a decline can be observed in the dollar's share of trading volume, from 45 percent to 41.5 percent, trading is still dollar dominated. In 1995 the dollar's share was larger than the next four currencies combined (deutsche mark, yen, pound sterling, French franc).

Other indicators of international currency use confirm the information in table 5.8. For example, in 1996 the dollar accounted for 75 percent of external bond issues, 64 percent of official holdings of foreign exchange, and 45 per-

Table 5.8. Shares of Selected Currencies in Global Gross Foreign Exchange Market Turnover

Currency	*April 1989*	*April 1992*	*April 1995*
U.S. dollar	45.0	41.0	41.5
Deutsche mark	13.5	20.0	18.5
Japanese yen	13.5	11.5	12.0
Pound sterling	7.5	7.0	5.0
French franc	1.0	2.0	4.0
Swiss franc	5.0	4.5	3.5
Other currencies	14.5	14.0	15.3
All currencies	100.0	100.0	100.0

Source: Bank for International Settlements, *Central Bank Survey of Foreign Exchange and Derivatives Market Activity* (Basel: BIS, 1995).
Note: Totals do not add up to 100.0 due to rounding.

cent of Eurocurrency deposits. These reflect the dominant role of the dollar as a unit of account and medium of exchange around the world.

CHALLENGE OF THE EURO

The international monetary system has experienced a major change with the advent of the European economic and monetary union. In fact, this is the most significant change in the international monetary system since the shift toward floating rates in the 1970s. The euro is widely described as a challenge to the dollar's hegemony in international finance. The EMU possesses the characteristics needed to establish the euro as a strong currency. The euro's potential to become a leading international currency will depend on the factors that contribute to international currency use described above relative to the U.S. dollar.

Basic Requirements for the Euro to Challenge the Dollar

Four basic requirements must be considered if the euro is to be able to challenge the dollar as an international currency. These include:

- Economic stability
- Financial markets
- Relative economic size
- Political factors

In the case of economic stability, we must focus on the ability of the new ECB to effectively control inflation. The ECB is an untested and unknown quantity in its early years. The ECB possesses several advantages. First, it enjoys a high degree of independence, as stipulated in the Maastricht treaty. Second, it will take over the reins from a number of national central banks that have earned themselves high credits as defenders against inflation. Third, it operates from Frankfurt and probably enjoys considerable support from the Deutsche Bundesbank, which has a tradition of effectively fighting inflation. Finally, it comes on the scene in an environment favorable to its mission. In 1998–1999, inflation rates across Europe were low and interest rates were declining.

On the eve of the EU, the financial markets of Europe were preparing for increased integration. Costs of financial transactions fell as the euro replaced national currencies. Narrower interest spreads were already in evidence across Europe in 1997–1998. An expanded supply of euro-denominated assets will be created as borrowers place bond and note issues in euros. Greater depth and breadth of financial markets denominated in the euro, compared with a former condition of financial markets splintered apart by currency differentials, will provide incentives for non-EMU nations to diversify their reserve holdings, bringing them more in line with their trade and financial transactions within the Eurozone.

The relative economic size of the Eurozone augurs well for the future role of the euro. The EU and United States each account for approximately 20 percent of world GDP and 15 percent of world exports. However, the U.S. dollar is used more widely as an international currency than all the European currencies combined (lower section of table 5.9).

The economic base of the euro is larger than that of individual European currencies. The use of the euro will reduce the transaction costs involved in exchanging European currencies. These two factors probably will lead to a

Table 5.9. U.S. and EU Relative Economic Size and Use of Currencies

Characteristic	*United States*	*European Union*
Economic size		
Share of world GDP, 1996	20.7	20.4
Share of world exports, 1996[a]	15.2	14.7
Use of currencies[b]		
World trade, 1995	51.0	31.0
International bond offerings, September 1997	45.1	41.90
Developing country debt, end of 1996	50.2	15.8
Global foreign exchange reserves, end of 1996	63.7	19.5
Foreign exchange transactions, April 1995	11.5	35.0

Source: International Monetary Fund, *World Economic Outlook Database and Annual Report*, 1997.
[a]Excluding intra-EU trade transactions.
[b]Share denominated in currency (or currencies) of country (or European Union).

gradual increase in the use of the euro as a unit of account in trade flows, especially in trade with some of the developing and transitional countries. This is discussed below.

If all fifteen of the EU countries eventually join the Eurozone, over 60 percent of their current foreign trade will become classified as domestic. This trade, plus the potential for the euro to be used for denominating foreign trade, will help make the Eurozone less exposed to exchange rate changes than individual European nations were up to January 1999. This could make the euro an attractive alternative to the dollar as a safe haven for investors and asset holders, protecting them from asset devaluations such as those that occurred during the oil price shocks of the 1970s.

Political factors also are important to the role of a currency in international finance. The role of the euro will be that of a currency used by a union of many nations. In the case of the dollar, a single nation is responsible for its management.

Political stability is a determinant of the international use of a currency, and differences in bilateral points of view on economic policy may arise. For example, Germany and Italy may disagree over the trend of interest rates in the Eurozone. The EMU will have to work such differences out. Until the EMU can demonstrate an ability to reconcile such potential differences, investors, asset holders, and foreign traders may exercise a cautious approach toward use of the euro.

Current Configuration of Forex Markets

In this section we examine recent and current patterns of currency use in the foreign exchange market, including the pattern of world payments and currency use within this pattern. Also, we consider possible scenarios of development and use of the euro.

As of 1998, the dollar was used in 83 percent of two-way forex transactions while the deutsche mark was used in 37 percent. Other EU currencies were used in 21 percent of transactions. Sterling is now used in 10 percent of transactions and the yen in 24 percent of transactions.[46] The EU accounts for a higher proportion of trade than the preceding figures indicate. For example, in 1992 the EU accounted for 17 percent of world exports, the United States 12 percent, and Japan 9 percent.[47] However, the dollar plays an intermediate and financing role for EU and third countries, as well as for trade between third countries. Low transaction costs in the forex markets involving the euro will make substitution a possibility.

EMU will bring almost exclusive invoicing in euros by European firms; however, there will be an initial one-off effect raising the dollar-denominated share of trade, as intra-EU trade becomes domestic and no longer enters into forex statistics. After this, the euro's role will grow as it captures dollar vehicle currency business. The pace of growth will depend on currency volatility.

Between 1985 and 1996 the share of U.S. dollar bonds in the international bond market fell from 62 percent to 38 percent. The share of yen-denominated bonds also fell (to 16 percent in 1996). It is believed that the euro money market will become highly liquid, so that derivative-related transactions will exceed both the dollar and yen derivative related markets.[48]

European institutional investors are little diversified into foreign assets. Initially they may prefer to diversify across countries within the newly integrated European capital markets, avoiding foreign exchange risks. At the same time U.S. institutional investors may find the new euro markets attractive as they diversify. Low correlation of returns on euro-denominated bonds vis-à-vis U.S. bonds will intensify the interest of U.S. institutional investors in bonds denominated in euros.

The attractiveness of the euro for governments and central banks deserves some attention as well. Between 1973 and 1994 there were significant shifts in the composition of official foreign exchange reserve holdings by currency of denomination. These are outlined in table 5.10. Most significantly, the dollar share fell as EU currencies and the yen rose in importance. The EMU process could very well reinforce this trend decline in the dollar share.[49] Outside the EU, the euro could become a major reserve currency if foreign exchange intervention by non-EU countries takes place in euros. Trends in the financial markets influence how important this development becomes, that is, how efficient and liquid the euro-denominated financial markets become vis-à-vis the dollar and yen.

Table 5.10. Currencies in Use as Official Reserve Holdings (percentage)

Currency	*1973*	*1994*
U.S. dollar	76.1	63.3
Major EU currencies	14.3	21.9
Deutsche mark	7.1	15.5
Yen	nil	8.5

Eurozone Alternative Scenarios

Portes and Rey construct alternative scenarios for development of the Eurozone. They presuppose that EMU represents a shock to the fundamentals of the world economy. They replace a set of EU currencies with the euro and note possible outcome.[50] A key element for internationalization of the euro will be the depth of the euro financial markets. The response and development in financial markets, not the goods markets, will determine the future of the euro. Basically, transaction costs in financial markets influence how well the euro can challenge the dollar.

Portes and Rey posit three scenarios:

- The pan-euro scenario: the euro replaces the dollar as the main currency for financial asset transactions between major regional blocs.
- The big euro scenario: the euro replaces the dollar as the main currency for financial asset transactions, but not for transactions between major regional blocs (such as dollar and yen).
- The medium euro scenario: the euro replaces the dollar as the main currency for financial asset transactions, with transactions between the dollar and yen regional blocs dominated by the dollar.

These scenarios are described in detail in table 5.11.

In the past, central banks outside the United States, particularly in Germany and Japan, sought to avoid internationalization of their currencies. With the introduction of the euro, it is possible that the new ECB may wish to promote international use of the euro. This will provide welfare gains (seigniorage). What policy measures will Europe follow to achieve this objective?

The previous discussion emphasizes transaction costs as a determinant of the international role of the euro. We expect transaction costs in the Eurozone to decline, due to "natural" financial integration, larger-scale financial markets that manifest themselves (leading to increased liquidity) and moderate success by European governments and monetary authorities in achieving financial deregulation. Further, banking competition will intensify, bringing about lower bank transaction costs.

Private market initiatives are operating to lower transaction costs. These include mergers and affiliations between stock exchanges and derivatives markets (discussed in chapters 6–8), coordination of efforts between securities markets association groups in Europe, and efforts to coordinate bond and equity market benchmarking.

EMU is introducing a financial market shock to the Eurozone, analogous to but greater in severity than the big bang in London and other financial centers. It remains to be observed whether the aftershock effects will be as significant.

Table 5.11. Alternative Scenarios under the Euro

Pan Euro Scenario	*Big Euro Scenario*	*Medium Euro Scenario*
1. Euro replaces dollar for financial asset transactions between blocs and as vehicle currency in Forex market.	1. Euro replaces dollar for financial asset transactions, but transactions between the dollar and yen blocs are dominated by the dollar.	1. Euro replaces dollar for financial asset transactions, but transactions between dollar and yen blocs are still dominated by the dollar.
2. All transactions between the dollar and yen blocs are intermediated through the euro.	2. The euro takes the role of vehicle currency on the Forex markets.	2. Euro has not taken the role of vehicle currency on the Forex market.
3. Use of euro in all financial transactions leads to its use as vehicle currency on Forex markets. There are no direct transactions between the dollar and yen. Transactions costs are low on euro/dollar and on euro/yen markets.	3. Transactions costs on the dollar/yen market is high, compared with the dollar/euro and euro/yen markets. This is because the vehicle currency role of the euro has increased trading volumes in these markets.	3. Some transactions will be intermediated through the dollar, some through the euro.
4. Scenario is unlikely, since post-euro the dollar and yen markets will be as liquid as pre-euro.	4. Scenario is more likely than the pan-euro scenario.	4. The less Europe and Asia are integrated (higher transaction costs on the euro/yen market), the more likely the dollar is to retain its vehicle currency role.

Source: R. Portes and H. Rey, "The Emergence of the Euro as an International Currency," NBER Working Paper 6424, February 1998, 10–14.

THE MANY HORIZONS FOR THE EURO

With the advent of the euro, developing and transition economies around the world will discern its impact on trade, financial flows, and exchange rate regimes. The degree to which developing and transition economies will be affected by the euro and the changes it brings will differ widely by country and by region. In part, this impact will depend on trade links with the Eurozone and investment ties of each country and region. In the following paragraphs, we examine these prospects for five regions—central and eastern Europe, Latin America, Asia, the Middle East and Mediterranean, and Africa.

Central and Eastern Europe

The countries of central and eastern Europe display wide differences in their economic interaction with the Eurozone countries. One group, consisting of former USSR countries such as Kazakhstan, Russia, and Ukraine, has only limited interaction with Eurozone countries. These countries depend on exports of dollar-priced commodities, such as oil, gas, cotton, and gold. Introduction of the euro will have only limited impact on these countries. Indirectly, they will benefit from the ability to utilize the large and liquid financial market in the Eurozone.

A second group comprises the ten central and eastern countries associated with the EU (known as the ACEEC-10)—Bulgaria, Czech Republic, Estonia, Hungary, Latvia, Lithuania, Poland, Romania, Slovakia, and Slovenia. This group also includes countries in the Balkans (Albania, Bosnia, Croatia, Macedonia, and Yugoslavia). The impact of the euro on these fifteen countries is more complex. As these countries develop closer links with the EU, euro-denominated debt will become a larger part of their external liabilities. In short, they will become more reliant on raising funds in the liquid financial markets of the Eurozone, and more affected by changing liquidity and interest rate trends in the EU countries.[51]

Trade and investment links between these fifteen central and eastern European countries and the EU are increasing. Investment links are expected to become especially important, since these countries will depend on foreign investment with technology for continued development and economic expansion.

Almost all of these countries have a peg (de facto or de jure) to a currency or currency basket. This peg generally includes at least one EU currency (most often the deutsche mark). The formal currency arrangement must change as the euro replaces the national currencies beginning in 1999. This may not take the form of a simple substitution of the euro for the national currency. More likely it will involve a reconsideration of the appropriate anchor to which to peg the central and eastern European currencies. These countries have replaced the deutsche mark with the euro as a currency anchor and in some cases have reweighted dual currency anchors, giving the euro an upward weight.

In 1998 three countries (Czech Republic, Slovenia, Romania) with a de facto floating currency had no apparent reason to alter this arrangement. As long as the floating rate system remains successful and viable, introduction of the euro may have little or no impact. However, a shift in capital flows may become a determining factor.

Latin America

Trade and financial links between Eurozone and Latin America are not strong. Approximately 15 percent of Latin American trade is with the European

Community. Therefore, the euro's introduction is not likely to exert a significant impact on countries in the Western Hemisphere. By contrast, North America accounts for half of Latin American trade flows, and regional trade agreements such as the North American Free Trade Association (NAFTA) are tending to reinforce the important role of dollar-related trading ties in Latin America.

Where European and Latin American producers compete in third markets, introduction of the euro will increase pressure for European firms to improve productivity, indirectly impacting producers in Latin America. These pressures are not expected to be strong, since buying patterns are slow to change, and productivity gains being achieved in Latin America are likely to offset a major part of the competitive gains achieved in Europe from the single currency.

Latin American countries are important borrowers in the international bond market. With varying current account deficits, Latin American countries can be expected to tap the international bond market for needed funding. On the eve of the euro, Latin American external debt was denominated mostly in U.S. dollars, but some countries have been diversifying the currency denomination of their borrowing (table 5.12). For example, in 1997 Argentina launched a 750 billion Italian lire-into-euro seven-year bond. Also, half of the Mexican issues in early 1997 were in nondollar currencies. Mexico was the first borrower to issue a euro-denominated Eurobond (September 1997), followed by Argentina (January 1998).[52]

The single European currency should be an attractive way to tap the European capital market, with investors focused more and more on Latin American economic development. As interest rates in Europe decline (based on convergence as well as perceived lower risk premiums), euro issues should become more interesting for Latin American issuers. This will allow governments in this region to better diversify their debt profile.

Table 5.12. Currency Composition of Latin American External Debt, Year-End 1997

Currency	*Percentage*
U.S. dollar	67
EU currencies	12
Japanese yen	11
Other	10

Source: Union Bank of Switzerland, *EMU Monitor*, April 1998.

Mediterranean and Middle East

Countries in this area will experience varying effects with the introduction of the euro. Almost all of them have (or are in the process of negotiating) free trade agreements with the EU. Countries likely to experience the greatest impact from EMU include those of the Maghreb and Turkey. These countries already have integrated closely with Europe through trade, investment, and other ties. Turkey enjoys customs union status with the EU, and Morocco and Tunisia are in the process of implementing their own free trade agreements with the EU. Maghreb countries would not gain any immediate advantages in pegging their currencies to the euro. The Moroccan and Indonesian currencies effectively shadow the French franc and may be expected to continue this pattern.

Turkey is seeking full EU membership. It must attain full price stability and will need to improve its performance in this area by a wide margin. In 1998 the Turkish lira informally followed a basket consisting of U.S.$1 and DM1.5. A severe liquidity crisis in the Turkish banking sector required increased commitment by the IMF to restore confidence in November 2000. But financial problems reemerged in February 2001 and led to the abandonment of a preannounced crawling peg regime. The crisis showed signs of easing after the Turkish lira was floated, and a set of policy measures designed to reduce inflation and support economic growth was announced.

The oil-exporting economies of the Gulf region will experience minimal impact. In 1998 members of the Gulf Cooperation Council (GCC) were negotiating a free trade agreement with the EU. However, their exports are mainly petroleum and petrochemicals. These commodities are priced largely in U.S. dollars. These countries are expected to remain more impacted by fluctuations in the dollar exchange rate and to maintain close financial ties with the United States.

In the Levant and Egypt implications of EMU are blurred. These economies depend on Europe for imports, but much less as a market for exports. Egypt depends on exporting dollar-priced commodities (cotton and oil). Lebanon obtains most of its imports from Europe but directs its exports largely to the GCC countries. Lebanon needs to reconsider its exchange rate policy, and the arrival of the euro may trigger action in this area. Israel's economy is more integrated with Europe, but the currency (shekel) follows a basket that includes the French franc and deutsche mark.

Asia

The euro presents Asian nations with new options for international reserve and exchange rate management. Asian central banks can take advantage of the euro-denominated Treasury bill market to diversify reserve holdings. While U.S. Treasury bills have dominated the reserve holdings of Asian central banks, launch of the euro will establish a liquid market alternative. An ample supply of euro-denominated bills issued by European governments will provide Asian central banks with the opportunity to diversify their portfolios of reserves.

While the euro will be one of the world's largest economies, it is not likely to replace the dollar as Asia's currency anchor. The dollar will remain dominant due to the importance of U.S.-Asia trade and the use of the U.S. dollar in the past in financing intra-Asian trade. The dollar and the yen will continue to play dominant roles in Asian borrowing (table 5.13). Nevertheless, Asia's euro-denominated borrowing will grow as Eurozone banking institutions compete for lending and bond issuance mandates.

Table 5.13. Currency Composition of Asian External Debt, Year-End 1997

Currency	*Percentage*
U.S. dollar	46
EU currencies	33
Japanese yen	16
Other	11

Source: Union Bank of Switzerland, *EMU Monitor*, April 1998.

Africa

As the euro comes into operation, three currencies will dominate Africa's monetary affairs: the euro, the U.S. dollar, and the rand. The euro will play a dominant role in the exchange rates of western and central African countries, most especially those in the CFA franc zone. By contrast, in southern Africa, export concentration in commodities will extend the important role of both the rand and U.S. dollar in the region's floating exchange rate regime.

The CFA franc is shared by fourteen western and central African nations, and it is pegged to the French franc. The French Treasury guarantees full convertibility of the CFA franc into the French franc, with overdraft facility available to the two regional central banks of the CFA franc zone. In exchange for this convertibility, French government authorities have an influence on zone monetary policy. The CFA exchange rate arrangement has been a matter of French fiscal policy, not central bank policy. Fiscal policies within the EU will remain under national authority, subject to the 3 percent of GDP budget deficit criterion, according to the Stability Pact. If the euro becomes a strong currency, the CFA franc will follow. This can provide the CFA zone with monetary stability. Absence of exchange rate risk favors capital inflows, particularly foreign direct investment.

In 1998 the French minister of economics, finance, and industry, Dominique Strauss-Kahn, announced that CFA franc countries will stick to the stability of exchange rates between the CFA franc and successor currency to the French franc (euro). A new parity for the CFA franc against the euro was to be fixed in January 1999, but present stability arrangements are not to be affected by the transition to the euro. With launch of the euro in 1999, France and the other ten members of the single currency will transfer competence for the external exchange rate of the euro to the ECB.[53]

Although exchange rates throughout southern Africa float freely, they move closely in line with the South African rand and U.S. dollar. The rand is actively traded on major financial markets and is used for regional transactions. The rand is affected by (and reacts against) the U.S. dollar, due to South Africa's export orientation (precious metals and agro-alimentary products priced in dollars). This is true of other African nations that export goods to the United States and goods priced in U.S. dollars, including oil exports from Nigeria, cocoa and coffee exports from Ghana, and precious metals exports from the Democratic Republic of Congo. Introduction of the euro probably will not displace the role of the rand and U.S. dollar in these cases.

PAYMENTS SYSTEM AND CRISIS MANAGEMENT

Overview of ECB Form and Structure

The coming of the euro and parallel establishment of a central banking system raises many questions and issues related to the form and structure of the new central bank. The following discussion considers these questions, as well as how they appear to have been resolved. The key questions considered here relate to three areas:

- What type of payments system should be established to serve the twelve-country Eurozone?
- As bank restructuring and expanded cross-border lending raise the level of systematic risk in the banking sector, what responsibility, if any, will the new ECB have for such problems?
- In the event of a bank liquidity crisis, what resort to monetary policy (open market operations) and liquidity support to private financial institutions may be expected from the ECB?

TARGET Payments System

TARGET is a central feature of the EMU financial infrastructure. TARGET is geared to safeguard the developing European financial markets and institutions from systemic events. The TARGET system is made up of national real-time gross settlement (RTGS) payments systems linked through a communications network. Cross-border payments are settled through accounts at national central banks. The RTGS systems make the payment final as it occurs, and it avoids accumulating large outstanding positions. This avoids the problems built into older payments systems in which all transactions were settled at the end of the day or were netted. In these older systems large open positions exposed counterparties to sizable risks that could materialize due to settlement failures.

Since TARGET is used for large value transactions, which require intraday credit, institutions will have to maintain collateral. This is costly, and alternative netting systems will be used, such as euro clearing system (ECS) and euro access Frankfurt 2.[54]

The TARGET price structure is outlined in table 5.14. The cost is lower than anticipated before TARGET came into operation. However, the price structure clearly is high relative to competing netting systems (line 4, table 5.14). In July 1998, the ECB announced the conditions under which London-based institutions and other non-euro based institutions are permitted to use TARGET. London-based institutions might access TARGET through subsidiaries or branches located in the Eurozone, and they will need to maintain a pool of eligible euro assets if they wish to receive intraday credit.

It has been suggested that TARGET would be used to a greater degree if lower charges were levied on its use, such as the low fees applied in the case of U.S. Fedwire. This would bring most settlements in real time, minimizing the potential for problems should a European bank experience liquidity difficulties.

Table 5.14. TARGET Price System Compared with Alternatives

System and Alternatives	*Cost per Transaction*
TARGET System	
1. First 100 transactions a month	€1.75
2. Next 900 transactions a month	€1.00
3. Each subsequent transaction over 1,000 a month alternatives	€0.80
4. Announced price for ECS and EAF2	€0.25

Source: IMF, *International Capital Markets*, September 1998, 105.

Financial Stability

In the early years of the euro, the ECB will be challenged to protect and maintain financial stability and avert liquidity crises. Several types of problems could manifest themselves. TARGET could fail to prevent a systemic outbreak of risk. Or, as trans-European financial markets assert themselves, rapid growth of cross-border interbank (unsecured) lending could lead to higher levels of risk and even contagion. Finally, inefficient and loss-making banks and financial institutions may continue to function, adding to the overall risks in the financial system.

As the euro system develops, trans-European financial markets and institutions will displace national ones. This in turn will increase the need for more centralized financial surveillance over risk management and more focused crisis resolution. While we may consider the central bank the logical place to centralize several of these functions, this is not exactly how the allocation of responsibilities has been structured relative to the Eurozone and the working of the new monetary and financial system.

There is a complicated separation of responsibilities between the ECB, the national central banks, national financial supervisors, and finance ministers. These are set by the Maastricht treaty and EU legislation. The Maastricht treaty[55] and the ESCB statute[56] assign the ESCB functions related to prudential supervision and financial stability. Also, they give the ESCB explicit responsibility in promoting smooth functioning of the payments system.[57] A specific advisory function of the ECB relative to prudential supervision of credit institutions is contained in article 25(1) of the ESCB statute. The ECB must be consulted on draft legislation in areas pertaining to its competency.[58]

The Maastricht treaty stipulates that the ESCB shall contribute to the smooth conduct of policies pursued relating to prudential supervision of credit institutions and financial stability.[59] This aims at ensuring effective interaction between the ESCB and national supervisory authorities. In the event of a banking crisis with systemic implications, national supervisors will inform the ESCB on a case-by-case basis.

Finally, article 105(6) of the treaty contemplates the possibility that the EU Council of Ministers, acting unanimously, may assign specific tasks to the ECB in the area of prudential supervision. This avoids "premature" transfer of supervisory powers from national authorities to the ECB but leaves it unclear how a bank crisis would be handled. In the case of a trans-European bank, where supervisory responsibilities would be shared, some understandings need to be put in place for the ESCB or national central banks to implement. At present, there is no framework that is seen as appropriate. It is understood that on the eve of euro phase-in, some understanding had been reached concerning how to deal with cross-border crises and implementation of lender of last resort activities.[60]

The question of moral hazard arises in connection with possible injections of liquidity by central banks or monetary authorities. A preference would operate for use of open market operations rather than injections of liquidity directly to the ailing institution.[61] In the United States, the Federal Reserve enjoys discretion in deciding the kind of collateral to accept in such cases. By contrast, in Germany the Bundesbank has little discretion concerning acceptable collateral. German experience is important, since ESCB rules are similar to those governing the

Bundesbank. Like the ECB, the Bundesbank does not have explicit responsibility for safeguarding financial stability or operating as lender of last resort.

There is uncertainty about the scope of authority national central banks might have in providing liquidity to troubled banks in the case of an emergency. Apparently the ECB would be required to inject funds into the system, given a general liquidity crisis, or work with the appropriate national central bank to achieve the necessary intervention. In the case of a fast-developing crisis, there might be inadequate exchange of information between the ECB and national supervisors so that timely action would become possible.

No clear lender of last resort function has been assigned to the ESCB, and there is no fully developed framework for crisis management. It is feasible that a national central bank or national supervisory authority would provide liquidity support, with close following assistance provided by other national authorities, if required. On the eve of euro phase-in, lack of transparency concerning the above described problem areas leaves one to wonder concerning the possibility of a speedy and effective response to market crisis. Currently there appears to be reliance on a decentralized approach toward liquidity problems and financial instability. As the euro has its expected positive effect on capital market development, banks and other credit institutions will become more exposed to liquidity and instability problems. As this occurs, the ECB will find itself at the center of European financial markets without the information and policy tools required to assess creditworthiness or provide support to illiquid institutions.

ECB CURRENCY INTERVENTION

In chapter 3 we traced the movement of dollar/euro exchange rates since January 1999. Over the period January 1999 to October 2000 the euro depreciated almost 30 percent. In the shorter period October 2000 to January 2001 the euro gained in value against the dollar, approximately 16 percent. Then in the period January 2001 to July 2001 the euro fell in value by 10.5 percent. In the following discussion we trace the evolution of ECB policy toward intervention and a more aggressive stance in the foreign exchange market, to stabilize the euro.

Disappointment on Foreign Exchanges

ECB Currency Intervention Disappointment on Foreign Exchanges

Over the period January 1, 1999, to October 26, 2000, the euro depreciated against the U.S. dollar by approximately 30 percent (from $1.17 to $0.82). At the same time continental European politicians and central bankers spent much of this period trying to improve investor confidence in the euro, without much success.

The falling euro presented real problems for the European Central Bank in the form of fostering inflationary pressures (via higher prices of importables), impairing the market credibility of the ECB and the new currency, and causing the ECB to adopt a higher interest rate posture than it otherwise might have followed. In the case of raising interest rates on several occasions during the second half of 2000, the ECB walked a tightrope between dampening Eurozone economic growth, and enhancing the relative attractiveness of holding financial assets denominated in the single currency.

During the period July–September 2000 the ECB has been depicted as caught in an unwelcome trap. According to Luigi Buttiglione, the former ECB economist who joined Deutsche Bank's staff, "Usually the weakness of the euro has been linked to divergence between Europe and the U.S. in growth. . . . The danger is that this may be exacerbated by more aggressive action by the ECB, and we might enter a vicious circle of lower growth and a lower exchange rate."[62]

Three Phases of Intervention

Since August 2000 the euro has moved through several distinct phases, in regard to central bank intervention in support of the currency. These phases reflect a growing assertiveness on the part of the ECB, and recognition of an increasing need to realign the foreign exchange valuation of the currency.

An initial phase began at mid-August, when the ECB governing council agreed to sell some of the dollar interest income earned on foreign exchange assets (table 5.15). In mid-September the ECB sold $2.2 billion of such reserve assets for euros. The ECB asserted, "Intervention in the market was not the motive."[63] This action came on the heels of press pronouncements that there was not much the ECB could do about the weak euro, that rising interest rates do not help, and that a tighter monetary policy could choke off the Eurozones economic expansion.[64]

A second phase began shortly later, on September 22, 2000, when the ECB initiated a coordinated foreign exchange market intervention with the United States and other G-7 central banks (table 5.15). At that time the euro rose slightly to above U.S.$0.88. This intervention did not appear to provide lasting gains in the value of the euro, and by early October the currency had fallen to U.S.$0.86. Some analysts asserted that ECB intervention suffered from diminishing returns.

Table 5.15. Chronology of Intervention on Forex Market by the European Central Bank

Date	*Description*
August 14, 2000	ECB announced it would convert into euros $2.2 billion in interest income earned from its foreign exchange reserves. The ECB had decided to take this action at a policy-making meeting of the ECB governing council.
September 6, 2000	Gerhard Schröder stated that he is not concerned about the euro's weakness on the foreign exchange markets. The weakness had helped spur exports from Germany and other Eurozone nations.
September 22, 2000	ECB conducted coordinated currency intervention with the United States and G-7 nations to support the euro.
October 24, 2000	Larry Summers, U.S. Treasury secretary, reaffirmed the U.S. commitment to a "strong dollar" policy and said that intervention would not be an ongoing practice.
October 26, 2000	Euro hit its lowest value vis-à-vis the dollar, at $0.8225.
November 3–6, 2000	ECB intervened to support the euro unilaterally, without support from other central banks.

The ECB explained its rationale for this intervention as "owing to the shared concern about the implications of recent movements in the euro exchange rate for the world economy."[65] The timing of the September 22 intervention reflected growing conviction that the currency tide was turning. Part of the goal was to capitalize on the modest upturn in the euro and on the weakening performance of the U.S. economy. Analysts noted a systematic ratcheting up of aggressive policy by the ECB to support the euro. On November 4, 2000, this aggressiveness took the form of the ECB raising interest rates, and this was followed in the next eight weeks by six additional interest rate tightenings.

The third phase of intervention began on Friday, November 3, and ended on Monday, November 6. In this case the European Central Bank displayed a new aggressiveness, unilaterally intervening in the currency markets. This round of intervention brought a brief bounce in the euro's value. On Monday, November 6, ECB Vice President Christian Noyer stated in an interview with France's Radio Classique that the large outflows of capital from the Eurozone to the United States was coming to an end.[66] Estimates of the amounts utilized in the November intervention ranged from $500 million to $1 billion.

Have the ECB interventions on foreign exchange markets in support of the euro been successful? The answer depends on the ECB objective in engaging in intervention. Was it to stabilize the euro, or to reverse undervaluation?

On November 23 in testimony to the European Parliament, Mr. Duisenberg said: "I do want to underline that we do not have an exchange rate target, we have a price stability target, so interventions are not supposed to achieve a certain exchange rate . . . mainly used to break a prevailing thinking . . . that market participants have only a one way risk. . . . Now they have a two way risk."[67]

Financial markets have found it difficult, at times, to understand the actions of the ECB. Thomas Mayer, economist at Goldman Sachs in Frankfurt, differentiates the ECB approach to monetary controls from the "Greenspan model." Greenspan is a strong leader who steers market expectations in a skillful manner. By contrast, Duisenberg of the ECB is more like a moderator of the ECB eighteen-member governing council that sets refinancing rates every fortnight.[68]

Road to Recovery

By December 1, 2000, the euro seemed to have bottomed out in its valuation against the dollar. Slowing U.S. growth and a declining fortune for U.S. high-tech companies were accompanied by a rise in the euro valuation to U.S.$0.87.[69]

By early January 2001 the euro had pushed beyond the U.S.$0.95 level. From October 26, 2000, to early January 2001 the euro had appreciated 16 percent against the U.S. dollar. However, this level was still considered too low for the ECB. A continued strengthening of the euro would constitute a de facto tightening of monetary conditions in the Eurozone, giving the ECB flexibility to lower interest rates.

This explains why Laurent Fabius, French finance minister, had stated that there was a strong margin for appreciation of the euro, at least to a parity against the dollar and even beyond.[70]

ECB MONETARY POLICY IN 2001

In mid-2001, the monetary policy of the European Central Bank was vacillating and largely ineffectual. The ECB was hobbled by its goal of keeping the twelve-nation Eurozone's inflation at less than 2 percent per annum with a consensus policy agreed on by the members of the ECB.[71]

In March 2001, Jean Claude Trichet, president of the Bank of France and a governor of the European Central Bank, first suggested a rate cut and then reversed himself, falling in line with the ECB chairman, Wim Duisenberg. But on May 10, the bank appeared to reverse course again.[72] Just as Duisenberg had persuaded market analysts that the bank would not relax rates, he announced a quarter point cut in the benchmark short-term interest rate, to 4.5 percent.

Part of this apparent uncertainty in monetary policy merely reflects the early stage of development of the merging Eurozone economies. During this early stage, it would be unreasonable to expect that ECB monetary policy would be appropriate for all twelve countries. Because of the differences in the twelve countries, *any* monetary policy would produce relatively obvious winners and losers. If the European Union is successful, though, over time, the differences in the economies will begin to blur. When the Eurozone economies become more similar this will make the crafting of an effective consensus Eurozone monetary policy much easier. Still though, the recent vacillations in ECB monetary policy point up interesting issues and problems in the management of the ECB.

A Bias in Favor of Small Countries

The eighteen-member board of governors of the ECB includes the presidents of all twelve national central banks, and each of these members has a vote on zone monetary policy. This one vote per country system leaves ECB monetary policy biased against the larger countries like Germany, France, and Spain, but in favor of the smaller countries like Ireland and the Netherlands.

These smaller countries have faster growth rates and more inflation than the larger countries. The smaller countries are not much worried about an economic slowdown. The larger countries, such as Germany, have slower growth and lower rates of inflation. But Germany is 150 times larger than Luxembourg. Thus the bias in favor of smaller countries has made for a monetary policy in favor of fighting inflation that risks Eurozone-wide deflation and higher unemployment by unduly deflating the large economies of Germany, France, and Spain (table 5.16).

The ECB's primary goal is still price stabilization, but its goal of keeping Eurozone inflation below 2 percent increasingly looks like an unfortunately rigid

Table 5.16. Eurozone Inflation and Unemployment in June 2001 (%)

Country	*Inflation Rate*	*Unemployment*
Netherlands	5.4	2.0
Ireland	4.1	n.a.
Germany	3.6	7.7 .
Average	3.3	8.1
France	2.5	8.5
Spain	n.a.	13.2

Source: Edmund L. Andrews, "A Central Bank in All Directions," *New York Times*, June 27, 2001, C1, C15.

stance. An inflation rate in the Eurozone of less than 2 percent would mean that large countries like Germany would have an inflation rate of only 1 percent. Such very low inflation rates are synonymous with deflation in the large German economy and thus in the Eurozone as well.

A further technical problem with ECB monetary policy is that it is based on statistically inaccurate estimates of the Eurozone money supply. The ECB's own research has shown that their measures of European monetary aggregates are inaccurate. This situation argues that the ECB, like the Fed, should focus its monetary policy on interest rate targets. But in mid-2001 the ECB continued to use its inaccurate monetary targets.

Eurozone Dissonance with U.S. Monetary Policy

The U.S. "Inventory Adjustment"

In late 2000 and the first half of 2001, the Fed cut interest rates six times to stimulate the flagging U.S. economy. The sixth U.S. rate cut in as many months came on June 27, 2001, when the Fed cut the federal funds rate a quarter of a point, down to 3.75 percent.[73] This cut indicated the beginning of a tentative shift in Fed policy from a highly stimulatory policy to one of more restraint. The shift to more restrained monetary stimulation came despite the fact that a vicious cycle of weaker earnings and corporate cutbacks in employment and capital spending continued. The forecasters expected that corporate earnings would decline 15 percent by the end of the year. In the IT sector, however, earnings were often down by as much as 50 percent. Because rate cuts generally take from six to nine months to work their way into the U.S. economy, the Fed expected that their six rate cuts would take U.S. first quarter growth rate of 1.3 percent back up to 3 percent by year's end.

Although the U.S. slowdown never technically qualified as a recession, this "inventory adjustment" involved a sharp drop in production that began in the fall of 2000. The slowdown was heralded by Intel's announcement of slackening profits because of softening exports to the Eurozone.[74] Slackening U.S. exports to the zone were followed by the realization that the global telecommunications sector had seriously overinvested. This meant that although the U.S. technology sector had led the U.S. economy sharply down toward recession, it would probably not be able to lead the economy back to prosperity.

This shift in economic fortunes was particularly swift because it was led by a downturn in the information technology (IT) sector. This sector had previously been responsible for a 47 percent increase in U.S. productivity, up from 1.35 percent in 1973–1995 to 2.67 percent from 1995 to 2000.[75] Because of this boost from IT, total U.S. factor productivity grew at an annual rate of

1.26 percent for 1995–1998, as compared to a rate of 0.40 percent for 1973–1995—a productivity increase of 68 percent.

The productivity boost was shared by and sharply limited to the industrial sectors that either produced or used the new information technology. The increase was caused by massive investment in IT equipment, especially in the twenty-six industries using this equipment. In 1999, U.S. firms invested $373 billion in IT assets that included computer hardware, computer software, and telecommunications equipment. This investment accounted for more than 30 percent of all nonresidential fixed investment. In 1989–1999, the stock of IT capital grew at an annual rate of 22.4 percent, far faster than the 2.5 percent rate for private fixed assets. As a result, the U.S. stock of IT assets has grown to nearly 9 percent of all business fixed capital in 1999.

When the U.S. IT sector turned down, it did so sharply, and the magnitude of the downturn was greater than expected.[76] The "Internet recession" turned the U.S. bull market into a bear. With IT companies no longer able to offer lucrative initial public offerings (IPOs), the U.S. venture capital markets that had been so successful in financing the large number of small, innovative IT companies collapsed for lack of adequate incentives to compensate their risk.[77]

Dissonant ECB Monetary Policy

The U.S. "inventory adjustment" was disconcerting because it threatened to spread to the global economy through U.S. trade adjustments. While the Fed made six consecutive interest rate cuts, the ECB vacillated between policies of inflationary restraint and those of faint stimulation. From the U.S. point of view these ECB policies were risky. By the first quarter of 2001, the Fed knew that although the U.S. IT sector could lead the economy toward recession, it would not lead it out of recession. Overinvestment in the telecommunications industry was so great, however, that it could not be adjusted in the short term.

Michael Mandel, an editor at *Newsweek,* proposed a popular scenario for the U.S. downturn late in 2000. According to Mandel, the collapse of the U.S. IT sector would cause a slackening in investment in, sales of, and use of information technology. The economy would simultaneously suffer decreasing productivity, price inflation, and a Fed contraction. Christopher Farrell[78] faulted Mandel's dark predictions of an Internet depression[79] by pointing out that the Fed did not continue to raise rates, but rather began to cut them to stimulate the economy. When the rate of economic growth of U.S. GDP fell to 1.1 percent in the fourth quarter of 2000 (virtually zero),[80] the Fed quit raising rates. When the University of Michigan's Survey Research Center's index of consumer confidence plunged in early February for the fourth consecutive month (declining 6.9 points to bring the index to 87.8, about where it was at the start of the last recession, in July 1990),[81] the Fed cut interest rates.

In the Eurozone, however, the ECB continued to raise rates, fight inflation, and support the euro. On October 5, 2000, the ECB raised interest rates by a quarter of a point.[82] The ECB did not join the rest of the world in cutting interest rates until May 11, 2001.[83]

The View from the Eurozone

From the ECB's point of view, there was little reason to mimic the Fed's stimulatory monetary policy:[84]

- The growth of Eurozone economies was slackening more slowly than the U.S. economy.
- The ECB's only strong mandate was to keep Eurozone inflation below 2 percent, although in the United States the Fed was equally concerned about employment and economic growth.
- With its recent productivity increases, the Fed thought that the United States could sustain 4 percent growth rates without encouraging inflation. In the Eurozone, however, with a slower growth rate, the ECB thought that European economies could not grow much more than 2.5 percent in the long run.
- A cut in Eurozone interest rates would also have encouraged an outflow of hot money at a time when the euro was still languishing at a 15 percent discount to the dollar. This fact may have encouraged the ECB to trade off the short-term protection of the euro for the longer-term health of Eurozone economies.

When the stage of development of the European Union is taken into account, along with the different political and economic goals in the Eurozone and the United States, the joint monetary policies of the ECB and the Fed seem reasonable enough, but often risky and not yet optimal.

NOTES

1. Jonathan A. C. Wise, "Variable Geometry and the European Central Bank: How the ECB Can Assert Itself against Attack from Member States with Derogations," *Boston College International and Comparative Law Review* 20, no. 2 (1997): 407.
2. "EU Takes First Steps toward Single Currency," *Wall Street Journal*, May 5, 1998, A17.
3. T. Kanam and B. Coleman, "Europe's Central Bank Draws Warm Welcome," *Wall Street Journal*, May 5, 1998, A6.
4. Samer Iskander, "Probe into French Central Bank Chief May Hit Plan for Him to Head ECB," *Financial Times*, April 29, 2000, 24.
5. European Central Bank, *Annual Report 1999* (Frankfurt, 2000), 134–137.

6. "Enter the Euro," *Economist*, May 9, 1998, 20.

7. Andrew Fisher, "Germans Pay Their Respects to the DMark," *Financial Times*, June 20, 1998, 2.

8. Wolfgang Münchau, "ECB Squares Up to Finance Ministers," *Financial Times*, July 10, 1998, 2.

9. C. Enoch, P. Hilbers, and A. Kovanen, "Monetary Operations in the European Economic and Monetary Union," *Finance and Development*, June 1998, 38–40.

10. ECB, *Annual Report 1999*, 48.

11. ECB, *Annual Report 1999*, 48–49.

12. ECB, *Annual Report 1999*, 49.

13. ECB, *Annual Report 1999*, 53.

14. Robert Graham, "Bank of France Claims a Continuing Role in the Eurozone," *Financial Times*, May 29, 2000, 2.

15. ECB, *Monthly Bulletin*, January 2000, 51.

16. G. T. Sims, "Finance Ministers Are Expected to Issue Statement Supporting Euro," *Wall Street Journal Europe*, May 8, 2000, 2.

17. Sims, "Finance Ministers Are Expected to Issue Statement Supporting Euro," 2.

18. G. T. Sims, "Will European Central Bank Step In to Support the Euro?" *Wall Street Journal Europe*, May 15, 2000, 15.

19. Robert L. Bartley, "The Mystery of the Vanishing Euro," *Wall Street Journal Europe*, May 15, 2000, 12.

20. ECB, *Monthly Bulletin*, January 2000, 56.

21. Lea Paterson, "Euro Hits New Lows despite ECB Rate Rise," *The Times* (London), April 28, 1000, 27.

22. Tony Barber, "ECB Seen as Powerless to Halt Euro's Decline," *Financial Times*, April 27, 2000, 3.

23. P. Norman and C. Adams, "Pressure Grows for Intervention to Halt Ailing Euro's Slide," *Financial Times*, May 8, 2000, 1.

24. John Schmid, "ECB Reassures Public on Euro," *International Herald Tribune*, May 6, 2000, 1, 10. Also T. Major and C. Swann, "ECB Chief Appeals to Public in Bid to Boost Support for Euro," *Financial Times*, May 6, 2000, 24.

25. G. T. Sims, "ECB Raises Growth Forecast amid Campaign to Boost Euro," *Wall Street Journal Europe*, May 16, 2000, 2.

26. J. Barrett, "Traders to Watch for Signs of Support for the Ailing Euro by Central Bankers," *Wall Street Journal*, May 22, 2000, C27.

27. C. Adams and A. Beattie, "Talk of ECB Intervention Gives Big Boost to euro against Dollar," *Financial Times*, May 27, 2000, 24.

28. Tony Barber, "Cheers in Eurozone as Economic Growth Hits Home," *Financial Times*, June 7, 2000, 2.

29. Tony Barber, "ECB Surprises with Half-Point Rate Rise," *Financial Times*, June 9, 2000, 1.

30. Tony Barber, "ECB Switches to Variable Rate Tenders," *Financial Times*, June 9, 2000, 2.

31. Kenneth Gooding, "ECB Seen as Active Market Participant," *Financial Times*, June 23, 1998, 30.

32. ECB, *Annual Report 1999*, 56–57.

33. ECB, *Monthly Bulletin*, November 1999, 41–51.

34. ECB, *Monthly Bulletin*, November 1999, 42. A unique feature of TARGET services is that its euro payments are available throughout the EU, including countries not participating in the single currency.

35. Wolfgang Münchau, "Teething Troubles in Store," *Financial Times*, June 1, 1998, 13.

36. Wolfgang Münchau, "Bank Must Define Its Target," *Financial Times*, June 2, 1998, 3.

37. W. Münchau and G. Graham, "ECB Decision on Reserves Attacked," *Financial Times*, July 9, 1998, 1.

38. The Luxembourg central bank was created recently to provide a working central bank institution for this implementation. Wolfgang Münchau, "Complex Relations Make Rows Certain," *Financial Times*, August 4, 1998, 3.

39. Wolfgang Münchau, "Encouraging Start but Problems Loom," *Financial Times*, August 4, 1998, 3.

40. ECB, *Annual Report 1999*, 87.

41. Martin Wolf, "Euro's World Test," *Financial Times*, July 7, 1998, 16.

42. Wolf, "Euro's World Test," 16.

43. Robert A. Mundell, "The International Impact of the Euro and Its Implications for the Transition Countries" (paper presented at the Dubrovnik conference on Transnational Economies, June 1998).

44. It has been speculated that large reserve holders such as China might wish to hold a large part of their reserves in euros. James Harding and James Kynge, "China May Use Euro in Reserves," *Financial Times*, May 6, 1998, 4.

45. George S. Tavlas, "The International Use of Currencies: The US Dollar and the Euro," *Finance and Development*, June 1998, 48.

46. We should remember that the global total here is 200 percent—there are two sides of each transaction. The Bank for International Settlements, *Central Bank Survey of Foreign Exchange and Derivatives Market Activity* (Basel, 1996).

47. R. Portes and H. Rey, "The Emergence of the Euro as an International Currency," Working Paper 6424 (Cambridge, Mass.: NBER, 1998), 10–14.

48. A. Prati and G. Schinasi, "European Monetary Union and International Capital Markets, Structural Implementation and Risks," IMF Working Paper, WP/97/62, 1997.

49. Portes and Rey, "Emergence," 15.

50. Portes and Rey, "Emergence," 22–37.

51. Union Bank of Switzerland, *EMU Monitor*, April 1998, 2.

52. UBS, *EMU Monitor*, 6.

53. Samir Iskander, "CFA Franc to Be Tied to Euro, Says Brussels," *Financial Times*, July 2, 1998, 9.

54. Euro Clearing System is the privately owned clearing system of the European Bankers Association. Euro Access Frankfurt 2 is system based in Germany allowing membership outside the country.

55. Article 105 (4, 5, 6).

56. Article 25 (1).

57. Statute article 22; Treaty article 105 (2).

58. Treaty article 105 (4). Also the ECB must be consulted on rules regarding financial institutions as they may influence the stability of financial institutions and markets.

59. Treaty article 105 (5).

60. International Monetary Fund, *International Capital Markets*, Washington, D.C., September 1998, 106.

61. M. Goodfriend and R. G. King, "Financial Deregulation, Monetary Policy, and Central Banking," *Economic Review*, Federal Reserve Bank of Richmond, May–June 1988, 3–22.

62. Ed Crooks and C. Swann, "ECB Takes the Plunge," *Financial Times*, August 31, 2000, 10.

63. Tony Barber, "ECB Ready to Support the Euro," *Financial Times*, September 15, 2000, 1.

64. "The Currency of Disappointment," *Financial Times*, August 26, 2000, 6.

65. European Central Bank, *Monthly Bulletin*, October 2000, 31.

66. "European Central Bank Intervenes Again," *Wall Street Journal*, November 7, 2000, C1.

67. Tony Barber, "Euro-Zone Interest Rates Unchanged," *Financial Times*, January 5, 2001, 2.

68. "The European Central Bank: The Terrible Twos Begin," *Economist*, January 6, 2001, 63–65.

69. C. Swann and A. Hill, "Slowdown Ends Dollar's Bull Run," *Financial Times*, December 1, 2000, 1.

70. Tony Barber, "Euro-Zone Interest Rates Unchanged," *Financial Times*, January 5, 2001, 20.

71. Edmund L. Andrews, "A Central Bank in All Directions," *New York Times*, June 27, 2001, C1, C15.

72. Edmund L. Andrews, "To the Thinnest of Applause, Europeans Cut Interest Rates," *New York Times*, May 11, 2001, C1, C4.

73. Greg Ip, "Vicious Cycle: Despite Rate Cuts, Mood in Boardrooms Is Darkening Further," *Wall Street Journal*, June 28, 2001, A1, A10.

74. Lawrence M. Fisher, "Intel Expects Its Revenue to Be Below Expectations," *New York Times*, September 22, 2000, C1, C2; and Jacob M. Schlesinger, Greg Ip, Yochi J. Dreazen, and David Wessel, "Power Veering: Policy Makers Face Confusing Crosswinds in Piloting Economy," *New York Times*, September 25, 2000, A1, A12.

75. Kevin J. Stiroh, "Information Technology and the U.S. Productivity Revival: What Do the Industry Data Say?" *Federal Reserve Bank of New York*, January 24, 2001, 1–45.

76. Ip, "Vicious Cycle," A10.

77. Michael J. Mandel, "The Next Downturn," *Business Week*, October 9, 2000, 173–176.

78. Christopher Farrell, "The Case for Optimism," *Business Week*, December 18, 2000, 54–57.

79. Michael J. Mandel, *The Coming Internet Depression* (New York: McGraw-Hill, 2000).

80. "U.S. Lowers Growth Rate in 4th Quarter," *New York Times*, February 1, 2001, C1, C11.

81. Louis Uchetelle, "Consumer Confidence Is Wild Card in the Nation's Economy," *New York Times*, February 17, 2001, C1, C14.

82. "ECB Raises Key Interest Rates by a Quarter Percentage Point," *Interactive Wall Street Journal*, October 5, 2000.

83. Edmund L. Andrews, "To the Thinnest of Applause, Europeans Cut Interest Rates," *New York Times*, May 11, 2001, C1, C4.

84. Edmund L. Andrews, "Asia Hails Fed Rate Cut, but Europe Snubs It," *New York Times*, April 20, 2001, W1.

Chapter Six

Capital Markets in the Eurozone

STRUCTURAL CHANGES IN EUROPEAN MARKETS

On January 1, 1999, with the commencement of stage 3 of European monetary union (EMU), the world's second largest capital market came into existence. Between 1996 and 1998 structural change was accelerating in European financial markets. This chapter considers the key trends in Europe, evaluates them, and analyzes the new dynamics of stock exchanges and their related market sectors.

On January 1, 1999, the irreversible fixing of exchange rates in Euroland introduced the following major changes for European capital markets:

- Currency risks between and among the E-11 countries were ended. Small differences in inflation between E-11 countries almost disappeared.
- A single currency area provides investors access to a wider range of securities. The currency areas are now more homogeneous in their susceptibility to exchange rate risk.
- The single currency eliminated fundamental distinguishing criteria between so-called domestic and foreign financial products. For German investors, this means abolition of the deutsche mark and the disappearance of a well-recognized seal of quality for German financial products.[1]
- The new, level corporate playing field induced unprecedented corporate restructuring and related Internet and technology stock volatility. Cross-border and hostile bids became part of the landscape.

Implications of Structural Change

These broad structural changes in European capital markets carry important implications. First, changing competition among investors, issuers, and financial intermediaries throughout Europe influence how capital is mobilized, the pace of financial innovations, the functioning of market systems, and the development of financial infrastructure. Second, the terms and conditions at which funds are provided in the bond and equity markets have improved. Spreads have narrowed through competition. Third, more attractive investment returns draw larger savings into investment channels, increasing economic growth in the Eurozone.

Institutional investors benefit handsomely from the dynamics of these changes. Institutional investors are now applying more professional techniques in making investment asset allocations, as well as in clearing/settling/inventorying their transaction and asset holdings. These professional groups are increasing the scope of their operations across European capital market sectors.

The French have been carrying out a rapid transformation of their economy in preparation for EMU. In 1986 a right-leaning government was elected, and political leaders quickly decided to reverse the nationalization process begun in 1981 when François Mitterand took power. Paribas, the French investment bank, was one of the first to be privatized, with industrial giants like Rhone-Poulenc, Saint-Gobain, and Alcatel quickly following. Financial companies such as Banque Nationale de Paris, Société Generale, and Union des Assurances de Paris (now merged with AXA) also became privatized. In 1999 several of these banks became involved in a three-way merger battle, discussed later in this chapter. This privatization program aimed at:

- Making French companies more efficient and competitive in the international market place
- Controlling the government budget deficit
- Developing the capital market via an expansion of shares listed and traded on the Paris Bourse

According to Eric Chaney, senior economist for Morgan Stanley Dean Witter in Paris, "European Monetary Union will dramatically increase competition within Euroland, as the government will probably have to accelerate privatizing companies where the state still has a stake."[2]

The French equity markets are modernizing rapidly. In March 1996 the Paris Bourse launched a special market for young high-growth companies called the Nouveau Marche. Several foreign companies are listed, including Stelax (UK), Astra (Israel), and Oxis International (U.S.). The Nouveau Marche is open to foreign brokers as well as foreign companies. The main idea, according to Jacques Nouvil, London representative of the Paris Bourse, was to create a network of cooperating exchanges. Four such new markets were created in Frankfurt, Brussels, and Amsterdam, as well as Paris. This allows companies to tap a larger investment pool by trading their shares through brokers registered with the four exchanges.[3]

Capital Market Comparisons

In the final run-up to EMU, German, French, and other European capital markets grew vigorously, measured by the volume of securities outstanding. The thirteen European countries included in table 6.1 experienced a median 9 percent growth in their bond markets and a 14 percent growth in their share markets. Among the E-11, Germany ranks first in bonds and shares outstanding, with a bond market value of DM3 trillion and a share market value of nearly DM1.5 trillion (table 6.1). The Italian, French, Belgian, and Spanish bond markets represent the four next rankings on the debt side. The French, Dutch, Italian, and Spanish share markets represent the four next rankings on the equity side.

As a percentage of gross domestic product (GDP), the European and especially the E-11 compare well with the U.S., the UK, and Japanese bond markets. The weighted average for the E-11 countries is 66 percent of GDP.

Table 6.1. International Comparison of Bond and Share Market Capitalization

	Bond Market			*Share Market*		
Country/ Group of Countries	*In DM Billions*	*As % of GDP*	*Annual Growth in the 1990s %*	*In DM Billions*	*As % of GDP*	*Annual Growth in the 1990s %*
Austria	242	53	9	66	15	6
Belgium	524	121	6	245	57	8
Denmark	292	88	5	168	51	12
Finland	92	37	13	132	54	16
France	1,191	42	7	1,209	42	9
Germany	3,025	81	12	1,479	39	11
Ireland	44	32	4	86	65	45
Italy	2,035	87	13	618	27	14
Netherlands	368	48	7	340	111	16
Portugal	82	39	13	70	33	61
Spain	390	41	19	520	54	16
Sweden	393	95	8	474	115	14
UK	827	35	10	3,707	155	12
EU-11	7,993	66		5,327	44	
Japan	6,998	90	6	3,737	48	-10
U.S.	17,264	117	8	19,028	129	18

Source: Duetsche Bundesbank, *Monthly Report,* April 1998.

On the equity side, the E-11 fall further below the United States and the UK, with the share market at 44 percent of GDP.

Changes in Debt Issuance and Investor Role

Germany was one of the government issuers of debt to introduce changes in financing in preparation for the single currency. It introduced regular auctions of five-year federal bonds (Bobls) and reopened issues of federal bonds (Bunds) and Bobls. A two-year Treasury note (Schatze) was introduced. Also, the government initiated regular issues of thirty-year Bunds and introduced the possibility of bond stripping. Finally, introduction of a futures contract on the two-year Schatze by the German Financial Futures Exchange (DTB) completed this set of innovations. Other changes in 1998 include the abolition of the Federal Bond Consortium, so that federal securities are now issued by auction through the so-called Bund Issues Auction Group. The federal government redenominated its old debt into euros on January 1, 1999. From that date, new issues were denominated in the single currency.

Since 1995 credit institutions have made their issues more liquid and more attractive to institutional investors. The jumbo Pfandbriefe are issued in amounts no less than DM1 billion. No fewer than three banks are required to quote buying and selling prices to ensure tradability. Related to this, communal bonds in Germany *(öffentliche Pfandbriefe)* are offered more frequently (158 issues in 1997) and in larger volumes.

While less pronounced, direct effects of EMU on share market issuance are observable, due to the basic characteristics of such markets. Enterprise-specific and country-specific factors generally are more important in the share market, and it is difficult to increase liquidity through the issuance of more homogeneous securities. Share markets tend to be viewed in a horizontal rather than a vertical way by investors. That means that pan-European industry sectors are becoming the focus, replacing the former attention given to top-down country investment allocations.

Important new issuing techniques have become widely applied in the German capital market and are spreading to other country markets. These techniques include the fixed price reoffer method for bonds, in which the issuer and syndicate banks agree on a minimum price that must be honored for a defined period in reselling underwritten tranches. For shares, the bookbuilding method has become more widely used. Bookbuilding is a method of determining the issue price of shares that takes into account the pricing suggestions of potential investors prior to the actual pl acement, in order to avoid the danger of mispricing. This is very different from the fixed price method that was previously used for share issuance.

International integration of the German and other European securities markets has proceeded rapidly. For example, in 1997 German investors purchased bonds issued by nonresidents worth DM77 billion, more than three times the 1996 amount. Conversely, purchases by foreign investors in the German bond market at DM122 billion attained the second highest level since 1993.

The arrival of EMU is associated with the new currency pattern in the foreign currency bonds marketed in Germany in 1997. Over DM26 billion of these instruments were lira-denominated. The prospects of the convergence of the related price gains in the Italian bond market exerted a major influence on investor decisions in this market. It is not yet certain whether this "convergence trade" presages a sustained, major diversification within the euro area. Currency-related preferences can no longer be a factor in choosing domestic financial instruments, but the risk profile of bonds is converging, a fact that argues against international diversification.

In the share market there also are indications of a trend toward international diversification. In 1997 German residents purchased DM52 billion of foreign shares while nonresidents purchased DM27 billion of German domestic equities. These are record levels of share purchases. Global orientation of investment strategies and global fund movements related to the coming of EMU both played a role in increasing the purchase of shares.

Changes in Market Infrastructure

Technical improvements in the market infrastructure are taking place in Europe, making stock exchange trading faster and more flexible. Since 1997 spot trading of securities has been given a new electronic basis. The new electronic trading system, Xetra, speeds up trading through the automatic matching of orders. Other innovations, already referred to, are the "new markets," such as Nouveau Marche in Paris and Neuer Markt in Frankfurt.

On the legal front, private market initiatives are supported by the Second and Third Financial Market Promotion Acts. The centerpiece of the Second Financial Market Promotion Act in 1994 was the reorganization of the securities supervision system and the methods for monitoring of trading activities.

STRUCTURAL CHANGE AND CAPITAL MARKET EFFICIENCY

With the onset of the euro, increased competition is promoting financial market efficiency. Market players are introducing broader product ranges, and competition is driving transactions costs to lower levels (e.g., electronic trading platforms discussed below). Market players are also providing more liquid financial instruments. All of this adds up to a gain in efficiency, since financial transactions can now be undertaken with less friction.

Efficiency an Important Capital Market Evaluator

Conflicts can occur between a macro- versus microeconomic capital market efficiency. Financial innovations can also lock up economic resources that might otherwise be used more productively (table 6.2). Over time the innovations must more than recover any short-term losses caused by their absorption in the innovation processes. In the European capital market, however, structural change seems to be exerting a positive effect on real economic trends.

New financial instruments assist in providing more complete capital markets. An entire body of literature supports this view with respect to the role of financial innovations in the United States. In the recent past, an important step in this direction was the creation of efficient forward and futures markets, making it possible to hedge microeconomic risk cheaply and flexibly. The heightened competition developing between the various stock exchanges and derivatives markets (described below) attests to this. Also, the application of new index products in Euroland indicates favorable trends relative to all definitions of efficiency, but most important are these innovations relative to information efficiency. As discussed below, the introduction of new capital

Table 6.2. Definitions of Financial Market Efficiency

Allocative efficiency: An economy is allocation efficient if it is not possible through further exchange operations to increase the utility of one economic agent without simultaneously reducing the utility of another individual. This Pareto optimality is enhanced when the financial markets act as a lubricant for frictionless exchange of goods.

Market completeness: Markets exist to permit agents to hedge against various economic risks via contracts. When such hedging is available, market structure is considered complete. Complete financial markets exist when all possible states of nature can be covered by combinations of hedges made with securities that possess independent features.

Transaction cost efficiency: Costs of financial market transactions must be as low as possible. Cost is very broadly defined, embracing all outlays of money, time, and effort involved in planning, executing, and settling a financial market transaction. Transaction costs drive a wedge between a borrower's financing costs and the return that lenders receive after deducting all charges, taxes, and other costs.

Information efficiency: Presupposes that all relevant information is reflected immediately, completely, and correctly on the price of a traded financial instrument. Correctly means that participants do not commit any systematic expectation errors in valuing the asset.

markets indexing for equities and debt in the Eurozone fills a large gap in information.

Until the euro, the European capital market was incomplete in regard to the marketability of credit risk. This was demonstrated by the relatively limited development of the corporate bond market. For example, in Germany the volume of corporate bonds in circulation early in 1998 was 0.1 percent of GDP. According to table 6.3, Germany has ranked behind other European Union (EU) countries in the development of a corporate bond market. This situation has changed since 1999, and the elimination of exchange rate risk has put the spotlight on credit risk for purposes of comparing European bond issues.

Table 6.3. Volume of Corporate Bonds Outstanding on Eve of Euro

Country	*Volume of Corporate Bonds Outstanding (DM billions)*
United States	3,025
Japan	766
France	55
Belgium	27
Germany	4
OECD countries	4,325
EU countries	149

Source: Deutsche Bundesbank, *Monthly Report,* April 1998, 65.

STRUCTURAL CHANGE AND CAPITAL MARKET EFFICIENCY

Index Products and Information Efficiency

The capital markets in the United States lead the world in developing market indexes that inform investors about market trends and changes in valuation. The introduction of the euro created a capital market base potentially as large as that in the United States. During the first year of single currency, European creators of capital market indexes responded quickly to the growing need for more complete information.

Capital market indexes cover three broad areas—equities, bonds, and derivatives. In 1999 new index products were introduced in all three areas (table 6.4). Stock and derivatives exchanges, investment banks, and commercial providers such as FTSE and Dow Jones sponsored these products.

These new equity indexes have been developed in response to the dynamic changes following the euro. Sector-based (rather than country-based) analysis allows comparison of trends and valuation changes on a cross-border basis (table 6.4). FTSE and Dow Jones indexes are constructed to facilitate a

Table 6.4. Securities Indices in Euroland

Security Type	*Name and Coverage*	*Sponsor*	*Description or Purpose*
Equities	Neuer Markt 50, stock blue chip index	Deutsche Börse AG	Aimed at institutional investors; index weights related to market cap and liquidity. No stock weight over 10 percent.
	Six new indexes, All Share, Small Cap, Mid Cap, others	Amsterdam Exchanges	For institutional investors on Amsterdam Exchanges, weighted by market cap.
	FTSE EStars "Magic 29"	Financial Times Stock Exchange International	Includes 29 stocks, DaimlerChrysler, Deutsche Bank, Unilever, Elf Aquitaine, largest and most liquid shares of Eurozone.
Bonds	Family of pan-Eurozone bond indexes	Deutsche Börse AG	For institutional and individual investors. Family of pan-European government bond indexes. Covers maturities of 1–10 years and longer. Basis for futures and options contracts on exchanges.
	CECE Bond Indexes	Wiener Börse	Covers central and eastern European government bond markets in Poland, Czech Republic, and Hungary. Separate price and total return indexes in euros and local currency.
	European Credit Indexes	Warburg Dillon Read	Designed for post-euro market; tracks highly liquid, large bonds in institutional market. Bonds must have minimum of €1.5 billion outstanding.
Derivatives	Futures and options contracts based on FTSE Eurobond 100, MSCI Euro, and MSCI Pan-euro indexes	LIFFE	Covers top 100 companies in Eurozone, FTSE Eurotop 300, and FTSE Eurotop 300 ex UK.

bottom-up approach to stock analysis. Companies in the Eurotop 300 and FTSE indexes are grouped into sectors and subsectors. In 2001 more changes were made in stock index weights. Morgan Stanley Capital International (MSCI), the largest indexing company, revamped its MSCI equity indexes. Two changes were made. First, MSCI moved to a free float weighting rather than simple market capitalization weighting. Free float considers the percentage of shares available to investors in the marketplace, rather than all shares issued and outstanding. Large stakeholdings not traded are deducted from total shares outstanding to arrive at the amount of free float. Second, the coverage of each country will rise from 60 percent of market capitalization to 85 percent of free float. MSCI follows similar initiatives by index providers Dow Jones and FTSE, the latter owned by *Financial Times* and London Stock Exchange.[4]

New bond indexes are needed because of the redenomination of newly issued bonds in euros. A benchmark euro-denominated yield curve is in the making, based on sovereign issues by several countries (including France, Germany, and Italy). The Deutsche Börse family of bond indexes will focus on individual European government bond markets as well as pan-European and the Eurozone indexes. The Deutsche Börse indexes are unique in that they are (1) pan-European and (2) exchange traded. At year-end 1998 the market for domestic and international fixed income securities denominated in euros equaled $6.6 trillion, compared with $13.1 trillion for U.S. dollar–denominated securities.[5]

With the introduction of equity and bond indexes, it is natural to follow with futures and options contracts on these products. The London International Financial Futures and Options Exchange (LIFFE) was quick to do so. In May 1999 the LIFFE and Amsterdam exchanges jointly launched futures and options contracts based on the FTSE Eurotop 100 companies, the FTSE Eurotop 300, and the FTSE Eurotop 300 ex UK. At the same time, futures and options on the MSCI Euro and MSCI Pan-euro Indexes were first-listed by the LIFFE.

In the future we can expect further development of European capital market indexes. For example, as the mutual fund industry expands across the Eurozone, exchange traded funds (ETFs) are likely to become accepted and utilized as a means of achieving efficient portfolio diversification. ETFs provide a new type of stock exchange tradable security that retains many attributes of a mutual fund while providing ready liquidity in a market context. The first ETF, the Standard & Poor's Depository Receipt (SPDR), was introduced on the American Stock Exchange in 1996. As of mid-1999, the fund held $10 billion in assets. Closely related are eleven other S&P index funds, seventeen World Equity Benchmark Shares (WEBS), based on the Morgan Stanley Capital International

(MSCI)[6] country indices, and the Diamond, based on the Dow Jones Industrial Average.[7] It is likely that ETFs will increase in number for investors in Europe as well as North America.

Credit Ratings

The increased use of credit ratings in the Eurozone is rapidly improving information efficiency. In 1999, the first year of single currency, the number of new credit ratings assigned by Standard & Poor's reached its highest level. This occurrence was directly related to the large number of European companies and financial institutions turning to the bond markets as a source of funds.

In 1999 the number of new S&P ratings increased by 30 percent, or 327 new ratings. There were eighty-two new corporate ratings. By year-end, S&P had 1,800 credit ratings in Europe, the Middle East, and Africa. Although European companies have traditionally used bank loans as the major source of financing, the euro gave strong impetus to use of the corporate bond market. A credit rating is essential if bonds are to be sold in the diverse international investment markets. Corporate issuance almost doubled in this international bond market in 1999, reaching $186 billion.

A large part of the increase in corporate bond issuance related to companies with a low investment grade seeking to diversify away from bank financing. Some of the increase in corporate bond issuance also relates to merger activity and the need to finance larger mergers and acquisitions (M&A) deals. But increased issuance volume does not mean higher debt quality. The reverse may be true. The number of corporate downgrades was four times as high as the number of upgrades in 1999, and a continuous weakening of credit quality may result from the new high levels of acquisitions, and the increased use of leverage to enhance returns to shareholders.

COMPETITIVE POSITIONING OF STOCK EXCHANGES AND RELATED MARKETS

The arrival of the single currency changed the competitive environment in Europe for securities trading markets. Old market sectors began to lose ground, as these sectors altered their delivery systems or affiliated with other sectors. Meanwhile, new exchange trading platforms were being created. These changes were not restricted to Europe and Euroland. In the United States, mergers between leading stock exchanges (American Stock Exchange, NASDAQ, and Philadelphia Exchange)[8] were associated with the declining price of seats on major U.S. financial markets (stock exchanges) in 1998,[9] and analysts are now asking how many exchanges will survive the new competitive environment.[10]

These changes are happening all around the world and are not peculiar to Euroland or the United States. But they have been heightened in intensity in Europe with the coming of the euro and the changes the euro is exerting on European capital markets. In the following section we analyze how the development of a pan-European capital market is shaping securities trading in Euroland, and how competition among exchanges is heating up.

Pan-European Markets

Two pan-European stock markets were operating in June 1998 and more were planned. These markets include EASDAQ and Euro Nouveau Marche. EASDAQ was organized in 1997 and was intended to offer Europe a trading market similar to NASDAQ in North America. EASDAQ was intended to trade high-growth companies. At midyear 1998 a French chemicals group, Chemunex, became the first company to have its shares listed on both EASDAQ and Euro Nouveau Marche. Chemunex is a microbiology and instrumentation company, which raised $11.1 million (FF67.5 million) when it listed on the Nouveau Marche in Paris. It was listed on EASDAQ in March 1997. By listing on Euro Nouveau Marche, the company broadened its investor base, targeted French institutional and retail investors, and improved its share liquidity. The share offering was underwritten by Nomura International and Meeschaert Rousselle, the French stockbroker. The proceeds will allow Chemunex to increase its business in the United States, an important location for the application of the firm's technology.

EASDAQ and Euro Nouveau Marche both claim to be leaders in replicating in Europe what NASDAQ has accomplished in the United States. At midyear 1998 there were twenty-seven companies listed on EASDAQ, with a market capitalization of $12.9 billion. Additional listings were scheduled in June 1998 for EASDAQ.[11]

Both exchanges have dual listings with NASDAQ. It is expected that if the joint EASDAQ/Euro Nouveau Marche listings of Chemunex prove positive, many European companies will seek joint listings. Euro Nouveau Marche had achieved its hundredth listing among its four member exchanges. These four include the Nouveau Marche (Paris), Neuer Markt (Frankfurt), and similar growth company markets in Brussels and Amsterdam.

On the eve of the euro's introduction, competition was intensifying between EASDAQ and the Euro Nouveau Marche alliance. Euro Nouveau Marche's ability to court Chemunex and gain its listing raised questions about EASDAQ's ability to provide market liquidity. Also in question was the access to French investors desired by Chemunex. Fighting back, EASDAQ unveiled five new listings of high-tech firms (including biotechnology) based in Austria, Switzerland, the Netherlands, the United States, and the United Kingdom. Beginning on July 1, 1998, EASDAQ launched a new index, the EASI All Share Index, to provide a portfolio benchmark.[12]

In mid-1998 the eighteen-month-old exchange complained to the European Commission about recent legislation in France and Italy that offered companies tax incentives if they would list on national exchanges. These tax concessions were exclusive to those countries and in effect constituted subsidies. EASDAQ's chairman Stanislas Yassukovich argued that they should be removed.

The EU is increasingly sympathetic to the need for greater company access to risk capital and the harmonization of listing requirements across Europe. But local regulatory bodies are reluctant to give up their powers. EASDAQ has fallen behind the Euro Nouveau Marche alliance in number of listings and market capitalization. At midyear 1998, the Euro Nouveau Marche celebrated its 101st listing, and a market capitalization of more than $20 billion. At that time, EASDAQ had a market capitalization of $13 billion and enjoyed a fast-track trading link with NASDAQ.

Global Graphics, a French graphic arts company, made its debut on EASDAQ (June 1998). It originally sought to list on EASDAQ, but it met with intense lobbying pressure from the Nouveau Marche and the Paris Bourse. Bringing a French company to EASDAQ was like committing a crime. EASDAQ, however, was able to offer Global Graphics (1) strong Belgian market exposure, since Belgians buy a lot of shares; (2) a good portfolio of high-tech companies; and (3) immediate access to NASDAQ if desired. A breakdown of the sources of demand for EASDAQ initial public offerings (at mid-1998) can be seen in table 6.5 below.

Table 6.5. Investors in EASDAQ IPOs

Country	*Percentage*
United Kingdom	34.2
United States	13.8
Germany	12.2
Austria	5.9
France	5.6
Belgium	5.5
Switzerland	5.1
Netherlands	3.5
Japan	1.8
Ireland	1.8
Scandinavia	1.6
Italy	1.6
All others	5.5%

Source: Vincent Boland, "Gloves Come Off in Battle for Europe's Answer to NASDAQ," *Financial Times,* March 23, 1998, 28.

At this point, EASDAQ needs to develop a European retail market to rival NASDAQ's following in the United States. But this requires that investors have the opportunity to participate in cross-border initial public offerings.

Competition among the Exchanges

The stock exchanges of the world continue to compete for listing and trading of shares and bonds, as well as the right to issue new securities to raise capital. This competition heated up on the eve of the introduction of the euro for several reasons:

- An expected realignment of European capital markets, accelerating in 1999 and beyond
- Accelerated corporate restructuring in Europe, as companies realign their competitive structures
- The expected rapid development of the European corporate bond market, presenting challenges to existing capital providers
- The expected realignment of the European equity market away from a national currency focus and toward a pan-European industry focus

Surrounded by Euroland, the Swiss banks, financial institutions, and stock exchanges have begun competing more aggressively to retain their strategic position. Two of Switzerland's leading banks announced plans to merge early in 1998, due to this changing competitive environment. Despite the euro, however, Switzerland's importance as a center for European initial public offerings (IPOs) is growing. This was emphasized in June 1998 as two global companies announced plans to raise $677 million on the Swiss stock exchange.[13] At that time there were seven other IPOs in the pipeline, including the flotation of Swisscom, which was expected to raise more than SF5 billion later in 1998.

The two global companies include Barry Callebaut, the world's biggest manufacturer of industrial chocolate, and Gretag Imaging, the world's leading manufacturer of photofinishing equipment. Both IPOs involve the issuance of new equity and the sale of shares by existing shareholders. Gretag was formed in 1990 from a management buyout from Ciba-Geigy. Gretag's chairman, Hans Zulliger, stated that the company had decided to seek a Swiss listing because valuations in Switzerland were similar to other markets, flotation costs were cheaper, and reporting requirements and legal restrictions were less onerous.

Markets Merge into One European Market

In May 2000, France, the Netherlands, and Belgium announced the merger of their securities markets into the new Euronext market. This announcement, coupled with the proposed merger of the LSE and Frankfurt exchanges in 2000, seemed to presage an eventual merger of all European stock exchanges. The institution of pan-European trading on Internet trading companies such as Tradepoint Financial Networks and the announcement that NASDAQ will commence pan-European trading in 2001 also seem to show that competition is pushing individually competitive exchanges into a single, large efficient European exchange that would encompass all securities trading in Euroland. Chapter 8 discusses the issues involved in these mergers and some of the impediments to their implementation.

New Technology

New technology is forcing stock exchanges and derivatives markets to rethink their competitive strategies. This issue is impacting European markets. Even in the United States, where derivatives markets have long enjoyed a strong lead over the rest of the world, new computerized trading programs are being compared with electronic trading very seriously.[14]

Open outcry trading, in which brokers and traders shout orders back and forth in a trading pit, used for over a century in the United States, is giving way. It is expected to be phased out over time. Business growth in the Chicago derivatives exchanges is coming mostly from computer screens, not traditional pit trading. The French Matif has also moved away from pit trading and has switched to a total electronic platform.[15]

LIFFE Faces Competition from Euroland

In 1990, German financial market leaders were espousing a *Finanzplatz Frankfurt.* This was based on the planned closer affiliation of the regional German stock exchanges with Frankfurt, inauguration of a new futures options exchange (Deutsche Termin Börse, DTB), and a more globally oriented strategy by German banks and financial institutions. The European currency crisis of 1992 and the unsettling changes due to EMU arrangements for the next several years caused the Germans to temporarily set aside ideas of any *Finanzplatz,* either German or pan-European.

With the likelihood of EMU strengthening in 1996–2000, continental European financial markets drew new inspiration to compete for global (or at least European) financial services business. One development early in 1998 was the success of the DTB. By May 1998 DTB overtook LIFFE in the volume of all contracts traded over a one-month period. In May 1998 LIFFE traded (overall) 15.1 million contracts while the DTB traded 15.5 million. For all 1997 LIFFE traded 220 million contracts while DTB traded 112 million.[16] The

DTB success was mostly accounted for by high turnover in the ten-year German government bond future contract, which the DTB has come to dominate. Overall, DTB doubled its volume in a twelve-month period ending May 1998, whereas LIFFE experienced only a 10 percent rise in the same period.

DTB increased its international membership from forty-seven institutional members in January 1997 to ninety-one a little over a year later. While the DTB leads LIFFE in derivatives markets for government bonds, LIFFE still enjoys a lead in short-term interest contracts.

Another development at midyear 1998 was a marketing and trading alliance between the NASDAQ stock market and the German stock exchange. If the linkup is completed, it will increase competitive pressure on London, Europe's premier stock exchange. The launching of the European currency also increased the pressure on Europe's thirty-two stock exchanges to consolidate. A working group of specialists in technology, marketing, and trading was looking into the various possible areas of cooperation. The announcement of the EU signifies that the German exchange, one-sixth the size of NASDAQ, believes that it does not need a pan-European alliance to take on London.[17]

An alliance with NASDAQ would provide the Germans with direct access to the U.S. market. SEC rules currently do not allow them to install their trading screens with dealers and institutional investors. This kind of cooperation threatens EASDAQ, but it would face obstacles. First, the two markets represent opposite trading styles. NASDAQ relies on dealers as market makers and intermediaries. The German exchange runs a continuous electronic order-matching system and is willing to cut out brokers by placing trading screens with large institutional investors. Second, joint listings require agreement on common accounting standards, and the SEC has been unwilling to accept anything other than U.S. accounting rules. German accounting standards, by comparison, are much less transparent and allow the buildup of hidden reserves.

The NASDAQ-German Stock Exchange alliance eventually gave way to a more European project. This was the announced merger of the London Stock Exchange and the Deutsche Börse in May 2000, the most far-reaching change in the European equity markets. The planned merger required approval of 75 percent of each exchange's members. The London and Frankfurt exchanges announced a full merger of their cash markets in equities and derivatives products into a market called iX—international exchanges.

The merger would create the world's third biggest stock market by turnover, accounting for 53 percent of daily trading in all European equities. Its size would make it the partner of choice for other European stock exchanges, under pressure to consolidate to cut the cost of buying and selling European shares. Ownership was to be split fifty-fifty between the LSE and Deutsche

Börse. One issue that arose early on was how a market regulator in two different jurisdictions will work in practice.[18] This merger is discussed further in chapter 8.

FRAGMENTED MARKETS

A final note is that competitive changes taking place in European financial markets may bring adverse effects in the form of technologically fragmented markets. This is due to two opposite and competing trends that have made themselves evident as Europe phases in the euro:

- Automation in communications and technology dramatically reduces the cost of trading, allowing large exchanges such as the New York Stock Exchange (NYSE) to do a large proportion of all stock trading.
- Standardized trading lowers costs but allows small, fragmented market systems to operate successfully.

For brokers and their customers, the new world of fragmented markets offers the expansion of the range of available trading services. Regulators (the SEC in the United States) must cope with new trading systems that do not fall into an easy regulatory category of "exchanges." Also, these trading systems are not "broker-dealers."[19] The electronic communications networks (ECNs) were permitted beginning in the mid-1990s. ECNs create separate points of access for matching trades, mainly in NASDAQ stocks (in the United States). Growth of ECNs has been dramatic, accounting for 30 percent of American trading volume in 1999.

How should this trend be evaluated? Is it good or bad? How far should European share markets be allowed to wander or compete in this direction of fragmentation? Will freely competitive markets give all investors—individual, European, and non-European-based financial institutions—the best execution? These remain critical questions.

LIFFE Responds to Competition

Early in June 1998, LIFFE members voted to overhaul the exchange and introduce electronic trading. As this was done, LIFFE changed from a mutual-type structure to a profit-seeking commercial company, a trend soon followed by other trading exchanges.

LIFFE encouraged outside shareholders to take a stake in the company and sever the link between membership and trading permits on its electronic platform. Electronic trading was introduced for equity options in November 1998 and for all other contracts in 1999.[20]

The LIFFE also indicated that it was considering moving its German and Italian government bond futures contracts to its after-hours screen trading system. By moving these two contracts to the automated pit trading system (APT), LIFFE could provide a cheaper alternative to its trading floor. As a LIFFE board member noted, "Undoubtedly, there is a move toward screen based trading."

DTB Invades England

As already noted, during the first five months of 1998, the DTB moved ahead of the LIFFE in the share of the German government bond futures contract trading. The DTB is seriously considering launching a rival contract to the UK gilt future traded on the LIFFE. This coincides with similar plans by the French derivatives exchange, Matif. This will escalate the battle between London and its continental competitors in the monetary union for dominance in the derivatives market. It is also possible that an alliance between Matif and DTB might bring a cooperative venture in gilt futures.

According to the agreement between the French and German exchanges, they would develop cross-membership and establish a common platform for clearing and settlement in 1999. By 2002 they would have a single clearing-house and common trading system listing joint products. LIFFE officials state that they have been expecting such a challenge in the wake of Frankfurt's success at winning control of German bond futures.

The LIFFE board of directors approved a plan to switch trading on its bond futures from the trading floor to an electronic platform. This was aimed at reducing the cost of trading government bond futures and the competitive threat of the French and German initiatives. LIFFE trailed behind continental exchange movement toward electronic trading, but in 1999 it established plans to introduce a permanent electronic platform.[21]

The DTB is also considering the launch of a Swedish government bond future, even though the OM, Sweden's exchange, plans to launch such a contract. UK and Swedish government bonds are regarded as increasingly important battlegrounds for Europe's derivatives exchanges, since neither country joined the first group of monetary union members in January 1999. A single government bond benchmark denominated in the euro is to be developed and is expected to be more efficient than the eleven separate government benchmarks in use when the euro was introduced.

To respond more quickly to the DTB challenge, in mid-June 1998, LIFFE decided to move the German government bond contract to computer screen trading. The Bund and two other contracts were moved to a trading system reserved for after-hours dealing on August 3, 1998, a year before the exchange was expected to roll out a state-of-the-art electronic system. This announcement came one week after exchange members agreed to the strategic reversal of a former policy based on the traditional open outcry trading. This about-face followed several months in which LIFFE's share of Bund futures trading fell sharply. The interim measure was used until the Bund contract could be moved to the new trading system, LIFFE Connect, in 1999. One LIFFE official indicated that these moves would save the Bund options contract, which is still traded on the London market.[22]

CORPORATE RESTRUCTURING AND MERGERS

The coming of the euro has intensified the need for corporate restructuring in Europe. Even before the single currency, European companies were developing strategies to compete more effectively. We discuss these trends in this chapter because they are in large part driven by capital market dynamics and are due to the fact that the "new, new thing" in corporate planning and strategy is itself introducing unexpected forces of change in the capital market sphere.[23] The following discussion considers incentives for, and techniques of, corporate restructuring. We also analyze several of the most important cases of corporate restructuring, and how and why they occurred. In all cases, these restructurings required capital market financing and valuation. But more importantly, they came about as a result of the markets in the Eurozone seeking to generate greater wealth from existing corporate assets.

Restructuring Incentives

We consider four important incentives for corporate restructuring in Europe:

- Growing importance and acceptance in Europe of the need to maximize shareholder wealth. Therefore, managers of companies whose aggregate share value (market capitalization) is low automatically become aware of the need for restructuring, or they face prospects of becoming a target for acquisition by other companies.
- Effect of the single currency in unifying bond markets and equity markets into one large capital market, where there no longer can be a "currency veil" or "money illusion" effect protecting corporate managements that do not succeed in maximizing shareholder value.
- Demonstration effects in the United States and the UK, taking the form of rising levels of mergers and divestitures, and more transparent financial re-

porting and disclosure. As a result, it became possible for European companies to witness the benefits to be served from focusing more carefully on the capital market as a mechanism for setting the value of corporate assets, as well as carrying out the financial transactions required to move forward the restructuring processes.

- Growing importance of information technology (IT) in global business. This is bringing about a distinction between old (traditional) and new (high-tech) industry sectors. Capital market pricing reinforces this distinction, with new sectors at times enjoying high share valuations and old sectors experiencing low valuations.

The change in attitude and perspective of European corporations has taken place gradually. During the 1990s it gathered momentum and by the year 2000 was accelerating. One of the first German companies to "see the light" was Daimler-Benz. In 1993 Daimler listed its shares on the New York Stock Exchange. Between 1993 and 1998, ten German company share issues had been listed on the NYSE (table 6.6). Many other German firms have adopted international accounting standards for the purpose of improving reported earnings and enhancing stock market capitalization value. German accounting rules allow companies to understate earnings through depreciation, low asset valuation, and special tax treatment. Volkswagen could be the last of the DAX 30 companies to undertake such a change. This may coincide with the retirement of Ferdinand Piech, chairman, and could increase the profits reported and market valuation by 20–30 percent, as well as assisting in fending off potential foreign raiders. The Vodafone Airtouch takeover of Mannesmann has

Table 6.6. German Company Share Listings on NYSE, Early 1999

Company	*Volume of Shares*	*Value of Shares Traded*	*Date of Listing*
Daimler-Benz AG (replaced by DaimlerChrysler)	86.9	8,196.9	10-5-93
DaimlerChrysler AG	84.1	7,316.2	11-17-98
Deutsche Telecom AG	33.5	883.2	11-18-96
Fresenius Medical Care AG	10.2	218.0	9-17-96
Fresenius Medical Care (Pfd)	0.1	1.8	11-25-96
Hoechst AG	31.9	1,338.7	9-24-97
Pfeiffer Vacuum Technology AG	4.2	227.4	7-16-96
SAP Aktiengesellschaft	67.9	2,870.6	8-3-98
SGL Carbon Aktiengesellschaft	0.7	24.7	6-5-96
VEBA AG	1.5	93.4	10-8-97

Source: New York Stock Exchange, *Fact Book for Year 1998*, 69.
Note: Shares and value of trading expressed in millions.

left many German companies feeling vulnerable. International comparisons show that the shares of many German companies are underpriced.[24]

Companies in sectors perceived to be traditional often are easy takeover targets for companies with high share valuations. This capital market pricing distinction is apparent also in Japan, where Softbank, an Internet company with a relatively high share price, has been able to acquire other companies with ease. In February 2000, Softbank had a market capitalization value of ¥18.2 trillion ($164.6 billion), ranking it third, only behind NTTDoCoMo and NTT. At that time Softbank's capitalization was equivalent to the total of Matsushita Electric, Nomura Securities, and Bank of Tokyo-Mitsubishi, combined.[25]

In February 2000 the government of Japan decided to sell Nippon Credit Bank to a consortium led by Softbank. The consortium offered to pay $9 million for National Central Bank (NCB) shares, and to inject ¥100 billion to support the NCB's capital base. This would give Softbank access to a banking operation that can support Nasdaq-Japan, the Internet-based stock market being launched by Softbank. From May to August 2000, Softbank's share price plummeted 65 percent in parallel with the general weakness in the Tokyo stock market. Softbank came under financial pressure when the Internet market began to suffer. Financial analysts criticized the company for investing in too many companies. The unwinding of cross shareholdings by Japanese banks extended the stock market's weakness into 2001 and increased the uncertainty about the status and potential success of Nasdaq-Japan.[26]

Restructuring Strategies

Corporate restructuring in Europe contains a number of interesting features. These include:

- New economic trends and positioning to benefit from these developments
- Consolidation of formerly splintered industry sectors
- Merger to create a geographically broader market position
- High-tech spin-offs to realize capital market valuation
- Creation of a company with a revised set of core businesses

An excellent example of new economy is the mobile phone sector, for example, in the UK. At mid-2000 more than one in two British adults owned a cellular phone. In the one-year period 1998–1999 the number of UK mobile phone users almost doubled to 24 million, spending an average £20.23 per month, with an industry total of £5.61 billion. The market appears to be shared equally by four operators (Vodafone Airtouch, BT Cellnet, Orange, and

One-2-One). Vodafone and BT Cellnet appear to be losing customers to the remaining two newcomers, as well as new entrants such as Virgin Mobile.[27] Vodafone's successful merger with Airtouch and its successful hostile bid for Mannesmann were in part based on the relatively high share valuations the capital market has given the new economy sector companies.

Ability to consolidate business sectors provides another opportunity for corporate restructuring. Two examples in the cable television and logistics sectors are presented. In February 2000 Deutsche Telekom revealed the first step in the disposal of its cable operations, selling a majority stake in its network in North Rhine and Westphalia to a consortium headed by Callahan Associates, a U.S. private equity group. This transaction, involving Callahan's taking a 55 percent stake in the cable network, is believed to be the largest European private equity deal. Callahan's stake is valued at DM3.7 billion, and the entire North Rhine network at DM6.8 billion.[28] The agreement is important in that a benchmark now exists for valuation of other components of DT's cable network. Cable is perceived as the best mechanism for delivery of high-speed Internet and interactive television into the home.

Callahan will consolidate its European cable operations, with the German components providing the possibility of creating a pan-European brand that will give the new cable entity more clout with providers and electronic commerce services. Callahan indicated that it would spend DM3 billion to upgrade the network and introduce some interactive content. According to Richard Callahan, president and chief executive, "We are going to be the largest cable company outside the United States." Ron Sommer, Deutsche Telekom's chief executive, said that sale of nine regional cable companies in the year 2000 could raise over DM30 billion.[29] A recent government tax reform makes it tax-free for German companies to sell stakes in other companies. Therefore DT could put off a transfer of control of several of the cable companies until January 2001, when the tax bill will take effect.

Another illustration of industry consolidation is the discussion being held between Lufthansa and Deutsche Post, for a three-way merger of their three logistics businesses, DHL International, Lufthansa Cargo, and Air Express International (AEI). The combined group would have a turnover of DM17 billion. With a merger, this would be the world's largest air freight forwarder, ahead of U.S.-based Federal Express. Deutsche Post purchased AEI in 1999 and is the biggest U.S. air freight forwarding service operating worldwide. AEI has no fleet of its own and makes a good fit with LH, which has a large fleet of its own.[30] Lufthansa and Deutsche Post each have a 25 percent stake plus one share in DHL.[31]

A third aspect of the restructuring involves creating a company with a revised set of core businesses. Siemens, the German technology group, in the year 2000 was in the midst of a radical change in core businesses. The company plans to focus on IT and communications for the medium term, and other divisions such as energy, transportation, medical technology, and light bulb making (Osram) could be sold. The plan is to turn Siemens into a narrowly focused two-tier company. Turnover could be halved from its 1999 level of DM134 billion in the process.[32]

While Siemens stock market capitalization doubled in the six months ending February 2000 (to €100 billion), the Vodafone takeover of Mannesmann has increased the urgency of raising their profit and share value. The core of the Siemens strategy is to make the company into an information technology, communications, Internet, and process automation enterprise. Siemens is expected to carry out several acquisitions from funds generated by sale of Infineon, its cutting edge semiconductor unit.

Early in 2000 Siemens announced plans to list (sell) 25–30 percent of Infineon, the world's eighth largest semiconductor group, which is valued at about €18 billion. This sale is part of a radical restructuring announced by Siemens late in 1998. Businesses with sales of DM17 billion will be sold to improve profitability and to reduce the cyclicality of core businesses. Infineon's core sectors include chips for mobile communications, multimedia, vehicles, and "smart cards." Infineon is expanding internationally, with R&D spending in excess of 18 percent of sales.[33]

Meanwhile, Siemens has plans to acquire e-business targets, including the mobile phone business of Bosch and Debis Systemhaus, DaimlerChrysler's information technology business. Siemens stated that it expects e-business to account for one-quarter of its sales from Internet businesses.[34] Debis is a purely German business, and Siemens needs to acquire other units that could carry its operations into other country markets.

Clearly, Siemens is implementing high-tech spin-offs as an important part of its restructuring. Technology and high-growth stocks, the main drivers of the European new issues market in 1999, continued to play that role in 2000. Among the largest such deals scheduled were DT's sale of T-Online using Goldman Sachs and Dresdner Kleinwort Benson as advisers. Valuations of Internet and mobile phone companies have been too compelling for parent companies not to consider carveouts or spin-offs.[35] Deutsche Telekom hopes that the public offering of its Internet subsidiary, T-Online, will realize $58 billion with plans to enter the European travel market. In February 2000 T-Online announced the purchase of Club Internet from the French media group Lagardere, as well as a cross shareholding with Commerzbank's direct banking arm Comdirekt. As the leading Internet services provider in Europe, T-Online could enjoy rising share value as it further develops synergistic ties with other companies. Therefore Deutsche Telecom is expected to sell only a relatively small initial stake (10 percent) of the company.[36]

Mergers Boom in Europe

In 1999 $1.2 trillion of merger transactions were announced in Europe. The mergers business in Europe is profitable and likely to grow as corporate restructuring takes on the highest priority. Citigroup, the world's largest financial institution, acquired the investment banking business of Schroders for $2.2 billion, due to the London merchant bank's ranking of sixteen in the league tables of European M&A advisers. In 1999 Schroders advised on deals worth $46 billion.[37]

In this section we undertake a detailed analysis of the European mergers that took place from 1999 to 2000, largely as a result of the introduction of Europe's single currency. The single currency wiped away the currency veil, fully exposing competitive forces across Europe. The new competitive environment in the Eurozone placed a premium on industry consolidation, especially in sectors in which services can be delivered more efficiently on a pan-European scale. These sectors include banking, telecommunications, and mobile phones, sectors for which our analysis of mergers follows.

Olivetti-Telecom Italia

On February 20, 1999, Olivetti SpA, a company one-fifth the size of Telecom Italia, made a $58.5 billion offer for the Italian telecommunications firm. This was the largest hostile bid ever launched in Europe. Formerly, Telecom Italia had enjoyed a state-regulated monopoly, but beginning with its privatization in 1997 and the deregulation of the European telecommunications sector in 1998 (table 6.7), the Italian firm was facing serious management problems. The transition from monopoly status to competitor in a dynamic telecommunications sector resulted in three changes in Telecom Italia's chief executive within one year.

To defend itself from the Olivetti bid, Telecom Italia organized and publicized a novel industrial plan. This consisted of a reorganization based on consumer services, combining their stationary and mobile units to achieve more effective marketing, with a new focus on their business customers.[38]

From February 20 to April 12, 1999, Telecom Italia appeared to enjoy an advantage over Olivetti. Investors were concerned over Olivetti's highly leveraged offer in cash, bonds, and shares. Telecom Italia scheduled a shareholder's meeting on April 10, with an appeal for shareholders to attend and vote against the Olivetti bid. Franco Bernabe, Telecom Italia's chief executive, attempted to gain support from shareholders in the United States, UK, and Italy with a plan based on a $24 billion cash buyback of a 40 percent stake in the cellular subsidiary, Telecom Italia Mobile.

Attendance at the April 10 meeting failed to meet the required one-third quorum, with only 22.3 percent attendance of shareholders represented. The

Table 6.7. Key Events in Olivetti-Telecom Italia

Date	*Event*
January 1, 1998	Deregulation of European telecommunications industry, including privatization of Deutsche Telekom, Telecom Italia, and France Telecom.
January 1999	One year after deregulation of telecommunications industry in Europe, Deutsche Telekom lost over one-third of its share in long distance and international market, more than British Telecom lost in a decade of competition in the UK.
February 20, 1999	Olivetti makes an unsolicited offer to acquire Telecom Italia for $58.5 billion.
March 11, 1999	Telecom Italia implements program to ward off Olivetti bid, including merger with its mobile phone subsidiary and buyback of 10 percent of its shares.
March 29, 1999	Olivetti raises its offer to $65 billion.
April 21, 1999	Telecom Italia and Deutsche Telekom agree to $81 billion deal that would leave Olivetti out.
May 21, 1999	Olivetti wins takeover battle for Telecom Italia.

Sources: Financial press, including *Wall Street Journal, Financial Times, International Herald Tribune,* and selected Web sites.

meeting ended with nothing accomplished, and it became clear that only a white knight could rescue Bernabe. During the following several weeks Telecom Italia entered into merger discussion with Deutsche Telekom (DT). A factor encouraging DT's interest was a need to broaden its sources of revenue. DT was facing tough competition at home. Mannesmann and others had secured 30 percent of the German long-distance market share and were moving aggressively into the local telephone market. Factors impeding DT's role in saving the Italian telecom company included the German government's continued ownership of DT (74 percent), a need for approval at the highest political levels of government in each country, and the existence of a strategic partnership between France Telecom and DT. Also, any deal between Telecom Italia and Deutsche Telekom would have been scrutinized by European Commission regulators.

On April 21, the Telecom Italia board gave conditional approval to the proposed merger with DT. On May 21 the Milan Bourse stated that Olivetti had won a 51 percent stake in Telecom Italia. After these events, the financial press reported gains by either Olivetti, or by Telecom Italia–Deutsche Telecom on a daily basis, as the pair moved closer to their respective objectives. The Olivetti victory confirmed the introduction of aggressive American-style capitalism in Europe. Further, it signaled a far-reaching change in the nature of corporate governance and competition in Euroland.

Three French Banks

Until the euro came onto the scene, the French government had long resisted foreign ownership and participation in domestic financial markets. But privatization of French banks, as well as the onset of more open and transparent competition in banking across Euroland, has compelled banks to prepare for intense competition. Early in 1999 Société Generale and Paribas announced that they were preparing to merge in order to create an institution better able to compete in the dynamic single currency market (table 6.8). The merger

Table 6.8. Chronology of Events in the Three-Way French Banking Merger

Date	*Event*
February 1, 1999	SG agrees to acquire Paribas in stock swap worth $17 billion.
March 9, 1999	BNP announces hostile bid of $37 billion for both SG and Paribas.
March 11, 1999	SG and Paribas reject bid launched by BNP.
March 16, 1999	CMF clears BNP's hostile offer.
March 26, 1999	SG and Paribas appeal against CMF decision to clear BNP offer.
March 29, 1999	CECEI Banque de France governor Trichet and COB clear BNP offer.
April 6, 1999	Boards of SG and Paribas meet to vote on BNP hostile bid, formally rejecting it.
April 9, 1999	BNP accuses SG and Paribas of entering into unfair stock market transactions affecting BNP share price.
April 19, 1999	Paribas announces it has a 10-year arrangement with AXA to protect each from hostile bids.
April 22, 1999	CMF announces that SG offer and BNP offer will end on same day and that the closing date for the offers will be delayed until eight days after the Paris court rules on suit brought by SG and Paribas against BNP offer.
May 4, 1999	COB invalidates a decades-long agreement between AXA and Paribas.
May 28, 1999	Banco Santander Central Hispano (BSCH) considers helping SG and Paribas to merge.
June 9, 1999	BSCH increases its stake in SG.
June 14, 1999	BSCH raises its friendly bid for Paribas.
June 17, 1999	SG and Paribas lose lawsuit to stop BNP hostile offer.
June 21, 1999	French authorities intervene to prevent bidding war.
June 22, 1999	French stock market regulators set deadline of July 21 for BNP bid.
June 24, 1999	Three banks meet at Banque de France for discussions.
June 25, 1999	SG and Partners criticize regulators' refusal to approve new SG offer.
June 28, 1999	Three banks meet second time for discussions.
June 30, 1999	Banque de France fails in attempt to end the battle between the three banks.
July 1, 1999	BNP raises its bid for SG and Paribas to $41 billion.
July 8, 1999	CMF gives Paribas shareholders until July 30 to choose between BNP and SG.
July 21, 1999	BNP garners over 65 percent of Paribas share tenders but only 35 percent of SG shares.

would take place through a stock swap worth $17 billion. Approximately six weeks later (March 9, 1999) Banque National de Paris (BNP) announced a hostile $37 billion offer to swap shares for the investment bank Paribas and the retail bank Société Generale (table 6.8). From this point until the end of July a series of maneuvers by the three banks, investors, and French regulatory agencies took place.

Four French regulatory authorities enjoy a determinative supervisory position in the three-way bank merger. The Conseil des Marches Financiers (CMF) was established in 1996 as a self-regulatory body to define the rules of good practice for investment service providers. The CMF must approve a takeover once it has been set forth. The takeover must be approved by the Comite des Establissement de Credit et des Enterprises d'Investissement (CECEI). Final clearance is necessary by the Commission des Operations de Bourse (COB), which has five days to respond. In addition, the Banque de France must approve any takeover bids.

The CMF rules on whether the value of an offer is compatible with the market. Also, the CMF sets the timetable for takeover bids. The CECEI was given power under the Banking Act of January 1984 to supervise credit institutions. An act of 1996 expanded these powers, giving them the power to regulate all firms providing investment services. The CECEI regulates new banking entities and is presided over by Jean-Claude Trichet, governor of the Banque de France.

The COB was set up in 1967 to rule on whether shareholders are given sufficient information to make a rational decision. COB investigates insider trading, share price manipulation, the validity of public offerings, and claims of misleading information. The COB is the French equivalent of the American Securities and Exchange Commission.

The role played by the four regulatory authorities was critical for several reasons.

- It would be the first major case of a hostile bid in the French banking sector.
- The government role, or absence of a government role, would set an important precedent in future possible takeovers.
- Decisions by the several regulatory bodies could place the decision regarding who purchases whom into a capital market context, that is, shareholders could tender to the preferred bidder.
- French banking needed a solution that would strengthen banking institutions in the more dynamic European market place.

Several critical turning points include March 16 (CMF clears BNP offer), March 29 (Trichet and COB clear BNP offer), April 22 (CMF sets same date for end of offer), and June 21 (French authorities intervene to prevent bidding war).[39]

By mid-July it was difficult to judge the outcome. The three banks appeared equal in terms of assets, profits, and return on equity (table 6.9). According to John Leonard, a banking analyst at Salomon Smith Barney in London, BNP might win its two bids, or it might win just one and the one it might win could be Paribas.[40] Leonard could not have been more correct. Paribas shareholders gave BNP support to acquire the investment bank.

Table 6.9. Comparison of BNP, Société Generale, and Paribas

	BNP	*Société Generale*	*Paribas*
Assets[a]	329.6	389.2	263.9
Net banking income[a]	7.47	9.37	5.68
Profits[a]	1.13	1.09	1.01
Tier 1 capital adequacy ratio[a]	6.4%	6.5%	9.1%
Return on equity	11.8%	11.2%	12.0%
Number of employees	56,286	58,600	21,100

Source: "French Bank Merger," *Wall Street Journal,* July 15, 1999, A15.
[a]In U.S.$ billions.

BNP garnered only 36.8 percent of the shares and 31.5 percent of the voting rights in SocGen. By contrast, BNP garnered over 65 percent of Paribas's shares. Using year-end 1998 standings, BNP plus Paribas became the third largest European bank measured by assets (table 6.10). Initial estimates by BNP put the savings through synergies at €600 million. Therefore, the challenge facing BNP was to keep the investment banking talent of Paribas intact.

Table 6.10. Europe's Top Banks by Assets (year-end 1998)

Bank	*Assets*
SBP	0.97
Deutsche Bank	0.84
BNP + Paribas	0.69
UBS	0.61
HSBC	0.57
Hypo Vereinsbank	0.50

Source: "Yes, but Who Won?" *Economist,* August 21, 1999, 63–64.
Note: Amounts in trillions of euros.

Vodafone-Mannesmann

In the final week of December 1999, Vodafone-Airtouch PLC indicated it would launch a $132 billion hostile takeover bid for Mannesmann AG. The bid would give Mannesmann investors until February 7, 2000, to decide whether to accept Vodafone's offer or not. This was midway through the 30–60 day period allowed under German takeover rules.[41] Vodafone is the largest cell phone company in Britain, whereas Mannesmann is a German industrial conglomerate with the largest mobile phone business.[42] Vodafone revealed its intent to make a bid a month earlier, on November 19, 1999, but Germany's takeover code only requires that the tender offer be published "without undue delay."[43]

By mid-December 1999 Vodafone had completed arrangements with eleven banks, setting up a €30 billion loan facility as part of its preparations. The one-year loan would have to be refinanced in the bond markets.[44]

Klaus Esser, chairman of Mannesmann, set out arguments against the hostile bid. He noted that Vodafone's offer should give Mannesmann shareholders 58 percent ownership of the combined entity rather than the 47.2 percent proposed by Chris Gent, Vodafone's chief executive. Further, Esser stated the merger offered nothing to Mannesmann shareholders of strategic value. The Vodafone offer did not reflect the growth potential of Mannesmann's wireless data, Internet, and e-commerce businesses.[45]

In January 2000 Mannesmann laid out its plans for the long-term development of Mannesmann, and their implications for shareholder wealth. These included taking an equity stake in AOL Europe. In return the Internet service provider would gain access to Mannesmann's fixed and mobile phone operations. Also, Mannesmann announced plans to form joint ventures on Internet activities with Gap Gemini, the French IT and consulting group. Further, Mannesmann announced it was joining with Deutsche Bank to create a pan-European Internet-based bank. This followed a recent decision by Lloyds TSB to develop similar European Internet-based banking.

Both Vodafone and Mannesmann utilized news advertising in the UK, the United States, and continental Europe. More than half of Mannesmann's shares were held outside Germany, hence the wide use of newspapers on several continents to win the battle for investor support. Because of the many investors and financial institutions involved, the advertising was informative rather than emotive.[46]

By February 2, 2000, both companies were discussing the terms of an agreement leading to takeover. Capitulation by the Mannesmann board was based on the unwillingness of German political leaders to become involved in actions contrary to the interests of investors and on the less-than-neutral stance of large institutional investors.[47] With Vodafone increasing its bid to give Mannesmann investors close to 50 percent ownership in the combined entity, there remained little opposition.

The two companies agreed to combine on February 4, 2000. The all-stock transaction became the largest merger on record, worth $183 billion (table

Table 6.11. Largest Agreed Merger Deals

Acquirer	*Target*	*Date Announced*	*Value (U.S.$ Billions)*
Vodafone-Airtouch	Mannesmann	February 3, 2000	183
America Online	Time Warner	January 10, 2000	165
MCI Worldcom	Sprint	October 5, 1999	115
Exxon	Mobil	December 1, 1998	80
Glaxo Wellcome	SmithKline Beecham	January 17, 2000	76

Source: L. Andrews and A. R. Sorkin, "$183 Billion Deal in Europe to Join Two Wireless Giants," *Wall Street Journal*, February 4, 2000, A1, C9.

6.11). This combined group is by far the world's largest wireless telephone company, with a major presence in the United States, Europe, Asia, and Africa. Never before had a European company carried out a hostile takeover on such a scale. Both companies employed armies of investment bankers to advise them. Goldman Sachs, Vodafone's lead adviser, earned about $75 million for its services. Mannesmann's advisers included Merrill Lynch, J.P. Morgan, Deutsche Bank, and Morgan Stanley Dean Witter.[48]

NOTES

1. Deutsche Bundesbank, "Structural Change in the German Capital Market in the Run-up to European Monetary Union," *Monthly Report*, April 1998, 55–56.
2. Robert Killhoffer, "Privatization Marches On," Newsweek, June 22, 1998, special advertising section. In 1999 several of these banks became involved in a three-way merger battle, discussed later in this chapter.
3. Robert Killhoffer, "Globalization of the Bourse," *Newsweek*, June 22, 1998, special advertising section.
4. "FTSE Grapples with Its Reclassification," *Indexes: The Journal of Index Issues in Investment*, July–September 1999, 47. Alex Skorecki, "Companies Index Shake-up May Spell Investor Earthquake," Financial Times, May 17, 2001, 22; and Alex Skorecki, "High Noon for Indices," Financial Times, May 21, 2001, 13.
5. "Just When You Thought It Was Only Stock Indexes," *Indexes: The Journal of Index Issues in Investment*, July–September 1999, 44.
6. James Clunie, "Active Countries, Passive Stocks," *Indexes: The Journal of Index Issues in Investment*, July–September 1999, 7–9.
7. Nathan Most, "Inside Your SPDRs and WEBs," *Indexes: The Journal of Index Issues in Investment*, July–September 1999, 36.
8. Greg Ip, "Philadelphia Exchange to Join NASDAQ, Amex," *Wall Street Journal*, June 10, 1998, C1, C22.
9. David Barboza, "Value of Seats on the Major Exchanges Declines," *New York Times*, June 12, 1998, 31, D1.
10. Greg Ip, "How Many Exchanges Can Survive?" *Wall Street Journal*, June 11, 1998, C1, C16.

11. Vincent Boland, "Chemunex to List on EASDAQ and Euro.NM," *Financial Times,* June 17, 1998, 24.

12. Vincent Boland, "Gloves Come Off in Battle for Europe's Answer to NASDAQ," *Financial Times,* June 23, 1998, 29.

13. William Hall, "Swiss Bourse Attracts Two More IPOs," *Financial Times,* June 3, 1998, 17.

14. B. Dowling and D. Rosenberg, "Open-Outcry Traders Ponder Electronic Threat," *Wall Street Journal,* June 8, 1998, C19.

15. J. R. Wu, "Futures Exchanges Face Challenges to Traditional Open Outcry System," *Wall Street Journal,* June 15, 1998, C17.

16. Edward Luce, "Frankfurt Exchange Overtakes LIFFE," *Financial Times,* June 3, 1998, 15.

17. Silvia Ascarelli, "NASDAQ, Deutsche Börse Plan Alliance, a Move That Could Pressure London," *Wall Street Journal,* June 23, 1998, C25.

18. Vincent Boland and Aline Van Duyn, "Deal with London Gives Frankfurt Added Weight," *Financial Times,* special survey on Germany, May 22, 2000, XII.

19. John O. Matthews, *Struggle and Survival on Wall Street* (New York: Oxford University Press, 1994), 237–238; and J. Labate and A. Hill, "Remaking Markets," *Financial Times,* March 6, 2000, 14.

20. Edward Luce, "LIFFE Members Vote Heavily in Favor of Electronic Trading," *Financial Times,* June 10, 1998, 17; Chip Cummins, "London Futures Exchange May Switch Two Contracts to Screen-Based System," *Wall Street Journal,* June 12, 1998, B9A.

21. Edward Luce, "DTB May Launch Rival to LIFFE's UK Gilt Future," *Financial Times,* June 16, 1998, 17.

22. Silvia Ascarelli, "London Exchange Going Electronic with German Bond," *Wall Street Journal,* June 18, 1998, B2.

23. The term "New, New Thing" is taken from the title of the book authored by Michael Lewis (New York: Norton, 2000).

24. Uta Hanischfeger, "Volkswagen Reluctantly Changes Lanes," *Financial Times,* February 21, 2000, 20.

25. Gillian Tett and Alexandra Nusbaum, "When the Distinctions between Old and New Blur," *Financial Times,* February 25, 2000, 19.

26. "Softbank," *Financial Times,* February 28, 2000, 16; Gillian Tett, "Nikkei Plunge Raises Fears of Bank Crisis," *Financial Times,* January 12, 2001, 1; and Alexandra Harney, "Softbank Chief in Attack on Analysts," *Financial Times,* November 25, 2000, 10.

27. Alan Cane, "Number of Mobile Phone Users to Hit 26.5m," *Financial Times,* February 21, 2000, 9.

28. Peter Larsen and Richard Rivlin, "DT Sells Stake in Network to Callahan," *Financial Times,* February 22, 2000, 15.

29. William Boston, "Callahan Accruing German Cable Assets," *Wall Street Journal,* February 23, 2000, A18.

30. Tasso Enzweiler, "Lufthansa and Deutsche Post in Talks," *Financial Times,* February 22, 2000, 15.

31. "Deutsche Post, Lufthansa Discuss Merger in Cargo," *Wall Street Journal,* February 23, 2000, A17.

32. Rudiger Koln, "Siemens Plans Radical Restructuring," *Financial Times,* February 21, 2000, 22.

33. Sarah Althaus, "Streamlined Infineon Feels Rapid Pace of Change," *Financial Times*, February 21, 2000, 22.

34. Bertrand Benoit, "Siemens on Acquisition Hunt," *Financial Times*, February 25, 2000, 18.

35. Arkady Ostrovsky, "Hi-Tech Spinoffs the Flavor of the Year," *Financial Times*, January 17, 2000, 23.

36. T. Enzweiler and G. Warlimont, "T-Online Aims at $58 bn Valuation," *Financial Times*, February 21, 2000, 17.

37. Charles Pretzlik, William Lewis, and Gary Silverman, "Citigroup Buys UK Business to Boost M&A Deals in Eurozone," *Financial Times*, January 19, 2000, 1.

38. Paul Betts, "Mother of All Takeovers Reflects Powerful Changes," *Financial Times*, March 18, 1999, 1.

39. "An Agency Clears Way for Three-Bank Deal in France," *New York Times*, March 17, 1999; and Rebecca Bream, "When Two's a Crowd Can Three Succeed?" *Euromoney*, May 1999, 41.

40. "Yes, But Who Won?" *Economist*, August 21, 1999, 63–64.

41. Richard Waters, "Vodafone Sets Date for Telecom Bid," *Financial Times*, December 21, 1999, 17.

42. William Boston, "Vodafone to Launch Hostile Bid, Biggest Ever, for Mannesmann," *Wall Street Journal*, December 21, 1999, A16.

43. R. Atkins and K. Bialdiga, "Vodafone to Publish Offer by Christmas," *Financial Times*, December 1, 1999, 22.

44. "Vodafone Sets Up 30 bn Facility," *Financial Times*, December 15, 1999, 32.

45. Ralph Atkins, "Esser Sets Out Case against Vodafone Takeover," *Financial Times*, December 9, 1999, 15.

46. Ralph Atkins and Richard Tomkins, "Ad Campaigns Lose Their Innocence," *Financial Times*, January 29, 2000, 11.

47. R. Atkins and K. Bialdiga, "Big Win for Vodafone Could Spark Legal Fight," *Financial Times*, February 2, 2000, 13.

48. E. L. Andres and A. R. Sorkin, "$183 Billion Deal in Europe to Join Two Wireless Giants," *Wall Street Journal*, February 4, 2000, A1, C9.

Chapter Seven

Bond Market Development

In 1999, the first year of the new single currency, European and other borrowers issued $602.2 billion of euro-denominated bonds. That accounted for 45 percent of all international bond issuance, surpassing the $572.5 billion (42 percent) of bonds denominated in U.S. dollars. An additional $174.2 billion (13 percent) were sold in other currencies (sterling, yen, Swiss francs).

The euro has played a big role in unifying the eleven national bond markets that served borrowers prior to 1999. The new currency achieved the depth and liquidity demanded by large institutional investors. The result is that the euro has created a pan-European bond market. No longer must investors deal within a fragmented European capital market. With greater liquidity in the bond market, large institutional investors, rather than individuals, are major buyers.

The euro has increased the financing options of European firms, which formerly had to rely primarily on bank loans. The funds raised by European companies in 1999 have financed mergers and corporate restructuring and have made companies more competitive.[1]

FINANCIAL STRUCTURE IN THE EURO AREA

During the initial year of operation of the Eurozone, euro member overall debt to gross domestic product (GDP) ratio remained above the reference levels set by the treaty establishing the European Community (EC). In 1999 the average ratio of debt to GDP declined slightly to 72.9 percent, reflecting efforts by E-11 governments to reduce budget deficits.

In its first *Annual Report*, the European Central Bank (ECB) noted that overall budget imbalances and government debt levels in the euro area remained higher than in the United States.[2] The size and structure of the government sector in the euro area differs significantly from that of the United States and Japan. Euro area government expenditure is higher, with government transfers to households relatively high, owing in part to the greater importance of European social security systems.

Euro Area Financial Structure

Early in 2000, the ECB noted that the financial structure of the euro area "can still at present be considered as being close to a bank-oriented financial structure." Domestic bank loans represented a larger percentage of GDP in 1999 than financing through domestic debt securities (100.4 percent versus 88.8 percent in table 7.1). This contrasts sharply with financial patterns in the United States, where bank loans and domestic debt securities represented 48.4 percent and 164.6 percent of GDP, respectively (table 7.1). Further, euro area

Table 7.1. Financial Structure in the Euro Area, the United States, and Japan

Structural Element	*Reporting Period*	*Unit*	*Euro Area*	*United States*	*Japan*
Bank deposits[a]	June 1999	€billions	4,752.2	4,742.8	4,467.5
	June 1999	% of GDP	77.8	55.2	111.7
Bank loans[b]	June 1999	€billions	6,136.1	4,145.8	4,280.8
	June 1999	% of GDP	100.4	48.4	107.0
Outstanding domestic debt securities	June 1999	€billions	5,422.7	14,140.8	5,061.1
	June 1999	% of GDP	88.8	164.6	126.5
• issued by corporates	June 1999	€billions	202.3	2,493.8	583.4
• issued by financial institutions	June 1999	€billions	1,891.5	3,900.1	753.7
• issued by the public sector	June 1999	€billions	3,329.0	7,746.8	3,723.9
Stock market	Oct. 1999	€billions	4,346.0	13,861.1	6,275.8
capitalization[c]	Oct. 1999	% of GDP	71.1	163.3	137.7

Sources: Bank for International Settlements (BIS) (domestic debt securities), ECB (bank deposits and Monetary Financial Institutions [MFIs] loans for the euro area), IMF (bank deposits and GDP forecasts in Japan and the United States), Eurostat (GDP forecast for the euro area, stock market capitalization), Federal Reserve (bank loans for the United States), Bank of Japan (bank loans for Japan).

[a]For the euro area, data cover demand deposits, deposits with an agreed maturity, and deposits redeemable at notice of MFIs other than national central banks (NCBs) and the ECB. For the United States, data include demand, time, and savings deposits from all banking institutions; for Japan, data include demand and time deposits from deposit money banks. For Japan, other banking institutions that offer close substitutes to deposits are not included.

[b]For the euro area, data cover loans to euro area residents from the consolidated balance sheet of euro area MFIs. For the United States, data cover total loans at commercial banks, savings institutions, and credit unions (from the flow of funds accounts of the United States from the Federal Reserve), while for Japan, data cover total lending at deposit money banks from the monetary survey from the Bank of Japan.

[c]Owing to the use of different reporting rules and calculation methods, data are not entirely comparable.

Source: European Central Bank, "Euro Area Financial Structure," *Monthly Bulletin*, January 2000, 39.

stock market capitalization was only 71.1 percent of GDP (October 1999), contrasted with 163.3 percent in the United States. The U.S. capital markets exhibit a securitized structure, with financing through issuance of domestic debt securities considerably larger than that via banks. The financial structure of Japan appears less securitized than the U.S. structure but more than the euro.

Financial Services Consolidation

In 1999 Europe experienced consolidation of the financial services industry. The number of monetary financial institutions (banks and near banks) decreased by about 4 percent in the euro area. This consolidation reflects the response of banks to changing market conditions, related to technology, deregulation, and liberalization. The euro has strengthened these forces. Most notable changes have taken place in wholesale banking. Changes in retail banking are more gradual.

In 1999 the money market experienced greater integration and standardization. The unsecured deposit market, in which banks exchange short-term liquidity without collateral, became highly integrated. Less integrated market segments include the repo market and the short-term securities markets (Treasury bills, commercial paper, and certificates of deposit).

Immediate and full acceptance by all market participants of EONIA (effective overnight average reference rate) and EURIBOR played a key role in providing a uniform price reference (euro interbank offered rate). This is reflected in almost identical risk-adjusted short-term interest rates across euro-area countries.[3]

The repo markets, in which participants exchange short-term liquidity against collateral, are not yet fully integrated in the euro area. This is indicated by the variety of prices prevailing in the general collateral market. The main reasons for this are as follows:

- Diverging prices of underlying bonds and their differing degrees of liquidity
- Lack of harmonization of the legal documentation used for repo agreements
- Difficulties in the cross-border management and settlement of collateral
- Different country tax treatment of bonds
- Uneven availability of collateral across the euro area
- With onset of the single currency, the integration and standardization of the short-term derivatives market increased considerably. The euro interest rate swap market (in which fixed interest rate payments are exchanged for floating interest rate payments) reflected an important increase. Depth and liquidity increased with the development of a single yield curve for the whole

euro area.[4] Bid-ask spreads narrowed to 1–2 basis points and standard deal size increased to €50 million.

The most active segment of the swap market is formed by the "overnight index swaps" in which the fixed-rate component of the transaction is exchanged for an overnight variable rate component (the EONIA rate).

Bond Market Development

According to the ECB *Annual Report*, the most spectacular development in 1999 was the rapid growth of the private bond market, which surpassed the expectations of many market observers.[5] The market gained momentum with the launch of large debt issues that financed sizable mergers. The smooth absorption of these large issues by the euro-denominated private bond market was a sign of the growing depth of this market. During the first nine months of 1999, nonfinancial corporate bond issues increased by 294 percent over the same period in 1998. The largest issuers were banks, which accounted for over half of issuance volume.

Several factors that make for a larger and more liquid market drove the strong growth of the euro-denominated bond market. One of these factors was the ongoing process of corporate restructuring in Europe. This corporate restructuring led to strong demand for funds by the private corporate sector. Introduction of the euro also stimulated integration of euro-area capital markets. Euro-area companies involved in mergers and acquisitions (M&A) financed these deals, to a large extent, with euro-denominated debt issues. These issues often were used to repay bridge facilities (syndicated loans).

In addition to the surge in merger activity in the euro area, investor behavior contributed to the growth of the euro-denominated bond market. Institutional investors increasingly started to invest in higher yield bonds, as the possibility to diversify risk in EU markets across the sovereign euro bond decreased. Growth of the euro-denominated bond market also wiped out currency diversification opportunities that had previously been used to achieve higher rates of return.

Strong growth of the European pension sector and high savings rates in Europe supported demand by pension funds for private sector bonds. Demand by insurance companies for investment in corporate bonds may have given additional support to development of this market.

Liquidity considerations have led retail investors to purchase corporate bonds via investment funds. These purchases further institutionalized the structure of finance and facilitated the absorption of large issues by European capital markets.

Finally, the choice between direct and indirect finance may be related to the financial structure of the euro area itself. Financial markets may have perceived that the risks of financial intermediaries have increased. This is a result of greater competition and deregulation in financial services as well as greater exposure of banks to risks in emerging markets. In this type of environment, corporate borrowers in the euro area have seen their ratings rise above those of many financial intermediaries.[6]

FINANCIAL MARKET FINANCING IN 1999

In this section we analyze the rapid growth of corporate financing in the euro area, which took place through the issuance of debt securities. Introduction of the single currency has acted as a catalyst for the development and integration of the euro-area capital markets. The rapid growth of the corporate bond markets surpassed the expectations of many observers prior to launch of the euro. This market gained momentum as successive large-size euro bond issues were floated to finance mergers and acquisitions. The ability of the euro-denominated debt market to absorb these issues was an important signal of its increased depth.[7]

Broad Trends

In the first year of operation, the Eurozone did not experience a "big bang" in corporate bond issuance. According to research provided by Merrill Lynch, the widely expected shift of European industrial companies away from bank loan financing into the bond market did not take place. Moreover, this shift is not likely to occur as long as European companies lack the scale of their counterparts in the United States.[8]

Table 7.1 shows that at midyear 1999 nonfinancial corporate bonds made up only 4 percent of bonds outstanding in the euro area (€202.3 billion). According to data released by the ECB, much of the growth in the market came from issues outside the Eurozone (79 percent of net issuance). A relatively small number of multinational companies adjusted quickly to the opportunities presented by the new currency and issued euro-denominated bonds that carried low coupon rates. It is important to note that the savings in net finance cost is less than the spread between euro interest rates and the rates on alternative currencies of denomination. This is due to additional costs that are incurred in the form of stock market listings, accounting and documentary procedures.

The substantial use of the euro-denominated bond market by nonresident corporations is confirmed by statistics published by the ECB. According to this data, in 1999, nonfinancial corporations tapped the developing euro-denominated bond market to the extent of $135 billion (table 7.2). Euro area resident corporations issued close to €65 billion of such securities and non-resident corporations issued over €70 billion.

Table 7.2. Long-Term Euro-Denominated Securities Issued by Nonfinancial Corporations, 1999

Quarter	*By Euro-Area Residents*	*By Nonresidents*
1	22.2	14.3
2	17.1	17.7
3	15.1	21.2
4	10.2	17.2
Total	64.6	70.4

Source: European Central Bank, "Euro Area Statistics," *Monthly Bulletin,* April 2000, 30.
Note: Amounts in €billions.

Some Eurozone countries have regulatory and accounting practices that prevent their companies from using the bond market. In Germany, for example, the law allowing pension provisions to be kept on company balance sheets reduces the number of firms that need to go to the capital market for financing.

The Merrill Lynch report concludes there are fewer potential industrial issuers of bonds in Europe than the United States, and this condition is likely to continue for some time. These smaller, less-known companies will continue to draw on alternative sources of funding, including bank loans.

Long Bond Yields Increase

There was a prolonged decline in long-term interest rates in industrial countries and Eurozone nations in the 1990s. In May 1999 these yields reversed direction. Brighter economic prospects for the euro area may have been one factor that turned the direction of these yields. Overall, the euro area experienced a 150 basis point increase in yields on ten-year government bonds. By year-end 1999, the yield on ten-year governments was close to 5.5 percent. Similar upturns in bond yields took place in the United States and Japan.

The euro area yield curve reflected these trends in bond yields. Between the first and last trading day of 1999, the slope of the yield curve, measured by the difference between ten-year euro area bond yields and three-month EURIBOR rates, increased by 140 basis points to 215 basis points.

Bond Scarcity

During the three-year period 1997–1999, European bond issuance consisted of two opposite trends. The amount of government bond issuance declined steadily, while the amount of corporate bond issuance grew without interruption. The decline in euro area government bond issuance mirrored trends in the United States and United Kingdom, and by late 1999 analysts were experiencing an increasing scarcity of sovereign debt both in Europe and North America.

A scarcity of long-term sovereign debt tends to raise price levels and lower yields. Persistent pressure of this nature could produce an inverted yield curve. The first signs that Eurozone government yield curves could become inverted were seen in mid-May 2000 as the yield gap between ten-year and thirty-year German bunds fell to its lowest level between April and May 2000. The yield difference between these two maturities fell from 40 basis points to 20 basis points.[9]

In May 2000 there was an expectation that governments would sharply reduce their supply of government bonds. These expectations may have driven the inversion of yield curves. The necessity of euro area governments to conform to the Stability and Growth Pact and lower their budget deficits also may have caused a shortage of government bonds. According to one analyst, "The perception of government bond scarcity is spreading to the Eurozone, with Germany's plans to use the proceeds of its mobile phone licenses later this year to repay debt."[10]

Inversion tends to coincide with rising interest rates. The phenomenon of falling bond supply is strengthened by an upswing in the economic growth rate, which generates higher tax revenues and pushes budget deficits lower.

Risk-averse investors in Europe face a future in which the "safe haven" investment afforded by government bonds may become more difficult and costly. The scarcer these relatively risk-free investments become, the higher their price will be. According to J.P. Morgan, net global issuance of government bonds is expected to be $247 billion in year 2000, the lowest level in a decade. The J.P. Morgan study indicates that net issuance of government bonds by the six largest euro area countries will fall by 50 percent in 2000 compared with 1999 (table 7.3). The UK gilt market also is likely to shrink in the fiscal year ending in 2001.[11]

The unprecedented economic growth in the euro area is expected to lower budget deficits from 1.2 percent of GDP (1999) to 0.7 percent (2000). European governments face the dilemma of wanting to reduce debt while maintaining liquid markets for government bonds.

The Dutch solution is to concentrate issuance on a few segments of the yield curve. The Netherlands was issuing primarily three-year and ten-year

Table 7.3. Projected Net Government Bond Issuance (in billions)

Country	*1999*	*2000*	*2001*	*2002*	*2003*	*2004*	*2005*
France	35.1	29.7	11.0	14.0	17.0	20.0	23.0
Germany	30.7	12.0	2.0	5.0	8.0	11.0	15.0
Italy	15.8	11.0	12.0	11.0	9.0	6.0	4.0
Belgium	3.0	0.4	0.0	0.0	1.0	1.0	2.0
Netherlands	0.9	-4.0	-3.0	-1.0	0.0	2.0	4.0
Spain	13.6	2.0	-1.0	0.0	2.0	4.0	7.0
Total	99.0	51.0	21.0	28.0	36.0	45.0	54.0

Source: Astrid Wendlandt, "Safe-Havens Become Endangered Species," *Financial Times*, March 30, 2000, 25.

paper to maintain market liquidity at those points on the yield curve. According to the J.P. Morgan analysis, the growing scarcity of government paper is particularly acute at the longer maturities.

The expected scarcity of government bonds in the euro area poses special problems for investors seeking to benchmark their portfolio performance. Bond scarcity also makes it difficult to get benchmark prices for other issues further down the credit curve. As Gary Jenkins, head of credit research at Barclays Capital stated, "Is it really correct to benchmark against something that is so difficult to buy?" Alternative methods to benchmark pricing include (1) the swap rate—the cost of borrowing in the interbank market, (2) rates on highly rated corporate bonds, (3) rates for supranational borrowers such as the World Bank, or (4) for agency borrowers. For example, in Europe, the huge amount of Pfandbrief issuance provides a liquid and secure asset base.[12]

Corporate Issuance Potential

The first year of single currency produced a successful crop of corporate bond issues. As noted in the previous sections, low interest rates in the euro-denominated bond market and a desire by European companies to tap the new liquidity source led an issuance level of €130 billion. The success of 1999 was not matched in first half 2000, as corporate bond issuance in euro-denominated securities was down modestly.

According to Lehman Brothers, the composition of the corporate bond market is quite different in Europe and the UK. Europe may have as many A-rated corporate issuers as the United States, but when we move lower on the rating scale, U.S. issuers outnumber European corporate borrowers. For example, in the rated category, there may be six U.S. rated corporate issuers for every one in Europe.[13] Since the introduction of the euro, Europe's corporate bond market has been growing at the bottom end of the credit rating range.

The proportion of European BBB bond issuance increased from first quarter 1999 to early 2000. For example, in first quarter 2000, BBB and below bond issuance accounted for 37 percent of euro-denominated corporate issuance.

Event risk has impacted the euro-denominated corporate bond market. Merger announcements, the auction of third-generation mobile phone licenses, and capital market volatility have impacted the European bond markets in a negative way. Consequently, investors are demanding protective covenants. Issuers can preempt the need for covenants by managing their issues in a way that gives investors greater comfort. But as corporations begin to issue debt to more sophisticated groups of institutional investors, issuers are offering more protection. For example, in June 2000, when Deutsche Telekom (DT) started the road shows for its giant bond issue, they offered investors protection against credit downgrades. DT plans to borrow at least $8 billion in a global bond issue denominated in U.S. dollars, euros, sterling, and yen. Investors will be offered a guarantee that the coupon will rise by 50 basis points if DT's credit ratings fall below the single A level.[14]

Such rating protection is becoming standard in the telecoms industry, where companies have large funding needs. Investors in this sector are wary of rating downgrades, which occur when companies take on too much debt to finance expansion.

Moody's thinks the telecom sector needs watching because of the high cost of obtaining third-generation licenses in Europe. Sectoral analysis, distinguishing the special problems and risks by industry, is fast becoming a key focus for analysts and investors in Europe.

A Merrill Lynch report questioned the ability of European corporate bond issuance to grow to the level found in the United States. The report noted that Europe does not have the same number of natural bond issuers as the United States does. Lehman Brothers conducted a similar analysis. Lehman assumed that listed companies with book equity over $500 million and operating income over $150 million are required for a company to be a natural candidate for bond issuance. Lehman found 142 companies in Western Europe that fit these criteria but were not yet rated. The Lehman report concluded that the structure of European industry remains very different from that in the United States. In Europe, there are many thriving family businesses (Germany, Italy) that are unlikely to take the route of ratings and bond issuance.

This analysis ignores several dynamics that could increase the number of European companies in need of bond financing. First, European companies are evolving through several stages of development as they make themselves eligible for bond financing. These stages include setting up a Euro-MTN program for shorter-term capital market use and tapping the floating rate note market. Second, diversification of funding sources is becoming a key objective for many companies. These sources include typical bank credits, MTN programs, equities, and bonds. Third, mergers are driving up volume in the bond markets. European M&A volume exceeded American levels in 1999. Bond financing is one of the methods needed to finance mergers. Finally, the number of corporations in Europe that restructure will increase. This restructuring will lead to more bond financing to support the restructuring, and also create more potential bond issuers.

SECTORAL ANALYSIS

Government Sector

We have noted the large size of the government bond market in the euro area (table 7.1). The government bond market provides a sector around which other corporate bond issues can be priced and benchmarked. While government budget deficits are getting smaller and government bond issues are declining in volume, the market continues to attract competition.

Competition is particularly keen in the bond trading business. Brokertec, a company backed by some of the biggest banks, launched its electronic trading system in late June 2000. Bond trading systems generally aim at two market segments—the interbank market and the trading of bonds between banks and their customers. While a considerable portion of bond trading continues to be done via the phone, this procedure is slow and costly. Brokertec aims at the interbank market, competing with Euro-MTS and eSpeed, which are both well-positioned trading platforms.

Brokertec initially will trade Eurozone government bonds and U.S. Treasuries. It also plans to expand into "basis trading" of cash versus futures to cover repurchase agreements and bonds from sovereigns and corporates. Euro-MTS was once a system for trading Italian government bonds but was expanded to include most other European government bond markets. To gain admission to these markets, bank traders require minimum trade amounts. These markets trade only bond issues that have €5 billion or more outstanding. About sixty bond issues meet these requirements.[15]

ESpeed has a different approach. It acts as a broker for the wholesale market, with no minimum trading amounts. It offers trades in a broad range of bonds and securities. Other systems that are being developed include the Bondclick market for institutional traders, which was set up by six banks.

Market players expect consolidation of these trading systems with only two or three survivors. Banks that use these trading platforms will not want to have too many parallel systems.

EIB Aims at Treasury Surrogate Status

The financing institution of the European Union (EU) is the European Investment Bank (EIB). This bank attempts to help integrate the Union, to balance its development, and to promote the social cohesion of the member countries.[16] To do this, it raises more funds than the largest of the private investment banks operating in the EU. In 1996 the EIB raised $23 billion from 109 issues.[17] These funds are used to finance projects that implement the Union's developing policies and aid the agreements promoting the cooperation of Union members.

At mid 1998, the EIB announced plans to exchange a number of outstanding bond issues, denominated in European currency units (ECUs) and other European currencies, into a handful of liquid, benchmarked, euro-denominated bonds. The EIB had €51 billion of outstanding issues eligible for this program.

As a part of its goals, the EIB aims at developing a liquid yield curve to equal that of the large sovereign issuers. The EIB would also like to reduce borrowing costs by encouraging more liquid, and therefore better priced, bond issuance. Paribas, the French investment bank, was appointed sole arranger of these issues, while six other European banks were appointed exchange agents. This left out in the cold the UK-based bulge-bracket investment houses that dominate the Eurobond markets.

The initial exchange operation covered seventeen bond issues denominated in DMarks, lire, and French francs worth €10 billion. The EIB offered to convert these issues into a small number of euro-tributary issues. Euro-tributary issues are bonds that were to be consolidated into one series of euro-denominated notes after the first coupon date following the launch of EMU in 1999.

Paribas spokesman David Ovenden stated, "They are saying they appreciate and want to appeal to an institutional investor base. They are trying to make EIB debt a Treasury surrogate."[18]

Bank Sector

National bond markets in Europe have experienced heavy use by bank issuers. This is the case in Germany, where various types of bank issues play an important role.

German bond issues include the Pfandbriefe, interest bearing securities backed by loans to the public sector or real estate. In 1998 the Pfandbrief market had over DM1.6 trillion ($904 billion) outstanding, according to Verband Deutscher Banken, the German mortgage bankers' association.

After the launch in 1995 of the jumbo Pfandbrief, this market experienced uninterrupted growth. By April 2000 the outstanding volume in the sector had reached €330 billion, 30 percent of the entire German Pfandbrief market.

Jumbos alone represent the fourth largest capital market segment in Europe. The German Pfandbrief market is exceeded only by the Italian, German, and French government bond sectors.

Germany's mortgage banks have sought to broaden the international appeal of the Pfandbrief by enhancing its liquidity. Institutional investors successfully targeted up to €5 billion of individual bonds. Enhanced liquidity has been realized through banks committed to making continuous markets and to developing a flourishing repo market, as well as to marketing internationalization.

Ratings awarded by the three leading rating agencies to the issuing mortgage banks are generally AAA with only one or two exceptions. Large refinancings are due to be carried out in 2001 and following years, reflecting the many five-year issues launched since the mid-1990s.[19]

The Pfandbrief is expected to remain the most important funding instrument, although Germany's mortgage banks will make increasing use of the mortgage-backed securities market. There are a number of fundamental differences between Pfandbriefe and mortgage-backed securitization structures, as summarized in table 7.4.

The Deutsche Termin Börse (DTB) launched a German jumbo Pfandbrief futures contract in July 1998 that enhances the hedging and arbitrage opportunities available in the European fixed income market. The new five-year

Table 7.4. Comparison of Pfandbrief and Mortgage-Backed Securitization

Balance Sheet Treatment	*Pfandbrief*	*MBS*
Source of principal	On-balance sheet	Generally off-balance sheet
Interest payment	Issuer's cash flow	Collateral cash flow
Collateral pool structure	Dynamic pool of infinite life	Secured by a pool of assets that are (in general) not substitutable
Collateral	Secured by a pool of assets of equal amount and equal average maturity that are substitutable	Secured by a pool of assets that are not substitutable
Pool loans	Mainly heterogeneous pools	Mainly homogeneous pools
Rating	Dependent on asset quality, issuer overcollateralization and quasi-bankruptcy remoteness	Dependent on quality and overcollateralization of underlying assets and/or quality of guarantor
Risk weighting	10% in Germany, Austria, Denmark, France and Spain; 20% in other countries	0% GNMA 20% other agencies 50% or 100% nonagency
Principal redemption	Bullet form	Amortization and prepayment

Source: "The German Pfandbrief," *Wall Street Journal*, May 22, 2000, B21.

Pfandbrief contract will also be traded on the German-Swiss futures trading partnership, Eurex, and provide a more efficient way of managing exposure to the German mortgage bond market. Until introduction of the new Pfandbrief futures, hedgers used government bond futures as a proxy. This left traders with a large basis risk. According to Peter Fertig of Dresdner Kleinwort Benson Research, the "Bund and Pfandbriefe markets are not 100 percent correlated, so there is an increased basis risk for hedging Pfandbriefe via Bund futures and swaps." Unstable spreads between Pfandbriefe and Bobls was illustrated in the Asian crisis in October 1997, when spreads widened significantly. At that time, the spread widened by 12 basis points in the five-year and by ten basis points in the ten-year segment.[20]

Michael Silberberg, a dealer at mortgage bank Rheinische Hypothekenbank, stated that his bank will be using jumbo Pfandbrief futures contracts rather than the interest rate swaps market for hedging exposure in cash Pfandbriefe. Pfandbrief futures will provide a cheaper means for hedging than the swaps market, where bid-ask spreads are wide. However, the Pfandbrief is not suitable for longer maturities (ten years), and the swaps market will continue to be used for hedging at that maturity and longer.

Corporate Sector

In 1998 investment banks were betting on the rapid development of the corporate euro bond sector.[21] Early in 1998 Salomon Smith Barney was increasing its research, trading, and merger staffs. According to Peter Middleton, chief executive in Europe for Salomon Smith Barney, issuance of corporate bonds in Europe is going to develop significantly over the next four or five years. Salomon Smith Barney wants to be a lead player in that market, which means that it must strengthen its continental European sales teams. Until recently, Salomon has been only a minor player on the Continent. According to Securities Data Company, the firm ranked eleventh in 1997 for Eurobond issuance with a volume of $17.4 billion, far behind the first two firms, Merrill Lynch and Deutsche Morgan Grenfell, with $34.8 billion and $28.5 billion, respectively.[22]

Expected Growth of the Corporate Sector

The corporate bond sector is expected to expand steadily with the euro currency in place.[23] This is based on the following factors:

- The Eurobond market already absorbs large volumes of deutsche mark, French franc, and other Euroland national currency bonds issued by corporations. A larger, more efficient euro sector will attract even larger amounts of corporate bonds.

- Relationship banking is under siege. Bank mergers in Europe will further reduce the role of relationship banking, and European banks will focus more on capital market activities, including bond issuance for corporations.
- European corporations are beginning to focus more on the Anglo-Saxon financial model, which emphasizes arm's-length financing in the capital market. Also, corporations are gradually adopting a shareholder value mentality, and this results in more transparent bond financing.
- Institutional investors are beginning to play a more important role in the development of European capital markets. This role will cause demand to grow for corporate bonds issued in euros.
- Foreign (non E-12) investors will be attracted to the euro as a way to achieve currency diversification in their investment portfolios.[24] This will bring them into the market for corporate debt denominated in the single currency.
- Although it is easier for U.S. corporations to do business in euro debt markets, where there are fewer litigation concerns and less regulation, until recently only the UK market offered governmental benchmarks for long-term debt issues. Now EU debt markets are expected to draw away U.S. corporate business from this UK "Yankee market."[25]

Convertible Bonds

In 2000 the issuance of convertible bonds was increasing in Europe and the United States. In the first three months, convertible issuance exceeded €7 billion, nearly a third of the total (€29.3 billion) issued in Europe in 1999. The growth is due to a rapidly expanding investor base and the cash needs of companies that cannot tap the equity or straight corporate debt markets.

In Europe, market observers expect high-growth stocks to make a strong showing on the European convertibles market. Traditionally, investment grade companies have dominated this market. In first half of 2000, technology, media, and telecommunications companies issued some 53 percent of European convertibles. The market correction of so-called new economy stocks may provide a favorable base for European companies to issue convertibles, a bet that equity prices will rise.[26]

European investors are starting to treat convertibles as a separate asset class. Funds dedicated to convertibles have increased in importance in year 2000. Given these expectations, some banks are developing or expanding their capacity for doing business in this sector. For example, in June 2000, ING Barings revealed a significant push into the convertible bond business. The bank identified the convertible bond business as a coproduct in efforts to renew its credentials as a global investment bank. In the eighteen months ending June 2000, the bank expanded its convertible bond team (sales, research, and origination) from twelve to forty-seven persons.[27]

High Yield Corporate Issues

If the euro helps the corporate euro bond market grow, can junk bonds be far behind? Several developments point in this direction:

- Individual European investors accustomed to high yields (Italian pensioners) have experienced a sharp decline in yields on domestic currency bonds, so they are searching for alternatives.[28] High yield bonds could be that alternative.
- Venture capital investing has taken solid root in Europe in anticipation of the newly dynamic corporate sector. Venture capital funds constitute a ready market for high yield debt.
- More aggressive corporate restructuring will take place. This restructuring will include leveraged buyouts, which create the need to issue high yield debt securities.

The telecom and media sectors dominated European high yield issuance in 1998 and 1999, representing 55–60 percent of issues. European issuance was in a high-growth phase between 1996 and 1999 (table 7.5), but in the first half of 2000, equity market losses hit high yield euro bonds as well, particularly in the telecom and media sectors.

Lower share prices are spurring leveraged buyouts, and this is expected to cause an increased issuance of high yield bonds. Although highly leveraged, leveraged buyout (LBO) borrowers are mature businesses with good cash flows.[29]

Investment bankers are trying to persuade industrial companies across Europe to access the high yield bond market as an alternative to bank debt. After postponing a bond deal in 1999, German television company Kirch Pay TV is expected to make another try at this market when conditions become more favorable.

Private equity transactions support this market. New private equity funds continue to be set up in Europe, supported by growing institutional investor

Table 7.5. European High Yield Issuance (U.S.$ billions)

Year	*Issuance*
1996	1.5
1997	3.5
1998	12.6
1999	17.6

Source: J. Chaffin and R. Bream, "European High Yield Market Matures," *Financial Times*, April 26, 2000, 24.

interest. A broader range of European money managers is entering the market, including insurance companies, pensions, and retail fund managers.

Municipals

Italy's Lazio was the first region or municipality to issue a bond denominated in the euro. The €250 million ($280 million) issue follows a jump in the number of bonds issued in euros in June 1998. With a thirty-year maturity, this was the longest dated bond issued in the new currency to mid-June 1998.

Investment bankers attribute the high activity in euro-denominated issues to the successful fixing of conversion rates between the E-11 member countries. These fixed conversion rates removed much of the uncertainty about the value of the euro vis-à-vis the other eleven currencies. The Lazio offering followed offerings by lead European banks and corporations, including Banco Centra Hispano, Spain's third ranked bank, and Olivetti.

Issues in typical European currencies such as the Dutch guilder, French franc, and the Italian lira, have fallen sharply. Lead investors such as pension funds[30] became comfortable with bonds issued in the euro, since they did not require redenomination[31] after January 1999, unlike bonds denominated in departing currencies.[32]

NOTES

1. Michael R. Sesit, "Euro, Despite Struggles against Dollar and Yen, Has Provided a Stable Investing Environment," *Wall Street Journal*, January 4, 2000, A17.
2. European Central Bank, *Annual Report 1999*, 38.
3. European Central Bank, *Annual Report 1999*, 41.
4. European Central Bank, *Annual Report 1999*, 43.
5. European Central Bank, *Annual Report 1999*, 43.
6. European Central Bank, *Annual Report 1999*, 46.
7. European Central Bank, *Annual Report 1999*, 15–16.
8. Rebecca Bream, "Big Bang in Euro Bonds Did Not Occur," *Financial Times*, April 17, 2000, 27.
9. Aline van Duyn, "Euro-Zone Yield Curve on Inversion Course," *Financial Times*, May 19, 2000, 32.
10. Van Duyn, "Euro-Zone," 32.
11. Astrid Wendlandt, "Safe-Havens Become Endangered Species," *Financial Times*, March 30, 2000, 25.
12. Rebecca Bream, "New Benchmark Sought as Bonds Dry Up," *Financial Times*, June 22, 2000, 27.
13. M. Peterson, "Pause for Thought," *Euromoney*, June 2000, 106.
14. Aline van Duyn, "DT to Offer Protection for Downgrading," *Financial Times*, June 16, 2000, 26.

15. Aline van Duyn, Rebecca Bream, and Nanna Hepke, "Bond Battle Hots Up with Brokertec Launch," *Financial Times*, June 23, 2000, 25.

16. "Overview," *European Investment Bank*, L-2950 Luxembourg, June 18, 1998, m.bello@eib.org.

17. Peter Lee, "The World's Best Borrower: EIB," *Euromoney*, June 1997, 73–78.

18. Simon Davies, "EIB to Exchange Bonds into Euro," *Financial Times*, June 16, 1998, 30.

19. "The German Pfandbrief," *Wall Street Journal*, May 22, 2000, B21.

20. Sabrina Ghani, "Pfandbriefe Futures Are Viewed as Solid Hedging, Arbitrage Tool," *Wall Street Journal*, May 22, 1998, 21.

21. Gavin Gray, "How EMU Will Change the Bond Market," *Euromoney*, December 1997, 89–90.

22. Sara Callan and Nicholas Bray, "Salomon Smith Barney Faces a Test in Europe," *Wall Street Journal*, March 30, 1998, B11E.

23. "Goodbye Yankees, Hello Euros" *Euroweek*, March 11, 1998, 54–56.

24. Because there is only mild market segmentation among European capital markets, there is little diversification effect available to Europeans who cross-invest in one another's markets. See Theodor Kohers and Gerald Kohers, "Recent Developments in European Stock Market," *Mid-Atlantic Journal of Business* 31, no. 3 (1995): 233–245.

25. "Goodbye Yankees, Hello Euros?" 54–56.

26. Astrid Wendlandt, "Demand for Convertible Bonds Gathers Pace," *Financial Times*, April 7, 2000, 25.

27. V. Boland, "ING Set to Move Into Convertible Sector," *Financial Times*, June 21, 2000, 25.

28. Joel Chernoff, "Sides Square Off in Battle over European Regs," *Pensions and Investments*, March 9, 1998.

29. J. Chaffin and R. Bream, "European's High Yield Market Matures," *Financial Times*, April 26, 2000, 24.

30. Chernoff, "Sides Square Off in Battle over European Regs."

31. Edward Murray, "Practical Approaches to Securities Redenomination" (IFR EMU Series conference on Evaluating the Impact of EMU on the Bond and Derivative Markets, October 2, 1997, London). Murray is a partner in the firm Allen & Overy.

32. Edward Luce, "Lazio First Region to Issue Bond in Euros, *Financial Times*, June 15, 1998, 17.

Chapter Eight

European Equity Markets

At midyear 1998 hopes were high that the euro would provide the impetus for the revitalization of the Continent's equity markets. There were a number of reasons for this optimism, including a new perspective on investing in equity shares after the euro removed the currency differentials between regional stock markets as well as greater competitive efficiency in share trading as the bourses prepared for more intermarket rivalry. There would also be a potential wealth effect, as the capital markets reappraised the valuation of securities, and a more active financing and corporate restructuring calendar as companies sought to position themselves better in the new Eurozone.

THE EURO BRINGS CHANGE

The period 1998–2000 was forecast to be the most change-oriented epoch ever for European stockbrokers. That forecast has proven to be conservative. Investors across Europe have been forced to rebalance and reorient their portfolios. These changes will make up "the mother of all program trades."[1]

The euro has brought a shift in European culture and behavior. The *Mittelstand,* Germany's privately held companies, is preparing to go public, and smaller companies across Europe are watching this development. This could create a two-tier corporate economy across Europe, with 200–300 big European corporations making up a pan-European share market. The smaller companies are likely to remain more local in their share listings and share trading. Meanwhile, Brussels-based EASDAQ is attempting to develop a European-wide new company stock market, as the Neuer Markt and Euro Nouveau Marche in Frankfurt and Paris seek to list small high-tech companies. These changes suggest that the old flagship national equity indices, DAX and

CAC 30, face a volatile future. A race is on to design and promote European share indices, such as the FTSE Eurotop index, introduced in 1998.

The labyrinth of regulated financial institutions and fund managers in Europe is being attacked by those aware of new opportunities in the equity markets. This means that insurance mergers, bank mergers, and new partnerships are forming to break through the tangle of restrictions that have limited European fund managers in the past. In 1999 a rising demand for cross-border equity investing became more apparent, although it was observed in 1998, when continental equity markets rose 28 percent in dollar terms (January–May 1998).

Although national borders are becoming fuzzy, stock market analysts are observing the ascendance of European-wide industry sector analysis and focusing away from national stock market sectors. One Brussels equity analysis firm notes that four European-wide stock market sectors are clearly identifiable: pharmaceuticals, financials, oils, and consumer brands. Others are following closely behind, including telecoms, motors, and utilities.

European corporations witnessed a decline in their cost of equity capital between 1997 and 1998. Not far behind this decline is European companies' acceptance of the shareholder value concept. For example, company attitudes toward equity buybacks still vary, but German legislation is moving ahead to provide a more permissive environment for share repurchases by companies.

EUROPEAN SHARE MARKETS IN AND OUT EURO

The inclusion of eleven nations in the euro system placed two stock markets, those of Germany and France, in a dominant position. The German and French markets accounted for over half of European market capitalization at mid 1998. Two other markets, those of Italy and the Netherlands, account for nearly 30 percent of the E-11 market value (table 8.1).

If we consider the E-15 countries, the London stock market is in first place with 37 percent of market capitalization, much more than Germany and France combined (table 8.1). If we consider the E-17 markets, half of market capitalization lies outside Euroland.

EXPECTED GROWTH OF EQUITY MARKETS

The European equity markets are expected to grow faster as the euro is phased in. This growth will result from changing demand and supply, structural changes in the equity markets, and the creation of new equity market components.

Table 8.1. Percentage Share of European Market Capitalization In and Out

	Percentage of		
Market Sector	*E-11*	*E-15*	*E-17*
E-11			
Germany	27.1	15.2	13.8
France	23.7	13.3	11.9
Italy	13.0	7.3	6.5
Netherlands	15.9	8.9	7.9
Belgium-Luxembourg	5.0	2.8	2.5
Spain	8.6	4.8	4.3
Austria	1.0	0.5	0.5
Finland	2.8	1.6	1.4
Portugal	1.3	0.7	0.7
Ireland	1.6	0.9	0.8
E-15			
United Kingdom		37.0	33.0
Sweden		5.1	4.5
Denmark		1.3	1.2
Greece		0.6	0.6
E-17			
Switzerland			10.0
Norway			0.7

Source: Barry Riley, "Aim for Bourse without Borders," *Financial Times*, May 18, 1998, 15. Authors' estimates.

Stronger Demand

A stronger demand already is manifesting itself in Europe's markets for equities. Several factors account for this:

- An equity culture is being fostered in countries such as Germany, which were long believed to lack interest in equity investment and financing.[2]
- European Union (EU) directives have provided the legal basis for the widespread issuance of mutual fund–type investment vehicles.
- A wealth effect across Europe based on the coming of the euro is taking place. This is explained below.

The euro will bring a positive wealth effect across Europe. There are three or more possible sources of this wealth effect, outlined in table 8.2. The sources consist of lower transaction costs in a wider capital market. These factors increase the value of both physical and financial assets as business entities across Euroland experience lower transaction costs (of approximately 0.25 percent); profit and valuation will rise by a similar amount.

Table 8.2. Sources of Increased Wealth Effect from Euro (U.S.$ billions)

Source	*Base Value (U.S.$bil)*	*Percentage Change*	*Wealth Effect (U.S.$bil)*
1. Lower transaction costs			
Company securities	3,800	0.25	9.5
Company assets	7,000	0.25	17.5
2. Lower interest rates and cost of capital			
Debt securities	2,000	2.00	40.0
Equity securities	1,800	2.00	36.0
3. Bond and credit quality upgrades related to euro-enhanced value of debt securities	2,000	4.00	80.0
4. Total	*16,600*		*183.0*

Source: Present value tables.
Note: Estimates are from authors' calculations.

Second, lower interest rates and cost of capital enhance wealth effects. A lower cost of capital implies higher security prices. These wealth effects could increase securities prices by two percent or more. These expectations are based on an assumption of a 0.5–1.0 percent reduction in interest rate levels (required yield on bonds or equity instruments). A 2 percent increase in value is a conservative estimate, as can be seen in table 8.3.

Third, bond and credit quality upgrades are expected because the euro should enhance the value of debt securities held by investors. Bond ratings should improve and valuations should rise by 4 percent or more. The numerical calculations for these expected increases can be found in table 8.2. Overall, we calculate a $183 billion wealth effect gain.

Table 8.3. Present Value of $1,000 Receivable in Five Years

Required Yield %	*Present Value*	*PV Differential*	*Differential as %*
5	783.50	36.20	4.84
6	747.30	34.30	4.81
7	713.00	32.40	4.76
8	680.60	30.70	4.73
9	649.90	29.00	4.67.
10	620.90		

Note: PV differential of 36.20 is calculated as 783.50–747.30.

Improved Supply

The growth prospects for European equity markets depend on an increased supply of securities coming into the market place. Several factors lead one to believe that the dynamics of equity markets with the euro will favor the increased issuance of equity. These factors include:

- A larger, more efficient, single currency equity market that has lower transaction costs, as well as a better information base. Currency transaction costs will disappear among the E-11 countries and investment bank fees will become more competitive for issuers of equity securities. The market will more readily facilitate the new issues of smaller companies. This was observed as early as 1998, when four "new markets" for high-tech start-up companies were organized for this purpose.
- There are many family-owned companies in Europe. In the past, it was not practical to expect to liquidate concentrated family ownership, due to the limited size and development of European stock markets. The new stock markets provide improved prospects for liquidation of these concentrated shareholdings. Similarly, relaxation or removal of capital gains tax (as in Germany) will allow shareholders to sell shares with more favorable after-tax results.
- The venture capital (VC) business will open up opportunities in European countries where such financing formerly has been difficult. (We return to the matter of venture capital in a later section of this chapter.)

The preceding factors translate into a higher level of initial public offerings (IPOs) throughout Europe. Writing in 1996, Erik Berglöf noted that the decision to go public affects the trade-off between control and liquidity in two ways. First, anonymity of transactions in a public market makes it easier for control investors to unwind positions, and, second, the increase in information asymmetry between large and small shareholders may have a negative impact on liquidity of equity shares.[3] As continental Europe evolves away from control-oriented and toward arm's-length financial markets, greater share issuance should result from:

- A larger number of firms listed on share markets (table 8.4, line 2)
- More dispersed ownership (table 8.4, line 3)
- More liquid share markets (table 8.4, line 5)
- Greater interest in equity markets via increasing numbers of hostile takeovers (table 8.4, line 8)

Table 8.4. Financial Systems, Capital Structure, and Share Issuance

	Type of Financial System	
Structural Element	*Control Oriented*	*Arm's-Length*
Share of control-oriented finance	High	Low
Share of firms listed on stock exchanges	Small	Large
Ownership of debt and equity	Concentrated	Dispersed
Investor orientation	Control	Portfolio
Turnover of control blocks of shares	Low	High
Dominant agency conflict	Controlling vs. minority	Shareholders vs.management
Role of external board of directors	Limited	Important
Role of hostile takeovers	Limited	Important

Source: Benn Steil, ed., *The European Equity Market* (London: Royal Institute of International Affairs, 1996). Materials adapted by authors.

Structural Change in Stock Markets

When Europe entered the third stage of the European monetary union (EMU), interest focused on how the capital markets adapted to provide more efficient and responsive trading systems for shares. We examine some of the structural approaches in the following section of this chapter. At this point we consider the question, What is a stock market? How do we distinguish the market mechanism from the broker-dealer securities firms that are traditionally viewed as no more than active participants in the equity markets?

Until the early 1980s there was a clear distinction between stock exchanges (or markets) and the broker-dealer securities firms that facilitated transactions on these markets. Several trends made this easy distinction fuzzy or even obsolete. More important, technology was changing the field of securities trading dramatically. We now speak about "trading platforms" or "electronic platforms" on which securities trading can take place. These platforms can be large or small, can accommodate one or several securities, and can be serviced by none, one, or several securities broker-dealers.

A second change is the proprietary nature of the markets in which securities are traded, notably the electronic trading platforms. Purveyors of electronic trading programs and systems developed these platforms. The platforms were sold or leased for use by securities broker-dealers or institutional investors needing a capacity to match block trade deals. Even the stock exchanges themselves have moved from the concept of markets affected by a public interest toward that of proprietary markets that generate bottom-line results.

MARKET STRUCTURES

With the advent of the euro, an already dynamic and changing European equity market structure became subject to even greater change. Some of these major changes began to occur as a result of the new euro currency. First, trading volume began to escalate as global investors became more interested in European equities and as fund managers began to conform to new benchmarks and weightings. Second, competition for this trading business began to intensify, which exerted pressure on the profit margins of broker-dealer operations in Europe.

In the following discussion we consider how equity trading in Europe may be expected to evolve, using the North American scenario as a reference point. Next we examine the specific changes occurring in Europe as it moves into a single currency system.

The North American Model

At first glance the North American equity trading system may seem to present a picture of stable maturity, but this is not the case. Behind the scenes, considerable change is going on. We view this, first, from the perspective of changes taking place in the large, mature market systems and, second, from the perspective of the subindustry that services equity trading, the information technology purveyors of screen-based trading systems.[4]

Mature Markets

The intense competition between leading market systems in North American equities trading is reflected by the following:[5]

- The New York Stock Exchange (NYSE) is aggressively visiting European and other non-U.S. companies to secure additional listings. Success in attracting the large German companies in recent years has whetted their appetite. This success is evidenced by the rapid growth in American Depository Receipt listings on U.S. markets.
- The merger between NASDAQ and the American Stock Exchange reflects a fear that intensified competition will leave some market systems obsolete. The different trading technologies of both of these partners provide protection against possible technological obsolescence.
- The Toronto Stock Exchange virtually closed down its trading floor in March 1997, as did the London Stock Exchange ten years earlier. Now computer-assisted trading systems (CATS) have provided the TSE with a window into the future and assures it of a competitive position for several years.

These competitive responses to a dynamic North American equity market environment should be placed in perspective. The United States has enjoyed a single currency for over two hundred years, and the central banking regime has eliminated the small regional currency differentials that distinguished New York from Chicago and San Francisco funds.

The North American equity markets now compete on a global basis. The European equity markets are just beginning to compete on a regional or continent-wide basis as the euro comes on the scene.

Reuters et al.

While stock exchanges provide "markets of place" for equity trading, the related transactions are shifting more and more to electronic "markets of execution." As a result, strong competition has developed for the business of providing screen-based trading services. We can observe the competitive status of providers of screen-based trading services in table 8.5. Close to 300,000 equity trading screens were in operation in North America in 1998, with the largest provider accounting for almost 40 percent of the total.

Screen-based trading originally meant providing price and trading volume data. There were no analytics and there was little capacity to complete the transaction within the system. This kind of system was superseded by more advanced programs that provided the ability to perform various kinds of information and analytics. The new screens also could generate bid-offer prices produced through broker-dealer networks and allowed users to close deals based on these prices. These facilities were supported by computerized back-office trade processing, another important dimension of screen trading.

Finally, screen-based computer systems allowed total matched transactions, where there was an automatic lock of buyers and sellers. Variations existed in terms of the number of participants who could have access to the platform and the trading volume capability.

Table 8.5. Trading Screens Used in North America by Equity Traders

Company Purveyor	*Number of Trading Screens*
Quotron	42,000
ADP	84,000
Bridge	54,000
Thompson	112,000
Subtotal	292,000
Estimated Total for North America	300,000

Source: Richard Waters, "Reuters Prepares Second Assault on U.S. Equities," *Financial Times*, May 27, 1998, 19.

European Markets

The equity markets in the E-11 country group and the four equity markets in the EU countries not in the group (UK, Sweden, Denmark, and Greece) faced many challenges as the euro came into existence. In London, the stock exchange made initiatives to retain its competitive position across all Europe.

London Initiatives

In October 1997 the London Stock Exchange (LSE) launched a new electronic trading system, SETS (Stock Exchange Trading System), to replace the old market makers that received tax and trading privileges in return for making dealer markets in equities. After four months in operation, the central electronic order book reduced spread costs from 62 basis points to 50. Wholesale or large order spreads benefited more than retail spreads. A typical retail trade was reported to enjoy a £4 (or 15 percent) saving from the new system. On March 1998 the question was how to get direct access to the system without using a broker.[6]

Six months after SETS was established, institutional investors in London indicated that they preferred a central counterparty so they could trade shares anonymously. While orders were posted anonymously on the exchange's electronic order book, the buyer-seller identity was revealed to anyone who matched an order. When one large order was filled by dozens of small counterpart deals, the investor had to pay settlement costs on each counterpart deal. A survey conducted by Tradepoint, the rival electronic market that uses a central counterparty, found that 85 percent of institutional investors considered a central counterparty to be important. Tradepoint has struggled to attract trading volume since it was established in 1995.[7]

Both listed companies and institutional investors found problems with the SETS trading system implemented by LSE. These complaints were based on excessive price volatility, low liquidity, and the speed at which trading takes place. Nevertheless, a number of market users found the overall cost of trading improved. The LSE proposed to shorten trading hours to improve liquidity.[8]

In May 1998 it was reported that 32 percent of FTSE 100 company share trades were done via the SETS system. The rest were traded through market makers that quote prices for shares, but they were no longer required to quote firm two-way prices to all callers at any time.[9]

Continental Initiatives

The continental stock exchanges have been aggressively preparing for the euro and for what is expected to be a more competitive climate. Beginning as early as 1995, new equity trading systems were being planned, including EASDAQ, a system for pan-European equity trading and other imitators. The basic problems in European equity trading have been a lack of pan-European equity trading, inability of smaller companies to gain listings, low liquidity, and limited institutional demand. The following initiatives focus on some of these problems.

- EASDAQ was initiated in 1995 as a pan-European equity trading system and operates a trading system closely modeled along the lines of NASDAQ in the United States.
- Four "new markets" were organized in Paris, Frankfurt, Amsterdam, and Brussels. These were intended to provide electronic trading for new high-tech European companies. The Neuer Markt was one of Germany's most successful exchanges. As of April 2001 it had listed some 339 companies. In calendar year 2000 the Neuer Markt received 108 initial public offerings, compared with 191 for NASDAQ and only three for EASDAQ. While the Neuer Markt experienced an 8.5 percent decrease in activity since its March 2000 to April 2001 peak, shareholder expectations continue to be high. In the case of the Neuer Markt, its shareholders are often also the managers of the companies that list their stocks. In fact, in the Neuer Markt, many companies are still owned and managed by the same people who started them. The range of ownership for managers of many of the listed companies is 30–60 percent. These Neuer Markt companies are still run like private companies. Managers view the IPO as a way to raise money, and are managing the companies along venture capital-private equity lines. Partly for these reasons, there has been only one takeover of a Neuer Markt company up to April 2001.[10]
- European stock exchanges are forming alliances. The German, French, and Swiss discussed teaming up to create an electronic network called Euro Alliance. This approach could lead to closer ties, shared costs of electronic trading facilities, and cross-listing of shares.[11]
- In May 2000 France, the Netherlands, and Belgium announced the formation of a new merged securities market called Euronext.
- In April 2000 the London Stock Exchange (LSE) announced renewed merger talks with the Frankfurt markets. This merger promises a new market with a market capitalization of $4.379 trillion, second only to the New York Stock Exchange's $11.2 trillion capitalization. These negotiations are discussed below.
- The Paris bourse is launching a European depository receipt market in 1999 for emerging market companies. This initiative challenges London's position as a regional financial center. The Paris bourse also linked with Citibank as its depository bank. A target of ten new listings is expected by

mid-1999. Funds in the Eurozone, which are restricted to investment in euro-denominated shares, could provide a ready market for such listings.[12]

- The Swedish stock exchange indicated plans to list securities in the euro. Like Britain, Sweden is one of the four nations that delayed entry into the single-currency system. Some Swedish companies have expressed concern that Stockholm's position as a financial center might be damaged if European investors decide to avoid currency risk in the kronor. The biggest company on the Swedish stock exchange, L.M. Ericsson, favors listing its shares in both currencies, similar to what London's exchange plans to do with its one hundred blue chips.[13]

Europe's Big Bang

In July 1998 the London and Frankfurt stock exchanges announced a cooperation agreement. A London-Frankfurt linkup would mark a change in tactics for the LSE, which had been aloof to the attempts of continental exchanges to establish an alliance. A new aggressiveness in London signals a sharp response to the success of the German Financial Futures Exchange (DTB) in wresting away control of Europe's benchmark government bond contract from the London International Financial Futures and Options Exchange (LIFFE).[14]

This alliance could reshape the operation of continental financial markets. At a press conference the LSE and Deutsche Börse signed a memorandum of understanding aimed at creating a common electronic trading platform for Europe's top blue chip stocks. They proclaimed that their bilateral agreement would become the nucleus of a new pan-European stock market. Brokers currently must deal with an array of different market structures and regulatory regimes, and they welcomed the pact as a step toward reducing trading costs. Gavin Corr, portfolio manager of American Express Management in London, stated that this has the potential to immediately increase the universe of stocks that we are able to analyze and invest in.[15]

Nevertheless, the new venture faced hurdles. Similar past projects have become stalemated. The impetus for the venture comes from the London brokerage community, fearful of being left out in the cold as eleven other European nations move toward full membership in the monetary union. Firms like Merrill Lynch, Union Bank of Switzerland, ABN Amro, and HSBC Holdings advised British stock exchange officials to accept the idea of a pan-European exchange and move forward in discussions with their German counterparts. American investors also seem to have an interest in European market alliances. According to Fred Taylor of U.S. Trust Corp. in New York, the development of a common trading platform will make investing in European stocks easier for American institutions.[16]

The move caused a lull in the bitter war between the London and Frankfurt stock exchanges for European supremacy. Gavin Casey, chief executive of the LSE, stated that the two exchanges hoped other European bourses would join. The two exchanges plan to harmonize their market rules, accounting standards, and conventions, and build a single electronic trading system.[17]

Negative responses to the London-Frankfurt initiative came from several sources. The LIFFE stated that it would threaten London's position as Europe's financial center. LIFFE has aimed at remaining the biggest derivatives market in Europe. It has introduced several trading innovations to counter competitive inroads from the DTB and the French derivatives exchange, Matif.[18] The concern in Paris is that the French stock exchange could become isolated.

A Strategic Alliance

The strategic alliance announced by the London and Frankfurt stock exchanges early in July 1998 called for significant changes in the trading systems of the two participants. The two exchanges planned to harmonize their listing rules and market conventions, offer reciprocal access to each other's members, and eventually build a single electronic trading platform for the three hundred largest European companies. In the single, market-driven Europe of the future, there will probably exist only one European-wide group of blue chip stocks and one market on which to trade them.

Stock exchanges are losing their hold on related services. For example, the LSE settlement system (formerly Talisman) has been displaced by an autonomous system named Crest. Some observers think that stock exchanges are headed for the dismal status of electronic bulletin boards, functioning only to centralize buy-and-sell orders.

Technology is an important driving force in the changes taking place in stock exchanges around the world. This technology is quite expensive. The Xetra trading system launched by Deutsche Börse in Frankfurt in November 1997 cost DM150 million, and the SETS electronic order book operating in London since October 1997 absorbed £20 million. Newer electronic trading systems like London's Tradepoint were expensed at £10 million, one-half of which was spent on technology.

Tradepoint is another contender in the race to create the first single electronic platform for trading European stocks. In February 2000, Tradepoint won the backing of two leading clearing and settlement houses. The London Clearing House, which clears Tradepoint's UK transactions, agreed to act as a central counterparty for settling and clearing cross-border trades made though Tradepoint. Euroclear will settle these trades.

Early in 2000, Tradepoint was handling 1 percent of trading in UK shares and had plans to launch a pan-European exchange later in the year, trading three hundred top European companies. Tradepoint plans to compete with others who aspire to organize the main platform for trading European equities. These competitors include NASDAQ, Deutsche Börse, the London Stock Exchange, and the OM Group, which operates the Swedish stock exchange. In early 2000 Tradepoint had eleven members, including Merrill Lynch, CSFB, Warburg Dillon Read, and Instinet. Tradepoint has targeted interdealer and institutional investors.[19]

Technology also is bringing about a redistribution of share trading. For example, the U.S. Securities and Exchange Commission estimated that alternative trading systems in 1997 handled 20 percent of the orders in NASDAQ listed shares, as well as 4 percent of the orders in NYSE-listed stocks. These orders included those from Instinet, which is run by Reuters electronic media group. In Instinet participants display firm-priced orders and execute them. The Arizona Stock Exchange also operates an electronic market that establishes a single price for order execution in the UK.

While Instinet and Tradepoint offer similar services, there is a legal distinction between the two companies. Instinet is considered a broker, whereas Tradepoint is considered an exchange. Regulators are searching for ways to deal with such anomalies. Meanwhile, in 1998 an estimated one-fifth of the orders in NASDAQ's electronic market came from personal computers via the World Wide Web.

The proliferation of computers, the impact of the Eurozone in focusing investors on a pan-European equity market, and competitive behavior of corporations should make European equity markets develop rapidly into more liquid and efficient trading systems.

The LSE-Frankfurt Merger

In April 2000, it was reported that the LSE and the Frankfurt stock exchanges were discussing a full-scale merger that would create Europe's largest market.[20] This move was spurred by a number of recent large-scale securities market mergers in Euroland:

- NASDAQ's announcement that it will begin pan-European trading in 2001
- The May 2000 merger of the securities markets in France, the Netherlands, and Belgium into the new Euronext market (The Paris Bourse probably will dominate this market.)
- Nimbler Internet trading companies such as Tradepoint Financial Networks offering electronic trading on a pan-European basis

In the long run, the LSE-Frankfurt merger seems to be inevitable. "The logic is that all Europe's exchanges should all be one big alliance," said David Donnelly, chief investment officer at Gordon House Asset Management.[21] Don Cruikshank, the new head of the LSE, said that he felt that the merger would be "the first major step toward the rationalization of securities trading across Europe."[22] Should the merger take place, it would create a market trading shares with a combined value of $4.3 trillion, as compared with $11.4 trillion of shares traded on the New York Stock Exchange and $2.2 trillion traded on the Euronext market. Table 8.6 compares European exchanges and proposed market mergers.

Table 8.6. Alternative Stock Markets in Europe

Market	*Location*	*Listings*	*Capitalization*	*Date Created*
Operating markets				
AIM	London	312	€9.900 billion	June 1995
EASDAQ	Brussels	35	€16.200 billion	Oct. 1996
NMAX	Amsterdam	12	€1.300 billion	Feb. 1997
Neuer Markt	Frankfurt	36	€16.400 billion	Mar. 1997
Nouveau Marche	Paris	59	€3.900 billion	Feb. 1996
LSE	London	2,775	$2.827 trillion	Jan. 1800
Frankfurt	Frankfurt	8,890	$1.552 trillion	n.a.
Pending mergers				
Euronext	Paris	n.a.	$2.200 trillion	May 2000
LSE-Frankfurt	n.a.	11,665	$4.379 trillion	n.a.

Source: Daniel Myzyka and Benoit Leleux, "Europe's New Equity Markets: A Delicate Balance," *QED,* October 1998, 18–20.

Despite the merger's appeal, it faces a number of daunting short-term obstacles:[23]

- Werner G. Seifert of the Frankfurt exchange is demanding two-thirds equity control of the merged exchange based on the faster growth and larger revenues of the German exchange ($635 million versus $240 million for the LSE).
- The two-hundred-year-old LSE feels that it is the oldest and most respected European stock exchange, based partly on the fact that it trades stocks with a greater market capitalization ($2.827 trillion) than does the Frankfurt exchange ($1.552 trillion). Thus the LSE feels that its "leading position in the trading of international securities gives it a pivotal role in the realignment of exchanges,"[24] and it has demanded a merger of equals. Should the demands not be met, the LSE would attribute the failure of talks to "the intransigence of Germans over regulation."[25]

- The Frankfurt exchange, however, generates a larger revenue, with 1999 revenue exceeding $635 million, as compared with revenues of only $240 million for the LSE.
- The British fear that a merger on Frankfurt's terms would be viewed as a competitive capitulation to the German markets. This point is particularly sensitive in light of BMW's recent sale of Rover to a venture capital firm.
- The electronic trading platforms of the LSE and Frankfurt markets are incompatible. The LSE uses the cumbersome SETS platform, whereas the Frankfurt exchange uses the more modern Xetra system. On April 5, 2000, the SETS system immobilized the British exchange for most of the day while the European exchanges were able to follow the wild swings on Wall Street using Xetra.
- The merged market must operate across different currency zones—British sterling and the euro—and also across both British and German regulatory regimes.

Enter the Top Tier

Frankfurt and other continental European stock exchanges can learn much from a linkup between London and Frankfurt. The main global investor contacts are in London. The Germans bring one important asset to the alliance—technology. In 1997 the Germans introduced Xetra to make trading more transparent and efficient. Technology and the new realities of the Eurozone lead Frankfurt's agenda for the future. The Vienna Stock Exchange is switching to Xetra, after merging the Vienna exchange and the formerly separate derivatives exchange market. The Germans and Swiss have combined their derivatives exchanges (DTB and Soffex) to form Eurex, which now plans to link up with France's Matif.[26]

The Deutsche Börse has positioned itself at the center of European share and derivatives alliances. It is exploring business ties with NASDAQ, itself interested in linkages in Europe. Deutsche Börse has teamed up with the French and Swiss exchanges and Dow Jones (U.S.) to produce the Eurostock index. This is in competition with the Eurotop indices operated by FTSE International. These alliances aim at making investment easier for both institutional and retail investors.

A successful alliance with London could catapult Frankfurt into the top tier of the world stock exchange industry. But there is a cost. Frankfurt will sacrifice its ability to operate independently and bring forth new strategies to enhance its competitive status. Frankfurt may think that top tier status is more important.

Common Rules and Systems

The London and Frankfurt exchanges must adopt common rules and systems for a successful alliance. This includes a "common access package" and single point of liquidity. Technical linkage will require standardized bank holidays and hours, trade reporting requirements, and exemption from special duties (stamp duty). Lack of liquidity on SETS must be addressed. The combined system will need to service the large block trades of institutional investors.

The development of a pan-European stock market will require regulatory adjustment. At present, unfortunately, there is no natural regulator of a pan-European stock exchange. Nevertheless, the regulators themselves state that "the proposed alliance should not pose regulatory problems."[27]

In Paris, the officials of the stock market were surprised by the negotiations for an LSE-Frankfurt alliance. These officials had already been discussing co-operation with the Frankfurt stock exchange. The Paris exchange had launched its "euro alliance" with the Stoxx index of European quoted companies and another index for derivatives. Also, it was building partnerships between its own Nouveau Marche for small and growing companies and similar trading systems in at least three other nations.[28]

Toward a Pan-European Equities Market

The alliance between the Frankfurt and London stock exchanges is what the EU and the euro is all about: removing barriers and creating a unified capital market.[29] Europe will not find it efficient or advantageous to continue with twenty-five or more different stock exchanges. The euro is creating a single European-wide pool of capital. This means to many observers a European equities market, using a single share-trading platform.

The link between the London and Frankfurt stock exchanges could be the most important step in the direction of this single market. The two-country alliance signifies that Europe's two largest equity markets have agreed to become central points for market participants to gain efficient access to a more unified equity market system. This could lead to another big bang on a pan-European scale, making prior big bang experiences (London, Spain, and Portugal) seem like insignificant blips on an electronic viewing screen.

Despite this, national efforts to become more important in equity trading will continue. This will include competition for listing, trading, and related services (benchmarks, indices, clearing facilities, and special platforms for trading block positions held by institutional investors).

With respect to large traders, it has become increasingly clear that Europe's exchanges must give big customers what they need—capacity for trading large volumes in single trades, temporary anonymity, and market liquidity. Michael

Marks, chairman of Merrill Lynch Europe and a board member of the LSE, stated that "the London and Frankfurt stock exchanges saw that the users would demand a pan-European market and if they hadn't set it up, someone else probably would have."[30] Werner Seifert, chief executive of Deutsche Börse, stated that the alliance should put an end to speculation about a battle between Frankfurt and London.

Many tricky details had to be worked out for the alliance to work well, including how revenues will be shared, where the office headquarters will be located, and what governance structure will be developed. Can a unified settlements system be developed? How will the selection of three hundred blue chip companies be carried out? London has already set up a benchmark called Eurotop. The two partners state that they would adopt a single benchmark. Other obstacles to be overcome include different accounting standards, tax regimes, and regulatory systems.

The many details weighed heavily in discussions between the LSE and Frankfurt stock exchange officials over the summer months of 2000. In September 2000 the LSE unilaterally withdrew from merger discussions. Shortly after that, the OM Group, representing the Swedish (Stockholm) stock exchange, initiated a hostile takeover bid for the LSE. Officials at the London Stock Exchange successfully rebuffed these advances.

In the nine months from September 2000 to May 2001 the LSE was busy transforming itself into a profit-seeking organization, demutualizing itself and initiating a privately traded market for its shares. The equity market specialist Cazenove served as market maker in this instance. In this period the LSE's privately traded shares outperformed OM Group's by 170 percent.[31] By the summer of 2001 the LSE's shares were trading at a relatively high multiple (21 times) of forward earnings, and the exchange anticipated merger synergies because of the high proportion of fixed costs in their share trading business. A full listing of the LSE's shares is scheduled for July 2001.

The LSE plan for a full listing of its shares is in line with the strategies of Deutsche Börse and Euronext. These plans will allow the stock exchange to raise new capital and maneuver for alliances or takeovers. Mergers may not be a panacea for them. First, traders have electronic access to all the important exchanges. Second, mergers of quoted exchanges could raise serious competition policy issues, especially when transactions costs are considered to be too high. One of the prime objectives of the bourses and their authorities is to reduce these costs. Cross-border clearing and settlement offer good scope for cost savings in this regard. Two incompatible approaches are emerging. First is Deutsche Börse's intent to acquire control of Clearstream, the Luxembourg integrated clearing and settlement provider. Second is Don Cruickshank's desire to separate the bourses from the clearing process. Cruickshank, chairman of the LSE, has a vision of a clearing system that will evolve into a single, not-for-profit, European-wide institution. Such an exchange could cut transactions costs to U.S. levels.[32]

In 2001 the LSE went through an organizational restructuring and experienced significant management changes. Clara Furst replaced Gavin Casey as chief executive in February 2001. Furst, who is Dutch and speaks five languages, is the first woman to head the exchange in its 228-year history. Her biggest challenge is to devise a plan for taking the exchange beyond London to create a trading system that spans Europe. Her earliest initiatives have been to shake up the board and to replace half the directors with executives from outside the financial community. The LSE needs to get its house in order before it can expand abroad. This means lowering trading costs, and adding new products. Furst has been holding discussions with her counterpart at the LIFFE to explore ways for the two exchanges to work more closely together.[33]

VALUATION, MERGERS, AND MARKET DISTORTIONS

The period 1998–2000 witnessed a surge in merger activity, with a number of mega-deals completed in this period. These merger transactions created serious problems for investors, who used stock market index weightings as a basis for setting their portfolio allocations. Underlying this problem was an apparent shift in investor demand toward high-tech securities and away from companies in traditional industry sectors.

Knock-Down and Super Prices

While the period 1998–1999 saw the introduction of the single currency, there was a related surge in mergers and corporate restructuring, and these changes put new pressures on equity prices. With the coming of euro, corporate executives expected, correctly, that share prices would become subject to more intense analysis, based in part on a horizontal stock market perspective throughout the Eurozone. The new emphasis on shareholder wealth placed a sharp focus on the stock market capitalization of European companies in evaluating success. Corporations could ignore such matters only at great peril, since depressed share prices would expose them to takeover bids. A previous chapter demonstrated this phenomenon dramatically using the Olivetti, BNP-Paribas, and Vodafone-Mannesmann cases.

In this period investors repriced equity securities to an extreme degree. Two distinct classes of equity securities became recognizable: the shares in technology, communications, and media and the traditional sector shares, including food producers, banks, chemicals, restaurants and breweries, and insurance. The technology stocks became priced in the penthouse, while the companies in traditional sectors experienced bargain basement pricing.

One interpretation of this phenomenon is that investors are uninterested in the safe and reliable and seek growth at any price. For example, British privatization companies lost one-fourth to one-third of their value in late 1999 and early 2000.[34] These companies included British Telecom, British Gas, and British Airways. In this "rush to growth" investors tended to ignore historic valuation methods when they assessed stocks.

A typical new technology IPO was the Interactive Investor International issue, floated in mid-February 2000. The offer was oversubscribed twenty-five times. At the close of first-day trading, the stock rose from 150 pence to 338.50 pence, more than doubling. Interactive is an online financial services group that provides information for retail investors and software for stockbrokers.

Interactive had net revenues of £2.6 million in 1999 and a first-day closing market capitalization value of £555 million, or almost 213 times annual sales of £2.6 million (table 8.7). In 1999 Interactive suffered a loss of £6.3 million. How do we value a company such as Interactive? In their recent book The *Internet Bubble,* Anthony Perkins and Michael Perkins use a model assuming 65 percent revenue growth, net margins of 5–15 percent, and a PE multiple of 40. They indicate that investors should demand a 20 percent annual return from equities, due to high risk.

These figures imply that Interactive should have revenues of £31.8 million in five years and pretax profits of £4.8 million (a 15 percent margin). These figures further imply that after-tax profits should provide a multiple of forty and this suggests that Interactive's market capitalization should be £134 million (table 8.7). The problem is that Interactive's actual estimated value in five years is less than one-fourth the first day's closing price. These discrepancies

Table 8.7. How to Misprice New Tech Stocks

	Year 0	*Year 5*
Revenues	2.6	31.80[a]
After-tax profit[b]	—	3.36
Profit (loss)	(6.3)	4.80[c]
Market capitalization	555.0[d]	134.5[e]
PE multiple	n.a.	40

[a]Growth at 65 percent annually.
[b]Taxes at 30 percent.
[c]Profit margin of 15 percent in year 5.
[d]First-day closing price.
[e]Apply PE multiples of forty to after-tax profit.

suggest that the market's valuation model is flawed or that investment bankers originally improperly priced the issue.

The pricing of new technology issues is not the only source of distorted equity valuations. Large mergers also have caused some problems. For example, if the mergers of Vodafone-Mannesmann, BP-Amoco-Arco, and Glaxo-Smith Kline go through, these three stocks, in descending order, would account for 15 percent, 9 percent, and 7 percent, respectively, of the FTSE 100 equities index.[35] This observation is based on valuations at end of January 2000. These percentages represent a full 31 percent of the FTSE 100 index. This level of market concentration does not exceed historic patterns, and it is much lower than in Finland, since Nokia alone accounts for two-thirds of Finland's entire stock market value. Thus an investor must reappraise the whole UK market, given the higher level of systematic (nondiversifiable) risk now present. This distortion is transmitted to institutional investor portfolios because of their adherence to market weight portfolio allocations. This results in a decrease in the diversification of institutional portfolios, which mirrors the decreased diversification of the market itself.

Index Problems

As noted in the previous section, leading stock market indexes are facing problems as a result of the mega-mergers of recent years and their effect on concentrations of value within the indexes. As giant stocks come to dominate the main benchmarks against which fund performance is judged, fund managers and trustees of pension funds are placed in a difficult position. Many of the trustees are directors of the companies whose shares must be dumped to reduce portfolio concentrations.[36]

It is reported that the Vodafone-Mannesmann group could be worth as much as 18 percent of the FTSE 100, using valuations current in mid-February 2000. The need to keep portfolios diversified dictates that under UK rules, their pension funds generally limit stock holdings in a given company to only 5 percent of their total holdings. For the same reason, in the UK, indexes tracking unit trusts cannot hold more than 10 percent of their portfolio in one stock. Keeping in mind this need to diversify away risk, unit trust managers have recently lobbied for a new series of benchmark indices that cap individual stocks at close to 10 percent of the tracking fund. FTSE International is expected to introduce indices that meet these requirements.

Pension funds, in contrast to unit trusts, have issues which are so difficult that actuarial consultants cannot agree on how to proceed. Pension funds agree that the 5 percent rule should continue but cannot agree on most other issues. One approach would be to rely on multinational indices rather than more instructive national stock indices. An alternate approach is to divide the pension portfolio into two or more components, UK equities and overseas equities.

These proposals boil down to a never ending circle of depressed share prices, incentives for merger, and disconforming equity indexes. Equity indexes continue to suffer from overly concentrated mega-issues and from a propensity to become fully loaded with tech stocks.

Depressed Prices Breed Takeover

In the first quarter of 2000, the share prices of traditional UK companies were seriously depressed. As noted earlier, the depressed prices of traditional companies reflected the penthouse pricing of top-tier technology shares, as compared with the depressed prices for companies in traditional lines of business. Companies like Whitbread, the brewing-restaurant group, were in danger of dropping out of the FTSE 100 index. Baltimore Technologies, a software group, was proposed as a candidate to replace Whitbread. This proposal went forward despite the fact that Baltimore expected losses of £20 million on net assets of £50 million, while holding a market capitalization of £4 billion.[37] As investors deserted "old economy" stocks, share values fell and the older companies became vulnerable to takeovers. A large number of big-name European companies were trading in early 2000 at single-digit price earning ratios, including Tate & Lyle (foods), Royal & Sun Alliance (insurance), National Power, and Abbey National (banking). While technology prices soared between 1999 and 2000, at least a dozen Footsie (FTSE 100) stocks saw their share prices fall as much as 40 percent.

Potential buyers of companies have looked at these trends. These buyers include institutional investors expecting that takeovers will help them bail out of risky positions at favorable prices. These institutional investors also expect to liquidate poorly performing shares through takeover releases of "hot issues" like Vodafone that have been purchased to pump up the valuations of portfolio funds. At severely depressed prices, consumer goods companies made tempting breakup targets. For example, Merrill Lynch placed a higher value on Whitbread's pubs (£2.54 billion) than on the market value of its shares, not counting its hotel, restaurant, and sports club interests. The same can be said for United Biscuits, which in 1999–2000 was subject to bids by several private equity specialist houses.

FROM BONDS TO EQUITIES

In the previous section we noted that in Europe, particularly in the UK, the equity markets are experiencing valuation and structural changes. These changes include a divergence between high low valuations, respectively, on technology and traditional sector companies. Another new factor is the rising level of mergers related to depressed valuations and the new takeover opportunities they cause among traditional sector companies. Rising concentrations of market capitalization in leading equity indices follow these mega-mergers.

Such changes reflect increasingly dynamic equity markets in Europe following the advent of the single currency. This dynamic aspect comes about when money in Europe flows out of the bond market and into equity sectors. In 1999, €90 billion went into European equity funds. This was a 32 percent increase over previous year flows. At the same time investments in bonds fell from €154 billion in 1998 to €16 billion in 1999. Data supplied by J.P. Morgan indicates that this will continue.[38]

The shift from bonds to equities is based on several factors:

- Falling interest rates in the Eurozone
- Concern about the sustainability of state-funded pension systems
- Improved equity performance in Europe for restructured companies and high-tech companies
- Increased retail participation in equity markets

The growing population of pensioners in Europe will stretch the state pension systems to the limits. Therefore, workers will be seeking other sources of retirement income. Locking investments in to equities is expected to generate high returns. Another factor is the increased corporate focus on maximizing shareholder value. Corporate restructuring in recent years is beginning to demonstrate results in terms of increased value, and this is stimulating the investor's appetite for equities. The Dutch pension fund ABP plans to increase the weight of equities in their portfolios to get higher returns.

Jeremy Toner at Foreign and Colonial in London believes that there is a repositioning of the whole European investor base. Many people are cashing in their savings deposits and putting the money into investment funds. The rush into equities has been most notable in Italy and Spain, countries with a history of inflation and high interest rates. Paolo Pizzoli, senior economist at ING Barings in Milan, noted that the fall in inflation sparked a commensurate increase in the appetite for equities. The equity weighting of Italian mutual funds jumped from 25.1 percent in 1998 to 38.9 percent in 1999.

VENTURE CAPITAL IN EUROPE

Continental Europe is catching on to the Anglo-Saxon notion of venture·capital. Corporate Europe is becoming more change oriented as the euro washes away protective national currency zones. In the UK, financing high-tech start-ups, management buyouts, and specialty venture capital funds has become a regular aspect of corporate finance.

Venture capital firms provide funding from private sources for investment in selected companies that offer special opportunities. In the United States, the focus tends to be on financing the early stage of high-risk (and return) ventures. In Europe the focus tends to be on financing buyouts or private equity transactions to alter management performance for higher returns. Firms typically invest for periods of three to seven years and expect returns in the area of 30 percent annually.

The cost of financing through venture capital or private equity is high, due to the perceived risk level and time required to achieve successful operations. Often, venture capital firms demand an equity interest of 20–40 percent in the company as well as the ability to monitor and perhaps exercise some degree of control through a position on the board of directors. In the American model, venture capital ownership takes the form of a straight equity interest plus ownership options. In the European model, equity ownership will be required, but also the opportunity to gain from the leveraged financing required to take the enterprise private.

There are several distinct stages of development in the life cycle of a business, and VC–private equity activities have a differential relationship to several of these stages:

- Seed investment funding for development of a business concept before production or trading
- Start-up investment funding for an enterprise in operation one or more years, to provide expansion capital (This stage is important in U.S. venture capital.)
- Replacement investment funding for the purchase of existing shares of venture-backed companies from other shareholders, perhaps due to a delay in business development
- Expansion of investment funding to facilitate the growth of established firms (private, venture capital–supported) that are operating but still require risk capital
- Buyout investment funding: buyouts or buyins to provide funding to help a management team acquire a company (This represents the largest portion of private equity investing in Europe.)

Exit mechanisms are necessary to allow entrepreneurs and venture capital investors to capture the value they have created. Without exit mechanisms, there could be no healthy venture capital industry. Three of the most common exit channels are the following:[39]

- Trade sale—cash sale of an enterprise to another company, institution, or individual

- Managerial acquisition—sale of a venture-backed company to another company (This method is difficult and only available to a buyer with a long-term perspective.)
- IPO—public sale of the invested company through a stock market distribution and listing (This often is the preferred exit method, based on the expectation of high returns in a market flotation.)

Europe is becoming more familiar with venture capital. Germany's Neuer Markt lists the shares of relatively young enterprises. Science students in the former East Germany are dreaming of commercializing technical and scientific processes. In 1997 European venture capital firms raised $22 billion, more than double the amount for 1996 (table 8.8). Over half of this came from Britain. Nevertheless, venture capital funding increased 650 percent in Germany and nearly 2,000 percent in Sweden.[40] This money is flowing into start-up companies that have few alternative sources of capital.[41]

Table 8.8. New Funds Raised by European Venture Capital and Private Equity Fund Managers

Year	*U.S.$ billions*
1990	6
1991	5
1992	6
1993	4
1994	8
1995	6
1996	10
1997	22

Source: "Europe's Great Experiment," *Economist,* June 13, 1998, 67–68.

Continental Catch-Up

The venture capital sector in Europe is unique. It is different from that in the United States for several reasons. First, Europeans have not manifested as much entrepreneurial spirit as Americans have. Socialist governments have established a tradition of publicly provided retirement and health care. The European educational system also emphasizes careers in government and big businesses. Few European schools offer courses in business or have departments teaching entrepreneurial skills. Government bureaucracy tends to stifle business start-ups, and the stigma of bankruptcy or failure is severe.

The European Venture Capital Association (EVCA) and British Venture Capital Association (BVCA) have worked to change governmental policy toward business, taxation, and innovation. Most specifically, EVCA has pressed for tax relief on capital gains and sought to reform tax systems to avoid double taxation of venture capital investment income.[42]

When the EU nominated Eckki Liikanen for the post of EU commissioner for enterprise in 1999, he vowed to combat unemployment through a broad program that sought to make Europe a real information society. He noted that the EU lacked a dynamic enterprise culture. According to Liikanen, "Without a pronounced turn for the better" in the next five years, Europe would have lost the game and settled permanently behind the United States. He pointed out that business start-ups in the EU take longer to arrange and are more costly than they are in the United States. Liikanen said he was prepared to review EU regulations to ensure their compatibility with the interests of small business. He noted the EU must further liberalize, as it did in the telecommunications industry, in order to improve access to risk capital. The EU must also help connect young people to networks at the primary school level and retrain women and older workers.[43]

Raising Capital and Stage Distribution

In Europe, banks and pension funds have been the two largest sources of venture capital, each providing 25 percent of the total. Venture capital and private equity funds in Europe raised an average of €4.5 billion in 1988–1991 and €4.55 billion in 1992–1995. The European funds raised in excess of €7.9 billion in 1996 and €20 billion in 1997. The amount of money invested inside Europe reached a record €9.7 billion in 1997, an increase of 42 percent over 1996. The discrepancy between new funds raised and private equity investment represents funds invested outside Europe. The United States, in particular, is an important destination for European venture capital investors, given the large number of start-ups in high-tech sectors and the need for European companies to close the technological lead the United States holds over Europe.

Buyouts represent the largest investment stage for European VC investors when ranked by the amount of funds invested. The expansion stage is the largest when measured by the number of investments.

Corporate governance arrangements vary in the venture capital and private equity sectors. 3i, the leading VC company in Europe with €20 billion invested in over 13,000 companies in 1999, follows a hands-off policy. 3i's only managerial efforts relate to the appointment of independent directors. In 1999 3i announced that it would only fund smaller companies that were involved in growth technology, and it would not transact buyouts with a total value under £5 million.[44]

In European buyouts, business advice and networking is not a high priority. Providing the funds needed for a buyout constitutes a vote of confidence in the management team. By contrast, seed capital and venture start-ups are usually required to give up part of the board of director seats to investors and their appointees in the United States. EVCA-sponsored research found that less than half of European entrepreneurs believed that financial backers contributed nothing more than cash for the success of their businesses.[45]

The vast majority of VC investors, 35 percent of the European total, are located in the UK. France, Germany, and Italy rank next, with 20 percent, 15 percent, and 6 percent of investment, respectively.

Exit Strategies

Until 1995 there were few public offerings of venture capital–backed companies in Europe. Institutional investors were just beginning to play an important role as buyers of small company shares. Europe did not have a second-tier market for small capitalization companies or technology-oriented enterprises. Beginning in 1995, this situation changed. In that year the Alternative Investment Market (AIM) was created in London, and in the next several years similar alternatives or new industry markets were established to list and trade newly issued venture company shares (table 8.6).

AIM became an important alternative for the flotation of the securities of small British companies. Similar alternative markets sprang up on the Continent. In the eighteen-month period ending June 1998, the number of companies listed on these five markets increased from 334 to 454. In the same period, the market capitalization of these markets grew from €14 billion to €48 billion.

Between June 1995 and February 2000 the Neuer Markt and other alternative markets began to grow rapidly. This growth is reflected in table 8.9, which shows that the aggregate capitalized value of the 210 listed companies is €175.8 billion, ten times as large as it was in mid-1998. The market has become more international with thirty-five non-German companies listed, representing over 27 percent of market capitalization.[46] Eight American companies and five Israeli companies are listed.

A healthy symbiosis developed between the venture capital and IPO markets, beginning in 1997–1998. Providers of capital for management buyouts and high-risk start-ups were flocking to Germany, as conditions for their "exits" via flotations were improving on the increasingly more liquid Neuer Markt. As the pace of corporate restructuring accelerates in Europe, noncore divisions, such as Veba's Stinnes distribution business, are being prepared for full or partial flotation.[47]

Table 8.9. Neuer Markt Capitalization, by Country of Listed Corporation

Country	*Market Cap. (€ billion)*	*Percentage of Total*
Germany	127.262	72.4
United States	20.606	11.7
Switzerland	10.322	5.9
Netherlands	5.986	3.4
Austria	3.387	1.9
United Kingdom	3.216	1.8
Ireland	2.581	1.5
France	1.213	0.7
Israel	1.200	0.7
Hungary	0.025	0.0
Total	175.796	100.0

Source: B. Benoit, "Foreigners See Opportunity in Neuer Markt," *Financial Times*, February 21, 2000, 25.

The management of the Neuer Markt positioned it as an ideal IPO platform for European growth companies, rather than as an antechamber for the DAX 30. The Neuer Markt is strong in media and entertainment stocks. This market will probably attract U.S. film studios and start-up film companies from other countries as well. A large number of U.S. Internet companies are considering separate listings for their European operations. For example, Lycos Europe, the Internet hub owned by Lycos of the United States and Germany's Bertelsmann, both plan to float stock issues in the second quarter of 2000.

Despite the growth of IPO activity on these new alternative markets, trade sales continue to be the most popular exit mechanism in Europe. In the late 1990s trade sales represented about 47 percent of exit transaction value, and IPOs accounted for 15–20 percent of exits.

Buyouts and Restructurings

The private equity market, which includes buyouts, is growing on the Continent. Figures compiled by Initiative Europe, the UK private equity analyst, show that large industry group selloffs and private deals were still the most common type of transactions, particularly in Sweden and Finland.[48]

Table 8.10 reflects the number and value of buyout deals in 1997 by country. France and Germany are far ahead of other continental nations, with £3.4 billion and £2.3 billion, respectively. Continued interest and sustained levels of buyouts reflect the belief among institutional investors that restructuring in the Eurozone will continue to generate lucrative opportunities. That trend led to £920 million worth of deals in Sweden alone. In 1997 the value of Finnish buyouts rose to £480 million, up from £320 million the previous year.

Table 8.10. Continental Europe Buyouts, 1997

Country	*Amount*	*No. of Deals*
France	3,400	123
Germany	2,300	84
Italy	1,850	20
Switzerland	1,500	63
Sweden	920	17
Netherlands	700	60
Finland	480	30
Belgium	280	10
Denmark	250	13
Spain	220	18
Norway	100	6
Austria	70	7
Greece	40	7
Portugal	30	4

Source: Tim Burt, "Outsiders Muscle In," *Financial Times*, June 5, 1998, 11.
Note: Amounts in millions of pound sterling.

Formerly, many buyout funds were national or regional in their focus. Now, more are taking a continental approach. One such private equity operator, Industri Kapital, a Swedish firm, intends to build its presence outside the Nordic markets. In 1997 it purchased the wholesale electrical goods business of German industrial giant Siemens. Due in part to the influence of the euro, corporate restructuring is taking hold across the European Continent. In France, a new type of life insurance policy is tax exempt if half of it is invested in shares, provided that at least 5 percent goes into small company stocks.

Industri Kapital announced the formation of an additional venture capital corporate restructuring fund in 1999. Exceeding €l.5 billion, it will be the largest fund outside the UK ever focused on Europe. It will aim at businesses that large European corporations no longer regard as core business. As the single market deepens, European companies are having to spread their divisions and capital over a wider market, so they must limit the number of activities in which they are involved. Therefore, the sale of peripheral or noncore units becomes a high priority. Industri Kapital's strategy is to purchase majority stakes in such units and reorganize them as stand-alone companies. The units are financed through a stock market flotation with an expected five-year turnaround between flotation and trade or sale.

In late 1999 Industri Kapital managed three funds with a market capitalization of over €l billion. Since its launch in 1989–1999, Industri Kapital has invested in thirty-one companies and divested thirteen, five through stock market listings. The larger size of the newest fund reflects an emphasis on the

German economy, where opportunities are on a larger scale than in Scandinavia and other countries in Europe.[49]

In 1999 a number of U.S. buyout houses were setting up in London, attracted by the promise of growth in corporate restructurings across Europe. Foremost among these was Kohlberg Kravis Roberts, the world's largest leveraged buyout specialist. KKR raised a $3 billion investment fund through its new London office. KKR follows a conservative, disciplined approach, having bought seventy-five companies over a twenty-three-year span, about three per year. Unlike some venture capital and private equity firms, KKR follows a policy of maintaining a firm grip on strategic matters. "This generally translates into the dominance of KKR executives on portfolio company boards."[50]

KKR is distinguished by its policy of long-termism. This policy means that they hold their investments an average of eight years. They exited Safeway in 1999, after a twelve-year investment in which an initial $131 million equity stake was turned into $5.9 billion.

Public-to-private deals are becoming popular in Europe, as companies in forgotten and fragmented industries suffer depressed share prices. European and U.S. buyout firms are taking these forgotten public companies private, merging them with other companies in their portfolios, to create regional leaders in their respective sectors. This strategy lies behind the fight for control of United Biscuits in 2000. In February 2000, KKR put up $627 million to take Wassall PLC private (Thorn Lighting Group). KKR plans to combine the Wassall assets with closely held Zumtobel, an Austrian lighting concern, to create a new multinational lighting company large enough to rival Philips NV.[51]

The aggregate value of public-to-private buyouts is on a strong uptrend. It appears that continental buyouts may catch and even surpass UK levels in a few years (table 8.11).

Table 8.11. Value of Public-to-Private Buyouts (U.S.$ billions)

	1997	*1998*	*1999*
United Kingdom	0.4	4.1	7.3
Continental Europe	—	0.2	5.1
Total	0.4	4.3	12.4

Source: Wall Street Journal, February 24, 2000.

The United Kingdom Speeds Up

The largest UK provider of venture capital, 3i, indicated that it plans to double its exposure in continental Europe between 1998 and 2003, partly through acquisitions. 3i is interested in purchasing venture capital companies with expertise in technology. 3i also manages pools of funds for other investors.[52]

The EU supports development of high-tech venture capital funds. Funds backed by EU capital totaling $390 million were unveiled in June1998 by Gordon Brown, UK chancellor of the Exchequer. These funds will support small and medium-sized businesses in high-tech sectors including biotechnology, communications, and electronics.[53] The largest fund is a development fund for the English regions set up by Baring Private Equity Partners in collaboration with Dutch parent ING and European Investment Bank (EIB). The challenge for Europe is to develop a stronger venture capital industry for investment in the high-risk high-technology sectors and investment in early-stage and start-up companies.

Venture capital investment is very risky. One estimate is that only one in twenty biotech companies are likely to succeed. Harold Baum, Emeritus Professor of Biochemistry of King's College, London, warned in 1998 that small investors should steer clear of such ventures. This followed in the wake of a scandal that engulfed British Biotech, the UK's biggest drug discovery company.[54]

Private Equity Secondaries

Private equity funds are catching on in Europe, and a new, second phase has taken root in which specialized funds buy out the interests of investors in other private equity managers' funds. These specialized funds are labeled "secondaries," based on the idea that they create a market for assets that otherwise would be illiquid.

In 1998 Jeremy Coller raised a specialist private equity fund of $220 million. His roster of investors included Calpers, the California state retirement fund. The investments of Coller Capital included the acquisition of the U.S.-based Shell Pension Trust's private equity portfolio valued at $265 million. Shell was disposing of a portfolio consisting of 169 private and 78 listed companies, with thirteen separate U.S. managers and two European firms. The bulk of the assets were buyout or venture capital investments. The assets of the Shell fund were purchased between 1989 and 1994 at multiples of from a half to a third of what private equity investors now pay for companies.[55] The proceeds will be invested in quoted European equities.

NOTES

1. Barry Riley, "Aim for Bourse without Borders," *Financial Times*, May 18, 1998, 15.
2. Deutsche Bundesbank, "Shares as Financing Instruments," *Monthly Report*, January 1997, 27–40.
3. Erik Berglöf, "Corporate Governance," in Benn Steil, ed., *The European Equity Markets* (London: Royal Institute of International Affairs, 1996), 156–157.

4. Richard Waters, "Reuters Prepares Second Assault on U.S. Equities," *Financial Times*, May 27, 1998, 19.

5. John Labate, "Stock Markets Jostle to Boost Share of Overseas Listings," *Financial Times*, April 29, 1998, 7.

6. George Graham, "Review of Electronic Order Book Opens Amid Criticism," *Financial Times*, March 31, 1998, 11.

7. George Graham, "Stock Trading Move Worries Institutions," *Financial Times*, April 29, 1998, 9.

8. George Graham, "Attack on Electronic System for Share Trading," *Financial Times*, April 30, 1998, 8.

9. Norma Cohen, "Exchange Set to Announce Dealing Reforms," *Financial Times*, May 26, 1998, 9.

10. B. Benoit "Ownership Culture Is Acquisition Barrier," *Financial Times*, May 14, 2001; and B. Benoit, "First Non-German Deal Will Spark No Rush," *Financial Times*, April 9, 2001, 27.

11. Thomas Vogel, "European Stock Markets Risk to Form Alliances," *Wall Street Journal*, May 6, 1998, 17.

12. Simon Davies, "Paris Bourse to Launch EDR Market," *Financial Times*, April 22, 1998, 18.

13 "Swedish Exchange Ponders a Switch to Euro Listings," *Wall Street Journal*, June 3, 1998, All.

14. Silvia Ascarelli, "London, Frankfurt Bourses Expected to Form Alliance," *Wall Street Journal*, July 7, 1998, C15.

15. R. McGee and S. Ascarelli, "European Market Link-Up Faces Hurdles," *Wall Street Journal*, July 8, 1998, C1.

16. McGee and Ascarelli, "European Market," C1.

17. G. Graham and S. Davies, "London-Frankfurt Link Paves Way for Pan-Europe Exchange," *Financial Times*, July 8, 1998, 1.

18. Edward Luce, "LIFFE Chief Attacks Frankfurt Trading Deal," *Financial Times*, July 11, 1998, 4.

19. A. Ostrovsky and A. Wendlandt, "Backing for Tradepoint on Stock Platform," *Financial Times*, February 11, 2000, 19.

20. Alan Cowell, "British-German Market Merger on the table," *New York Times*, April 21, 2000, C1–C2.

21. Cowell, "British-German Market Merger," C1–C2.

22. Cowell, "British-German Market Merger," C1–C2.

23. Cowell, "British-German Market Merger," C1–C2.

24. Cowell, "British-German Market Merger," C2.

25. Cowell, "British-German Market Merger," C2.

26. Andrew Fisher, "London Link Offers Way into Top Tier," *Financial Times*, July 8, 1998, 20.

27. George Graham, "Partnership Must Aim for Common Rules and Systems," *Financial Times*, July 8, 1998, 20.

28. Andrew Jack, "News Takes Paris Exchange by Surprise," *Financial Times*, July 8, 1998, 20.

29. Simon Davies and George Graham, "Europe's Big Bang," *Financial Times*, July 8, 1998, 15.

30. Davies and Graham, "Europe's Big Bang," 15.

31. The Lex column, *Financial Times*, May 25, 2001, 16; and Vincent Boland, "A Buying Opportunity for the LSE," *Financial Times*, May 24, 2001, 13.

32. "Bourses Afloat," *Financial Times*, May 25, 2001, 14.

33. Suzanne Kapner, "London Bourse Gets Breath of Fresh Air," *Financial Times*, June 5, 2001, 11.

34. Philip Coggan, "The World Turned Upside Down," *Financial Times*, February 19, 2000, 24.

35. "UK Equities," *Financial Times*, February 2, 2000, 12.

36. Simon Targett, "Giant Stocks Bring Nightmare Choice to Fund Managers," *Financial Times*, February 18, 2000, 20.

37. Philip Coggan and John Willman, "Knock-Down Stocks," *Financial Times*, February 19, 2000, 6.

38. "No Light at the End of the Bond Tunnel," *Financial Times*, February 18, 2000, 23.

39. Shawn Neidorf, "Venture-Backed IPOs Take a Comeback," *Venture Capital Journal*, August 1999, 18.

40. "Europe's Great Experiment," *Economist*, June 13, 1998, 67–68.

41. Katherine Campbell, "A Big Business Is Going Global," *Financial Times*, June 5, 1998, I.

42. Jonathan Blake, ed., *Venture Capital Fund Structures in Europe* (Zaventen, Belgium: European Venture Capital Association, 1998), 9.

43. Peter Norman, "Liikanen Pledges Jobs Drive through EU Small Business," *Financial Times*, September 1, 1999, 3.

44. Katharine Campbell, "3i Moves Away From Buyouts Below £5 m," *Financial Times*, September 10, 1999, 18.

45. Raynier D'Ydewalle, *1998 EVCA Yearbook*, Zaventen, Belgium, European Venture Capital Association, 1998, 37.

46. Bertrand Benoit, "Foreigners See Opportunity in Neuer Markt," *Financial Times*, February 21, 2000, 25.

47. "German IPOs," *Financial Times*, December 7, 1998, 18.

48. Tim Burt, "Outsiders Muscle In," *Financial Times*, June 5, 1998, XI.

49. Nicholas George, "Industri Kapital's E 1.5 bn Fund," *Financial Times*, August 11, 1999, 21.

50. Katharine Campbell, "Giant Settles in for the Long Haul," *Financial Times*, July 1, 1999, 8.

51. Charles Fleming, "In Europe, Buyout Specialists Are Snapping Up Unglamorous Firms Forgotten in Tech Gold Rush," *Wall Street Journal*, February 24, 2000, A14.

52. Katherine Campbell, "3i to Raise Presence in Europe," *Financial Times*, June 5, 1998, 24.

53. Brian Groom, "EU Supports High Tech Venture Capital Funds," *Financial Times*, June 3, 1998, 10.

54. Julia Finch, "Biotech Business Built on a Wing and a Prayer," *Guardian*, London, May 21, 1998, 24.

55. Katherine Campbell, "Secondaries Come to the Forefront," *Financial Times*, July 17, 1998, 24.

Chapter Nine

Dollarization: Extending the Single Currency Concept

The 1990s witnessed two significant and related developments in the international currency realm: the introduction of the European single currency and proposals for dollarization as a relief measure for nations experiencing financial crisis and currency instability. These developments are related in that (1) both are viewed as solutions to the general question of how an individual nation or a group of nations can achieve currency stability and (2) proponents of dollarization consider such an initiative an extension of some of the basic principles built into the European single currency system, with the specific objective of neutralizing instabilities associated with financial crises in emerging market nations.

DOLLARIZATION AND THE EURO

Comparison with the Euro

The introduction of the euro was the final step in a multidecade process of achieving a high degree of economic and monetary integration for the countries within the Eurozone. The same cannot be said concerning proposals for dollarization. Dollarization, in part, is a response to repeated financial and currency crises, particularly for emerging market nations. These crises appear to be related to a combination of internal and external factors which destabilize nations that use a number of different foreign exchange systems, including pegged to the dollar, currency board, and floating rate currency systems. We examine these crises within the context of dollarization later in this chapter.

The innovation of the euro completed the creation of a European single market for goods, services, and capital by removing the foreign exchange–

related costs of cross-border transactions. Proposals for dollarization in Argentina, Russia, and other nations have little or nothing to do with completing any single market, with the possible exception of proposals to dollarize the North American Free Trade Association (NAFTA) group of countries, and similar proposals to dollarize the Mercosur four.

The euro and proposals for dollarization are similar in that they (1) remove or reduce currency transaction costs and risks incurred in cross-border transactions and (2) provide a wider and broader zone of currency stability. The dollarization proposals also minimize or remove incentives for capital flight, since a dollar currency base would leave local and other investors with little or no likelihood of gain from such activities. Capital flight was an important element in the several financial crises of the 1990s.

Different Meanings

Dollarization proposals and discussions of dollarization vary considerably in conceptual content. Some writers refer to Russian dollarization almost as an accomplished fact, given the widespread use of U.S. currency (Federal Reserve notes) in that country and the periodic speculative rushes to shift away from rubles and into dollars. These discussions link currency preferences with informal economic activity and even illicit activities such as smuggling and tax evasion. Thus discussions of Russian dollarization differ considerably from those in Latin America, where discussions stress dollarization as a method for avoiding instability in trade and investment caused by imprudent economic policies.

Panama is officially on a dollar currency system, and the dollar is used as the circulating medium. Nevertheless, Panama faces all of the problems associated with excessive external debt: rural poverty, fiscal slippage during the presidency of Ernesto Perez Balladares, and the need to accelerate privatization in order to supplement the available resources for government debt service.[1] According to Standard & Poor's, Panama's credit rating on sovereign is BB+, a notch below investment grade. The country spends over 20 percent of its budget servicing government debt, which at year-end 1999 was $7.1 billion, nearly three-fourths of gross domestic product (GDP).[2] The new president, Mireya Moscoso, enjoys an inflow of new fiscal revenues as Panama was officially given administrative control of the Panama Canal at year-end 1999.[3]

Another totally different meaning of dollarization relates to the successful debut of the euro and the prospects for creating a similar dollar bloc in the Western Hemisphere.[4] Mexican and Canadian support of dollarization across NAFTA envisions corporate and private investors putting money in places where they don't have to fear wide currency swings. Foreign trade would be simpler and cheaper without currency hedging costs. According to Michael

Walker, executive director of Vancouver's Fraser Institute, dollarization would create a single economic space.

The dollar is already embraced throughout the Western Hemisphere. Commodities such as Canadian pulp and paper and Venezuelan oil have long been traded in dollars, and the elite in Latin America use the greenback as the benchmark currency for evaluating high value items such as real estate. Argentina operates a currency board with U.S. dollar reserves backing the peso. The country with the highest percentage of dollars in total money is Bolivia, where 82 percent of the money supply consists of dollars.

Problems with establishing a dollarized NAFTA region include the lack of harmonization in Canadian and Mexican tax and budget policies at variance with those in the United States. Few countries in Latin America may be ready for a single currency. But if the euro gives European companies a competitive edge, it would be logical for Western Hemisphere companies to seek similar advantages through a NAFTA dollar.

Dollarization also reflects the increasing need for competition between currencies and currency zones. Dollarization proposals gain new relevance when countries as large as Argentina propose them. Currency competition is already a reality, based on the amount of foreign currency notes held for domestic use around the world. A recent International Monetary Fund report on dollarized economies suggested that over half of the $470 billion of dollar notes in circulation are held outside the United States. Similarly, large quantities of German currency circulate outside Germany.

Financial crises in emerging market countries provide a key source of inspiration for dollarization. During the 1990s these nations gained more regular access to international capital markets. But when financial market crises occur, capital flows are interrupted, triggering collapses in output and severe damage to national banking and financial sectors of the more fragile economies. As crises become more frequent and severe, they are forcing emerging market countries to seek ways to make themselves less vulnerable to such interruptions in capital inflows. Dollarization is coming to be viewed as a long-term market-friendly solution. Strong currency pegs, like dollarization, are also viewed as a way to reduce the incidence of external shocks.[5]

THEORY OF DOLLARIZATION

In this section we consider two of the mainstay theoretical bases for dollarization. The first, the theory of optimum currency areas, is discussed in detail in chapter 2. The second, the choice of an appropriate exchange rate regime, is more controversial, leading different writers to alternative conclusions.

Optimum Currency Area

The requirements for an optimum currency area have been outlined in chapter 2. Four criteria from this discussion are presented in table 9.1, with comments regarding how well EU countries conform to these criteria, and how well the Mercosur four conform to these criteria. The Mercosur four include Argentina, Brazil, Paraguay, and Uruguay. We have utilized a wide range of data to make these assessments, including total and directional trade flow, various references found in chapter 2 concerning capital and labor mobility, and data from *World Development Report* publications concerning industrial and trade diversification.

The Eurozone countries satisfy three of the four requirements (table 9.1). Therefore, the EU may be considered an appropriate but somewhat imperfect application of the single currency concept, albeit one that has high expectations of succeeding. Most EU countries enjoy high-intensity trade with other EU countries. The EU falls short primarily on the criterion of labor mobility. This is discussed in detail in chapter 2, where we note that labor mobility is growing at all levels of skills and compensation.

By contrast, the Mercosur four satisfy only two of the four conditions (intensity of trade and industrial diversification). Domestically, capital mobility is low but increasing. This increase is related to structural reforms, including a rapidly developing equity market, privatization of state enterprises, and liberalization of foreign capital participation in the domestic economy.

Table 9.1. Conditions Required for Optimal Currency Area

Conditions Required	*Satisfied by EU*	*Satisfied by Mercosur*
High intensity of trade between subregions	Satisfied by most countries	Satisfied by Paraguay, and Uruguay; almost satisfied by Argentina[a]
High labor mobility	Low mobility, but increasing	Low mobility of labor
High capital mobility	Six mechanisms facilitate capital mobility, as described in chapter 2	Low capital mobility domestically, but increasing; intermittent mobility of external capital
Industrial diversification	Satisfied very well	Satisfied by all countries except Paraguay[b]

Sources: World Bank, *World Development Report*, various issues. Materials in chapter 2 relating to labor and capital mobility.

[a]Brazil trade with Mercosur partners accounts for only 17 percent and 16 percent of exports and imports, respectively.

[b]Paraguay still depends heavily on agricultural output for one-quarter of its GDP. Manufacturing exports account for only 17 percent of total exports.

An Exchange Rate Regime

The second aspect of theory of optimal currency areas focuses on selection of exchange rate regime. This discussion follows three distinct channels of thought in the literature.

- Follow fixed rates, dollarize, and maintain an economy highly integrated into the rest of the world.
- Follow floating rates, since only individual special circumstances can allow fixed rates or dollarization to be an effective exchange rate system.
- Partial dollarization based on use of dollar-denominated debt limits the exchange rate options open to a country.

FLOATING RATES

Adherents of floating exchange rate regimes argue that exchange depreciation is a necessary shock absorber. Using the example of an oil exporter faced with declining petroleum prices, they argue that allowing the oil exporter's currency to depreciate vis-à-vis the dollar would provide the simplest solution to restore external payments equilibrium. The country's export products would become cheaper in world markets, and increased demand for nonoil exports would compensate for the fall in oil earnings. The same writers hold that "in theory fixed exchange rates may be appropriate under some conditions and flexible rates under others, recent practical experience suggests that most emerging markets are better off with the latter."[6]

Supporters of flexible exchange rates hold that what is good for the anchor currency country under a system of fixed rates (United States) in many cases is not necessarily good for other countries. Country X may need a monetary expansion, even if the anchor country does not. Citing recent financial crises of the 1990s, these writers hold that many countries have been unable to resist the pressure that builds up when markets come to expect exchange rates to depreciate. Mexico (1994), Thailand and South Korea (1997), and Russia and Brazil (1998, 1999), all experienced the collapse of pegged exchange rates. Expectations of a currency collapse can be very costly, as was the case in Mexico (1994) and South Korea (1997). The collapse of the pegged exchange rate in these two cases was followed by a financial panic in which foreign banks demanded the repayment of loans. Domestic banks were unable to meet these demands and defaulted.

Proponents of floating rates admit that under appropriate conditions dollarization is an acceptable alternative:

- The economy is tightly integrated with that of the United States. Clearly, commodity exporters (petroleum, coffee, sugar, and copper) do not meet this requirement.
- The economy is relatively small, most prices are related to dollar prices, and most goods enter into international trade. Panama, with a population of 2.7 million and a GDP of $8.7 billion, meets this requirement, and it is dollarized.
- The economy must have flexible labor markets in which domestic wages can adjust up or down to make prolonged periods of unemployment unlikely.
- The country's central bank can be relieved of monetary management without loss of effective control over financial stability. In countries where the central bank has been required to capitulate to populist demands or finance excessive budget deficits, dollarization may become a preferred alternative.

As noted above, some countries meet the standards for successful dollarization better than others. Clearly, Argentina is in a better position to benefit from dollarization than Russia. This does not mean that Argentina should dollarize, and Russia should not.

FIXED RATE DOLLARIZATION

In his 1972 Horowitz Lectures, Nobel laureate Milton Friedman presented a clear analysis of the currency problem facing developing countries. He concluded that unifying a developing country currency with a strong currency, via a currency board system or official dollarization, provided a viable alternative. Related to this, Steve Hanke evaluated data from ninety-eight developing countries between 1950 and 1993. The countries were separated into (1) those with central banks and (2) those that were operating with currency boards or had already been dollarized. The former group had the capacity to engage in discretionary monetary policy, but the latter did not.

Hanke found that countries without central banks had average per capita GDP growth rates 5.4 percent higher than countries with central banks. Moreover, the variability of these growth rates (measured by standard deviation) was virtually identical, suggesting that a lack of discretionary monetary policy resulted in no greater vulnerability to economic shocks. Also, the performance of countries with central banks was inferior with regard to inflation.

Average inflation rates were 4.9 times higher and 4.2 times more variable than in countries without central banks. Finally, budget deficit was on average *65 percent* higher in the central bank countries.[7]

Hanke noted that there are two ways in which developing countries can unify their currencies with stronger ones: by establishing a currency board or by replacing a national currency with a strong foreign currency (official dollarization). Although currency boards have performed well (e.g., Hong Kong and Argentina), they are not trouble free. The currency board deviates from the pure dollarization approach in that it may engage in lender-of-last-resort activity, it may use flexible reserve requirements on bank deposits, and it may deal in government bonds, using the dollar reserves for this purpose.

PARTIAL DOLLARIZATION

The decade of the 1990s has witnessed a new international environment in which emerging market countries have gained access to large amounts of international capital. This has been accompanied by a greater incidence of financial crises, associated with changing rates of capital inflow to emerging market countries. During these crises, emerging market countries routinely lose access to international capital markets. The problem becomes compounded when short-term loans must be repaid, denominated in foreign currency. Abrupt reversals of capital inflows can push a country toward insolvency. Once a crisis has erupted, policy options become very restricted.

Sudden reversals in capital inflows severely damage financial sectors, especially the domestic banking industry. When a devaluation occurs, exports can recover quickly, but when a devaluation and banking crisis come together, exports take much longer to recover. Banking crises endure longer than other forms of crises. This is because asset prices become depressed, with negative wealth effects that depress consumer and investment spending.

Liability dollarization refers to emerging nations' external debt being denominated in foreign currency. It is often argued that domestic investors would be less willing to incur foreign currency–denominated debt under a floating exchange rate than under a fixed rate. This argument misses two points. First, most emerging market countries start from a situation of partial (liability) dollarization, and, second, they rarely ignore exchange rate volatility. Fear of floating can, in fact, raise the cost of external funds due to the possible higher estimate of country risk it may engender. Whereas analysis may view shocks as exogenous, evidence suggests that reputation and the estimated sustainability of creditworthiness are critical factors in determining how hard an emerging market economy is hit by financial crisis.[8]

The Currency Board Alternative

As already noted, the currency board may be viewed as a halfway point between a fixed exchange rate system, managed by the nation's central bank, and dollarization, in which the national central bank no longer has responsibility for controlling the supply of circulating money or liquidity.

During the 1990s there was renewed interest in currency boards, and early in 1999 fourteen countries were operating such systems as a means of managing the domestic money supply.[9] A currency board was used to stabilize the economy in the aftermath of Argentina's hyperinflation in 1991. Additional benefits from this technique became evident when Estonia and Lithuania, transitional economies, established credible currency boards (table 9.2). Since 1998 there have been repeated suggestions to study the

Table 9.2. Currency Boards in Operation

Country/Region	*Years in Operation*	*Peg Currency*	*Special Features*
Antigua and Barbuda	32	U.S. dollar	Member of East Caribbean Central Bank (ECCB)
Argentina	6	U.S. dollar	One-third of coverage can be in U.S. dollar–denominated government bonds
Bosnia and Herzegovina	1	Deutsche mark	
Brunei Darussalam	30	Singapore dollar	
Bulgaria	1	Deutsche mark	Excess coverage in banking department to deal with banking sector weaknesses
Djibouti	48	U.S. dollar	Switched peg currency from French franc to U.S. dollar
Dominica	32	U.S. dollar	Member of ECCB
Estonia	6	Deutsche mark	Excess coverage for domestic monetary intervention
Grenada	32	U.S. dollar	Member of ECCB
Hong Kong SAR	14	U.S. dollar	
Lithuania	4	U.S. dollar	Central bank has the right to appreciate the exchange rate
St. Kitts and Nevis	32	U.S. dollar	Member of ECCB
St. Lucia	32	U.S. dollar	Member of ECCB
St. Vincent and the Grenadines	32	U.S. dollar	Member of ECCB

Source: Charles Enoch and Ann-Marie Gulde, "Are Currency Boards a Cure for All Monetary Problems?" *Finance and Development*, December 1998, 40.

feasibility of stabilizing the Russian ruble under a currency board (or dollarization).

A currency board combines three elements: an exchange rate tied to an anchor currency (U.S. dollar or other strong currency), automatic convertibility at a fixed rate, and long-term commitment to maintain the system. A currency board can be credible only if the central bank holds sufficient foreign exchange reserves to cover the narrowly defined money supply. In this case the financial markets and money holders can be assured that every unit of currency is backed by an equivalent amount of foreign (hard) currency.

The mechanism works through changes in money supply within the currency board country (contraction in the case of flight into the anchor currency), which leads to changes in the interest rate and in turn induces investors to move funds. This is essentially the same mechanism that operates under a fixed exchange rate. But the exchange rate guarantee implied in the currency board ensures that necessary interest rate changes and related economic costs will be lower.

The obvious advantages from a successful currency board are credibility, low inflation, and low nominal cost of capital. But for countries that have weak banking systems or are prone to economic shock, the currency board may prove to be a limiting structure. This is because under a currency board the central bank cannot easily function as lender of last resort to banks in financial difficulty. Also, policies to adjust interest rates or exchange rates to influence the economy are necessarily limited. Under a currency board much of the economic adjustment must take the form of wage and price adjustment, a slower and more painful path.

Empirical analysis suggests that countries using currency board arrangements have done better than other fixed exchange rate regimes. The presence of a currency board is found to lower annual inflation by about 3.5 percent, with no negative effects on growth.

Several important points should be noted with respect to the success and further applicability of currency boards. First, they have been used in smaller countries. Applicability to larger countries has yet to be fully proven. Second, a successful currency board requires time for building consensus, careful implementation, and institutional-legal changes. Third, countries with weak banks may have to rehabilitate them before changing their monetary regimes.

Pros and Cons

One analyst suggested that Washington must make up its mind about a regional dollar for Latin American countries. Pointing to the gathering support in Latin American countries and officials in the Inter-American Development

Bank, Clive Crook notes that Argentina is already close to putting theory into practice. Although pesos circulate, the currency board fixes their value to the dollar.[10]

With dollarization, Latin America would be importing not just the currency of the United States but also its interest rates and monetary policy. If the Federal Reserve can be relied on to keep inflation low, countries that dollarize should gain the ability to borrow abroad at long maturities and lower interest costs. One of the reasons for the financial difficulties (crises) of many emerging market countries in the 1990s has been that much of their external borrowing has been at relatively short term. When panicked lenders decided to not roll over these short-term borrowings, the country faced a financial squeeze. The resulting currency devaluations magnified this problem by forcing borrowers into illiquidity and insolvency. This scenario can be better avoided with longer-term borrowing in a stable currency. Thus there can be sizable advantages from dollarization, but there may be offsetting disadvantages as well, which Crook identifies as the following:

- Loss of seigniorage
- The need for central bank or alternate lender of last resort to the country's banks
- The loss of flexibility to devalue the currency in the case of an independent (nondollarized) currency

Seigniorage is a windfall that is collected by the government when it prints money. On average in Latin America seigniorage amounts to half a percent of national income. Any dollarizing government is likely to ask Washington to reimburse this loss of seigniorage. In the European single currency, the governments have agreed to share seigniorage among all the members of the Eurozone.

When a dollarizing country central bank shuts down, there is no lender of last resort to the banking system. In the case of a liquidity crisis, or run on the banks, a central bank ordinarily stands ready to provide liquidity to banks to avoid a deeper financial crisis. In a dollarized economy there is no agency or institution with a clear mandate to carry out this function. Possible solutions could include having emergency lines of credit with foreign lenders and enabling the finance ministry to arrange lines of credit to banks facing cash shortages.

A final disadvantage is the inability to devalue the currency once dollarization is in place. The economies of many countries for which dollarization has been proposed rely heavily on commodity exports, such as petroleum, copper, coffee, and sugar. When world commodity prices fall, these countries experience reduced incomes. If the exchange rate remains unchanged, the commodity-exporting country experiences a recession with falling output and rising unemployment. Alternately, if the currency depreciates, income is reduced in real terms. But this depreciation also reduces the price of exports, elevating foreign purchases of the country's export products. This tends to soften the recessionary impact. The fixed exchange rate recession is the more burdensome adjustment to falling commodity prices.

Therefore, a key advantage of a flexible exchange rate (absence of dollarization) is the possibility of a softer landing, given world commodity price downswings. In the case of dollarization, the Federal Reserve response to a downswing in world commodity prices might be inappropriate to the needs of the developing countries.

FINANCIAL CRISES

The past two decades have witnessed several serious financial crises impacting the emerging market nations and the global economy. The first in 1982, labeled "debt crisis," resulted in zero growth in that decade for the Latin American region. Hence the decade was given the name "lost decade." The second was the Mexican crisis of 1994–1995, in which spillover effects were important. This gave rise to a theory of contagion affecting emerging market economies. The third, or Asian, crisis tended to be restricted to a number of Asian nations, although some spillover effects appeared in 1997–1998, which tended to destabilize Russia and Brazil. Financial crises are important to the discussion of dollarization in several respects. First, each of the crises described included important elements of currency imbalance and volatility. Second, currency volatility and exchange rate depreciation have helped intensify the extent of crisis and cause spillover effect.

Three Crises: Differences and Similarities

Three crises in Latin America (1982), Mexico (1984–1988), and Asia (1997) demonstrated numerous similarities and differences (outlined in table 9.3). They were preceded by a surge in capital inflows to the crisis countries, resulting in larger unhedged interest rate and currency exposures.[11] Weak financial systems and regulatory regimes were in operation, evidenced by directed credits, nonperforming loans, and liquidity problems. All three crises took investors by surprise, and spillover effects caused other countries to experience serious financial volatility. Debt restructuring was a necessary factor in resolving these crises.

Table 9.3. Three Crises: Similarities and Differences

Similarities

1. Capital inflows to emerging market countries surged in months preceding crisis.
2. Unhedged currency and interest rate exposures played a central role. In some cases governments increased their exposures on the eve of the crisis.
3. Weak financial systems and regulatory regimes. Both the controlled financial systems of the 1980s and liberalized systems of the 1990s had serious structural weaknesses. These included directed credit allocations, nonperforming loans, reduced liquidity requirements, and weak risk management.
4. All three crises took investors by surprise. Initial policy responses by affected governments were unexpected, such as Mexico's decision in December 1994 to float the peso. Interest spreads did not spike until the crisis was well underway.
5. Spillover effects were extensive in all three crises. Contagion was made more virulent by weak banking systems and inadequate internal financial markets.
6. Debt restructuring a key element in resolution of all three crises.

Differences

1. Macroeconomic conditions varied in emerging market countries in the periods leading up to each of the three crises. Economic fundamentals were stronger in Latin America and Mexico prior to the 1994 crisis than in the years leading to the 1982 debt crisis. The macroeconomic situation of Asian countries in 1996 was better than that of Mexico in 1994.
2. Global economic conditions also differed on the eve of these crises. In the early 1980s industrial countries were headed into recession, while in the 1990s the world economy was more favorable via-à-vis export market growth and interest rate costs on debt.
3. In the 1980s official capital flows to emerging markets played an important role, accounting for 49.5 percent of flows to these countries between 1970 and 1981. They were only 9.5 percent of flows in 1990–1996. The share of foreign direct investment and portfolio investment in private flows increased relative to bank lending in the 1990s.
4. Development strategies differed between the 1980s and later periods. In earlier periods import substitution and capital controls prevailed. In the 1990s many emerging countries embraced more outward oriented policies, including trade liberalization, freer financial transactions, structural reforms, and more conservative fiscal regimes.

Source: D. Mathieson, A. Richards, and S. Sharma, "Financial Crises in Emerging Markets," *Finance and Development,* December 1998, 28–31.

Despite these common features, numerous differences are apparent. Macroeconomic and global economic environments differed vis-à-vis the three crises, and capital flows operated under varying degrees of economic policy liberalization. Finally, capital flow components experienced a changing role. In the first crisis bank syndicated lending proved to be the culprit, with floating exchange rate and interest rate shocks triggering near default. In the two crises of the 1990s official capital flows were reduced in importance. Foreign direct investment and portfolio capital played a dominant role (table 9.4). Emerging market borrowers enjoyed larger private capital inflows relative to GDP and longer-term credits via issuance of international bonds. The use of international bonds made these financings a central aspect of attempts to understand more recent crises and policy options for the future. In the following section we analyze these crises from this perspective.

Table 9.4. Relative Size of Capital Inflows to Emerging Market Countries, 1973–1982, 1991–1996

Time Period	*Private Capital Inflows as % of GDP*	*Private Capital Inflows, Billions*	*Average Maturity of Borrowings*	*Cost Basis of External Loans to Emerging Nations*
1973–1982	1	$165	Varied, mostly medium-term syndicated loans	Moderate spread over LIBOR, sometimes at negative real interest rates
1991–1996	3	$1,040	Average maturities on new Eurobond issues grew from 4.4 years to 8 years	Yield spreads on Brady bonds fell from an average of 1,100 basis points over U.S. Treasury securities to 350 basis points (1990–1997)

Source: D. Mathieson, A. Richards, and S. Sharma, "Financial Crises in Emerging Markets," *Finance and Development,* December 1998, 28–31.

Foreign Exchange Aspects

The financial problems in these cases center on the inability of national debtors to service their external debt on a timely basis. In a typical crisis the central bank of the country has pegged the domestic currency, buying and selling international reserve currencies at the pegged rate. During a crisis the central bank faces a rising demand (and declining supply) of international reserve currencies. This is due to a number of factors, including liquidation of domestic bank deposits and conversion of funds, investor sale of local equity securities. This causes a decline in stock market values, and international lenders refuse to renew or roll over maturing loans. All financial asset holders attempt to liquidate their claims and convert their funds into hard currency. To honor depositors and external lenders' demands for payment, financial institutions in the crisis-affected country are compelled to liquidate assets by canceling loans and selling the marketable securities they hold. This imposes strains on debtors and those who have issued marketable securities. In this scenario, loan default rates escalate, and entities (firms and households) become less liquid with some approaching bankruptcy. The domestic central bank is caught between two potentially conflicting needs:

- The need to inject liquidity into the system accompanied by lower interest rates
- The need to raise interest rates to lessen the incentives to liquidate on the part of both domestic and foreign creditors

The first course of action can intensify capital outflow and trigger capital flight, assuming it has not already taken place. The second will intensify economic contraction and lead to a higher rate of insolvencies and bankruptcy. When the public observes this central bank dilemma, a further loss of confidence takes place and capital outflows accelerate. International reserves are depleted, and the crisis has reached its nadir. The central bank reaches a point where it can no longer support the exchange rate, and the currency is allowed to float freely. The financial system is in disarray, and the economy enters a recession.[12]

The most notable aspect of crises in the 1990s is that currencies depreciated by large margins (table 9.5). The national currencies of the Asian five (South Korea, Indonesia, Malaysia, Philippines, and Thailand) lost over 30 percent of their value in the second half of 1998. Loss of significant amounts of international reserves left central banks helpless to defend their currencies. Mexico lost over half of its $16 billion of official reserves in the six weeks leading to year-end 1994 crisis. Similarly, Thailand's international reserves fell from $33 billion to $25 billion in the six-month period surrounding the crisis.

Capital flows also were heavily impacted by the 1990s crises. Capital inflows to Asia moved from plus $93 billion in 1996 to minus $12 billion in 1997. The total swing (U.S.$105 billion) represents 11 percent of regional GDP.

The foreign exchange aspects of these crises play a central role in the following respects. First, capital inflows are common factors that tend to magnify the currency and interest rate exposures of borrowing countries. Second, these exposures generally are unhedged, a fact well known to the financial markets.

Table 9.5. Exchange Rate Movements during Crises

Crisis Event	*Exchange Rate Adjustment*[a]
Mexico (November 1994)	42%
South Korea (November 1997)	45%
Thailand (June 1997)	33%

[a]Percentage depreciation in three months following the onset of the crisis.

Finally, capital flows exert a high leverage on the capacity of the borrower country to maintain its fixed exchange rate system. Shifting expectations or any signs of a change in the confidence level of international investors can exercise a heavy impact on the international reserve position of the country and the ability of the central bank to sustain the existing rate of exchange.

Argentine Currency Board Experience

As noted above, the ability of the monetary authority to sustain the existing exchange rate is a central question in the minds of capital market participants. The level of confidence moves with changes in financial indicators. Unfortunately, many emerging market countries do not provide timely data that can be used to anticipate the onset of crises due to the nature of the data and collection process. For example, quarterly data suffers from at least a three- or four-month time lag, and governments face limited budget resources for statistical data collection and processing. Finally, concern by some officials and authorities that published data will trigger speculative activity and precipitate a deeper crisis could lead to deliberate delay in releasing such information. For these and other reasons, surprise is a factor common to all crises experienced in the past two decades.

Struggling with the problem of stabilizing its exchange rate, Argentina adopted the currency board model in 1991. In March of that year the Argentine congress enacted the "convertibility law" that established the convertibility of the currency (at that time the Austral) vis-à-vis the U.S. dollar. Early in 1992 the peso replaced the currency. Under the convertibility law, the central bank is ready to sell dollars at the rate of $1 per peso. Reserves consist of gold, foreign currency deposits, and foreign currency bonds, equal to at least 100 percent of the monetary base. The convertibility law forbids the central bank from monetizing government deficits. Sound fiscal discipline is an integral part of the financial system in the Argentine model. In relation to this, the government has privatized many state enterprises and carried out numerous reforms, including trade liberalization, freeing international capital flows, and bank deregulation.

The economic benefits from this system are impressive. Throughout the 1980s Argentina was plagued by hyperinflation, with annual rates exceeding 1,000 percent in the final years of the decade. By contrast, annual inflation was only 4.6 percent between 1992 and 1998. Growth of gross domestic product was negative in the 1980s but averaged over 5 percent per annum in the 1990s (table 9.6). This growth could have been higher, but it was interrupted by the Mexican payments crisis (Tequila effect) in 1995 and the Asian crisis in 1998. Argentina now is able to accumulate larger international reserves, has

Table 9.6. Basic Data for the Argentine Economy

Element of Economy	*Years*	*U.S.$ Billions*
Gross domestic product	1998	$324.1
GDP growth	1980–1990	–0.4%
GDP growth	1990–1998	5.3%
International reserves	1980	$9.3
International reserves	1998	$24.8
Stock market capitalization	1990	$3.2
Stock market capitalization	1998	$45.3
Inward foreign direct investment	1990	$1,836.0
Inward foreign direct investment	1997	$6,645.0
External debt	1990	$62.2
External debt	1997	$123.2

Source: World Bank, *Entering the Twenty-First Century* (New York: Oxford University Press, 1999).

enjoyed a rising stock market value, has attracted much higher levels of foreign business investment, and is regarded as more creditworthy internationally (table 9.6)

The devaluation of the Brazilian real in January 1999 put extreme pressure on the Argentine currency. At that point President Menem asked his finance minister to look into the possibility of dollarization. Since then a working group was organized to study the prospects for this initiative and meetings were held with U.S. officials.

The currency board and other Argentine reforms have been successful in providing a more stable financial and monetary environment but have not led to Argentina's gaining full credibility on the international capital markets. Interest rate spreads remain wide and subject to large adjustment in Argentine peso- and dollar-denominated debt paper. To illustrate, the Asian and Russian ruble crises caused interest rate spreads to spike by approximately 400 basis points.

The Argentine and U.S. inflation rates are quite close, suggesting that wide and fluctuating interest rate spreads are caused by "other factors," including lack of monetary credibility and fear that the political authority in Argentina may lack the will to stand firm against speculative attack. For this reason, many have suggested that the Argentine peso be replaced by the U.S. dollar.

When Brazil depreciated its currency, Mercosur trade flows reacted against Argentine exports, and Argentina's economy went into a three-year recession that lasted from 1998 to 2001. In June 2001 Argentina initiated measures to pull the country out of recession. These measures included the introduction of a complex, unorthodox currency system. This currency system provides a second exchange rate for foreign trade without devaluing the currency. The new commercial peso gives exporters a preferential exchange rate based on the average value of the U.S. dollar and the euro. This new exchange rate for importers and exporters effectively devalued Argentina's peso for foreign trade, leaving the dollar peg untouched for domestic transactions. International investors were uncomfortable with the changes, and Argentine bonds fell in trading following announcement of the new currency arrangement.[13]

Prospects for Argentine Dollarization

What gains and losses would Argentina experience if it decided to dollarize? Losses would include inability to pursue an independent monetary policy and loss of the seigniorage on issuing peso money. Gains would include the greater stability and economic growth from a system not subject to contagion effects (Tequila effect).

The loss of independent monetary policy occurred when the currency board was adopted in 1991. The convertibility law leaves Argentina with no option but to allow the money supply to adapt to current need levels, a large part of which is the international flow of payments, including foreign capital. Repeated speculative attacks have taken place and are costly. They are based on the belief that Argentina will decide to resume an independent monetary policy and initiate a policy mix that includes exchange rate adjustment.

A cost-benefit analysis is useful to ascertain the balance between economic growth and seigniorage effects. In 1997 the Argentine central bank earned $781 million interest income on liquid international reserves, of which $658 million represents interest income on the monetary base. This is the estimated annual seigniorage loss, approximately 0.2 percent of GDP (table 9.7). Taking a 6 percent required return, we estimate the present value of this (constant) flow at $10.996 billion.

The gain from better economic performance is based on a once-a-decade interruption in economic growth resulting from contagion effects when other nations experience a financial crisis. For example, a 7 percent fall in GDP, in lieu of a 7 percent rise in GDP when a contagion effect occurs, implies a full 14 percent GDP loss in a single year. Assuming that this happens once in a decade, we have a $45.36 billion gain by adopting a dollar-based currency, which should enable Argentina to avoid such spillover or contagion effects (table 9.7).

A comparison of the gains and losses (table 9.7, lines 5–7) indicates that Argentina could benefit handsomely from a unilateral dollarization. A single-year seigniorage loss is a minuscule part of GDP. A one-decade loss of seigniorage at 1997 rates represents only 14.5 percent of the gain from improved economic performance. The gain from improved economic performance (in a given decade) is over four times as large as the present value of the

Table 9.7. Gains and Losses from Argentine Dollarization

Gain or Loss Element	*$U.S. Millions*
Loss in Seignorage, dollar amount, 1997[a]	$658.00
Decade amount of seigniorage loss	$6,580.00
Present value of future seigniorage taken at 6 percent required rate	$10,966.00
Gain from better economic performance[b]	$45,360.00
Gains and Losses	*Percentage*
One-year seigniorage loss as a percentage of GDP (1997)	0.2%
Decade loss as percentage of the gain from better economic performance[c]	14.5%
Gain in economic performance as a multiple of the present value of future seignorage[d]	4.14x

Source: World Development Report, 1999; F. R. Velde and M. Veracierte, "Dollarization in Argentina," *Chicago Fed Letter,* June 1999, 1–3.

[a]Loss in seigniorage estimated at 1997, when central bank reported $781 million income on liquid reserves, of which $658 million was attributed to earnings on reserves on monetary base.

[b]Calculated as potential one-year loss in GDP, at 14 percent of 1997 level.

[c]Calculated as decade loss relative to potential one-year loss in GDP.

[d]Calculated by dividing present value of future seigniorage into gain from better economic performance.

future seigniorage flow. A formal or bilateral dollarization could be even more beneficial to Argentina, seigniorage benefits being shared with the United States.[14]

Argentine dollarization is described by some analysts as preferable to the often rumored floating of the peso, which would import inflation. Excessive depreciation would raise the cost of servicing foreign debt in local currency terms and put the nation into a worsened fiscal crisis.[15]

A central part of the discussion for Argentina to dollarize is the trade-off between greater credibility (and confidence) in the exchange rate system that can be purchased through dollarization and the loss of options inherent in monetary sovereignty. An area of particular concern is the prospect that dissolution of the central bank can make the country more susceptible to external shocks that require the support of the financial system by a lender of last resort.[16] For this reason, some proponents of dollarization prefer it occur with the dollarizing country having access to the Federal Reserve discount window.

An important question is whether dollarization can be instituted while leaving Argentina with sufficient monetary flexibility. Argentina can retain monetary flexibility through several avenues. First, the money supply and liquidity tend to adjust to demand automatically. Market forces and mechanisms allow this to happen via changes in money turnover and capital inflows and/or outflows.

Second, although Argentine financial institutions may not have direct access to the U.S. money market, they will enjoy correspondent relations with international institutions that do. Third, after the convertibility law of 1991, Argentina's banking system has become more international. Foreign banks are reported to account for 41 percent of the banking system's total deposits and 64 percent of the deposits in private banks.[17] This has increased the liquidity provided by international financial markets. The contingent repurchase facility established in 1996 offers temporary funds to illiquid banks, a type of lender of last resort facility. This gives Argentina the opportunity to sell bonds to international banks under a repurchase agreement. This facility gives protections to the banks but invalidates the agreement if Argentina defaults on international debts.

Finally, dollarization does not prevent the government from being a lender of last resort directly to the banks.

Suggested Procedure for Argentine Dollarization

Hanke and Schuler[18] suggest specific steps and conditions that Argentina can take for a successful dollarization:

- Ensure that central bank international reserves are equal to the monetary base. This was satisfied in 1999.
- Establish a transparent policy of converting all prices, wages, and claims at a rate of 1 peso = 1 dollar. This leaves all monetary and financial (deposits, loans, bonds) assets and liabilities in the same relation after dollarization as before. Dollarization will bring some income redistribution, as new borrowers of dollars can expect to pay less interest and new lenders of dollars can expect to receive less interest. The offsetting benefits are (1) no fear of devaluation and (2) lower cost of capital, which should encourage higher levels of business investment spending.
- Replace the peso with the dollar as a unit of account.
- Replace peso deposits at the central bank with U.S. dollar assets.
- Retire peso currency from circulation. A transition period will be required to carry this step out in an orderly fashion.
- Reorganize the central bank so that it no longer issues money but continues to play a role by regulating financial institutions and providing monetary statistics.

To summarize, Argentina's next logical step toward enhancing monetary stability is to consider dollarization. The currency board can be viewed as an intermediate stage that prepared Argentina for dollarization. The benefits should easily outweigh the costs. The single remaining question asks if dollarization is appropriate for one country that is a member of the Mercosur customs union. If Brazil will not or cannot dollarize, will the Mercosur experiment be interrupted or fail? A parallel case exists in the European Union. Originally eleven countries adopted the euro and four did not. The status of the UK in particular is viewed as an important question for the future extension of the euro system. Nevertheless, there is no evidence to date that the euro system or the customs union itself is in any particular difficulty due to the UK opting out of the single currency. We analyze prospects for UK entry into the euro system in the following chapter.

Proposals for Regional Dollarization

Three cases of dollarization, or possible dollarization, are discussed, to provide a richer perspective.

A NAFTA Dollar

With successful introduction of the euro on January 1, 1999, proposals soon followed for a dollar bloc in the Western Hemisphere. One such proposal is for a North American Free Trade Area (NAFTA) monetary union embracing the United States, with the dollar as its single currency. The perceived advantages of this bloc are (1) ending the risk of speculators causing currency disorder for Mexico and (2) reinforcing the single market concept by removing the currency-related costs and risks of cross-border trade and payments.

Interestingly, there is no widespread support for such a move. Canadian fears of U.S. dominance are a major issue, even though leading Canadian exports, such as pulp and paper, petroleum and grain, have already been traded in dollars.[19]

The basic factors that favored adoption of the euro are not present in NAFTA. These include a highly integrated and competitive economic structure, fiscal harmonization, very similar monetary and interest rate conditions (via convergence), and a political machinery (European Union) that supports the monetary transition.

U.S. Officials Cautious

Given the lack of basic factors favoring monetary integration within NAFTA, the U.S. government has taken a cautious and conservative approach toward dollarization. Although Argentina gave dollarization serious consideration and other nations thought about the idea, Federal Reserve chairman Alan Greenspan and Treasury secretary Summers called for a cautious approach.

One consideration prompting Washington's caution is fear that the United States will take the blame whenever dollarized country economies experience economic setback. American officials note that dollarization would promote closer ties with the United States, which is a clear benefit. However, the dollarizer would lose domestic monetary sovereignty. This could foster resentment and encourage foreign policy makers to deflect blame for problems onto the United States.[20]

Ecuador Dollarizes

Although Washington remains cautious, serious problems confront political leaders in emerging market countries. Ecuador is a case in point. In September 1999 Ecuador became the first country to default on Brady bonds and entered into negotiations with creditors to restructure its $13 billion official foreign debt. From September 1999, when default took place, to early January 2000, Ecuador's central bank denied that it would dollarize its economy. Early in January 2000, however, President Jamil Mahuad declared a state of national emergency as protests over economic policy intensified.[21] In the twelve months before early January, the sucre, Ecuador's currency, dropped in value by more than 70 percent against the U.S. dollar.

On January 9, 2000, President Mahuad announced that Ecuador would convert its monetary base to dollars, and the next day the central bank approved the introduction of U.S. dollars as the nation's medium of exchange. This action followed unsuccessful efforts to stabilize the sucre against the dollar. After this 1999 stabilization program failed, the currency was "floated" and went quickly from 7,300 sucres to the dollar to 25,000 to the dollar. The 1999 depreciation of the sucre hit the economy hard, and the International Monetary Fund pressed Ecuador for a Brady bond default.

During the six-month period ending September 9, 2000, Ecuador carried out a transition phase, ending in full dollarization of the economy. Effective on that date, the dollar replaced the sucre as legal tender. Transition problems included shopkeepers adjusting to the conversion rates between the sucre and dollar, and a shortage of coins in circulation.

While dollarization has been implemented with only minimal side problems, the challenge for the government is to move forward with structural reforms needed to move the economy ahead. These are required in the areas of tax and fiscal reform, strengthening of the banking sector, and privatization.[22]

El Salvador Dollarizes

El Salvador allowed the U.S. dollar to circulate alongside its own currency in 2001. But the monetary law sent to the El Salvadorian congress in November 2000 by President Francisco Flores stopped short of full dollarization. In this respect, the dollarization of El Salvador differs from Ecuador's full dollarization, where the sucre was completely removed and replaced by U.S. coin and currency.

El Salvador's currency board fixed the exchange rate for eight years prior to dollarization. The exchange rate was enforced by $2 billion in central bank reserves. The El Salvadorian economy is tied closely to that of the United States. Almost one-fifth of the population (1.2 million persons) lives in the United States, sending back annual remittances of $1.5 billion. A booming maquila-type industry imports and exports U.S. textiles, and much of their remaining export base consists of coffee trade. The U.S. government and the International Monetary Fund supported dollarization and encouraged the government of El Salvador to proceed with economic reforms that would further integrate the nation into the global economy.[23] Dollarization will cause the country's central bank to lose seigniorage from issuing local currency that is estimated at $40 million, or 0.2 percent of El Salvador's GDP.[24]

El Salvador is the third Latin American country to adopt the U.S. dollar, following Panama and Ecuador. For El Salvador, dollarization came at a time when its economy was in reasonably good condition. With a population of 6.5 million, the country held $2 billion in foreign reserves to back the $450 million of currency in circulation. Most of El Salvador's tariffs on Mexican goods were removed on January 1, 2001, and other tariff barriers have been reduced across the board. The World Heritage Foundation rates El Salvador as the twelfth most open economy in the world.

Dollarization will expose El Salvador's economic weaknesses, such as undiversified exports, a fiscal deficit, and a lack of international competitiveness. Despite these problems, neighboring countries may follow the monetary change in El Salvador. In December 2000 Guatemala permitted foreign currency bank deposits and salaries. In Costa Rica, where half of business is already conducted in dollars, the central bank president called for full conversion to the dollar. In Nicaragua ATMs dispense U.S. dollars. Half of Central America's trade is with the United States.

Mercosur

Mercosur is a better prospect for dollarization than NAFTA. First, Mercosur more easily satisfies two of the four conditions described in table 9.1, and it partially satisfies a third. Mercosur has developed a high intensity of regional trade, and three of the four countries (except Paraguay) satisfy the condition of industrial diversification.

Second, Mercosur is a customs union, whereas NAFTA is only a free trade area. The customs union commits to a uniform external tariff and free mobility of capital and labor. Finally, Mercosur includes four national economies that are more competitive with one another. By contrast, NAFTA members are more complementary, suggesting greater trade diversion than trade creation effects.[25]

THE MACK PROPOSAL

In 1999 Senator Connie Mack (D-Fla.), chairman of the Joint Economic Committee and the U.S. Senate Banking Subcommittee on Economic Policy, proposed a bill that would give the United States an opportunity to "export" a key factor behind U.S. economic success: monetary stability. Senator Mack's legislative proposal calls for official dollarization, whereby emerging market countries may opt to abolish their own currencies and adopt the U.S. dollar as legal tender. Senator Mack refers to the dollar as the world's best currency and has noted that Latin Americans already hold large amounts of greenbacks as a hedge.

Senator Mack's proposal, the International Monetary Stability Act, would not oblige the Federal Reserve to act as a lender of last resort to dollarizing countries. Nor would it have responsibility for supervising banks in other countries. The proposal calls for the U.S. Treasury to share increases in U.S. seigniorage with countries that dollarize, removing one of the most widely discussed disadvantages for countries moving in this direction.

Senator Mack notes that "the decision to dollarize is one that each country must make for itself, without coercion." Dollarization is not a panacea for every economic problem in emerging market countries. But it is a step in the right direction. It should not be used as an excuse to avoid needed reforms, better tax systems, and less government control and interference in the economy.[26]

Senator Mack expects dollarization to provide a better opportunity for financial stability. Inflation and interest rates would fall toward U.S. levels in countries that dollarize, and governments would no longer be able to print money to finance wasteful programs. The result would be higher levels of saving and investment, greater liquidity in financial markets, and improved fiscal discipline.

This legislative proposal adds to the growing competition between lead currencies around the world. The euro, U.S. dollar, and Japanese yen are competing for use in third countries (emerging market nations). This competition is useful, since it tends to assure that market-imposed discipline will operate more widely as a constraint against abuse of the privilege to coin and print money.

NOTES

1. Sathnam Sanghera, "Panama in Plan to Cut Brady Debt," *Financial Times*, December 21, 1999, 26.
2. James Wilson, "Panama Wants President to Add Substance to Her Style," *Financial Times*, December 21, 1999, 3.

3. Wilson, "Panama Wants President to Add Substance to Her Style," 6.
4. Joseph Weber, "A NAFTA Dollar: Not Now, Maybe Later," *Business Week*, February 22, 1999, 34.
5. Guillermo A. Calvo and Carmen M. Rinehart, "Capital Reversals, the Exchange Rate Debate, and Dollarization," *Finance and Development*, September 1999, 13–15.
6. J. Sachs and F. Larrain, "Why Dollarization Is More Straitjacket Than Salvation," *Foreign Policy*, Fall 1999, 80–92.
7. Steve Hanke, "Three Cheers for Dollarization," *Euromoney*, March 1999, 96.
8. Calvo and Rinehart, "Capital Reversals," 13–15.
9. Charles Enoch and Ann-Marie Gulde, "Are Currency Boards a Cure for All Monetary Problems?" *Finance and Development*, December 1998, 39–40.
10. Clive Crook, "The Pan-American Greenback: Coming Soon?" *National Journal*, October 9, 1999.
11. D. Mathieson, A. Richards, and S. Sharma, "Financial Crises in Emerging Markets," *Finance and Development*, December 1998, 28–31.
12. R. Chang, "Understanding Recent Crises in Emerging Markets," *Economic Review*, Federal Reserve Bank of Atlanta (Second Quarter 1999), 7–8.
13. S. Fidler and S. Newport, "Drowning Ecuador Grasps the Dollar," *Financial Times*, January 11, 2000, 5; Thomas Caton, "Alarm over Argentina Measures," *Financial Times*, June 19, 2001, 6.
14. F. R. Velde and M. Veracierto, "Dollarization in Argentina," *Chicago Fed Letter*, June 1999, 1–3.
15. Mike Halls, "Argentina Dollarization Looks Inevitable," *Corporate Finance* (London), July 1999, 44–45.
16. David Altig and Owen Humpage, "Dollarization and Monetary Sovereignty: The Case of Argentina," *Economic Commentary* (Federal Reserve Bank of Cleveland), September 15, 1999.
17. Steve Hanke and Kurt Schuler, "A Monetary Constitution for Argentina: Rules for Dollarization," *Cato Journal*, Winter 1999, 405–419.
18. Hanke and Schuler, "Monetary Constitution," 405–419.
19. Joseph Weber, "A NAFTA Dollar: Not Now, Maybe Later," *Business Week*, February 22, 1999, 34.
20. Michael M. Phillips, "U.S. Officials Urge Cautious Approach to Dollarization by Foreign Countries," *Wall Street Journal*, April 23, 1999, A4.
21. Thomas Vogel, "Emergency Is Declared in Ecuador amid Protests," *Wall Street Journal*, January 7, 2000, A12.
22. Nicholas Moss, "Dollar's Embrace Leaves Ecuadorians Tender for Passing of Their Sucre," *Financial Times*, September 21, 2000, 9.
23. Andrew Bounds, "El Salvador to Use Dollar as a Local Currency," *Financial Times*, November 24, 2000, 4.
24. Andrew Bounds, "Salvadorians Embrace the Dollar," *Financial Times*, December 29, 2000, 2.
25. The trade creation effect implies greater efficiency of ultimate suppliers after the preferential trade union is formed. Trade diversion implies the opposite.
26. Connie Mack, "Time to Reap the Dollar's Rewards," *Financial Times*, December 16, 1999, 15.

Chapter Ten

The European Union and Eurozone Expansion

Expansion of the European Union (EU) or enlargement of the Eurozone: which is more critical? Why is enlargement or expansion so problematical? Why is the UK positive on EU expansion but unwilling to come to grips with its own decision to enter (or not) the single currency system? Do the proponents of a united Europe represent old socialist ideals clothed in the sheepskin of pan-Europeanism?

A key fear within continental countries is overcrowding of the labor market, should east Europeans become freely mobile within an expanded European Union. A German electrician working in Berlin may be paid the equivalent of $9.80 an hour, but he hears that east Europeans are willing to do similar work for one-eighth the going Berlin wage.[1]

Concerns about immigration are forcing their way up the political agenda as the EU reaches a critical stage in accession talks with leading candidate countries—the Czech Republic, Cyprus, Estonia, Hungary, Poland, and Slovenia. In the short run immigration can hit vulnerable low-skill workers. Xenophobia raises its head where risk of job loss can be heightened from immigration. The most eastern EU nations (Austria, Germany) are the most sensitive to this issue. Consequently, in these countries attitudes toward east European worker mobility are the least tolerant (table 10.1).

The central and eastern European (CEE) countries are transforming themselves, but at the same time the EU is becoming a more complex monetary and economic union. The single currency is causing western European nations to rethink their willingness to support CEE preparations via fiscal transfers. An enlarged EU would contain more social and economic diversity, perhaps complicating political consensus. European nations avoid grappling with difficult issues until they are forced to do so by circumstances. Enlargement is another one of these difficult issues, and western

Table 10.1. EU Attitudes toward Eastern European Worker Mobility in an Expanded Single Market (percentage of total)

Country	*Accepts without Restriction*	*Accepts with Restriction*	*Does Not Accept*
Spain	37	50	4
Portugal	24	53	13
Italy	18	66	13
Sweden	16	70	7
EU-15	12	59	23
Finland	11	75	12
Ireland	11	68	10
Netherlands	11	67	21
Luxembourg	9	59	20
France	8	63	26
UK	8	59	25
Greece	7	60	30
Belgium	7	51	37
Denmark	6	75	16
Austria	6	55	31
Germany	3	54	37

Source: Stefan Wagstyl, "Moving Targets," *Financial Times*, June 16, 2000, 14.

Europe does not appear to sense any urgency to decide on the issue of eastward expansion.

In the longer run, convergence will close the income gap between the EU countries and accession states. This requires sound economic management in the east, support from the west, and change in EU countries. As Horst Köhler, the managing director of the International Monetary Fund (IMF) says, "convergence is a two-way street." Transition periods will be needed, during which immigration levels may be limited in order to control labor market disruption. Meanwhile, within EU countries, labor market reforms are necessary to create a more flexible and adaptive environment. In 1998 there were 853,000 east European residents in EU countries. This number is projected to rise to 2.9 million in 2010 and 3.9 million in 2030. The impact of this will be uneven. Germany is expected to accept almost 70 percent of these immigrants, Spain only a little over 1 percent.

Successful introduction of the single currency in the eighteen-month period from January 1999 to June 2000 gave the fifteen-nation European Union a needed stimulus. The eleven-nation monetary union brought rapid change in European financial markets, democratized share ownership, and led to a dynamic corporate restructuring. At the same time, the EU experienced growing concern over the issues of EU enlargement, entry of the UK into the monetary union, and the need for reorganizing EU political arrangements to facilitate continued progress toward economic cooperation and integration. The January 2001 entry of Greece into the single currency system added to this stimulus.

A UNITED OR WORKABLE EUROPE?

In his famous Humboldt speech, Joschka Fischer, Germany's foreign minister, stated that "without the closest German-French cooperation, no future European project will succeed."[2] Fischer was referring to the need for Franco-German cooperation to promote further progress in attaining political integration in Europe.

Political integration has many meanings. For British conservatives like Michael Portillo, it means an agenda to create a European superstate that would intrude seriously on national prerogatives. Many British conservatives believe that the vast majority of European politicians want EMU to lead to full political union and a new political entity—the United States of Europe. By contrast, Fischer states that he merely intends to promote a more federal system in Europe that could give a boost to European integration. Fischer would allow a small core group of countries to lead the way in this respect, so that doubters could observe "how it works" before making deeper commitments.

London has been feeling excluded from the Euro-12 group of finance ministers, who participate in the single currency. Fischer sees closer cooperation between the Eurozone countries on their economic policy as a first step toward a federal Europe. Eventually a European government would probably want a new constitution and direct elections, but this would not mean junking the nation-state. Fischer thinks it necessary for the EU to complete urgently needed internal reforms to allow the speedy admission of countries located in central and eastern Europe.

Joschka Fischer comes from the Green Party, a passionate pro-European partner of Chancellor Schröder's government. Fischer thinks the European Union is fundamentally flawed as presently constructed. He thinks the Union is not capable of accommodating the reunification of Europe, both east and west, unless radical action is taken. He believes that enlargement of the EU, doubling it from fifteen, as it is presently constituted, to perhaps thirty members could destroy the edifice.

But Fischer also dared to say that the nation-states of Europe are here to stay, suggesting that a future European government could be intergovernmental rather than directly elected. He dared to speak out on a subject that most politicians would rather ignore—the contradiction between a united Europe and a workable Europe. Whereas Europeans see enlargement as a political imperative, this issue is of low priority to voters.[3] Some 59 percent of voters say enlargement is not a priority.

A TWO-TIER EUROPE

Fischer would like to revive the Franco-German motor of European integration. On the French side, President Jacques Chirac called for a two-tier Europe, in which France and Germany would lead a pioneer group of member states toward deeper integration. A "light secretariat" could coordinate the affairs of this faster-moving tier.

Chirac's vision of a two-tier Europe was set out in his June 2000 address to the German Bundestag in Berlin. The new initiative might include issues in foreign affairs and defense that have received considerable discussion.[4]

Creation of a new inner core is likely to worry Britain, as well as candidate countries that are concerned about entering the EU as second-class members. The government of Poland stated that it is not opposed to closer integration as long as the process is open to all.

INSTITUTIONAL SCLEROSIS

The EU is the world's largest trading area and has plans to double its membership, but its institutions are not working very well. Bodies such as the European Parliament and European Commission find it difficult to take decisive action. National leaders must consider more ambitious projects at special European Council summit meetings. One such need is a program of social-economic reforms designed to create 20 million jobs by 2010. There is a growing sense of crisis over EU institutions and methods of government.

An Intergovernmental Conference (IGC) on EU institutional reform was established in February 2000. But the IGC has not made much progress. Peter Ludlow, founding director of the Brussels-based Centre for European Policy Studies, believes that the EU is becoming dangerously dependent on the ability of national leaders who assume its presidency every six months.[5]

In mid-June 2000, member states of the EU agreed to put plans for closer cooperation between smaller groups of countries on the reform agenda. This is likely to be the subject of fierce controversy, especially in nations such as the UK, Spain, and the Scandinavian countries. The controversy could lead to the emergence of an "inner" and an "outer" core within the EU. The founding members (Belgium, Netherlands, Luxembourg, Germany, and France) strongly back this two-tier approach.[6]

Fischer and Chirac want a two-speed Europe in which finance ministers play a stronger role at E-12 group meetings. The British are skeptical and concerned about these Fischer-Chirac ideas. Tony Blair, British prime minister, fears that his country will be squeezed out of all economic policy discussions and policy decisions if the E-12 solidify their increasing role in monetary and economic matters. The UK Treasury also worries about proposals put forward by the European Commission and France for a group of three to five "wise men." Alexandre Lamfalussy, a former top central banker, has led a review of management in the EU financial services market. Britain fears that this could lead to bureaucratic restrictions and undermine the success of the London and Frankfurt stock markets.[7]

At midyear 2000, these proposals put heavy pressure on the British to decide whether and how they might enter the EMU or single currency. The possibility of the UK joining the single currency involves the interconnected problems of how to manage its entry, and how to define Britain's possible role in a reformed and enlarged EU.

UK AND THE EURO

When eleven countries decided to enter a single currency system in 1998, the Blair Labor government had less than a year of operational experience. At that time, Britain opted out of the single currency on a temporary basis. Chancellor of Exchequer Gordon Brown indicated that Britain would enter the monetary union when the following five tests were met:

- Has Britain achieved sustainable convergence?
- Is there sufficient flexibility in the British economy?
- Will joining create better conditions for long-term decision making?
- Will joining be good for jobs and employment?
- What will be the extent of impact on financial services?

In May 2000 the Institute of Directors, the UK business leader organization, assessed these five tests and said that there was nothing to suggest that the British economy was converging with its European neighbors.[8] The report closely followed the comments of Eddie George, governor of the Bank of England, and was seized on by antieuro lobbyists. The effect of the report was to cast doubt on the timing of a UK entry. Eddie George dismissed arguments that the city of London financial industry would suffer if Britain delayed joining. According to George, the city was thriving outside the euro and would continue to prosper whether or not Britain hastened to join.[9] George's comments disappointed proeuro ministers who were pressing Tony Blair to make a more aggressive case for membership in the single currency. Governor George's comments were in agreement with a survey showing that foreign banks did not regard British membership in the single currency as a key factor in determining whether or not they located in London.

Although financial services in London appeared neutral on euro membership, this was not the case for British exporters. According to one analysis, the UK could triple its trade with Eurozone nations within three decades if it joined the single currency. The study was commissioned by pro-euro business groups concerned with their loss of trading opportunities from failure to join the single currency.[10]

Unfortunately, British companies have not prepared well for a possible UK entry. The government has established committees that many believe have accomplished very little. The financial sector is said to be more advanced than most in contingency planning for entry into the Eurozone. But in January 2000 no banks had spent any of the $3.3 billion needed to change their computer and IT systems for euro transactions.[11]

High Pound

Tony Blair was subject to repeated criticism in the first half of 2000 for his vacillation on the single currency issue. He failed to take a decisive, positive policy position on UK entry into the euro system. Early in 2000, Blair acknowledged that "the British people are opposed to the single currency." Speaking on BBC's Breakfast with Frost, he noted "the economics aren't right." However, he also said that he remained in favor of taking Britain into the euro when the necessary economic conditions were met. But the public needed to be convinced.[12]

Speaking in January 2000, Blair faced a high and rising pound sterling valuation vis-à-vis the euro. When the Laborite government took office at mid-1997 the pound–synthetic euro exchange rate was 0.8 (pounds per euro). A year later, when the British opted out of EMU, the rate was down to almost 0.6. By February 2000 it was 0.58 and still falling. In the three-year period ending May 5, 2000, sterling had appreciated 30 percent against the euro.

The strong pound (weak euro) had a devastating effect on British industry. All across the UK industrial heartland companies were shutting down and cutting back. Britain lost some 100,000 manufacturing jobs in the twelve months ending February 29, 2000. Michael Kitson, economic adviser to the Institute for Manufacturing, said, "It's almost like the Rover case magnified."[13]

The exchange rate conditions in the first half of 2000 made it clear that several of the "tests" enunciated by Gordon Brown were not met. In earlier chapters we discussed the problem of the weak euro facing the ECB in its first eighteen months of operation. The opposite side of the coin was the high pound and the inability of those favoring UK entry into the single currency to do anything about this dilemma.

Foreign Investment

One of the great economic successes of the UK economy has been its strong participatory role in foreign business investment. The UK has operated like a magnet, attracting large amounts of business investment from the Eurozone, North America, and Japan. Unfortunately, the period of sterling appreciation (mid-1997–mid-2000) created serious problems.

Many segments of the British manufacturing industry are owned by Japanese, American, and European companies. For example, Japanese car manufacturers Honda and Nissan play a prominent role as producers in the UK. Much of the production is exported to the Eurozone. The rising pound sterling was squeezing profits out of these operations. In 2000, Nissan joined Honda and Ford to complain about the high pound. The high pound was forcing the companies to consider shifting new investment to the Eurozone. Nissan lost ¥38 billion in the European region in 1999. Nissan officials were saying that production at their Sunderland factory could fall by almost 50 percent due to the pressure on profit.[14] Similarly, Honda warned in June 2000 that it would shift more of its component sourcing from Britain to suppliers inside the Eurozone to reduce their losses.[15]

In general, Britain was facing strong pressures from inward business investors to hold its planned referendum on adoption of the euro. Stephen Byers, then minister of trade and industry, stated, "For the first time big inward investors are telling me that we need to make a decision on the euro early in the next parliament."[16] Robin Cook, British foreign minister, stated that in the next six months the priority must be to build public support among the British people for UK entry into the single currency.

A respected think tank, the National Institute of Economic and Social Research, published a report in February 2000. The report states that if the UK withdraws from the EU, the stock of inward manufacturing investment will eventually be about one-third lower.

The Aznar-Blair Statement

The debate on UK membership in the Eurozone heated up during first half of 2000. Even Tony Blair, the British prime minister, saw fit to stoke the flames. In June 2000, Blair and Jose Maria Aznar, Spain's prime minister, penned a statement published in the *Financial Times* entitled "Britain and Spain Will Continue to Drive Forward Reform."

Martin Wolf analyzed the situation and choices facing the UK at midyear 2000 as follows:[17]

- Stability would be greater outside the zone with a monetary policy aimed at that objective.
- Britain would gain in efficiency by being a full-fledged member of a broad single market.
- The economic costs of staying outside the Eurozone are related to a floating exchange rate. Sterling fluctuations are extremely uncomfortable for the one-sixth of the economy directly exposed to trade with the Eurozone.
- To raise living standards, Britain needs to belong to a large market, and a single currency adds to these benefits.
- Euro entry is irreversible. All sterling contracts would be redenominated in euros.

The Aznar-Blair statement made several key points and reflected their unified perspective on the need to move away from government interference in the marketplace that "could drive investment and jobs out of Europe."

They noted the importance of European reunification as the "greatest challenge" and the greatest opportunity. They noted the "huge benefits to prosperity and stability in Europe that enlargement will bring."[18] In a later section we discuss the different perspectives on enlargement held by the fifteen EU members.

Pro- and Anti-Euro Sentiment *before* the Election in 2001

During the first two years of the single currency Britain's official policy regarding entry into the Eurozone was that it should stay out of the launch phase of monetary union, making preparations to join later. The UK should proceed with entering the euro system when three requirements are satisfied:

- The euro must be launched and operate successfully.
- There must be a clear economic case in favor of UK joining (Gordon Brown's five tests).
- Voters must approve Britain joining in a referendum. With parliamentary elections set for June 2001, the five economic tests are to be assessed post-election, and if conditions warrant, a referendum is to be scheduled.

In the run-up to the June 2001 election Conservatives campaigned against membership in the single currency. The democracy movement organized a march late in 2000 to keep the pound and stop the Eurostate. The Labor government walked a narrow line, avoiding any battle over the euro until after elections.

Business for Sterling, an anti-euro pressure group, has argued that only a minority of companies trade directly with the Eurozone. With New Europe, it is a joint organizer of a "No" publicity campaign. New Europe asserts a pro-European but anti-euro policy. New Europe is headed by Lord David Owen, a former Labor foreign secretary who split from the party in protest against left-wing policies such as withdrawal from the European Economic Community.

In September 2000 Lord Owen's New Europe and Business for Sterling united to campaign under the banner "No—Europe Yes, Euro No." If a euro referendum is called, this group is expected to link up with the Tories to form the official No campaign. Lord Owen hoped Blair would shy away from a referendum. The No campaign is slick, smart, and well funded. In late 2000 it was leading rivals by three-to-one in opinion polls. Lord Owen warns that joining the euro will mean loss of control of economic, foreign, and defense policy.

Economic arguments have been persuasive regarding the economic costs borne by the UK from remaining outside the euro. A report issued by Britain in Europe, based on an analysis of 41,262 jobs lost in manufacturing companies, stated that up to 66,000 jobs may have been lost in Britain during the year 2000 because of the volatility between sterling and the euro. Kitty Usher, BIE's chief economist, suggests that additional effects further up the supply chain could increase the number of jobs affected by remaining outside the Eurozone.[19]

While there may be costs associated with not joining the euro, there also are significant costs from entering the euro system. A parliamentary inquiry reported in late 2000 that the conversion costs that must be borne by UK businesses could reach $30 billion. Martin O'Neill, the pro-euro chairman of the House of Commons committee conducting the inquiry, provided these figures.[20] The Treasury rejected criticism that followed the release of the report, stating that it would not speculate on conversion costs.

British voters have been polled frequently to test their views on joining the euro. Late in year 2000, a majority said that in the long run they expected Britain to use the euro, but also expressed clear doubts about entry in the shorter run.[21] The poll found that 61 percent believed that Britain would use euro notes and coins in ten years. A majority believed in the inevitability of the single currency. Voters are not convinced that euro membership is imminent. Some 52 percent believed that it was unlikely that the euro would be used in five years.

As the June 2001 election approached, the Conservative candidate, Hague, repeated a warning: "Save the pound." Long before Blair's victory he was convinced that he could win a referendum on the euro early in the next Parliament. He promised an assessment concerning whether or not the "five tests" were satisfied within two years of the election. On the eve of election the pound fell sharply against the euro, anticipating a Labor victory, and a more favorable governmental policy stance toward entering the euro system.[22]

One economic analysis of the choices facing the UK observed that Britain had a divided economy, with a relatively prosperous services sector that included financial services, and that these sectors accounted for five-sevenths of total output. The manufacturing sector, which accounted for the remaining two-sevenths of UK output, has exhibited sluggish growth. Should the re-elected Labor government promote policies that prepare the UK for entry into the Eurozone, this might intensify the sluggish performance of the manufacturing sector. Or the government might follow a more expansive policy mix that would undermine the UK ability to satisfy Brown's five tests, which would be required before a pro-euro decision could be made.[23]

Pro- and Anti-Euro Sentiment *after* the Election in 2001

Before the June 2001 election, the pro-euro forces in Britain pushed for a referendum on whether or not UK should join the European Union. But, paradoxically, after the June 2001 landslide election of Tony Blair and the Labor Party, two-thirds of Britons would vote against joining. Polling after the election showed that the camps break down into three groups with almost no overlap:[24]

- Small businesses objected to being forced to convert cash tills, computers, and accounting systems to euro use at great cost and for little obvious benefit.
- Medium-sized national companies that do business mainly in sterling were either neutral or hostile to the euro.
- Large multinational firms that already did more business in the euro than sterling favored joining the single currency EU.

Muddled Opinion

The issues were muddled from almost every point of view. Polling after the election revealed that British sentiment for or against joining the EU was based mostly on whether or not businesses thought joining the euro would increase or decrease their firm's expenses. Simon Wolfson, a euro opponent and the chief executive of Next, a clothing retail chain, took a longer view based on the issue's effect on the British economy. "It comes down to economics," he said. "We just don't believe that it's possible to manage the entire economy of Europe with just one interest rate policy. How do you alleviate recession in Germany and curb inflation in Ireland [with one monetary policy]?"[25] But Next imports only 20 percent of its merchandise from the Eurozone, and its $2.1 billion in annual sales were almost all in sterling. This point of view ultimately asked whether a single currency monetary policy could effectively deal with the needs of a disparate group of twelve Eurozone economies. This issue is discussed at the end of this chapter.

Uncertain Effect on Capital Flows

There was also a lot of controversy over whether or not joining would help or hurt investment in Britain. Britain had attracted far more investment than European countries while they remained outside the union. Anti-euro forces argue that this was because British law made it cheaper to do business in UK. But pro-euro executives like Lord Haskins and Unilever's cochairman, Niall Fitzgerald, insisted that the flow of capital would dry up if investors believed that Britain would stay forever outside the Eurozone, which accounted for half the nation's trade. Lord Haskins is chairman of Northern Foods, a company that buys raw materials like meat, grain, and milk that are priced in euros. Haskins felt that investment in the border-free Eurozone would minimize the effect of exchange rate fluctuations on European operations. Others, like Simon Wolfson of Next, felt that exchange rate fluctuations could be adequately dealt with through the traditional process of hedging in foreign exchange markets.

Effect on Trade Flows

Another short-term consideration was that joining in June 2001 would reduce British trade flows to the Eurozone, since the low value of the euro relative to sterling would make Eurozone goods cheaper than British goods. Chancellor Brown argued that Britain should postpone a decision until currency conditions were more favorable.

The Government Debates the Issue

After the election, pro- and anti-euro sentiment remained undecided, and the British government has done little to clarify this situation. Although it appears that Blair would like to be associated with a decision to join the EU, the chancellor of the Exchequer, Gordon Brown, laid out what he called a "considered and cautious" approach to jettisoning the pound in favor of the euro. The two-year period of assessment recommended by Brown was seen to be putting the brakes on a decision by delaying an ultimate referendum on the issue. Brown and Blair continued to debate the issue.

GREECE, DENMARK, AND SWEDEN

When the E-11 decided to move forward with a single currency in May 1998, four of the EU countries remained outside the monetary union. The UK opted out, in part due to an exchange rate alignment that was prejudicial to UK economic stability. Greece did not satisfy the convergence criteria. Denmark and Sweden opted to remain out of the Eurozone, with the expectation that they would decide to join at a future date.

Greece

The European Commission officially endorsed Greece's bid to become the twelfth country to adopt the euro. This all but guaranteed that Greece's bid would be approved and move forward. In mid-2000, Greece was expected to become a full euro member by early 2001.[26] Although Greece accounts for barely 2 percent of Eurozone gross domestic product (GDP), Greece is important because of the precedent that its entry will establish for over a dozen other countries in eastern Europe, each waiting to become a member of EU and its single currency system.

At mid-2000, Greece continued to face minor uncertainties over the drachma's valuation. Greek short-term interest rates need to fall sharply to converge with those in the Eurozone. Their official interest rates in June 2000 were still 500 basis points over those in the Eurozone, and although they had fallen 250 basis points in the first six months of 2000.[27]

Greece has worked hard to reduce inflation. In the fourth quarter of 1999 the inflation rate was 2.2 percent and was only 2.3 percent for the full year (table 10.2). Main factors contributing to the falling rate of inflation were the Bank of Greece's stability-oriented policy and a decline in the rate of increase in unit labor costs (table 10.2). Greece also achieved a sizable reduction in governmental deficits. Its deficit fell from 10.0 percent of GDP in 1994 to 1.6 percent in 1999. This decrease can be attributed to strong improvement in budget revenues.

On January 1, 2001, Greece formally became the twelfth member of the Eurozone. Opinion polls reported over 70 percent of Greeks to be in favor joining the single currency. Greeks were prepared to give up their currency—the drachma, the second oldest in Europe—in return for membership. Greece was able to prepare for entry into the euro system due to favorable economic trends in 2000–2001, including a growth rate of 4.1–5.0 percent, a projected budget surplus, and a declining trend in inflation.

During the month of December 2000 the Bank of Greece was making final preparations to bring the nation into the monetary union. Greek interest rates started the year 2000 above 10 percent, and the final weeks of 2000 required

Table 10.2. Macroeconomic Indicators for Greece (annual percentage change)

Indicator	*1994*	*1995*	*1996*	*1997*	*1998*	*1999*	*1999 Q4*
Real GDP	2.0	2.1	2.4	3.4	3.7	3.5	—
Inflation rate	—	—	7.9	5.4	4.5	2.3	2.2
Compensation per employee	10.8	12.9	8.8	12.4	5.8	4.8	—
Employment	1.9	0.9	–0.4	–0.3	3.4	1.2	—
Unemployment[a]	8.9	9.1	9.8	9.7	10.9	10.5	—
Fiscal balance[b]	–10.0	–10.2	–7.4	–3.9	–2.5	–1.6	—
Consolidated gross debt[c]	109.3	108.7	111.3	108.5	105.4	104.4	—
Three-month interest rate	26.7	16.4	13.8	12.9	13.9	10.3	10.4

Source: ECB, *Annual Report 1999*, 67.
[a]Denotes unemployment as percentage of total labor force.
[b]Denotes fiscal budget deficit as percentage of GDP.
[c]Denotes government debt as percentage of GDP.

aligning rates with those in the Eurozone. December 2000 saw no hint of speculative attack on the drachma. Banks had been practicing trading in euro–dollar trades over the final three months of the year.[28]

Greece serves as a beacon for aspiring EU and euro members from central and eastern Europe. But the entry of Greece will also provide more monetary policy problems for the ECB. The idea that one level of interest rates can fit the needs of twelve countries will be more fully stress-tested. Greek inflation was reported at 4.2 percent in November 2000, and together with Ireland it presents the ECB with a pair of Eurozone countries in which inflation rates press closely on interest rate levels.

Denmark and Sweden

During the year 2000, the Danish prime minister, Poul Nyrup Rasmussen, implemented an upbeat campaign to bring about a favorable referendum on the euro. However, the outcome of the September 2000 referendum looked extremely doubtful at midyear 2000. In 1992 Denmark shook the European Union to its core when it repudiated the Maastricht treaty. Eight years later Danish voters had a second opportunity. Four opinion polls published in May–June 2000 placed euro opponents in the lead. A second rejection of the euro carries important implications. First, EU efforts to carry out structural and institutional reform in preparation for planned enlargement could be affected. Second, in Britain, public opinion at mid-2000 was against relinquishing the pound. A Danish "no" would make Tony Blair's EMU drive more difficult. Finally, in Sweden there is the likelihood that a Danish "yes" could lead to a referendum on the euro. A reverse outcome in Denmark would likely delay a Swedish referendum and put the question of euro membership on the back burner.[29]

EASTWARD EXPANSION

At mid-2000, the integration process of central and eastern European (CEE) countries into the European Union seemingly had lost momentum. A prime reason was member states' growing concern that enlargement might cause mass labor migration to the west. In Austria and Germany, the two nations likely to be most directly affected by migration, there is insistence that migration restrictions be established, at least on a temporary basis.

Many EU leaders recognize that the zero immigration stance of the past several decades is no longer appropriate as the EU working population declines. The European Commission estimates that the EU working population will start to fall in the early years of the twenty-first century. Also, the number of persons over sixty-five will rise to reach 22 percent of the population by 2025. To gain a joint EU approach toward immigration, the Commission wants EU countries to complete two reports, the first reviewing current policy and the second setting out future intentions on immigration.

The debate on immigration has centered on the need to attract relevant skilled personnel. Other concerns must be avoiding a brain drain from immigrant countries and distinguishing between problems of asylum seekers and the need to remedy worker skill shortages. The EU estimates it may need to admit 50–75 million immigrants over the next fifty years. What is missing in Europe is a coordinated approach toward immigration. Accession for CEE nations is one means of limiting the size and scope of these issues.[30]

Several negative consequences might follow from a delay in the overall process of EU expansion. There would be a loss of credibility in the EU commitment to enlargement. A reduced commitment to enlargement would dampen private investor interest in eastern Europe. Candidate countries for accession likely would find it politically more difficult to implement the reforms necessary for accession. Finally, a delay means slower convergence of per capita incomes of CEE countries with EU countries.[31]

If E-15 member countries immediately opened their labor markets to migrants from the accession countries, the EU commitment to eastward expansion would become more credible. At midyear 2000 most of the migrants from CEE nations were living in Austria and Germany. With macroeconomic conditions improving in these two countries, the business cycle upswing would ease the absorption of migration flows and alleviate the impact of immigration on EU resident jobs.

Enlarging the EU

In 1997 French President Jacques Chirac told Poland and the Czech Republic they could be members of the European Union by the year 2000. By June 2000 Chirac and other EU leaders had fallen silent. Ten years after the collapse of communism, the EU says it will be ready to accept new members from the year 2003 onward. But this does not necessarily mean that the EU will be willing to let them in. In June 2000 six of the applicants asked jointly for assurance that the doors would be open by 2003 but did not receive it.

Several problems within the EU are blocking progress on setting a timetable for accession:

- Germany and Austria are concerned about migrant workers from CEE countries (table 10.1).
- The EU is struggling with the changes needed to revive its own political institutions and ensure that these institutions will not break down under the pressure of an increasing number of member states.
- The European Commission wants the candidates to achieve near perfect conformity with the EU's voluminous laws and directives.

These obstacles can be overcome, but only with much more political goodwill than has been demonstrated.[32]

The French government is expected to prepare a "road map" for EU enlargement that details the problems lying ahead and indicates how to deal with them. France is the most hesitant of all the EU countries concerning enlargement. EU countries located close to the CEE ten have greater concerns for security and stability. Other countries (e.g., France) are more ambivalent. The reunification of Germany has awakened its interest in closer economic ties and more direct business and investment links. This contrasts with Portugal, which has little reason to favor eastward enlargement.

In January 1998 the European Commission warned countries planning to join the European Union that they should not expect entry to be quick or easy. Nikolaus van der Pas warned that it could take five years from the start of negotiations for countries to establish the institutions required for EU entry. As director general of the task force for accession negotiations, he stated that thus far discussions have dealt with the easy aspects of entry and that applicants should not expect very much flexibility on the EU side.[33] On the other hand, Percy Barnavik, chairman of Investor, the Swedish group, warned the EU not to create a new "iron curtain" mentality by conducting negotiations that make accession seem almost impossible.

Regional differences abound. The Scandinavian countries express concern about stabilizing the three Baltic states, while Germany is focused on neighboring Poland. Greece is more interested in the transition in closely neighboring Romania and Bulgaria.

Economic Integration for CEE Nations

The six accession countries that are the likely first wave to enter the EU entered a more difficult phase on May 26, 2000. At that point the EU was demanding additional information on the possible impact of enlargement on immigration and border security. The six countries expressed fear that these requirements could further delay the process.

The six countries—Hungary, Poland, Estonia, the Czech Republic, Slovenia, and Cyprus—must satisfy requirements in thirty specific areas of inquiry ranging from agriculture to bank system stability and safety. For example, Slovenia's cooperative banks have two years to adopt capital adequacy rules. Hungary neared completion of negotiations on the free movement of goods in cross-border trade. Poland expected to complete its negotiations on accession by midyear 2001, with discussions on agriculture playing a key role in these negotiations.[34]

Factors impelling accession to EU and the single currency include historical precedent, geographic proximity, and sociopsychological compatibility. In discussions driven by foreign policy, economic benefits are regarded as less important than psychological and political factors. Poland regards security aspects of EU membership as paramount. Moving into the EU and decisively out of the Russian circle of influence is particularly important for the three Baltic states.

Another factor that draws central and eastern European countries closer to the euro is the possibility for improving their access to the vast pool of capital in western Europe.[35] Charles Frank, the acting president of the European Bank for Reconstruction and Development (EBRD), made this point. Poland already is considering changing its currency peg in the direction of the euro. At midyear 1998 the zloty was pegged to a base of currencies in which the U.S. dollar held a 45 percent weight. According to Gronkiewicz-Wiltz, former president of the National Bank of Poland (central bank), in the future, Poland could give an increasing weight to the euro in this market basket.

One sign of greater opening came in December 1999, when the EU accepted Turkey as an accession candidate. In 1995 Turkey had completed a long phase-in to become a member of the customs union. A large majority of the Turkish population favors joining. But it is likely that most Turks do not appreciate what EU membership means and what is required to achieve it. If Turkey does join the EU, it will replace Britain as the most difficult and obstreperous member.[36]

When Turkey becomes an EU member, it will rank second (to Germany) in population (table 10.3). Turkey's high birth rate could easily place it first in population within a quarter century. Turkey has more farmers than Belgium has people. Its income per capita is approximately one-third the EU average but is in line with other possible accession countries (table 10.3).

Table 10.3. Comparative Data on Five Possible Accession Countries

Country	*Population*	*Average Annual Population Growth*	*GDP per Capita, U.S.$*	*Trade Balance with EU*	*Workforce in Agriculture*	*Freedom Score*
Czech Republic	10.3	0.0	$5,220	-1,496	5.2	1.5
Estonia	1.1	0.1	3,730	-520	13.55	1.5
Poland	38.7	0.5	4,030	-11,368	19.0	1.5
Romania	22.5	0.1	1,480	-543	12.6	2.0
Turkey	65.5	2.0	3,050	-5,489	43.0	4.5

Source: Economist.
Note: Population in millions. Population growth for 1980–1998, annual average percentage. Trade balance with EU in € millions. Workforce in agriculture as percentage total. Degree of freedom is 1 for high, and 7 for low.

Turkey's accession will provide a younger population and workforce. Two million Turkish workers are already resident in western Europe. Turkey has addressed preparations for EU membership and has enacted various human rights reforms. Military judges have been removed from its civilian courts, and greater protection has been given to dissident political parties. But Turkey still needs to address questions of the role of Islam, the status and rights of the Kurds, and the constitutional role of the military.

Foreign Trade

The EU is the key economic partner for CEE countries relative to their foreign trade and investment. Since 1989 the CEE countries have shifted a major part of their foreign trade away from the Council for Mutual Economic Assistance (CMEA) region to the EU.[37] This changeover was carried out rapidly, as can be observed in table 10.4. As of 1995 the EU had become the most important market for CEE exports. EU markets are of vital importance for CEE countries, but the reverse is not true. CEE countries took barely 10 percent of EU exports outside the region. Future expansion of EU exports to the CEE is likely to be in line with GDP growth in the CEE.

Table 10.4. Shifting of Trade Focus of CEE 6 (percentage of total)

Component	*1989*	*1995*
To CMEA	47	23
To EU-15	35	63
To U.S.	2	2

Source: H. Grabbe and K. Hughes, *Enlarging the EU Eastwards* (London: Royal Institute of International Affairs, 1998), 13.
Note: The six include Bulgaria, Czech Republic, Hungary, Poland, Romania, and Slovakia.

Poland is the EU's largest CEE trading partner, with the Czech Republic second. Hungary and Slovenia rank third and fourth. These four countries account for three-fourths of EU-CEE trade.

EU countries are not equally dependent on CEE trade. Smaller countries such as Austria focus their exports on the CEE. Austria's trade with eastern Europe has more than doubled since 1989.[38] Based on proximity and investment ties, Germany also exports heavily to the CEE. Finland also has a high CEE trade direction. But for most of the remaining fifteen countries in the EU, the CEE share of trade is low, around 5 percent of total (UK, Netherlands, France).

We should note that the EU is the single most important trading partner with CEE. The EU enjoys an overall trade surplus with the CEE, and CEE countries complain that the EU needs to remove its restrictions on CEE exports. Exports of agricultural products are considered especially in need of EU liberalization.

Foreign Direct Investment

Foreign direct investment flows into central and eastern Europe were at low levels in 1989–1991 but have risen steadily since 1991. Inflows to the CEE-10 account for the bulk of inflows into transition countries. The United Nations estimated that there were cumulative inflows of $47 billion into transition economies from 1990 to 1996. Of this total, $39 billion was directed into the CEE-10 countries, with over $4 billion going to the Russian Federation. Close to $4 billion went into other CIS (Commonwealth of Independent States) and CEE countries.[39]

Among the CEE-10, Poland received nearly a third of total investment inflows (over $13 billion). Hungary was close behind Poland, receiving over $12 billion of foreign direct investment (FDI) inflows. The Czech Republic received over $6 billion of FDI inflows in this period. Factors such as market size, economic success, and political stability influence these flows.

Table 10.5. FDI by Source Country for Poland and the Czech Republic

Country	*Percentage of Total*
Germany	21.0
Netherlands	9.3
Switzerland	7.3
France	7.1
Austria	6.6
UK	4.5

Source: H. Grabbe and K. Hughes, *Enlarging the EU Eastwards* (London: Royal Institute of International Affairs, 1998), 23.

Source countries for FDI inflows to Poland and the Czech Republic are indicated in table 10.5. The United States and Germany lead, accounting for over 43 percent of flows to these two countries. As a tollgate country lying between eastern and western Europe, Austria accounts for a disproportionate amount of FDI inflows.

FDI data reflect uneven economic interest in the CEE countries in the EU. Germany plays an important role, but so does the UK. Shares of FDI flows tell almost the same story told by shares of trade. EU member states each have a unique and varying inclination to trade and invest in the CEE countries. These varying trade and investment propensities act as constraints on the timetable for accession of CEE countries into the EU single currency area.

The Economics of EU Enlargement

At present, European leaders are wrestling with the question of how much institutional adaptation and reform the EU should achieve before taking on new eastern members. The French president, Jacques Chirac, suggested strengthening the European Commission. This proposal was quickly taken up by Jacques Delors, now head of a high-level think tank called Notre Europe. Apparently some European leaders fear the early entry of new members, which suggests that the institutional reforms required for entry may become more difficult if the accession of eastern European countries comes too quickly.[40] Another view was expressed in publications such as the Economist, which stated that the EU dash for western integration should be deplored. According to the Economist, the EU also should have been dashing for eastern widening.[41]

Accession by CEE countries could impact the economic integration process in several ways. First, accession by CEE countries will give them a participatory role in the decision process within EU. This power is an important issue because of past EU difficulty in persuading members to agree.

A second factor is the effect that accession could have on opening up economic progress, one important area being the liberalization of EU trade in agricultural products. CEE countries that become full members of the EU will gain access to EU markets for their agricultural products.

Another area of change will be access to the single market. This is expected to give CEE exporters great benefits. Since the timetable for accession is not certain, there is no way to anticipate the length and timing of transition periods and the special treatment or status that might be accorded specific categories of goods.

EU countries will be minimally affected by enlargement because CEE countries are generally smaller than EU countries. But accession could still cause structural changes in western European industry. This would occur if low-cost CEE inputs and EU firm linkages with CEE countries increased the competitiveness of the firms. The industrial sectors in the EU most integrated with the CEE might enjoy significant benefits. For this reason we might expect many German firms to benefit most. To achieve cost advantages, German industry might partially relocate to CEE areas. This could expand German competitiveness relative to other EU industry sectors.

The EU must deal with this restructuring issue. In addition to using trade- and investment-oriented policies, the EU can avail itself of incentives for corporate restructuring and capital market–related policies.

STRATEGIES FOR ACCESSION

Not until 1989 was it thought possible for any central or eastern European country to become a member of the EU. But since 1989, the EU has developed institutional structures and policy approaches that can be interpreted as a commitment to enlargement.

The EU has set three goals for itself: (1) economic and monetary union, (2) institutional reform, and (3) enlargement. All three goals are linked to the phenomenon of globalization.[42] The third goal, enlargement, poses a serious challenge. Like a growing child, Europe does not know where its body ends. Because there is no clear geographical definition of Europe, the EU must redefine its own identity as well as the meaning of sovereignty.

Until the publication of Agenda 2000 in 1997, there were four elements of a strategy leading to accession. These elements included the Europe Agreements, the Single Market white paper, the Phare Program, and the structured dialogue.

The Europe Agreements

From 1993 on, a series of bilateral agreements were signed with CEE countries to establish a free trade area for a ten-year transitional period. Deadines for EU market opening were brought into the 1993 European Council in Copenhagen. Duties and quotas were removed on a major part of Visegrad country exports, with restraints decreasing almost yearly. Agricultural products are still subject to a regime of tariff and quota limits. This trade component continues to be a sensitive issue across Europe.

The Europe Agreements have benefited CEE-EU trade, providing a framework for discussions as well as real reductions in trade barriers. The remaining key issues are contingent protection and agricultural product treatment. It is not likely that much progress will be made in these areas until negotiations for accession are begun.

The Single Market White Paper

The Single Market white paper, which was endorsed by the European Council in 1995, sets out key legislation for trade in the EU internal market. Applicant countries must set priorities and maintain the pace of their progress. Because of the absence of agreements with the EU concerning these strategies, these countries need to make serious commitments as they attempt to align their systems. The white paper does not provide any reciprocal commitments on the part of the EU.

However, the white paper does provide guidelines for applicants' preparations. Following these guidelines, the CEE countries have surprised the EU with their speedy translation and incorporation of single market legislation into their own national systems. While the white paper provides an institutional framework for monitoring, many years of work remain for all CEE nations to conform their national systems. They must move from the enactment of single market legislation to implementation. Enormous administrative burdens are imposed by the white paper, stretching the legal and technical capacity of applicant countries at a time when their economies have been experiencing dynamic and systemic change.

A central question addresses the degree of conformity to trade and other legislation necessary to qualify for accession. Some EU countries were given liberal treatment in this regard prior to their own accession (Greece and Portugal). Is full implementation of the four freedoms (goods, services, capital, and labor) necessary at accession time? Faster enlargement of the EU requires liberal treatment in these areas. Yet enlargement that is too rapid may lead to severe competitive problems after accession.

The business sector often lags behind government initiatives in the EU. Are businesses actually adopting single market standards? Are governments able to monitor and enforce EU legislation? What will it cost business to prepare for the single market in the CEE countries?

The Phare Program

This program was established in 1989 at the Group of 24 meeting to support Poland and Hungary in their early reform process. The program also sought to provide aid and *technical* assistance for economic restructuring and transition.[43] The program covers all ten applicants for membership, plus Albania, Bosnia-Herzegovina, and Macedonia. Allocated funds have tripled. The program covers many types of restructuring activities, and it complements bilateral and multilateral aid.

Between 1990 and 1996, Phare receipts ranged between a low of ECU32 per capita (Romania) and a high of ECU80 per capita (Estonia). In this period, the ten countries received a total of ECU4.4 billion. Administrative problems, including unused funds and administrative bottlenecks, have reduced the effectiveness of this program.

The Structured Dialogue

The fourth element in accession strategies, the structured dialogue, was intended as a forum for the discussion of multilateral issues. This part of the preparation for accession has helped resolve disputes between Slovenia and Italy. But in general, policy makers in the EU agree that the structured dialogue has been ineffective. The European Commission has recommended in Agenda 2000 that it be abandoned or replaced by other kinds of dialogue.

Agenda 2000

In 1997, the European Commission reviewed ten CEE countries as potential participants in the eastward enlargement of EU. The EU considered the applicants as medium-term prospects for membership. An assessment was made of how close these countries might come to being ready to join EU in five years (2002).

Agenda 2000 offers a clear vision of the European Union as it enters the twenty-first century. The agenda is essentially an incremental approach toward reform. A debate has taken place within EU about which CEE countries should be first to gain accession. The agenda has also offered an opportunity to discuss the approaches to be followed in making such distinctions.

Agenda 2000 proposes a formal multilateral structure—a standing European conference on enlargement. In the areas of foreign policy and security, the conference would be used for general consultation. In the field of justice and home affairs, the conference would facilitate cooperation. It would meet once a year at heads of state level and at the ministerial level when necessary.

The first new members might joint the EU sometime between 2002 and 2006. In 1997 the European Commission recommended negotiations with five central European nations (Czech Republic, Estonia, Hungary, Poland, and Slovenia) for accession. These five appear to satisfy preliminary eligibility criteria and possess democratic governments, market-type economies, and the ability to embrace the responsibility of EU membership.

PREPARING FOR EASTWARD EXPANSION

Budget Considerations

Integration imposes the costs of transition and structural adjustment on the new members of the economic bloc. Over the past four decades, the EU has used fiscal transfers as a means of offsetting these costs of adaptation. Past practices have been based on a relatively generous approach. More recently the EU has indicated unwillingness to increase the budget as a percentage of GNP of member states. Therefore, to encourage accession, some "solution" to this budget constraint is needed.

The Common Agricultural Policy (CAP) and structured funds account for 75–80 percent of EU budget expenditures. The lobby groups represented in these expenditure areas (farmers and regional aid recipients) are powerful. Several competing pressures are critical to budget reform. First, the EMU criteria impose budget limits as a percentage of EU regional GNP. Germany and the Netherlands consider these limits sacrosanct. Second, countries receiving structural funds (Spain) would attempt to prevent accession if it required reduced transfers. Third, a central aspect of the EU is the requirement for equal treatment for all members. Therefore, extended transitional conditions on new members would violate the principle of equal treatment by creating a multitier EU.

Budget Projections and Compromise

In 1997 the Commission proposed that the budget operate from 2000 to 2006 with no increase in the ceiling of 1.27 percent of GNP. Actual economic growth will allow absolute increases that are closely related to trends in income. With growth rates of 4.0 percent and 2.5 percent respectively for the CEE and the EU, by 2006 there would be an additional €20 billion of budget resources.

These estimates allow for small increments to CAP, somewhat reduced regional aid for the EU-15, and small increments in aid to the CEE group. Whether this compromise will maintain peace and harmony within an expanding EU cum CEE depends on several key developments. First, will the pattern of fiscal transfers balance the needs of CAP, shifting regional requirements and evolving political pressures? Second, are the economic assumptions on which the above projections were based reasonably on target? Third, will all member states consider and accept this compromise as fair?

Enlargement and the Budget

Based on European Commission projections, the EU budget for 2000–2006 will be ECU745.5 billion. From this the CEE countries would receive transfers of ECU74.8 billion (table 10.6). Considering the massive economic restructuring ahead as the transition continues, these transfers do not reflect any robust commitment by the EU. As the CEE countries gain membership, they can be expected to argue for larger transfers and/or other benefits.

Table 10.6. Basic Parameters of Budget Compromise to Year 2000

Parameters	*€ Billions*	*Percentage*
Total EU budget, 2000–2006	754.5	
CEE transfers	74.8	
CEE share of budget in 2006		16

Source: H. Grabbe and K. Hughes, *Enlarging the EU Eastwards* (London: Royal Institute of International Affairs, 1998), 97.

Agricultural Policy

Agricultural policy is one of the most difficult issues related to accession. A big agricultural reform does not appear likely. Nor is it expected that any of the first tier countries would accept second-class status with regard to the treatment of their agricultural exports within an enlarged EU. CAP accounts for close to half of the EU budget (close to ECU40 billion in 1999). Extending CAP, without alteration, to CEE countries with less efficient agricultural sectors than current EU countries carries stark implications vis-à-vis budget control. The fifteen EU member states must first reform the Common Agricultural Policy and produce a new budget deal to cope with the costs of expansion.[44]

In CEE countries agricultural prices are one-half to three-fourths of the levels in the EU. Price supports keep farm product prices higher in the EU, although productivity and efficiency levels are superior. On the other hand, CEE countries have the potential to expand agricultural output whereas EU countries do not. This expansion depends on improving efficiency and productivity in the CEE via reorganizing land ownership and use, as well as adopting new techniques and technology.

The EU is involved in complex discussions with six accession candidates on agricultural reforms, one of the thirty "chapters" in which integration is required. The EU will insist on full implementation of the laws and standards covering agriculture. This implementation includes dealing with 630 legal texts and ninety directives covering veterinary issues alone.

Poland and other candidates have requested temporary exemptions. They will try to persuade the EU that its farmers should benefit from the price subsidies already available in the EU. The EU will argue that domestic reform, rather than new subsidies, provides the best solution for eastern region farmers.

Farming in eastern Europe is not the most efficient. For example, Poland's agricultural sector is undercapitalized, with the average farm size only seven hectares. Many Polish farmers fear they could lose markets to the EU after membership.[45]

Several factors press heavily for CAP reform in the EU:

- Enlargement toward the east with potential for higher levels of competition
- Cost reduction, since many sectors within the EU are experiencing diseconomies from intensive methods
- Environmental considerations
- Pressure from outside Europe (United States, World Trade Organization, and former colonial areas)

The Nice Treaty, 2001

In 2001 the EU countries endorsed the Treaty of Nice, which included complex new voting arrangements for an enlarged EU, as well as articles to allow the creation of a new European rapid reaction peacekeeping force. On June 8, 2001, the voters of Ireland rejected the Treaty of Nice by a 54–46 margin. This rejection posed a threat to the process of admitting new member states, and it was greeted with alarm in Brussels and other European capitals.[46]

The Irish rejection could provoke a crisis for the EU similar to the one that occurred when Denmark rejected the Maastricht treaty in 1992. Romano Prodi, the president of the European Commission, stated that EU enlargement could continue despite the Irish rejection. This amounted to a decision that, legally, ratification of the Nice treaty would not be necessary for enlargement.[47]

Commission officials said that, although it was legally possible to enlarge the EU under its existing Treaty of Amsterdam, the reforms of EU decision-making procedures in the Treaty of Nice would help applicants once they became EU members.

CONCLUSION

Accession inevitably will affect not only the EU budget but also the dynamics of the entire European Union. Given the number of CEE countries and the strong likelihood that enlargement will be spread over as many as twenty years, EU reforms can be expected to take place in stages. There will be no "great leap forward."

The process of enlargement can be expected to suffer setbacks from time to time. Reversals may stem from the need to negotiate budget reform or revisions in CAP. CEE applicants will receive no more than modest transfers, owing to the high unemployment levels prevailing in many EU countries, as well as the slow economic growth that imposes internal and external budget constraints.

While the enlargement process is under way, we must remember there is no generally accepted strategy for developing a European Union of twenty-six members. The process suffers from lack of leadership and a focused strategy. Each member state has its own perspective. Nevertheless, the EU has reaffirmed its commitment to expand its membership to include the CEE countries.

Eastward enlargement is a difficult process and will require leadership and commitment. Very probably, the leaders who will be at the helm nationally and regionally when the final stages of enlargement take place are individuals now in the early stages of their own professional careers.

NOTES

1. Stefan Wagstyl, "Moving Targets," *Financial Times*, June 16, 2000, 14.
2. Ian Black, "Berlin Minister's Federal EU Vision," *Guardian Europe*, May 13, 2000, 7.
3. Quentin Peel, "A Salutary Lesson for Europe," *Financial Times*, May 29, 2000, 15.
4. Haig Simonian, "Chirac Calls for a French and German Led Europe, *Financial Times*, June 28, 2000, 14.
5. Peter Norman, "Europe Seeks a Heart," *Financial Times*, June 6, 2000, 16.

6. Quentin Peel and Michael Smith, "EU States Open Way for More Diverse Europe," *Financial Times*, June 14, 2000, 2.

7. Brian Groom, "Blair to Question Schröder over Two-Speed Europe," *Financial Times*, June 29, 2000, 3.

8. Christopher Adams, "Economy Years Away from Meeting Criteria to Join Euro," *Financial Times*, May 29, 2000, 6.

9. C. Adams and R. Shrimsley, "Central Bank Chief Dismisses Euro Arguments," *Financial Times*, June 14, 2000, 10.

10. R. Shrimsley and R. Bennett, "Britain Could Triple Trade with Euro-Zone States," *Financial Times*, June 26, 2000, 9.

11. Ed Crooks, "Support for Euro Is in Doubt over Forum Inactivity," *Financial Times*, January 10, 2000, 5.

12. Cathy Newman, "Blair Admits British Are Opposed to Euro," *Financial Times*, January 17, 2000, 6.

13. Marc Champion, "Strong Pound Hits UK Manufacturers at a Bad Moment, *Wall Street Journal Europe*, May 5, 2000, 1, 6.

14. Tim Burt and David Owen, "Nissan May Order Switch in European Investment Policy," *Financial Times*, June 30, 2000, 1.

15. Tim Burt, "Honda Threat to Bust Euro Components," *Financial Times*, June 6, 2000, 4.

16. "Inward Investors Press for a Vote on the Euro," *Financial Times*, January 7, 2000, 9.

17. Martin Wolf, "The Chancellor at the Controls," *Financial Times*, June 14, 2000, 15.

18. Tony Blair and Jose Maria Aznar, "A Europe Bolstered by a Single Currency," *Financial Times*, June 13, 2000, 15.

19. Brian Groom, "Lord of the Anti-Euro Campaign," *Financial Times*, September 9, 2000, 9; and Alan Beattie, "Up to 66,000 Jobs Lost outside the Euro," *Financial Times*, December 30, 2000, 5.

20. R. Shrimsley and B. Groom, "Joining Euro May Cost Business $43 Bn," *Financial Times*, November 17, 2000, 12.

21. Rosemary Bennett, "Majority Expect Britain Will Use Euro by 2010," *Financial Times*, October 9, 2000, 8.

22. David White, "Pound Falls on Prospect of Blair Taking UK into Euro," *Financial Times*, June 7, 2001, 1.

23. Samuel Brittan, "Blair's Problems of Success," *Financial Times*, June 7, 2001, 13.

24. Alan Cowell, "Nuanced Conflict over Euro in Britain," *New York Times*, June 21, 2001, W1.

25. Cowell, "Nuanced Conflict," W1.

26. Geoff Winestock, "EU Commission Backs Greece's Euro-Zone Bid," *Wall Street Journal Europe*, May 4, 2000, 1, 5.

27. Kerin Hope and Christopher Swann, "Drachma Faces Final Hurdle to Euro-Entry," *Financial Times*, June 1, 2000, 25.

28. Kerin Hope, "Athens Lines Up a Smooth Entry," *Financial Times* [Greek supplement], December 13, 2000, II; C. Swann, "Few Regrets at Demise of the Drachma," *Financial Times*, December 29, 2000, 3.

29. Clare McCarthy, "Danes Set to Give Euro Supporters a Hard Time, *Financial Times*, June 3, 2000, 3.

30. Deborah Hargreaves, "Demography Is Destiny for the Old World," *Financial Times*, special section on Europe reinvented, March 2001, 12–13.

31. Tito Boeri and Herbert Brucher, "An Opening Gambit," *Financial Times*, June 27, 2000, 15.

32. "Make It Ten, Set a Date," *Economist*, June 10, 2000, 16–17.

33. Stefan Wagstyl, "EU Hopefuls Told Talks Will Be Tough," *Financial Times*, June 25, 1998, 3.

34. Peter Norman, "Brussels Stance Irritates EU Hopefuls," *Financial Times*, May 27, 2000, 2.

35. Stefan Wagstyl, "One up to Euro, East Europeans Told," *Financial Times*, May 11, 1998, 2.

36. "Why Are We Waiting?" *Economist*, June 10, 2000, 6–9.

37. The Soviet Union and its satellite nations.

38. "Austria and Its Eastern Neighbors," *Economist*, May 9, 1995, 35.

39. H. Grabbe and K. Hughes, *Enlarging the EU Eastwards* (London: Royal Institute of International Affairs, 1998), 20–21.

40. "Delor's Way," *Economist*, May 23, 1998, 52.

41. "Europe Takes Flight," *Economist*, May 2, 1998, 13.

42. Dominique Moisi, "The World Moves On," *Financial Times*, June 8, 1981, 14.

43. Phare stands for the Poland and Hungary Assistance Reconstruction Economic program. Christopher M. Dent, *The European Economy: The Global Context* (New York: Routledge, 1997), 117.

44. Lionel Barber, "In the Beginning," *Financial Times*, May 1, 1998, 13.

45. Michael Smith and John Redd, "EU and Poles at Odds over Direct Subsidies," *Financial Times*, June 13, 2000, 2.

46. Quentin Peel and Peter Norman, "Irish Reject European Treaty," *Financial Times*, June 9, 2001, 24.

47. Peter Norman and John Murray Brown, "EU Strategy Thrown into Confusion," *Financial Times*, June 22, 2001, 14.

INDEX

About the Authors

Edward B. Flowers is professor of finance and international business at the Peter J. Tobin College of Business, St. John's University. A former officer of the U.S. Treasury Department, Dr. Flowers has authored and coauthored five books covering corporate finance, the global utilities industry, direct foreign investment, and Asian-Pacific economics and finance. He is now working on a book on nanotechnology as it affects investment and business cycles.

Francis A. Lees is the Theis Professor of Global Finance at the Peter J. Tobin College of Business, St. John's University. Dr. Lees has authored and co-authored ten books covering international finance, national financial development, and world capital markets. He has been a consultant for The Conference Board, Central Intelligence Agency, New York Clearing House Association, and other organizations. In 1987–1988 he was a Fulbright Research Fellow in Brazil, researching and writing about the evolution of that nation's financial system. Currently he is coeditor of the *Journal of Emerging Markets.*

www.ingramcontent.com/pod-product-compliance
Ingram Content Group UK Ltd.
Pitfield, Milton Keynes, MK11 3LW, UK
UKHW041103150926
475561UK00001BA/20

9 780742 513051